D1473979

THE RISE AND FALL
OF THE ASSOCIATED NEGRO PRESS

The Rise and Fall
of the Associated Negro Press

*Claude Barnett's Pan-African News
and the Jim Crow Paradox*

GERALD HORNE

**UNIVERSITY OF
ILLINOIS PRESS**
Urbana, Chicago, and Springfield

Library of Congress Cataloging-in-Publication Data
Names: Horne, Gerald, author.
Title: The rise and fall of the Associated Negro Press : Claude Barnett's
    pan-African news and the Jim Crow paradox / Gerald Horne.
Description: Urbana : University of Illinois, [2017] | Includes
    bibliographical references and index. |
Identifiers: LCCN 2016058968 (print) | LCCN 2017016657 (ebook) | ISBN
    9780252099762 (e-book) | ISBN 9780252041198 (hardcover : alk.
    paper) | ISBN 9780252082733 (pbk. : alk. paper)
Subjects: LCSH: Associated Negro Press—History. | Barnett, Claude,
    1890–1967.
Classification: LCC PN4841.A73 (ebook) | LCC PN4841.A73 H67 2017
    (print) | DDC 070.4/3508996073—dc23
LC record available at https://lccn.loc.gov/2016058968

CONTENTS

Claude Barnett stands in homage before the statue of Haitian national hero Toussaint
L'Ouverture in Port-au-Prince in May 1952. Barnett was a frequent visitor to the island
in pursuit of a kind of "commercial Pan-Africanism." Courtesy of the Chicago History
Museum.

THE RISE AND FALL
OF THE ASSOCIATED NEGRO PRESS

Introduction

Claude A. Barnett was delighted.

In late 1958 this Chicagoan found himself in West Africa, sitting at a small dinner table with the prime minister of Ghana, Kwame Nkrumah, who had led his nation to independence the previous year, inaugurating a new era of African independence. He sat in the glass-enclosed dining room on the top floor of the famed Christiansborg Castle as three white-coated waiters hovered about, ready to respond to his most quotidian requests. The two men were offered fragrant cigars and cigarettes and brandy of the finest sort, though the prime minister graciously declined to partake.[1] Nkrumah was simply reciprocating because Barnett had just hosted him in Chicago weeks earlier.[2]

This Ghanaian tête-à-tête was nothing new for Barnett. Although he is largely forgotten today, at one juncture, he was undoubtedly one of the most influential of African Americans, particularly in Africa. By late 1960, for example, he had completed his third journey to Africa that year. In Congo–Brazzaville, he observed at the time that he was "entertained pleasantly" by President Fulbert Youlou. "His nephew was a guest of ours," he acknowledged, "during the Pan American Games in Chicago last year." He then ferried across the Congo River, where he met the man he called "Col. [Joseph] Mobutu"; he was unable to confer with Congo–Kinshasa's then top leader, Patrice Lumumba. He did notice the unrest that rather shortly was to lead to Lumumba's murder and the ascension of Mobutu's thieving dictatorship.[3]

It was shortly after Lumumba's assassination that Adlai Stevenson, the U.S. emissary at the United Nations, offered to cooperate with Barnett during this fraught moment,[4] leaving the implication that Barnett had been passing on to the United States national security establishment insights that may not have been in the best interests of those like Lumumba.

Surely Barnett, who had been propelled into eminence because of his close ties to the Republican Party, was in a unique position to provide useful intelligence to the U.S. authorities. Those three African journeys in 1960 also involved a trip to Liberia, where he and his spouse, he told Stevenson, were "guests of President William V. S. Tubman"; then they went to Tunis and Tripoli, then to Accra, "again as guests of the Ghana government." From there Barnett traveled to Freetown and Dakar. In November "we were guests of the Nigerian Government during its independence celebrations." In Congo–Kinshasa he "did not get to see President Kasavubu while there but did so at the Savoy Hotel in New York" subsequently. "I feel certain," he told Stevenson, already dodging charges of U.S. complicity in Lumumba's murder, "we can work closely with you and the U.N. Mission" since "our service can be important."[5]

Yet Barnett was a contradictory figure, which reflected his anomalous post as a member of the black elite and thus feeling the tug of the progressive black masses, while also being an aspiring member of the U.S. elite, which pulled him in an opposing direction. Thus, by 1963, Barnett's Associated Negro Press was reporting without sadness that "half of U.S. Negroes in Congo boycott[ed] [the] July 4th celebration to protest racial discrimination back home," including fifteen of thirty in the city that became Kinshasa. This included "United Nations officials, teachers, technicians, secretaries and housewives"; only "10 Negroes attended the celebration," but "six or seven" were "military men who indicated that they were not permitted to join a boycott."[6]

By 1961, largely as a result of Barnett's influence, Supreme Life Insurance Company of Chicago had entertained African visitors from nineteen nations during the previous four years, creating mutually beneficial business opportunities on both sides of the Atlantic.[7]

That same year Barnett informed Nnamdi Azikiwe, a founding father of independent Nigeria, that Supreme Life "is the largest and most successful Negro business in the northern section of the United States," which is why this influential leader was asked to come to Chicago to address executives and policyholders.[8] Earlier, Barnett—along with Congressman Adam Clayton Powell and a number of British Embassy officials—was invited to attend a luncheon at Blair House in Washington sponsored by the U.S. State Department in honor of Dr. Azikiwe, who was to emerge as his nation's first president by 1963.[9]

Over the years Barnett had, according to his publicist, been "intimately associated" with Booker T. Washington, Marcus Garvey, Ralph Bunche, Sékou Touré (founding father of Guinea-Conakry), Gamal Abdul Nasser of Egypt, Jawaharlal Nehru of India—and many other luminaries.[10] It was in November 1949, for example, that Barnett was in Manhattan, where he conferred privately with Prime Minister Jawaharlal Nehru of India on pressing antiapartheid and anti–Jim Crow measures.[11] It was in 1955 that Barnett confided that it was "through the kindness of Mr. Nehru's people" that he would "get reports directly from Bandung,"[12] the trail-blazing meeting in Indonesian of mostly African and Asian nations.

Barnett was sufficiently perspicacious to understand India's importance for black folk generally. Thus, when Lawrence Burr was en route to an India on the cusp of independence, Barnett told him when "England begins to loosen her grip upon this great multitude of colored people and they themselves find a way to become self-sustaining and lifted out of the realm of poverty, who knows what it may presage for all darker folk?"[13]

Barnett knew more than most that foreign and domestic policies were tied together inextricably. By 1954, weeks before the high court in the United States sought to nullify Jim Crow, former secretary of state Dean Acheson told Barnett, then in his sixties, that it was "obvious that the existence of discrimination against minority groups in the United States is a handicap in our relations with other countries."[14] By 1965, when both Barnett and the Associated Negro Press (ANP) were writhing in the throes of death, the press baron still found the time to contact "all of the African Heads of State whom I know," encouraging them to continue to press the White House for anti–Jim Crow concessions. "A new day appears to be dawning for people of color," he exulted, adding that "whatever happens to us in the United States is important to black people everywhere"; for "if racial bias is destroyed in the United States it can be a harbinger that it can be abolished in most of the world and bring about a surge of progress for blacks and people of color everywhere. I am confident," he noted diplomatically, "that President Johnson will appreciate a word from you."[15]

Barnett realized—and the ANP exemplified—the historic tendency among African Americans to acknowledge that African-American progress was heavily dependent upon global currents.[16] Moreover, like Barnett, many Negro leaders— David Ruggles, James Forten, William C. Nell, Samuel Cornish, David Walker, Frederick Douglass—either came from the ranks of printers, editors, agents, or patrons of newspapers or solidified their reputations there.[17] When Barnett died in 1967, one of his main competitors, John H. Sengstacke of the *Chicago Defender*, asserted that Barnett "was more than a pioneering genius in the field of journalism" because "no man was ever more dedicated to the liberation of Africa" and "to the cause of Negro freedom from oppression and segregation"; thus, "his death is an irreparable loss."[18]

Similarly, the ANP correspondent in Mexico, Earl Morris, in 1957 termed Barnett, an "unofficial Secretary of State" and "probably the best informed American on Negro countries in the world." Indeed, he said, "many American Negroes who served as Liberian consuls or representatives of the United States received their appointments only after Liberia had cleared them with Claude A. Barnett." When John Robinson, a noted Negro pilot, was sent to Ethiopia in the 1930s to fight Italian invaders, he "owed his appointment almost directly to Barnett." As was typical of Barnett's praxis, Robinson then filed regular dispatches via the ANP, updating African Americans on battlefield developments. It was not just pilots whom he helped to send abroad, for Barnett also was "instrumental in sending teachers, doctors, mechanics, etc. to foreign black countries. He has been an unofficial adviser to many such countries for more than 30 years." Thus, said

Morris accurately in 1957, "every incident, everything of major influence which occurred in foreign countries where there were Negroes, American or foreign, Claude A. Barnett had a correspondent through which flowed the happenings of those countries."[19]

Barnett being termed an "unofficial Secretary of State" was accurate. "I have known you for a long time," said P. B. Young of the *Norfolk Journal and Guide*, "and you have always impressed me as being a natural born diplomat."[20] A relentless letter writer and a tireless networker, Barnett's diplomacy not only benefited himself but the Negro community from which he sprang. By 1950 he was continuing to press Guatemala and Brazil because, he said, both were "finding it difficult to let Negroes in" as either tourists or immigrants. "The latter does not even want visitors," he said with a scoff. "Think up a group of questions," he instructed his Washington correspondent, Alice Dunnigan, "and ask the ambassadors point blank, what their attitude is on Negroes? Tell them your home office has proof that their Chicago consuls have refused Negroes and you wish to know why."[21]

It was not as though Barnett had chosen the easiest road to eminence, for it was well known that—not least because of its importance and influence—the Negro press was disfavored by Jim Crow advocates. The city of Pine Bluff, Arkansas, sought an injunction barring the *Chicago Defender* during this journal's hey-day during the 1920s. In 1921 a correspondent of the *Philadelphia American* was burned at the stake. Harassment of Negro journalists was customary.[22] This was

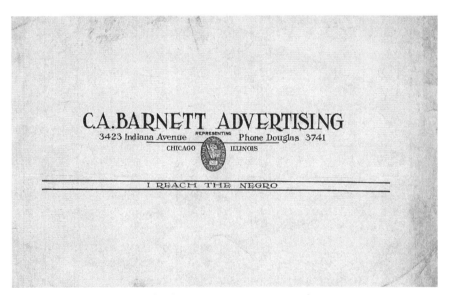

An advertisement for Barnett's advertising company: Barnett's various companies not only covered the news but also created ads that could then be placed in Negro newspapers. Courtesy of the Chicago History Museum.

generated not just externally, because newspapers with a captive Negro market could be lucrative. In 1934, A. S. Scott was convinced that his brother, who had founded the *Atlanta Daily World*, was murdered as a result of a "well laid plot for control of his newspaper"; he had been "asked to sign a will that he did not read" and then "lived in constant fear for his life"; he "left about thirty thousand to his children," paltry consolation but admittedly a king's ransom for a Negro in that era: no one was ever convicted for this presumed murder.[23]

Nothing so horrendous occurred during World War II, but it was then that the prominent columnist Westbrook Pegler claimed that the "majority of the Negro papers, during this war, so undermined the national loyalty of the Negro servicemen that they became unmistakably responsible for episodes humiliating to their own racial clientele"; he railed against the "evil influence of the Negro press on Negro units," an opinion that was reflected in the surveillance of the ANP during this titanic war.[24]

After the war, problems for ANP did not cease. There was difficulty in getting White House credentials for their correspondent. Then by 1957 Alice Dunnigan was complaining that President Eisenhower "ignores Negro reporters at press conferences . . . whom he apparently believes will ask him some embarrassing questions regarding civil rights," an accurate assumption in retrospect.[25]

*   *   *

What had led Barnett to this position of prominence was his role as—perhaps—the leading press baron in Black America. It was in 1919 that he had become a publisher's representative tasked with selling advertising in Negro newspapers. This took him from his then hometown of Chicago westward to California. As he contacted these periodicals, he found that there was no dependable service to supply a constant stream of news to their thousands of faithful readers, something along the line of today's Associated Press, for example. He rushed back to Illinois and contacted a group of colleagues who had invested in another one of this entrepreneur's enterprises. He formed a corporation, brought in Nahum Daniel Brascher, a newsman from Cleveland, as an executive, opened an office at 312 South Clark Street in Chicago—and thus was born the Associated Negro Press, which at one time served 150 U.S. Negro newspapers and 100 more in Africa in French and English.[26]

One observer has termed the ANP "the most ambitious black press institution in the country before the advent of Johnson Publishing," renowned for producing *Ebony* magazine, though it is evident that the reach of the ANP was much more extensive.[27]

Yet Barnett's success as a press baron was difficult to separate from his overall entrepreneurial skill—and from the dire portrayal of African Americans in the mainstream media, which he countered assiduously. Barnett later acknowledged that "it was amazing to see how little the Negro figures in the news columns [of

Nahum Brascher (no date): This veteran journalist worked closely with Claude Barnett in building the ANP. Courtesy of the Chicago History Museum.

the mainstream press]. When he did, it was in crime, violence or a descriptive article."[28]

As for the former factor, Barnett adroitly took advantage of the openings that Jim Crow created. Truman K. Gibson—a colleague of Barnett's—noted that "black real estate speculators made a killing. I represented Claude Barnett," he recalled when "he bought three buildings and confided to me that they were the best investments he had had ever made because they came at so little cost." But even Gibson, agog at Barnett's financial acumen, also knew that he too "had an intense interest in Africa" that was not solely due to his remunerative holdings there.[29]

There were other elements in his success. On the eve of his death, he admitted, "I have never been a 'Casanova' not even 30 or 40 years ago when I was a true philanderer";[30] this self-contradictory comment can be explained by reference to his long-term and loving marriage to Etta Moten, with which his bachelor-hood was contrasted. This union served as a rock of stability; moreover, Moten too was an operator of rare skill converting this marriage into a partnership that enhanced his own abilities.

His marriage—and the market—ensured that the ANP would have an outstanding chance of becoming a rousing success. Enoch Waters, who worked alongside Barnett for years, felt that "half, maybe three fourths of [Negro] papers could not have existed without the copy provided by ANP, just as most white papers would have folded had it not been for AP and UPI [United Press International]."[31]

*   *   *

Barnett and the ANP performed yeoman service in crusading against Jim Crow and colonialism but in the process created a catastrophic success in that once these walls of inequity began to crumble, the mainstream press began to hire more black journalists and pay more attention to the black community, thereby eroding Barnett's competitive and commercial advantage, leading directly to the ANP's demise in the 1960s. The paradox of the anti–Jim Crow crusade was that as entities like the ANP (or ebony colleges and sports teams too) became more successful in eroding Jim Crow, they became their own gravediggers, preparing the ground for their burial.[32]

The undermining of the Negro press was no minor matter. For as one scholar observed recently, "without the black press, the movement might well have foundered";[33] for this institution was in many ways the nerve center, the communications axis of the anti–Jim Crow campaign. The Swedish social scientist Gunnar Myrdal stressed accurately in the 1940s that "the press defines the Negro group to the Negro themselves," as "the individual Negro is invited to share in the sufferings, grievances, and pretensions of the millions of Negroes outside the narrow community. This creates a feeling of strength and solidarity."[34] Myrdal added that by the mid-twentieth century no other institution within the black community was as powerful as the Negro press, a claim that could be challenged credibly only by the black church.[35]

Modestly, Barnett declared that "next to the Negro church," the black press was "the most powerful influence operating within" the Negro community.[36] The ANP's columnist, the moderate Gordon Hancock, argued in 1948 that "in the Negro's fight for deliverance, the Negro press is a great right arm. The Negro who does not subscribe to one or more Negro newspapers and magazines" was contemptible as a result.[37] As the head of an octopus whose tentacles reached into virtually every nook and cranny where black folk resided, this suggested that Barnett was one of the most influential African Americans of the twentieth century.

Dr. Martin Luther King Jr. could have provided expert testimony on this point. It was in early 1962 that Dr. King provided "heartfelt thanks" to Barnett "for your prodigious efforts in giving coverage to the work" of his organization. He sought to "get together for a pleasant chat" that would include their respective spouses.[38]

Barnett reciprocated when he provided Dr. King press clippings on the 1963 March on Washington from a paper in Dakar, Senegal, along with a supportive editorial from the *Manchester Guardian*.[39] Weeks after this historic event, a close adviser to His Imperial Majesty, Emperor Haile Selassie of Ethiopia urgently instructed Barnett that it was "imperative you get Dr. King or one of the top civil rights leaders [to] request an audience" with the emperor so he could "declare publicly" his support of "U.S. civil rights," which would "help freedom fighters all over."[40]

Because of the ANP's critical role as the megaphone of the movement, it was not surprising that Barnett was in close touch with Lee Lorch, one of the few Euro Americans to back desegregation of Central High School in Little Rock, Arkansas, in 1957. In fact, he told the mathematician, "the day before your first letter arrived Carl Braden and E. D. Nixon of Montgomery were both in our office," a reference to a premier anti–Jim Crow crusader in Louisville and the trade union organizer who sparked the bus boycott in Alabama that marked a new stage in the movement.[41]

*   *   *

Barnett was born on 16 September 1889 in Sanford, Florida. He was a graduate of Tuskegee University and a faithful disciple of its founder, Booker T. Washington. On 24 June 1934 he married Etta Moten, a noted singer and actor.[42] She was born in San Antonio, Texas, and brought three daughters from a prior union to their marriage. She matriculated at the University of Kansas and Northwestern University and appeared in such Hollywood productions as "Flying Down to Rio" and "Gold Diggers of 1933" and performed recitals in South America and Africa besides.[43] She received an Oscar nomination for her work in the former film. She dubbed vocals for Barbara Stanwyck in "Ladies of the House" in 1932 and did the same for Ginger Rogers in "Professional Sweetheart" in 1933. In 1934 President Franklin Roosevelt invited her to sing "My Forgotten Man" for his birthday celebration.[44]

Moten's star wattage did not hurt when the ANP wooed the leading musician, Quincy Jones, who then contributed columns. Langston Hughes and Jackie Robinson also wrote for the ANP.[45] In 1936 Barnett told the Federal Theater in Chicago that "you have a young man on your staff who has newspaper talent. His name is Richard Wright," referring to a soon-to-be famous novelist. With his typical business savvy, Barnett wanted Wright to be assigned to the ANP to work "on publicity," that is, "spend half of each day or all of it . . . working out of our office" while being paid by the federal authorities.[46] By 1948, Wright was a renowned author; yet he still insisted on a "big favor" in the form of "accreditation as one of your correspondents here in Paris," reminding Barnett "that I once proudly carried a press card from the [ANP]."[47]

One of Wright's closest friends in Chicago was Frank Marshall Davis, who served for thirteen years as an ANP editor. In 1940, after Wright had attained a

Frank Marshall Davis, a long-time ANP staffer in Chicago, moved to Honolulu in 1948, where he eventually came to befriend a fellow Hawaiian who became president of the United States of America. Courtesy of the Chicago History Museum.

measure of eminence, he apologized to Barnett for being unable to write a poem for his Christmas card to him since he was "involved in a tremendous amount of work," though he was not too busy to send "my warmest regards to the genius of photography, F. M. D."[48] Barnett thought the versatile Davis was "one of the most capable among the current generation of Negro writers," possessing a "great native ability" besides, along with "unusual sensitivity"; he also was "entirely dependable" and "faithful."[49] Davis also was thought to be close to the Communist Party—in 1949 he sent fulsome "birthday greetings to Premier Joseph Stalin"[50]—but the flexible Barnett did not find Davis's sympathies to be a bar to positive relations with him. In 1948 Davis moved to Honolulu, where he befriended a young man who was to become a U.S. president.[51]

Indeed, it is difficult to separate what has been called the "Black Chicago Renaissance," a complement of the better-known Harlem Renaissance, without consideration of Barnett, the ANP, and the lifeline it provided to so many writers. The ampler point was that Barnett provided an outlet for writers to reach an audience that they may not have reached otherwise. The ANP was, perhaps, the premier intermediary between the black masses and black intellectuals. As for Barnett, though ANP was not necessarily a profitable enterprise, it provided him entrée to many whom he may not have reached otherwise, including corporate titans for whom he could open doors in Africa and the Caribbean.

Zora Neale Hurston was primarily associated with cultural trends in Harlem, but she too was quite close to Barnett and his spouse, referring to the latter as the "scrumptious Etta Moten," once suggesting that it "would be fun if Etta and I made a tour of Europe. Let her sing and me speak."[52] Hurston seemed to possess a searching fondness for "that luscious piece of gal-meat known as Etta. . . . Etta knows she is one of my enthusiasms," she confessed.[53] She was similarly fond of Moten's husband, once querying him about his "libido," while adding, "plenty of men would like to know the secret of your charms. You are intellectual, of course, have a charming personality and physical attractions."[54]

Hurston was not the only woman who sought to enter Barnett's circle. In 1930 the doyenne Mary Church Terrell was explicit about it: "I wish I could have a hand in the Associated Negro Press. I have so much to say that I really think it would be interesting to the public. Subjects and articles are dancing in my head all the time."[55] She may have noticed (and may have wanted to emulate) Alice Dunbar Nelson, yet another leading black woman intellectual, who was a frequent contributor to the ANP.[56]

It was in 1955, via Hurston's frequent sparring partner—Hughes—that Ezekiel Mphahlele, the famed South African writer, was suggested to Barnett as a correspondent in the land of apartheid for the ANP. Promptly, Hughes scribbled a note to "Claude," informing him that "this fellow is a good writer" and should be hired forthwith.[57] As early as 1936 the *African Liberator* in Johannesburg sought a cooperation agreement with the ANP.[58] Years later, the noted South African writer Nathaniel Nakasa gave "thanks" to the ANP for "sending some cash," the "25 dollars I got served well." Still, he added, "I find your pay rates quite unacceptable," a frequent plaint heard from writers who did not have much leverage in a buyer's market, particularly if they wanted access to the agency's vast audience.[59]

In any case, Nakasa's contributions and Mphahlele's request were consonant with the comprehensiveness of ANP's global coverage. By July 1945 Rudolph Dunbar, ANP's correspondent in London, was in Berlin and from there sent Barnett a dispatch on the stationery of "Adolf Hitler Berlin W8." "Don't assume that that I am Hitler," he reassured. "I carried away a considerable amount of this stationery when I paid a visit to Reich Chancellery when I was in Berlin."[60]

In October 1962 in a typical gesture, ANP contacted future powerbroker Vernon Jordan, who was then a budding lawyer in Atlanta. "We can provide you with credentials," he was told, along with "stamped and addressed envelopes" to facilitate his becoming a correspondent.[61] Jordan, who was to lead the National Urban League, was joined in his ANP tie by Roy Wilkins, who was to lead the National Association for the Advancement of Colored People (NAACP). For in

Don't Depend on Others When You Grow Old!

THE parents who trust their children for comfort in those days when old age leaves them helpless may trust in vain.

Perhaps the children whom you work and plan for may be better than the average. They may not be so thoughtless and carried away with the pleasures of the day that they will ever be forgetful of your needs. But why trust to uncertainty? Women especially should secure life insurance to guard against old age dependence. Statistics show that 90 per cent of the women in this country over 60 spend their last days supported by some relative, friend or charity.

Before age creeps upon you and you find yourself unable to work—helpless perhaps—see to it that you have used just a little of the money you acquire to provide for your declining years. A life insurance policy will make your future secure. Remember you are always welcome when you are independent.

Protect Yourself Now!

Many people do not know how to use their life insurance properly. It can help you alive as well as provide for others when you are gone. Any good insurance man will show you how. Take out an insurance policy to provide for old age independence. The cost is low if you begin early.

Let These Companies Provide for You:

CENTURY LIFE INS. CO., Little Rock, Arkansas
DOMESTIC LIFE & ACCIDENT INSURANCE CO.
Louisville, Kentucky
GOLDEN STATE INSURANCE CO., Los Angeles, California
SUPREME LIBERTY LIFE INSURANCE CO., Chicago, Illinois
PYRAMID MUTUAL LIFE INSURANCE CO., Chicago, Illinois
SOUTHERN AID SOCIETY OF VIRGINIA
Richmond, Virginia
UNITY INDUSTRIAL LIFE INSURANCE CO.
New Orleans, Louisiana
UNDERWRITERS MUTUAL LIFE INSURANCE CO.
Chicago, Illinois
VICTORY LIFE INSURANCE CO., Chicago, Illinois

Members of
THE NATIONAL NEGRO INSURANCE ASSOCIATION

An advertisement, circa 1930s: Barnett also had close ties to insurance companies that served African Americans: with desegregation—and the extension of social security benefits to the African-American community—this particular investment faced a stiff challenge. Courtesy of the Chicago History Museum.

1930 Wilkins was the ANP correspondent in Kansas City, a position from which he reprimanded "Dear Claude" about ANP references to Jewish Americans.[62]

The nimbly opportunistic ANP also took advantage of the fact that with the advent of air travel—which combined with the pre-existing trend of Negro expatriation—the possibility of hiring more freelance correspondents arose. When Amy Ashwood Garvey contemplated a journey to Ethiopia during the apex of the 1930s war with Italy, she was quick to tell Barnett "if you think you can use any articles from me, let me know immediately."[63] When the orchestra of Duke Ellington was on the verge of a world tour, Barnett chose to "remind" his vocalist, Ivy Anderson, "of the quite solemn promise which you made a couple of weeks ago to serve the [ANP] in the capacity of correspondent while you and the Ellington group are abroad."[64]

Barnett encouraged expatriation, particularly for the proliferating number of Negro artists, instructing Marian Anderson, the worthy contralto, that "the more Europe appreciates you the more America will"[65]—so stay away and send newsy items besides to aid ANP.

En route to Europe, the preeminent Negro scholar Merze Tate offered to write for ANP.[66] This was not an unusual offer, because those African Americans sufficiently lucky to travel abroad seemed to feel that it was their duty to report on world events and provide an alternative to the routine suffocation of Jim Crow.

Thus, it did not take much prodding to push many African Americans toward expatriation. Passing through London in 1937, the ANP's Fay Jackson was stunned to "have not met the first sign of prejudice, even when I was dining with a pure African gentlemen in one of the swankiest cafes here"[67]—this would have been well-nigh impossible to replicate on the west bank of the Atlantic.

In its role as a mini State Department for Black America, the ANP recognized that some of the more effective ambassadors were musicians. As the ANP was slipping into desuetude, the noteworthy composer and stride pianist Luckey Roberts recalled for "Dear Claude" a time when Roberts was regarded as "the man who introduced [George] Gershwin to Jazz"; Roberts had legendary close encounters with the Duke of Windsor, the would-be "King of England," during his 1917 sojourn in the United States. "I remember playing at receptions in his honor for seventeen successive nights," said Roberts. "At one in particular, the Sanfords (Laddie—a famous polo player) spent $180,000 for a single night's entertainment" in honor of this important British royal, who "was crazy about our music. He hung around the bandstand all night and never seemed happier than when I let him sit in on the drums. He sort of fancied himself with the brushes. From that time on I became his mentor and gave him lessons in rhythms. Later . . . I used to send him records and sheet music so he could keep up with jazz."[68] Black musicians like Roberts had access to elites globally—and capital ($180,000 for one night)—both of which proved useful to Barnett and the ANP, not least as anti–Jim Crow campaigns were pressed in the global arena.

But as his relationship to Adlai Stevenson suggested, Barnett had a curious alliance with Anglo American elites in any case. He came to know then vice president Richard M. Nixon when they both traveled to the ceremony inaugurating Ghana's independence. Later that year, Nixon's secretary, Rose Mary Woods, told Etta Moten how it was "so sweet of you to write me" after the power couple had been invited to a lunch with the Duke of Windsor's relatives, Her Royal Highness Queen Elizabeth and Prince Philip: "you were invited both as friends," said Woods, "and as representatives of the Negro race who would add dignity and charm."[69] It was unclear whether Barnett and Moten upheld their end of Woods's stated bargain, but doubtlessly the presence of the ANP's founder at this exclusive luncheon did little to hurt his business prospects.

The aforementioned kerfuffle with Wilkins was a rare misstep by Barnett, a canny businessman. Early on he combined newsgathering with public relations and, thus, proposed to Negro beauticians that they take an "associated membership" with ANP and in return he would offer "counsel" on "public relations problems," for example, converting their ordinary doings into news items that would place them in a favorable light.[70] In 1950 ANP converted an ordinary account of a European jaunt by the chief executive of Virginia Mutual Benefit Life Insurance Company into a news item, which was part of an overall strategy of publicizing black businesses and serving as a hub to connect them to others who could use their services.[71]

The black Communist lawyer William Patterson argued in defending the Scottsboro 9 and other prisoners that although he saw these cases in the broader scheme of things as a way to discredit capitalism, that did not relieve attorneys like himself from the primary responsibility of providing the most expert counsel possible to these beleaguered defendants.[72] In a similar vein, Barnett did not shirk in promoting adroitness in newsgathering, even when he bent ethics to benefit a favored client—though, admittedly, as a dedicated entrepreneur, his ethical mandate was harder to uphold than Patterson's. The ANP acknowledged that "we, no more than the white papers try to [but] cannot always adhere strictly to an ideal of journalistic ethics," which was all too true. The tension was seen as between "the dissemination of news and the fight against injustice in many forms," but the search for profit was actually the transcendent factor.[73]

Still, Barnett once reproached his London correspondent because "you deal in the profound. News is of the earthy, the immediate and the common. You philosophize. What we need is description. . . . [W]e want to know," speaking of England in 1944, "whether it is true that there is a considerable deluge of brown babies" because of miscegenation involving U.S. Negro soldiers. "Things which are human, things which are real," was his prescription for first-rate journalism.[74] Thus, the ANP style sheet counseled its many writers to "use simple words. Avoid long and rare words" and, above all, "do not editorialize" but "tell both sides of the story. Of course, 'colored' can be used as a synonym for Negro but under no circumstances is 'race man' permissible." And, "remember news is a most perishable commodity," so timeliness was essential.[75] Those who now are denoted widely as "African American" wrestled with the proper words to characterize themselves as a group.[76]

Just as Barnett was not averse to collaborating with Adlai Stevenson after the tragic murder of Lumumba, when the United States came under assault in 1951 because of Jim Crow, he saw it as a business opportunity. He proposed a collaboration with the U.S. Information Service on "a film or series of films showing the progress made in Negro life in the United States," which would could have "tremendous influence" in "undeveloped countries"; the production was to be "sponsored by Liggett & Myers Tobacco," with whom he had collaborated on a series of films targeting Negro consumers and distributed widely abroad.[77] The latter series featured Barnett, extending his brand—and tobacco's too: "when I am happy I light up a Chesterfield," he asserted.[78] The films were so successful overseas that the entrepreneurial Barnett was then involved in "breaking Liggett & Myers and Chesterfield into as important a market as the Negro represents" in the United States "through this series of films for Negro patronized theatres," which "may just be scratching the surface of a big opportunity."[79] Reputedly, the latter series played to an audience of 3 million in more than three hundred theaters and ninety-six universities, colleges, and schools nationally—then it was exhibited in Liberia and Haiti, where, it was said, it was "expected" to "play to an even greater audience."[80]

When antitobacco sentiment began to grow, Barnett offered to "hook up" again with Liggett and Myers to beat back the "sharp attack on cigarette smoking" that "is sweeping the country today," meaning "that the tobacco people need to do some real new selling."[81]

Neither was Barnett's interest in Africa wholly altruistic. He had substantial investments in Liberia and boasted of his ties to "Republic Steel Corporation of Cleveland," which lusted after the iron ore in West Africa.[82] Often he offered to open doors for U.S. corporations in Africa, including a potentially lucrative deal for mahogany.[83]

In 1938, Gabriel Dennis, secretary of the treasury in Liberia, praised Barnett for arranging "several favorable articles" via ANP and "as a token of appreciation for the friendly attitude you have shown towards" Monrovia, graciously he gifted ANP "twenty pounds, sixteen shillings and eight pence" in hopes "you will also continue your friendly attitude towards the people of Liberia."[84] Barnett collaborated frequently with Lester Walton, a U.S. Negro who—quite unusually—held an ambassadorship, albeit in Liberia. In 1941 Barnett worried that "now my friend Dennis is out of the picture, I presume our honorariums are at an end."[85]

Later Barnett told Dennis, at the time restored to influence, that "Liberia has had more publicity in the Negro papers of the United States since my visit there than it ever had before." This is "a fact," he insisted, "not vainglorious." Hinting subtly, he added, "I believe you could use a public relations man to do specific things when there were important issues you wished placed before the American public";[86] in other words, give Barnett a contract and, most likely, there would be even more favorable publicity for Monrovia.

When the ANP reported on the fate in June 1940 of U.S. envoy James Carter, who had been seized by German occupation forces in Calais, France, the reporter went on to note that in 1912 he was posted in Madagascar: "Next to the American Minister at Monrovia," it was said, this African island was "the most important foreign post held by Negroes."[87] In detailing Carter's plight and posts, one did not have to be a cynic to suspect that Barnett's news agency was angling for future advantage in case this diplomat were rescued.

The wily Barnett was capable of sharing his sharp-witted tactics. In 1935 his friend, the singer Marian Anderson, was worried that her using a European accompanist in her concerts—and not a Negro—would be a public-relations disaster among African Americans. He assured her that the Negro press, particularly his own ANP, would not object and reminded her of his top correspondent, Percival Leroy (P. L.) Prattis, who had been "with me for a number of years" and "will I am certain back you one hundred percent." As for another influential scribe (who likely was as ill compensated as most Negro journalists), he counseled, "slip a small bill in his hand in appreciation" and he too would be compliant.[88]

Barnett's many journeys to Africa also had a purpose beyond seeking investment opportunities for himself and his many business partners. "I have the most extensive collection of West African and East African carvings of any person in Chicago, if not in the country," he boasted with accuracy to South Africa's Alfred Xuma, whom he wanted to connect him to "dealers" in the latter's homeland.[89] But Barnett's saving grace was that he was not simply involved in shameless profiteering. When the anticolonial leader of Malawi, Hastings Banda, was jailed in 1960, it was Barnett who arranged to send him books, which brought the leader's profuse thanks.[90]

*   *   *

Part of the business model of the ANP included offering their news service to newspapers in exchange for advertising space paid for by black-owned businesses, especially successful cosmetic businesses, including his own.[91] Despite Barnett's craftiness as an entrepreneur, the ANP rarely broke even, and most of the Chicago staff—which was rarely more than eight individuals during its history—held secondary jobs.[92] The same held true for many of their correspondents. Their Hollywood correspondent, Harry Levette, was a movie extra. R. C. Fisher, their correspondent in St. Louis, was a clerk in the circuit court there. Another key correspondent, Trezzvant Anderson, was a railway mail clerk.[93] But note: all these posts tended to place these scribes in proximity to critical streams of news.

One of the agency's best connected staffers was Albert Graham Barnett, no relation to the founder but the stepson of the sainted antilynch crusader Ida B. Wells-Barnett. He was with the ANP founder from 1918 until the bitter end in the 1960s, though he spent time intermittently with the rival *Chicago Defender.* He was the son of Ferdinand Barnett Jr., who founded Chicago's first Negro newspaper and, thus, brought considerable experience to the table. His birth mother, who died in his infancy, was a graduate of the University of Michigan, and he himself was a law graduate of De Paul; his revealing nickname was "Garibaldi," an indicator of his formidable skill as an intellect and organizer.[94]

In sum, Barnett was an essential fixture in Negro elite circles, a status enhanced by his marriage to Etta Moten, a certified celebrity. In 1958, cannily taking advantage of "white flight" driven by housing desegregation, the couple purchased a baronial brownstone in Chicago's fabled Bronzeville. Their purchase price was a bargain $45,000.[95] Since in 1956 his bank balance was a hefty $46,000 plus, this he could well afford.[96] In 2008, however, providing an indication of the size of the estate the formidable couple left to heirs, this spacious five-thousand-square-foot house on a quarter-acre lot sold for a hefty $1.13 million.[97]

*   *   *

The ANP came along at an opportune moment, as Barnett's shrewd business dealings tended to suggest. From 1865 to 1900 nearly twelve thousand newspapers sprouted that catered to African Americans. Most wilted and died; on the eve of World War II, there were over two hundred Negro newspapers with all but one appearing weekly. From 1933 to 1940 their circulation more than doubled to 1.27 million, and this figure understates their reach, since each issue had multiple readers: The Office of War Information reckoned that 4 million blacks read an African American newspaper each week. Yet, says historian John Maxwell Hamilton, the ANP was "the first and only systematic effort to field African American foreign correspondents."[98]

Still, the fact that the Negro press generally was expanding—including global coverage—provided ballast for the ANP. The *Pittsburgh Courier,* which by the 1940s had an estimated circulation of three hundred thousand, was said to cover every corner of the United States, but it also was extending, it was said, "coverage [of] events of colored peoples in Africa, South America, Asia and the Caribbean nations."[99] By 1947 this periodical had a reported $2 million in revenues and its circulation was a reported three hundred thirty thousand. The paper operated twelve branch offices, published fourteen editions around the nation, and employed 165 workers.

By 1915 the *Chicago Defender* reached its peak circulation of about two hundred thirty thousand, though because railway porters circulated the journal nationally, its actual readership may have surpassed one million. By 1916 it was the largest-selling black newspaper in the nation.[100] A rival of theirs, the *Afro-American*, headquartered in Baltimore; although it had a small staff of ten, this periodical had subscribers in Africa as early as 1915. Their circulation more than doubled between 1930 and 1940 from 45,689 to 104,936. During World War II, the *Afro-American* had correspondents in Italy, France, the South Pacific, North Africa, and even the Aleutian Islands.[101]

Being a news service and thus able to avoid spending on the infrastructure of publishing—printing press, barrels of ink, et cetera—allowed ANP to spend more heavily on newsgathering and take advantage of this enhanced global turn evidenced among African Americans. By 1948 Barnett informed a correspondent that ANP received "most of the newspapers from Lagos and even the *Southern Nigeria Defender* from Ibadan," and the same held true for other key regions. A keen observer, when visiting Nigeria during that time, he compiled twelve hundred feet of motion pictures in Africa, including three hundred at the Booker T. Washington Institute in Liberia.[102] (Barnett was particularly helpful to the BTWI since he was—arguably—Tuskegee's most exemplary graduate of the twentieth century.[103]) The ANP also received, said Barnett, "all of the government news bulletins issued in Lagos and since those come by air mail, that is what enables us to have so many stories from Nigeria."[104]

Naturally, ANP paid careful attention to the home base. In 1960 Barnett asserted that the agency was "subscribing to daily papers all over the U.S., about 50 or more. We read them carefully," he said; as for "the Negro weeklies . . . we read the hell out of them too."[105]

*　*　*

Though not often recognized as such, Claude Barnett was one of the leading Pan-Africanists of the twentieth century, just as the ANP was an exemplar of the often discussed but little implemented doctrine of Pan-Africanism. Yet his very success carried the seeds of its demise; that is, as his anti–Jim Crow and anticolonial campaigns gained traction, it opened both Black America and Africa to incursions by mainstream entities that theretofore either had ignored these sizable communities or winked at (or worse, participated in) their bludgeoning. (It is easy to infer—as shall be seen—that if the left-wing of this progressive campaign, as exemplified by Paul Robeson and W. E. B. Du Bois, had not been battered so relentlessly, the demise of the ANP and like institutions may have been avoided).

In early 1944 as the destiny of the world teetered, Reverend Robert Williams proclaimed that "American Negroes ought to take more interest in the affairs" of "Foreign Negroes."[106] What ANP accomplished prior to this admonition and afterward was not only to promote a "Pan-Africanism" that encompassed "Foreign Negroes" but, as well, the entire planet. What ANP accomplished was to provide an assessment of the balance of global forces that historically had been essential in plotting the way forward for African Americans not least. Yet as the prize of anti–Jim Crow came within reach, ironically the way had been paved for the ultimate liquidation of the ANP.

ANP was a loss leader for Barnett, providing him with entrée to rarified circles, though not very profitable. As shall be seen, it was structured as a non-profit organization. The agency also did not prove to be remunerative for the many writers it deployed. Writing from Paris in 1949, William Rutherford offered himself, Richard Wright, and George Padmore—eminent analysts and writers all—"and as many of the African and Indian journalists as I can get to participate" to pen "articles and news items" at the rate of "say $5.00 per week," which was probably more than many ANP writers were paid.[107] Frank Marshall Davis, who by 1945 was the executive editor of the ANP, was thought by the FBI to be the highest paid member of the Chicago staff, garnering $37.50 per week. The FBI thought that the ANP had "not made a great deal of money."[108] Alice Dunnigan, ANP's postwar Washington correspondent, would have agreed in that, she said, she was hired at the rate of "half a cent per word" and at the end of her first month, received a paltry check "for thirty dollars," this despite generating a "load of copy each week."[109] It was a buyer's market, not least since there were so many literate intellectuals who ached to have access to an outlet that could reach masses, a vehicle that Barnett could provide.

Still, it often incurred deficits to its detriment. Enoch Waters of the ANP saw the agency as the "principal supplier of news and features for practically every Negro newspaper in the country," though this was not as profitable as it seemed, given the reluctance of those receiving the service to pay for it. Still, said Waters, "our greatest advantage over the dailies was our ability to call upon our frustrated journalists forced by economic necessity to earn a living at other occupations. They were our auxiliary volunteer staff, each possessing a highly prized press card," which they could leverage—in lieu of payment from the ANP—to their benefit.[110] ANP correspondents—before the advent of "integration"—also were loyal, perhaps because of the dearth of opportunity available to them. Harry Levette became their Los Angeles correspondent in 1926—and was still filing stories in 1961.[111]

Thus, in early 1939, W.E.B. Du Bois proposed to write a "monthly letter of interpretation" for the "Negro Press." He had "planned something of the sort" for the *Pittsburgh Courier,* but the journal "wanted something else." The NAACP founder wanted to prepare "an interpretation of certain outstanding events in world news and their relation to the American Negro, to general history and to the history of the Negro race."[112] But Barnett could not afford to pay for this proposal and turned him down because "our sole source of support is the pittance which the papers pay for the upkeep of the organization."[113]

In some ways, the ANP complemented the NAACP in that it too sought to knock down the walls of Jim Crow. In 1939 the news agency proposed a kind of merger with the association but, gently, Roy Wilkins, then with the NAACP, rejected the idea, though he went to great lengths to do so in order, he said, to bar "misunderstanding" that would compromise their de facto alliance.[114] In other ways, the ANP was a competitor of the NAACP in that blacks in distress often were prone to contact the former before the latter, which meant they competed at times for the same pot of funds and, at times, there was sniping between the two.[115] At times the two titans ran a kind of "good cop/bad cop" routine with U.S. elites. When the NAACP in 1942 issued a stinging rebuke of the National Association of Manufacturers, Barnett—whose sideline business as a public relations consultant was lucrative—advised this elite body on how to respond.[116]

Assuredly, Barnett, an astute businessman, cooperated with others of this class to their mutual benefit. In 1941, C. C. Spaulding, chief executive of North Carolina Mutual Insurance Company, one of the leading black businesses, in a note labeled "personal" and "confidential," told Barnett that he encouraged businesses to collaborate with ANP.[117]

ANP allowed Barnett's entry into elevated circles that might otherwise have been closed to him and facilitated his gaining contacts in Haiti, Liberia, and the Pan-African world generally. In the midst of an ongoing scandal about forced-labor practices in Liberia, Barnett contacted Harvey Firestone, a major investor in rubber plantations there, about an interview that could be leveraged for the advantage of the ebony press baron's own interests in West Africa.[118] When Firestone died, his company importuned Barnett to publicize the tribute that had been paid to his "memory by the Negro community of Akron."[119]

Hence, in 1937 Barnett asked John Hamilton, chair of the Republican National Committee, to secure for him "an introduction to several persons of means such as Messrs. Paul Mellon, Chauncey McCormick, and "Arthur Packard [the] personal representative of John D. Rockefeller."[120] Barnett, who was personally close to executives at Sears Roebuck, managed to get a grant for the ANP from that firm's Julius Rosenwald.[121]

To be sure, ANP provided a useful service—or product—in informing a broad audience about the horrors of Jim Crow, the evils of colonialism, the plight of black people (and the oppressed generally) worldwide. In doing so, it accomplished the purpose of amelioration of these terrible conditions and, for that reason alone, Claude Barnett merits remembrance.

*   *   *

In January 1965 one analyst seemed to be baffled by the closing of the ANP. For then it had a membership of "more than 75 American Negro newspapers" and "some 200 African newspapers," along with "two radio stations, two magazines and several individuals and institutions. During the 1962–63 fiscal year, its membership represented 21 states and 53.8 percent of the total number of newspapers published in the United States." About "50 percent of the news contained in the ANP releases were gathered by the headquarters staff of six" and "the other 50 percent came mainly from 72 correspondents strategically located." Even at the bitter end, the ANP mailed a news packet of "29 mimeographed" lengthy pages on Fridays and "27 pages" on Wednesdays and "16 pages" on Mondays. On its fortieth anniversary in 1959, the ANP launched a World News Service that was distributed weekly and was "designed mainly for the African press," both in English and French. Solidifying Pan-African solidarity was the fact that "French speaking students attending colleges in Chicago translated the English copy into French." This fifteen-page packet went to "97 newspapers, organizations and individuals in the French language," and "two Portuguese [language] newspapers received the French translation" too. These African correspondents were sited in Kenya, Tanganyika, Southern Rhodesia, Congo, Nigeria, Ghana and Liberia. ANP also clipped from some 100 African newspapers for this packet, and encouragement was "extended [to] young journalists" who wished to contribute, as ANP was on its way to forming a "Negro Press International."

With this apparent strength, how did it collapse? This analyst felt the reason was "something called 'integration.'"[122] That is, desegregation was a laudable goal, in that in would smash the lineaments of Jim Crow exclusion, but integration seemed to point toward the disintegration of the ANP at a time when the AP and UPI and the mainstream press generally were turning their dedicated attention to the victims of Jim Crow and colonialism, eroding the innards and the rationale of the ANP. Like the African slave trade,[123] the ANP was collapsing when it seemed to be at its height.

*   *   *

The paradox of the struggle against Jim Crow has been exposed further today. Despite the promise that the demise of black entities like the ANP would usher into existence a bounteous era of integration, a little more than a decade after the demise of the ANP, fewer than 4 percent of all journalists working in the nation's newspapers were from a minority—and fewer than that were African American. By 1989, 7.4 percent of the nation's editorial employees were minority and by 2008 the figure was 13.41 percent. By 2005 some 37 percent of the 691 newspapers participating in a respected survey reported that their newsrooms had no minorities. The membership of the National Association of Black Journalists has been shrinking steadily in recent years.[124] A 2015 report indicated that, for the most part, the nation's newspapers have not increased the percentage of African Americans in newsrooms above 1968 levels and may have even cut those paltry numbers: Then and now the figure hovers at an embarrassing 5 percent.[125]

Black journalists suffered—and journalism itself was wounded—when Barnett's ANP collapsed: such has been the strange career of Jim Crow in journalism. But more than this, African Americans generally did not benefit when the ANP collapsed in that this often-besieged community lost a staunch defender, a megaphone, and a crusader for human rights.

In any event, this book is designed to recollect the largely forgotten story of Barnett and the ANP and restore both to a well-deserved place in the anti–Jim Crow and Pan-African pantheon, as it relates the paradoxical story of how their very success paved the way for their demise. Barnett may be the most important unrecognized African American of the twentieth century, and the agency he built, the ANP, was surely one of the most important institutions of that era. This book recounts not only his story but also tries to braid his activity into a larger story of how his agency narrated critical events of this period. In sum, this is not just a biographical study but, more than this, a story of decades of epochal and often forgotten events told through the eyes of a sadly forgotten news agency.

CHAPTER 1

Beginnings

Barnett's great-great grandparents were free Negroes in antebellum Raleigh, North Carolina. His father was a hotel worker in Florida who learned enough Spanish on frequent trips to Cuba that he was able to supplement his income as an interpreter at a plush hotel on the St. Johns River. His mother, Celena Belle Barnett, was a native of Lost Creek, Indiana.

Shortly after his 1889 birth in Florida, Barnett was brought to Mattoon, Illinois, to live with his maternal grandmother, where he grew up, eventually attending schools in Oak Park and Chicago. A friend of his mother secured a job for him when he was twelve years old with the Sears family, which presided over a major retail enterprise. "I admired him tremendously," he said of his prime patron "and he not only talked intimately with me but used to give me tickets to theater and concerts." Sears was thought to be "colored" by many Negroes because his mail-order system of purchasing goods, which Barnett was to emulate in one of his first businesses, undermined plantation stores and their high prices. It was at the Sears home that he met Julius Rosenwald, a major philanthropist.

Barnett entered Tuskegee Institute in 1904, still under the deep influence of Booker T. Washington, who left a profound impression upon him. Then it was back to Chicago after his 1906 graduation, where he found employment in the post office. There, he recalled later, during the ordinary course of business, he saw "thousands of newspapers, magazines and advertising. . . . I found myself studying them for longer periods of time" and the seed was planted that this was a business he should enter. Not yet twenty, his future plans had not yet congealed, however, as he continued to harbor dreams of becoming an engineer. But even then he had an entrepreneurial sense, evidenced in 1913 at the time of the fiftieth anniversary of the Emancipation Proclamation, when he produced a series of portraits of famous Negroes and others, which were snapped up at a dollar each, providing a comfortable cushion of income. This provided the capital for him to organize a mail-order business in his uncle's garage that distributed portraits of famous Negroes. From there he began selling advertising space to newspapers.

Mrs. Annie M. Pope Turnbo-Malone
Founder and Owner

Annie Malone, a leading African-American entrepreneur, worked closely with Barnett from her headquarters in St. Louis. Courtesy of the Chicago History Museum.

By 1918 he was working nights in the post office and selling ads in the daytime, but then he moved to initiate Kashmir Chemical, a cosmetics company, the name emerging, he said, from "having heard or read somewhere that the most beautiful women in the world live in Kashmir." There was plenty of competition, including the eminent Madam C. J. Walker and Annie Malone, but the inventive Barnett lured a number of popular entertainers, including Ada "Bricktop" Smith and Florence Mills to appear in his advertisements. The business was wildly successful, to the point that Colgate's Cashmere Bouquet after charging consumer confusion, pressured him to change the name of this product to "Nile Queen." That change, however, contributed to the product's demise.

It was also in 1918 that the tall, lanky, and dark-skinned Barnett headed westward, spending three months arranging appointments on behalf of the *Chicago Defender*. In every city along the way, he encountered editors complaining about obtaining news. He sped back to Chicago, retired from the post office, and asked Robert Abbott, the patron of this periodical, for funding for a news service. Abbott balked. But he arranged a deal instead whereby Kashmir received ad space in newspapers and the newly born Associated Negro Press (ANP) got capital in return. The ANP was modeled after the Associated Press; thus all papers receiving the service were asked in return to submit items to be shared by others. There also were ANP correspondents and stringers who supplied copy regularly. Barnett recollected that news-hungry newspapers "virtually stood in line" to sign up. "Several publishers," he said, "agreed to swap advertising space for ANP service" and "Kashmir Chemical Company benefited" as a result.

Nahum Brascher, a Cleveland journalist who had worked for President War-ren G. Harding, came aboard, bringing numerous contacts with him. Brascher brought panache too, as he rarely left home without an elegant walking stick and an ever-present cigar, which, along with a stentorian voice, gave him a certain presence. At the end of the first year, 80 of an estimated 350 Negro newspapers had joined the ANP. Perhaps because of Brascher's influence, the ANP also received an endorsement from Harding. By 1920 ANP and Brascher offered Republican politician and former military hero Leonard Wood their services as publicists in Wood's attempt to receive the Republican Party presidential nomination. Wood lost and owed them $4,000 for their services, leading Brascher to appeal to the son of famed evangelist Billy Sunday to wield his influence to ensure payment, but to no avail. Then they turned to Wood's mentor—Colonel William Procter of the rising consumer products company Procter and Gamble—and were suc-cessful in wheedling money out of the campaign. This led to an agreement with the Republican Party to work on Harding's behalf, and this, in turn, led to con-tacts with other leading Republicans, including Herbert Hoover, whom Barnett admired, and Calvin Coolidge, who rubbed Barnett the wrong way.[1]

Barnett had toiled on Wood's behalf, admitting in 1920 that the ANP had planned to "carry in the . . . weekly news service . . . approved articles favoring Gen. Wood."[2] His allied firm, C. A. Barnett Advertising, which was housed in the same office as the ANP on Clark Street in Chicago, had plumped openly for Wood.[3]

Barnett had entered a field that had yet to exhaust its full potential. As early as 1880 Negro editors and publishers banded together to advance their common interests. In 1883 the *Washington Bee* had sought to organize a news bureau to broaden the paper's coverage beyond the merely local. By 1910 Chicago alone was supporting fifteen Negro newspapers, as it was estimated that as many as 70 percent of Negro families there bought at least one of these journals.[4]

Despite the untapped potential, the ambitious Barnett initially sought to pro-vide a service that was not limited to the Negro press. He had sought to recruit white-owned periodicals in Nashville and Columbia, South Carolina, but they were uninterested and thus missed the opportunity to receive the ANP's carefully curated news packet that was dispatched with major news on Fridays and gen-eral news on Mondays, just in time for the Wednesday deadline for publication observed by many of their clients.

Nevertheless, his business plan pointed to the hundreds of Negro periodicals that the ANP could draw upon that would be buoyed by the growing number of businesses emerging in Black America.[5] "Their businesses increased in the pe-riod of freedom by 588,000," he said in 1920, while the "per cent literate" in this community was 80 percent. The "value of church property [was] $85,900,000," he estimated, indicative of a wealth that could be built upon. Illustrative of the importance of the Negro press was the greater attention it was receiving from the U.S. attorney general, A. Mitchell Palmer, who was concerned that it was becoming a vector for radicalism. This too figured into Barnett's calculation on the reasonable assumption that such concern was an indicator of importance: "During the last year," said Barnett in 1920, "for the first time in history the office of the [A.G.] made a special investigation and public report of the Colored Newspapers of the country." Palmer thought that "agitators of the Radical Socialist Revolutionary conspiracy have devoted time and money and thought toward stirring up a spirit of sedition among the Negroes in America."[6]

Palmer may have been reassured if he had gotten a peek at ANP's correspondence with the Pullman Company, which employed numerous black workers as railway porters. The company was unhappy about the agency's coverage of unrest among these laborers, but ANP was unmoved: "Colored men broke the strike," it observed neutrally about a recent job action, "but the company has now turned its back on them," as the "foremen use every means to force us out."[7] It was unclear what role was played in the ANP's opportunistic position by the fact that the agency was planning a publication aimed at Pullman workers[8] and hotel waiters[9] with no discernible leaning to the left.

Barnett was torn when it came to dealing with unions. He was attracted for class and financial reasons to captains of industry, such as Firestone and Ford, but he could hardly ignore porters and waiters, a bulwark if the drift to the extreme right—which could imperil him too—was to be arrested. Thus, in 1934 Barnett, along with P. L. Prattis, then of the ANP, were to be found at a sizable "get together gathering" of "organized groups of Colored Railway Unions of America," convening at the Hotel Vincennes in Chicago.[10]

Assuredly, Barnett was ambivalent—at best—about the rise of unions, be they railway porters or auto workers.[11] When an organizing drive took place at a critical plant of the Ford Motor Corporation in Dearborn, Michigan, he argued that the company provided "Negro workmen one of the finest opportunities they have." Keen to capitalize on "opportunities" himself, Barnett took the time to send Ford executives "enclosed stories" hailing their (alleged) good works and added, "I wish to propose a plan" that "will do much to overcome the efforts of the CIO [Congress of Industrial Organizations, the union] insofar as colored workers are concerned." He proposed further to report on the "fallacies" of the CIO drive and the "advantage of [Negroes] remaining loyal" to the company,[12] because he was lukewarm toward this campaign and other unions.[13] But "Henry Ford," the CIO antagonist, Barnett chortled, "is one of the great present day benefactors of the Negro race"; hence, the Ford automobile "should be universally the car for the average Negro buyer." Seemingly, the ANP was willing to accept presumed emoluments in return for favorable press coverage.[14]

*   *   *

Because it scoured newspapers nationally and solicited articles from subscribers to its service, the ANP was also capable of providing a more capacious view of Jim Crow than most Negro journals. Of course, this was a particular concern of Barnett personally because his various business ventures often involved traveling by segregated trains.[15] He was right to be concerned when he found that the "Rock Island between Houston and Dallas has the lousiest arrangement I have ever seen on a railroad, a luxurious new streamliner with two seats in the baggage car to accommodate Negro passengers."[16] If there was any consolation, it was not just Barnett who faced this indignity. His congressman, Arthur Mitchell, informed him that "Mrs. Marjorie Joiner, a highly respected business woman in Chicago [was forced] to ride in the baggage car" too, but in her case "with a corpse" when "passing through Texas."[17]

There was a concordance between and among Barnett's various business interests in that there was an even larger market abroad for cosmetics than at home. He had a soft spot for cosmetics, as his Kashmir venture suggested. "About thirty five years ago after some experimentation," he said in 1933, "the idea of using irons on kinky hair was discovered. I don't know who made the first discovery," he said, "but it seems well authenticated that Mrs. [Annie] Malone was the first to successfully commercialize the idea" and that "Mrs. [C. J.] Walker was an agent of hers" in a business in which "profits were huge."[18]

Thus, with little apparent awareness of the social and psychological aspects of hair straightening, particularly among women, the ANP lavished positive press coverage on these fellow entrepreneurs. Edna Oyerinde was tied to Malone and by 1927 was marketing her products in Nigeria. Malone's Poro College was already established in eastern and southern Africa. Like Barnett, Malone was a Pan-Africanist of sorts, and classes at Poro College often opened with a recitation

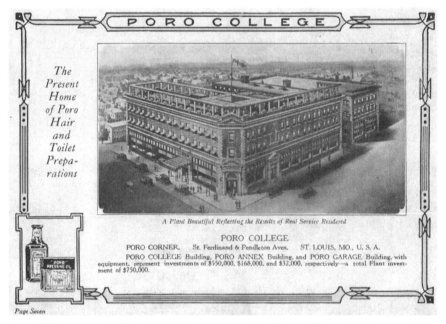

Poro College, controlled by Ms. Malone, was a major client of Barnett's. Courtesy of the Chicago History Museum.

NILE QUEEN
THE PERFECT PREPARATIONS
"FOR HAIR and SKIN"

On sale at all drug stores and first class beauty shops. If your dealer or beauty specialist cannot supply you—send us his or her name with your order.

NILE QUEEN Wonder Bleach
NILE QUEEN Hair Grower and Beautifier
NILE QUEEN Cold Cream
NILE QUEEN Vanishing Cream
NILE QUEEN Liquid Cold Cream
NILE QUEEN Face Powder

Pink, Flesh, White, Brunette and Cream Brown
50c each — postage 5c extra

FREE Beauty Book FREE

KASHMIR CHEMICAL CO.
Dept. 00   3423 Indiana Ave.,
CHICAGO, ILL.

This hair-care product was developed by Barnett as he first launched his entrepreneurial career in the aftermath of World War I. Courtesy of the Chicago History Museum.

of Paul Laurence Dunbar's "Ode to Ethiopia."[19] Malone and Barnett cooperated on West African investments.[20] At this point, Malone was more active abroad than Barnett, for as early as 1922 her Poro College boasted of "enthusiastic agents in every state in the United States and in Africa, Cuba, the Bahamas, Central America, Nova Scotia and Canada."[21] The ANP was kept abreast of Malone's varied activities, for example, her European tour in 1924.[22]

Barnett already had announced that the "salvation of the little group of capitalists which the race boasts," and of which he was a member, "lies in developing an absolutely independent press"; that is, his overall business interests turned on the success of his ANP. As early as 1928, however, Barnett was told that "colored people have already lost control of the Negro press." This was a shaky assertion based on the idea that the soon-to-be defunct "*Chicago Bee* is subsidized to the extent of $3000 weekly by the Overton interests."[23] Still, this assertion was an early indication that non-Negroes smelled the profits to be made in this realm, which signaled what was to come. Certainly, Barnett and his "little group of capitalists"—to a degree—benefited from the captive market that Jim Crow delivered, while chafing at the repetitive indignities of such seemingly ordinary activity as taking a train. Ironically, when Jim Crow began to erode, so did his hold on a captive market.

Barnett's own difficulties with Jim Crow at home also gave him added incentive to pursue opportunities abroad. Like many African Americans—before and since—he found that this praxis of prejudice seemed to be more inured in his homeland and, as well, when it did materialize overseas it was often at the behest of Euro Americans. Moreover, global press coverage facilitated the possibility of press coverage abroad of U.S. Jim Crow, placing this pestilence in the spotlight to its detriment.

At that point, in addition to the scores of newspapers that had joined the ANP, the agency claimed that it possessed a "bona fide mailing list of 125,000 names" and could easily "procure 400,000 additional names at a minimum cost of one cent each," giving Barnett a rare, if not unparalleled ability to reach African Americans and their allies globally. [24] Though Barnett and the ANP were perceived understandably as being a virtual arm of the Republican Party, their very letterhead urged readers to distinguish between, for example, the Democratic Party of New York and their counterparts in the "Solid South. Many of our friends are Democrats," it was said, "while many of our worst enemies are Republicans. Ask any colored lawyer what judges are the real square friends of the colored people," it was noted in anticipation of the massive decadal shift to the party of Franklin D. Roosevelt.[25] When a protest erupted at the 1928 Republican convention over the seating of the "Lily Whites from Louisiana," Barnett was contacted immediately because it was thought that he was well positioned to broadcast the "reactionary effect on [the] Colored Electorate in Northern States."[26]

Though at times it seemed that way, the ANP was not a one-man band. The staff included Irene Rowland, a fast and accurate stencil cutter, who toiled alongside Barnett for decades, from shortly after her high school graduation. She also served as his bookkeeper and secretary. There was also J. Henry Randall, father of a large family, who was a good mechanic and a fast typist. He was also a good rewrite man and, because of his knowledge of French, he was important for Africa coverage. Leahman Reid and Charles Livingston worked part-time at the post office and part-time with ANP. Staffers often were fielding frantic calls from newspapers when packets were delayed because these periodicals were so often bereft of both journalists and news. Fees were based on circulation, and very few of these journals—less than 25 percent—paid their bills on time, compelling Barnett to expand his businesses in various directions. Barnett warned these deadbeats and threatened them too, but he rarely deleted any of these journals from the ANP packet list.[27]

The flirtation with the Democratic Party, which was to flower in 1932, was not readily apparent in the pivotal presidential election of 1928. Then, even the successful nominee, Herbert Hoover, thanked Barnett for the "very fine support you have given me in the past months."[28] Others were not as convinced of the beneficence of the Republican nominee.[29]

Choices were sparse, a reality exposed by the controversy that erupted when African American delegates at the 1928 Democratic Party convention in Houston were, as the ANP put it, forced into a "chicken-wire enclosure," segregating them effectively.[30] The ANP's attacks on the party were all the more important because many of the leading organs of the Negro press proclaimed support for the Democrat nominee, Governor Al Smith of New York.[31]

A survey indicated that an increasing percentage of Negro newspapers were declaring their political affiliation as independent, eroding a decades-long trend.[32] Still, Barnett continued to back the Republican Party.[33]

Later, Barnett was working closely with his comrade P. L. Prattis, a Republican stalwart, in what was termed a "Kansas syndicate headed by Alf Landon," that "in strictest [confidence]" was seeking to buy Negro newspapers. "Find out if the [Chicago] *Defender* can be purchased outright," Barnett was told, though "these whites would be completely out of the picture" and would need a Prattis—or Barnett—to run the show. "You need not let [Robert] Abbott," the Chicago paper's major owner, "know any of this." The "money is available," he continued, and so "move with some speed." "$50,000 is a fair price" for "the purchase of a 51% interest," and "the fruition of this idea" could mean that Barnett could "shuck ANP," which was presumably worth much less. "You have remained a good Republican,"[34] Barnett was told—not exactly a revelation—which is why he was being brought into the deal. Such dealings also indicated why Barnett remained loathe to desert the Republican Party, even as many of his readers did leave.[35]

In short, Barnett, a skilled businessmen, recruited other Negroes in this category on behalf of the Republican Party and used the ANP as an enticement for the party, because it could provide favorable publicity if need be. In this capacity he had outmaneuvered such heavyweights as Robert Vann of the potent *Pittsburgh Courier*, whom the Republican Party listed sourly as "disloyal and bitter."[36]

Despite trepidations, Barnett and others among the Negro elite were reluctant to abandon the Republican Party; this lengthy list included the sainted antilynching campaigner Ida B. Wells-Barnett, who wrote a pamphlet entitled "Why I Am for Hoover" in her capacity as "National Organizer of Colored Women of Illinois."[37]

Increasingly Barnett—and those of similar outlook—found it difficult to back the Republican Party as it accommodated itself more forthrightly to Jim Crow. With the massive migration of African Americans northward and westward from Dixie and as more Jamaicans and others from the Caribbean headed to the mainland, they found it easier to ally with the Democrats, as symbolized by liberals such as Franklin D. Roosevelt. This alliance was particularly eased by markets beginning to gyrate and economic misery descending, facilitating migration to Democratic Party strongholds. As a result, New York City had a larger Virginia-born population than Norfolk did, though this did not necessarily erode the circulation of the *Norfolk Journal and Guide*, one of the leading black weeklies in Dixie, because migrants often sought to follow the news back home.[38]

*   *   *

The ANP provided value to its subscribers most notably in depicting global trends, which in some ways provided more uplifting news than the often dismal tales of lynching and oppression that characterized the domestic scene. Besides, foreign news was certainly one area that financially strapped Negro newspapers found it difficult to provide for themselves and that mainstream organs seemed incapable of providing. ANP foreign coverage too fed the drift away from the Republican Party in that stories often concerned the attempt by Euro American elites, the bedrock of the party, to impose Jim Crow abroad. Moreover, as their rivals—particularly the *Chicago Defender*—noticed the success attained by the ANP in this realm, they moved in a similar direction. Thus, from 1929 to 1940 the *Defender* had a formal foreign news service that included a steady stream of African news and regular reports from Russia, South America, and Asia.[39]

There were numerous reasons for otherwise less-than-munificent Negro organs to venture into the expensive business of gathering foreign news. A notable example arose just after the election of Herbert Hoover when the affluent Negro publisher Robert Abbott of Chicago was turned away from a number of London hotels for reasons that reeked of racism. William Pickens, soon to be a leading NAACP official but then an ANP correspondent, was irate, denouncing the British as "the nearest kin of the American white man." Pickens, who spoke German, observed that "Mr. Abbott and I talked over the matter with some German friends in Berlin, where a black man is really free. Abbott was staying at one of the finest hotels in Berlin." This was no small matter as transatlantic tensions rose. "Even Paris was found to be slightly infected, in spots at least, with the American color poison. . . . By the way, Vienna in Austria is another place where there are no color maniacs."[40] In other words, how could a Negro businessman like Abbott make money abroad when subjected to the indignity of Jim Crow? And what signal was sent by the fact that Berlin and Vienna seemed to be more advanced than London—and Washington?[41]

Marian Anderson bolstered this potentially seditious notion. In 1930 she told Barnett that she was "studying on a Rosenwald Scholarship" in Berlin, learning German and "the traditional way of singing German songs," which "I could not get in America,"[42] a repetitive message that could complicate the routine execution of U.S. foreign policy.

By early 1930 the ANP reported that Pickens was slated to edit a German language newspaper "with contributions from Negroes all over the world"[43] and by 1932 he was giving six lectures in Austria.[44] As matters evolved, however, so did the ANP, which by 1933 reported that "Germans bar jazz," a policy that had been "pursued by the followers of Adolf Hitler."[45]

Yet when Berlin replied in 1935 to a condemnation of their racist policies by pointing to Jim Crow, Pickens was quick to underscore this point too. The ANP was unsparing in its condemnation of Berlin's policies. Their correspondent was appalled to witness Julius Streicher, the "King of Germany's Jew Haters" speaking before "25,000 Nazis"; but this dispatch also "scored the Americans for their inconsistency based on the treatment accorded Negroes in the States." This was a repetitive theme: not only castigating troubling events abroad but reporting the events in a way that reflected malignly on Jim Crow.[46] Likewise, the ANP in scouring "Nazi papers" noticed the use of the "U.S. example in asking Jim Crow laws for Jews," for example, "Jim Crow sections on all trains for Jews traveling in Germany."[47]

By 1939 the ANP was following the story of Adolf Morgens, "son of a colored father and white German mother" who escaped Germany though he was born there; his parents were circus acrobats and had moved to a once amenable Vienna—but now had to flee.[48]

It did not take an oracle to sense that the rise of fascism could buoy Jim Crow. This struck the educator Horace Mann Bond, one of Barnett's closest associates, who in 1934 envisioned "An American Fascist Party to be formed . . . based on anti-Jewism [sic] in the North and anti-Negroism in the South." They could "sweep the country, take over the reins of power in 1936, pass laws expelling all Negroes from jobs of all descriptions except domestic employment, segregating them completely in a ghetto, requiring passes of those who travel." Which way out then? "The only thing which can save this situation is an international world war," he mused. "The coming clash of color seems to me to be more significant than the coming clash of class."[49] This private opinion was reflective of a larger discussion. The ANP repeatedly during the 1930s reported on what Negroes—Angelenos in this instance—were discussing: the "growing menace of fascism," it was said, was "the subject of great debate."[50]

What is also clear is that Barnett was among those who sought to rescue threatened European Jewry by lobbying to increase their immigration to Palestine in the 1930s.[51] "The action of the British Government in barring admission of homeless Jews to Palestine" was reprehensible, Barnett thundered. How could London turn away "Jews who are driven like animals and criminals from their native homes in many parts of Europe," he lamented.[52] This may explain why *Dynamite*, a Chicago journal that sought to push African Americans in the direction of anti-Jewish fervor carried a banner headline at the same time denouncing "Claude 'Giraffe' Barnett" who "serves his white folks."[53]

In short, Barnett possessed a global awareness, as did many of his correspondents. When Pickens told Barnett that "colored people are traveling more and more," he was commenting not only on his own peripatetic nature but was pointing ANP toward a realm of reporting that it was inclined to pursue in any case.[54]

The ANP perceived early on that it could undermine Jim Crow abroad in a way that it was difficult to do at home. The tendency to blame Euro Americans for Jim Crow abroad was magnified when the ANP ascertained "miscegenation" was "prevalent in Wales . . . chiefly among Negro sailors and white women."[55] Thus, when shortly thereafter the Haitian diplomat Stephen Alexis was denied entry to a Paris cabaret, the ANP cited a reputable source asserting that this was because his admittance would have been "displeasing to our American clients"[56] Subsequently, the ANP interviewed a French parliamentarian who addressed France's "fairness" to "her black citizens" and went on to make a lengthy comparison of France and the United States on the question of racism—to the detriment of the latter.[57]

Similarly, when Abbott journeyed to Brazil, he attributed whatever racial bias he encountered to the presence of Euro Americans.[58] Brazil was a repetitive concern for both the ANP and the Negro press. As Abbott was encountering difficulty in Brazil, the ANP was quoting Will Irwin of Tuskegee to the effect that "South America is [the] land of opportunity."[59]

Reflective of Barnett's interest in Brazil was his being asked to join the bibliophile Arthur Schomburg and the scholar Franz Boas to sponsor "a series of lectures on the Brazilian situation at each of the leading white and Negro academic institutions in the South," with the partial purpose being convincing the "white students" that the "Southern racial attitude is not the only solution" and to "counteract provincialism" in Dixie.[60]

Cuba, which also had a sizable population of African descent, also was a prime concern of the ANP and, likewise, the conclusion was reached that "without American influence, there would be nothing in Cuba like a color line, not ever."[61]

But it was not just the affluent with disposable income for travel who were affected by this disturbing trend. In February 1929 the U.S. Congress passed a bill that permitted the mothers and widows of U.S. servicemen interred in Europe as a result of the Great War to visit the graves of the deceased. Women were to be furnished first-class accommodations on government-owned or chartered vessels. Typically, women defined as "white" sailed separately, apart from those not so designated, and besides, lodged in the finest hotels—black mothers, by way of contrast, were offered decrepit boarding houses. The Negro press was infuriated.[62]

So was U.S. Congressman Oscar De Priest of Chicago, one of the rare African Americans in the House of Representatives. Speaking before a mammoth crowd in Philadelphia, he denounced this rank bias.[63] The maltreatment of these mothers was a landmark on the road to Negro alienation from the Republican Party. Just before the 1932 election, attorney Joseph Harris, writing Barnett from St. Louis, was still "harboring resentment" because of this episode; "it should not be easily forgotten," he warned, as—like legions of others—he made a forceful "demand that the treatment of our women be the same as that of other women."[64]

This incident reflected and propelled a growing radicalism among African Americans that Barnett and the ANP could hardly ignore. George Padmore, a Trinidad-born Pan-Africanist who crossed paths repeatedly with Barnett, particularly during the time of Kwame Nkrumah's reign in Ghana,[65] captured the prevailing mood nicely when in a dispatch to the ANP he espied a "growing internationalism and a steady shift to the left among Negro workers through the world," which he said was "the most significant sign of the times today"; writing from pre-Nazi Germany, he found that the demand was for "self government of all darker peoples, including American Negroes."[66]

It turned out that the ANP had quite a bit to be infuriated about.[67] But overriding all else for the ANP was coverage of Africa, a continent that became the locus of some of Barnett's most lucrative investments. The National Negro Business League, which was the epitome of the Tuskegee model of which Barnett was a part, as early as 1921 met in Atlanta alongside President Charles King of Liberia. Reflecting the commercial aspect of Pan-Africanism, he was introduced by Booker T. Washington's successor, R. R. Moton, who saluted this executive's presence "because Africa is part of us and we are part of Africa." For his part, President King exemplified why Barnett could seek to profit in Africa and push for anticolonialism simultaneously by exclaiming "we in Africa take a great deal of interest in American Negroes. . . . we hear of lynching, ostracism and of the hardships of every kind." But it was not just Africa that attracted attention at this NNBL confab. There was a stern protest also of "atrocities perpetrated by the Turks upon the Armenian and Assyrian races in the Near East representing the oldest Christian nations in the world"; delegates also "had the privilege of [meeting] Dr. Isaac Yonan, a native of Persia."[68]

There was an implicit recognition that Africa—and African Americans—could not be free from atrocity as long as the scourge of racism was tolerated generally. But, again, Barnett and his ilk had a dual agenda: Upholding Liberia as a rare exemplar of African sovereignty was surely a priority. Shortly thereafter, however, Moton had spoken with Barnett on "certain ideas which he [Barnett] has for developing behind the Firestone Liberian project a sound Negro public opinion" to sustain it; that is, the ANP would be used to exploit the nation's vast rubber resources on behalf of U.S. capital.[69]

Pan-Africanism and the news could be leveraged profitably, in other words. As early as 1931, Barnett was speaking at length about "a firm, in which I am interested, [which] receives every month or so, orders from various points on the West Coast of Africa," including "Sierra Leone, Liberia [and] Gold Coast."[70]

Despite Barnett's interest in Liberia, which was also characteristic of many of the disciples of Booker T. Washington, the ANP did not stint in reporting on the less savory side of this nation. The agency interviewed Dr. Ottawa Jefferson Saunders, a U.S.-born dentist in Liberia, who blasted the American Colonization Society, which helped to found the nation in order to "create a 'dumping ground'" for Dixie's "illegitimate" children with Negroes. Yet the Negro settlers persisted in maintaining a "superiority complex" vis-à-vis the indigenous Africans. This did not bode well for African Americans, he said. "Something similar to Hitlerism may yet [ensnare] the American Negro and he might find himself like the Jew, without a country," he warned ominously.[71]

Despite Barnett's capital investments and the accommodations they necessitated with colonial (and neocolonial) powers, the ANP generally provided more detailed and critical coverage of Africa than mainstream organs of that era, making the disappearance of the agency by the 1960s all the more poignant. "Rum, Syphilis and Illegitimate Children are the outstanding results of fifty years' missionary work of white people in the Congo," was the conclusion reached in 1929. "The black people of Africa are crying out for the advent of their blood brothers from America," was the message because "they know more about Marcus Garvey than they know about Jesus Christ"; in fact, "the only thing the Europeans fear in Africa is the name of Marcus Garvey." Contrary to the prevailing mainstream wisdom, the ANP reported that "there is not much hope for the Africans as long as white missionaries from Mississippi, Texas and Alabama predominate" because their "sole purpose is to live a life of ease under the tropical sun with black servants at their beck and call."[72] The ANP was quick to report, as a result, on "revolt in the Congo."[73] Solidifying the ANP's ties with a region that happened to produce a countless number of African Americans, the agency regularly referred to Black Chicago as "Chicago's Congo."[74]

Though this report was stingingly critical of missionaries, this approach was not wholly reflective of the ANP's attitude toward them. The ANP blared the accomplishments of Dr. Aaron B. McMillan of Omaha, who received an M.D. from the University of Lisbon and by 1931 was en route to Angola where, it was said beamingly, he "will become a member of a mission station wholly manned by American Negroes," where he planned to learn the Ovimbundu language. Born in Cotton Plant, Arkansas, and educated at Bishop College and Meharry, the erudite Dr. McMillan also served a term in the Nebraska legislature.[75]

Such reports of figures who rarely—if ever—were noticed by the mainstream press insured that the ANP and Barnett would have a chance to survive, even during the harshest moments of the Great Depression. Though the ANP was willing to shape coverage to appease burghers like Ford and Firestone, there was a recognition that their prime constituency was not in the castles but the cottages. This came clear as the crisis in Haiti deepened and as radicalism inspired by Moscow proliferated.

CHAPTER 2

Haiti and the Bolshevik Revolution

Claude Barnett was sufficiently perspicacious to realize that the U.S. occupation of Haiti, which had commenced in 1915 and was to last until 1934, was not in his or his class's interests. Moreover, as numerous African Americans moved leftward during this same period under the influence of the Bolshevik Revolution and the emergent U.S. Communist Party, Barnett—though a staunch Republican—demonstrated his flexibility by seeking to accommodate them too. Unlike some in his class, Barnett did not instinctively bow to either colonialism or anticommunism.[1]

*   *   *

Reflective of black concerns,[2] when Congressman Oscar De Priest gave his maiden speech in the House, Haiti was the subject.[3]

The ANP conceded that illiteracy was an issue in Haiti but stressed the "formidable list of composers" and writers that resided there.[4] Barnett's staunch opposition to the occupation may also have been influenced by what Haiti president Sténio Vincent told the ANP: "it was Franklin D. Roosevelt," he said, who in past years "drafted the much-hated Haitian constitution which was rammed down the throats of the Haitian people with the muzzle of a gun."[5]

It was in 1929 that another ANP correspondent objected sternly to the "slave trade between Cuba, Haiti and Jamaica" promoted by rapacious "American capitalists." The objection was to the horrid conditions in which cheap labor moved to Cuba, a practice facilitated by the U.S. occupation of Haiti and the dislocation and terror it delivered. Barnett's ANP could not ignore the point that "hotels, restaurants and other public places" that now were "operated by Americans" chose to "freely discriminate against Negroes, in spite of Cuban law."[6]

Naturally, the ANP gave extensive coverage to Haitian protests against the occupation, W. E. B. DuBois's backing of it,[7] and the like sentiments expressed by ANP correspondent William Pickens.[8]

Barnett's Tuskegee comrade, R. R. Moton, was instrumental in forming a commission to travel to the island to investigate the sordid conditions there, though the commission was compromised by its alleged ties to U.S. president Hoover.

Still, upon its arrival in 1930, huge crowds of Haitians greeted the commission rapturously. Though their ostensible mission was to study the plight of education in Haiti, the ANP's coverage indicated a larger unease with the U.S. role there.[9] Besides questioning the U.S. role, ANP correspondent P. L. Prattis detected another benefit of his journey with Moton to Haiti: "strangely enough," he said wondrously, "southern white Americans have been among those who have been most pleasant with us during our stay in Haiti."[10] The ANP was able to communicate to its audience that there was a certain cynical opportunism exuded by the promulgators of Jim Crow in that they were willing to compromise their alleged sacred principles if they found themselves in an environment where they were outnumbered and surrounded by those clearly unwilling to acquiesce; even a Haiti with limited sovereignty conveyed this important message, which left the conclusion that full sovereignty would deliver an even more robust retreat from Jim Crow.

Moreover, since Jim Crow was being exported from the United States, the ANP felt duty-bound to track the phenomenon, sensing that the overseas reinforcement of this system of iniquity could not be good news for African Americans. Thus, during the U.S. intervention in Nicaragua in 1931, it was almost with glee that the ANP reported that "Nicaraguans slay roaming Southerners" as "Uncle Sam's Marines and business men" were now under attack.[11]

The ANP floated a "theory that when Uncle Sam's Marines and businessmen go to the countries of the Caribbean and of South America where there is a large percentage of dark people, white Southerners who have little respect for dark peoples form a large proportion of both the Marines and the business army," with Managua being the latest example. "These southerners," the ANP charged, "as a rule go to those countries to be straw bosses and overseers on the plantations operated by big financial interests in the United States," based mostly in the North. Thus, it was in the interest of U.S. Negroes to fight their staunchest antagonist—Dixie—abroad as well as at home.[12]

Still, there were troubling signals in the bilateral relations between Haiti and Black America, said the ANP, in that the "Haitian attitude toward [the] American Negro is not inviting." These islanders, it was said, "like some other West Indians, think that they are better than American Negroes." In Washington, site of the Haitian embassy, "members of the legation have no social contacts with the American Negro" and preferred consorting with "white people."[13]

This reaction in Harlem was driven in part by the sharp reaction to the decision by President Hoover to appoint a body, which excluded African Americans, to scrutinize the occupation.[14] Hoover claimed that he did so at the behest of the Haitian leadership, which did little to improve relations between the latter and African Americans.[15]

Thus, when Dantès Bellegarde, a Haitian comrade of DuBois, was posted to Washington in 1931, the ANP exulted that "relations between colored Americans and Haitians are going to be much closer and friendlier."[16] The ANP erupted in glee when this Haitian envoy spoke to a "large and select" audience in Harlem.[17] Soon thereafter, Harlem received a premonition of better times to come when a French army captain—a Negro with roots in Guadeloupe—visited this community accompanied by a Haitian American translator who had just arrived from the percolating battlefields of Indochina.[18]

It was Barnett who consulted with Emmett Scott, the former right-hand man of Booker T. Washington but then at Howard University, about shoring up frayed ties by writing an article about Bellegarde "and his fine relationship with the colored people."[19] At this point Barnett also was considering recruitment of Zora Neale Hurston and her writing skill for this assignment because she had "spent some time in Haiti and the West Indies and knows all about zombies and witchcraft too."[20]

Thus, as the occupation was expiring in 1934, Albon Holsey of the Haitian Afro-American Chamber of Commerce in New York City was informing Barnett that "His Excellency, President Sténio Vincent" was inviting him to a luncheon in Harlem before his meeting with President Roosevelt. The president wanted to "welcome to the shores of Haiti a delegation of Negro agricultural experts[,] . . . engineers," and "business leaders" and wanted Barnett, who had been essential in publicizing his nation, to suggest names. This placed Barnett in the enviable position of being the indispensable broker, allowing him to profit handsomely from an already flourishing network of contacts,[21] a reality that had emerged when the Haitian president was greeted warmly in Harlem in April 1933.[22] It is not surprising that Barnett found this proposal intriguing, and he went further to propose an "entente cordiale" between "our Haytian brothers and our American groups," with his presence being essential to this process.[23]

With misunderstandings between the two groups dissolving, African Americans sprang into action on behalf of Haitians: Emmett Scott responded angrily from his post at the Republican National Committee when President Vincent arrived in Washington and somehow "no presidential salute of 21 guns" was forthcoming: there was "no fanfare, no military parade. . . . Why? Why?? Why???" Why "pomp and circumstance" for "dictators," such as Fulgencio Batista of Cuba and a "virtual snub" of the Haitian leader?[24] A hint as to why was evidenced in May 1934 when the ANP reported that when officers and members of a French naval vessel docked in New Orleans, all except a dark-skinned member of the crew with roots in Martinique were allowed entry into the St. Charles Hotel.[25]

Undeterred, a colleague of Barnett, Dr. A. L. Lewis of the Afro-American Life Insurance Company of Jacksonville, went to Haiti after the occupation ended and, as the ANP put it satisfactorily, "important developments regarding Haitian export and import business resulted."[26] A few years later, L. D. Reddick, a scholar and future adviser to Dr. Martin Luther King Jr., was in Pétionville, a posh neighborhood in the Haitian capital. "Yesterday I had a 45 minute tête-a-tête with the Haitian president," he confided to Barnett, and this leader "made some of the

soldiers once brought [there]." In any case, as he saw things, "today all traces of discrimination are disappearing" in Russia, so how could it be said that Jim Crow in the United States was immutable?[43] Miller may have known about what another ANP correspondent reported on in the Crimea: a huge Negro colony composed of "dissatisfied elements" existed, with roots in the United States, France, "English colonies . . . South Africa" and the "Belgian Congo." Many were artists, some were medics.[44]

Ted Poston, a black journalist not a part of the radical left, echoed the Marxists when he told the ANP that "the future of the Negro in America and the outlook of all oppressed groups throughout the world, will of necessity be greatly influenced by a fight which is being waged in the Soviet Union today."[45] The two passions of the ANP merged when the agency reported that the leading Soviet director, Sergei Eisenstein, was preparing to produce an epic film on Haiti's grand revolution.[46]

*   *   *

Though African-American writers had all manner of difficulty in getting published at home, "works of Negro poets" were "to be published in Russia" as of 1932.[47] Always alert to business opportunities, it was in January 1931 that the ANP carried the headline "Soviet Seeks Negro Business," a reference to "candy manufactured by the Soviets and featured at an extremely low price" and "of excellent quality" that was seeking successfully placement in stores catering to African Americans: "Harlem thus contributes to the USSR" was the accurate conclusion.[48]

In Brooklyn, the agency covered a debate between H. G. Mudgal, editor of Garvey's *Negro World,* and his interlocutor, Edward Welsh, on "whether Garveyism or Communism [is] best for Negro"—"there was no decision" who the victor was, apparently, and certainly not in Barnett's own mind either.[49] Thus, Barnett did not hesitate in urging Paul Robeson, even then known to be a friend of Moscow, to contact the ANP's London correspondent, Rudolph Dunbar.[50]

Surely, the efflorescence of both the ANP's and Black America's positive attitude toward Moscow occurred when the Soviet-backed International Labor Defense rode to the rescue of the Scottsboro 9. Miller thought that the campaign surrounding this case involving false claims of rape in Alabama meant that "the cause of the American Negro has been put before world opinion as never before in our history."[51] The case was known widely in the Soviet Union, said Miller in September 1932; "Russian opinion" was "saturated" with it, he said, since "this [was] one country in which the Negro problem has received serious study." Scottsboro, he declared, "has been the means of carrying the case of the Negro before the public opinion of continental Europe"[52]—and he could have added: the world at large.

The International Labor Defense, backed by the Communist Party and advocates for the Scottsboro defendants, whose case became a cause célèbre, had what the ANP deemed to be a "an active news service known as [the] Crusader News

Service" and, said Barnett's agency, had "a definite policy of magnifying every disadvantage which occurs to Negroes in America"; uncannily, a similar charge could be leveled at the ANP too, but in words probably intended for the agency's corporate benefactors, it was said instead that the ANP "doubtlessly serves as a bulwark against the activities of this organization."[53] In sum, those within the orbit of the Communists also were competitors. Suggestive of the fecundity of the market was the report that even the Socialist Party, not known for devoting special attention to African Americans, was seeking to launch a "News Service for Negro Papers."[54]

"The international complex of the Communist movement and its inner unity guarantees the Negro active allies everywhere," said a pleased Miller.[55] Backing up Miller's assertion, in 1931—early in the launch of the campaign to rescue the Scottsboro defendants—the ANP reported that "Russian Communists" were "stirred by fight for Scottsboro victims." Then they reported that the U.S. consulate in Dresden was assaulted as a result of this case,[56] as was its counterpart in Leipzig.[57]

William Pickens, an ANP correspondent known to be close to the NAACP, was not part of the amen chorus tossing hosannas at the Communists because of Scottsboro. In fact, he reproved "Communist Mendacity" in this important case.[58] But he also conceded that "everywhere" Communists and their allies were in the antiracist trenches on this case, even, he said wondrously, "in Oklahoma—think of it." Yes, he said with sobriety, "the soundness of the Communist ideal of ultimate and absolute racial equality, no Negro with both brains and guts can deny."[59] Symptomatic of the times, it was in early 1935 that NAACP stalwart James Weldon Johnson was heckled in Black Chicago when he critiqued the Communist Party and the "Back-to-Africa" movement.[60] Meanwhile, ANP correspondent Drusilla Dunjee Houston asked pointedly in June 1931, "Will Negroes be Communists?"[61]

Miller made his portentous pronouncements during a tour of the Soviet Union, but after his six-month stay there, where he reported vigorously for the ANP, he reproved the "provincial mindedness of the Negro," which was "one of the greatest single obstacles to intelligent action on his part"; thus, said Miller in words that received the editorial imprimatur of Barnett's ANP and could have stood for their credo, "if we are to find relief we must be alive to international currents."[62]

This is why, in August 1932, an ANP correspondent was to be found at the League of Nations headquarters in Geneva covering an important disarmament meeting. "Why don't the American Negroes maintain a representative here," he asked querulously; "if it cost you five or ten thousand dollars a year, it would be one of the best investments ever made" because "such work would have more influence in the United States than if done in the U.S. They can ignore you over there but they would have to consider you if you worked from this international layout in Geneva."[63] The de facto division of labor among African Americans then was that if this challenge were to be taken up, the ANP—and not the NAACP—would be the one to do so.

Barnett, the Republican, was of a like mind with Miller, the presumed Communist. Miller also wrote for an ANP affiliate, the *California Eagle* in Los Angeles, and it was from there that he chose to congratulate Barnett on his Scottsboro coverage: "your zeal in covering the most important case of [this] generation should merit the applause of your member papers."[64] Actually, the "member papers" were pushing the ANP for even more. "We desire to have you send us all wires in regard to the Scottsboro case," said Clarence Scott of the *Indianapolis Recorder*, "particularly those which contain dramatic elements that might form [the] basis of good news stories."[65] Reflecting the sensitivity of a case that involved inflammatory allegations of interracial rape, Jasper T. Duncan of the *San Antonio Register* adopted an opposing tack.[66]

The global nature of the case made the need clear to Barnett to send more correspondents abroad to measure the depth of support. The ANP reported on Cuba protests about the case[67] and was on the scene as one of the mothers of the defendants—Ada Wright in this case—headed to rallies in Europe.

Shortly after Miller returned from the Soviet Union, Barnett was angling to send another Californian there, with Scottsboro on the agenda. "One of our correspondents located in Los Angeles," he told a Communist leader, "is exceptionally competent. Her name is Fay Jackson" and "she would like to make a trip to Soviet Russia serving as correspondent for us. Could such a thing be arranged?" he asked hopefully.[68] Barnett also sought to cooperate with the left-leaning journalist Eugene Gordon, then residing in Moscow. In 1936 he sought to extend to him "the use of these columns whenever you wish to send material."[69] Like many thinking persons, Barnett was quite concerned about the rise of fascism in the 1930s and saw the rise of socialism as a countervailing force.[70] The mercantile Barnett considered arranging tours of the curious to the Soviet Union.[71]

Fay Jackson wound up reporting mostly from Western Europe, but that did not unduly hamper the ANP's ability to cover Communist affairs. A regular ANP correspondent from throughout Europe was Nancy Cunard, a dissident left-wing heiress to a British fortune. In 1935 she organized a written protest against a conservative attack on Moscow and Communists prepared by George Schuyler, the noted conservative writer, that was reprinted in the ANP and cosigned by Chatwood Hall, the ANP's correspondent in Moscow.[72] Perhaps because of her connection to capital, Cunard seemed to be a favorite of Barnett, her radical views notwithstanding.[73]

Being an heiress, Cunard was unlikely to press Barnett for better pay for her journalism. Such forbearance was not displayed by Rudolph Dunbar, the ANP's London correspondent, who continually pressed for more money. On the other hand, the talented Dunbar, with roots in British Guiana, who admitted that "I think like an Englishman," was pleased that "my status here is not like a Negro journalist in America. I receive all respect, courtesy and dignity of the press just the same as white journalists,"[74] a praxis that he would have been spared in the United States.

Similarly, when Irene Dobbs, who taught French at Spelman College—and was the mother of the future Atlanta mayor, Maynard Jackson—married in Toulouse, France, in 1933, the ANP was eager to note that the ceremony was "performed by the Mayor," which would have been unthinkable in her hometown in Jim Crow Georgia.[75]

The ANP did quite a bit to destabilize the view that has yet to be eliminated among many African Americans: that all those defined as white tended to be as retrograde as the most reactionary of their group in the United States. Though the nation was born in a revolt against London, the ANP continued to portray Britain as being friendlier to those like their readers. Thyra Edwards, a left-wing African American activist who contributed to the agency, reported from London in 1934 that "Indians who come to America quickly learn [of] the disfavor in which the Negro is held, so they carefully cling to their turbans (absolutely not seen in London or Oxford) and thus have access to all the privileges of the whites" while the "ever ingenious [U.S.] Negro had, in emergencies, 'donned the rag,'" in order to emulate turbaned Indians and escape routine censure at home.[76]

Thyra Edwards also reported to Barnett about events in Moscow,[77] informing him in 1936 about an upcoming "Pushkin Jubilee" there.[78] She would join Chatwood Hall, the ANP correspondent there, who was lionized by the ANP.[79] Barnett sought to secure a "correspondent's visa" for Edwards for the Soviet Union, with stories on "national minorities" being central to her mission.[80] It was Hall who told ANP readers that "tens of thousands of Russians gathered at the . . . Pushkin monument" in Moscow to mark the hundredth anniversary of Pushkin's death.[81] It was also Hall who called attention to George Tynes, a black alumnus of Wilberforce and Virginia State universities, then in exile in the Soviet Union, and Robert Robinson, yet another U.S. Negro, who by 1937 was sitting as a deputy in the plenum of Moscow.[82] A once jobless black graduate of Columbia University, Richard Williams, found employment at the "immense Ural Aluminum Combinat" in the Soviet Union.[83] He was joined by a "former Virginia State and Omega Psi Phi man" who was "head agronomist of [a] huge collective farm," with a son who "speaks Jewish [*sic*], Russian and Uzbek but not English." Also in Uzbekistan was the former Sadie Russell of Norfolk, whose son was born in Uzbekistan.[84]

Anthony Overton, an agricultural specialist from North Carolina then in exile in the Soviet Union, said that "oddly enough . . . I'll have to make some unpleasant adjustments in order to accommodate myself to my own native country" because, he declared, "I pleasantly dovetailed into the free and equal life to which all colored people aspire." His interviewer, Hall, chimed in by denouncing the "criminal sabotage and wrecking activity of the enemies" of socialism, including "traitors" aligned with the "fascist Trotskyite spy [Viktor] Chernov."[85] Overton agreed. This U.S. Negro, who had graduated from North Carolina A&T University in 1929 and was supervising a huge Soviet livestock farm by 1937, said movingly, "I only began to feel like a real human being after reaching Soviet Russia."[86]

The ANP coverage of the Soviet Union was stunningly positive and in contrast to its U.S. counterparts, which focused on human-rights violations. But the ANP merely anticipated its peers, for when the United States allied with Moscow by 1941, the mainstream's coverage shifted too, for then mainstream employers—like the ANP in the 1930s—were concerned about survival and were desperate for allies. Hence, the ANP correspondent responded breathlessly in 1937 at the height of the purges in Moscow that Soviet speakers at a rally assailed disfranchisement laws in Dixie.[87]

Thus, Chatwood Hall visited Abkhazia in 1937 to report on "Soviet Negroes" residing there. But what shocked Hall was the clerk at the hotel he visited there that "never heard of 'We don't take N——ers'" in this socialist hotel. Indeed, he mused, the bourgeoisie there along with their regressive attitudes were "Gone with the Wind."[88] These Africans arrived in Abkhazia almost two centuries earlier when it was under Turkish rule. "They are the only really free Negroes in the world in every sense of the word," said Hall.[89] Hall ascertained that "Negro and other Abkhazians" tended "to love Stalin most," for he had done "early revolutionary work" there and "showed the Abkhazian masses the path to national liberation."[90]

Similarly, it was with seeming gratitude that the ANP reported that Howard University's leader, Mordecai Johnson, denied he was a Communist by echoing the words of Harlem's Adam Clayton Powell Jr., who said, "I don't mind being called a Communist" because "the day will come when being called a Communist will be the highest honor that can be paid to any individual . . . and that day is coming soon."[91] Tellingly, the ANP provided coverage of Jane Emery Newton, a Euro American, who fled to the Soviet Union with her spouse, an African-American Communist, after tiring of various forms of harassment.[92] Frank Marshall Davis of the ANP echoed these praiseworthy words tossed at "Red Russia."[93] Likewise, Barnett contacted Governor Eugene Talmadge of Georgia in 1935 about the case of the imprisoned young Negro Communist organizer Angelo Herndon.[94]

Consequently, the ANP was probably the leading entity among U.S. Negroes that publicized the Spanish Civil War, which featured communists and republicans defending a government that was to be toppled with the crucial aid of German and Italian fascists. The coverage had a Pan-African cast in that it stressed black combatants globally—from the United States as well—who fought alongside partisans of the progressive regime.[95]

"I want to go to Spain," Thyra Edwards told Barnett in mid-1937,[96] and soon she was in Barcelona providing intelligence to him.[97] The multilingual Edwards was well equipped for this difficult assignment. In 1929 she was reporting for ANP from North Africa, where many of the troops opposing the Spanish Republicans originated.[98] The ANP foreshadowed this titanic conflict between fascism and antifascism by covering extensively the congresses of the latter in the prelude to the war in Spain.[99]

The ANP also covered the European jaunts of the activist African American Edward Strong when he traveled to Geneva on behalf of the left-leaning National Negro Congress[100] and then sped to the war zone in Spain.[101] The ANP covered the trip even though a "fellow traveler" had told Barnett that "Edward Strong was a dyed-in-the-wool Communist"[102] and even though Barnett realized that the NNC "has been accused of relationships with Soviet officials and has probably received some support from that source."[103] It was the ANP that highlighted a report when NNC cofounder John Davis made a "radio speech" that began "greetings to the Soviet people from the masses of Negro people of America."[104]

Presumably, mainstream U.S. Negro leadership agreed with Edwards and Strong too in that serving alongside Robeson in the "Negro Peoples Committee with the Medical Bureau and North American Committee to Aid Spanish Democracy" were the leader of the National Urban League Lester Granger, educator Mary McLeod Bethune, NAACP leader Channing Tobias, union leader A. Philip Randolph, and William Pickens.[105]

Potential correspondents in Spain volunteered to write for ANP,[106] not an unusual occurrence. Among them were Roy Woodson, former head of the "Colored" YMCA in Indianapolis. Writing from Valencia, he evinced the sentiment that had gripped a good deal of Black America in arguing that fascism spelled doom for U.S. Negroes,[107] a sentiment echoed by Fay Jackson.[108]

Their fervor was matched by that of Nancy Cunard, who reported to the ANP about the multifold activities of the Negro nurse from Harlem, Salaria Kee, and the "two new Negros" who had "just arrived" in Spain.[109] Langston Hughes, also on the Spanish battlefront, concurred with the idea that fighting in Spain would weaken Jim Crow.[110]

So did an Irishman, W. J. Smith, who proclaimed that the "toughest fighters in Spain" were brigades that included "a number of Negroes, Cubans and West Coast Americans," perhaps because they were more aware of the larger stakes, not least in their own hemisphere.[111] Pickens, who also was on the front lines, saw little to discourage this viewpoint as he sang the praises of "Luchelle McDaniels" of San Francisco who "defeated a whole company of fascists with 30 hand-grenades at the Ebro [River]."[112]

It was Ted Poston, a Negro journalist not aligned with the Communists, who told the ANP that U.S. Negroes in Spain were "accorded opportunities of advancement denied them" at home. There were "Negro volunteers from . . . Cuba, the West Indies, Ethiopia and parts of Africa" there too. His informants were Hughes and Louise Thompson, the youthful black Communist, who also participated in international broadcasts about these feats that targeted the United States before heading to Paris for a solidarity conference featuring delegates from Haiti, Madagascar, Mauretania, Senegal, and other far-flung outposts of French colonialism.[113] There they were to find Pickens, Edwards, and others tied to the then like-minded ANP.[114]

Driven by the desperation embedded in the Great Depression and the shift leftward signaled by the growing influence of left-wingers like Robeson, propelled by Moscow, the ANP too was flirting with a radicalism that seemed ascendant. And as African Americans moved leftward, the political spectrum as a whole edged in that direction too. But this process was not without bumpiness, for the erosion of Jim Crow that this portended had grave implications for black businesses built in no small part on control of a captive Negro market. (An ANP brochure asserted that "American Negroes live as a 'country within a country'" and as a "'city within a city.' This is the Negro market."[115])

For it was during that same time that Barnett was told that one of the leading lights of the Negro press—the *New York Amsterdam News*—was broke.[116] If a newspaper in the city with, perhaps, the largest black population nationally could not survive, what did that mean for the ANP? Soon the ANP was carrying a story castigating "Jim Crow pages in Southern" periodicals, not per se because of the immorality of segregation but more because, according to the preeminent Negro journalist P. B. Young, this trend "may by their invasion of the colored newspapers throw out of employment hundreds of reporters, stenographers, bookkeepers and mechanics."[117] Already unleashed, said one observer, was a "scramble among current magazines to corner Negro circulation" as "the White Press," it was said with sarcasm, "discovered that the Negro is literate."[118]

Then there were the gaps in ANP's network. Fay Jackson was told in 1933 that though the agency served "more than 100 papers," this list did not include the *New York Age* or the *Chicago Defender*. Abbott of the latter journal was still smarting over how Barnett organized the ANP right under his nose and, said the ANP, he "thinks that everything important must originate in the *Defender*."[119] The ANP saw Abbott as a formidable foe and even when he became—in their words—a "decrepit invalid" by 1934, they continued to fear and respect his prowess.[120]

Of course, the actual—and imagined—leftward drift of the ANP did not escape the attention of conservatives. Unavoidably, Barnett's reproach of the right was not accepted with equanimity. Vincent Fitzpatrick, leader of the Catholic Press Association, in a detailed and vitriolic four-page single-spaced upbraiding, concluded that "never in my thirty years of journalism have I read even in the Ku Klux Klan papers such slanders" as those propounded by the "filth" of Barnett and his ANP. Barnett, he charged, was doing little more than "appealing to the Negroes to become Communists," that is, "to join the United Front."[121]

The editor of the *Catholic Review* also reprimanded Barnett when the ANP targeted the depredations perpetrated in Spain by the forces led by General Francisco Franco. An enraged Barnett proclaimed that "far seeing white papers of America . . . choose the side of fascism against that of communism, inasmuch as the papers are businesses and therefore capitalistic concerns and would apparently fare better under a Fascist's control." In fact, Barnett continued with asperity, "should America ever be forced to choose between the two," meaning fascism and communism, "which would seem to be not so much of an impossibility as some may think," he would decidedly not be with the fascists. Why? "Every intelligent Negro who has observed Russia's attitude toward Negroes and the Communist credo with regard to this race, and has compared it with anti-Negro Germany, a fascist nation and the theft of Ethiopia by the Fascist Italians," would fight the latter fiercely since "communism may be regarded as more liberal" and thus, "for his own safety, the intelligent Negro is forced to at least consider the import of Communism against Fascism."[122]

* * *

The cases of Loren Miller and Fay Jackson and their city of residence, Los Angeles, also illustrated neatly the problems faced by Barnett and the ANP. Lawrence La Mar of the *California Eagle* averred as early as 1928 that "we are privileged to be right in the middle of the youngest of the . . . largest industries in the world," speaking of the motion picture industry.[123]

The ANP was closer to the *Eagle* than was its competitor, the *Los Angeles Sentinel*, which stood to the right of the periodical that employed Loren Miller. The publishers of the *Eagle*, Charlotta and J. D. Bass, were firmly in the firmament of the left, unlike Leon Washington of the *Sentinel*. In 1933 Mr. Bass informed "Dear Friend Claude" that "Washington has no legitimate newspaper. He gets out a handbill financed by white merchants and deadly foes to Negro Progress who should be [ignored] . . . let alone by [the] Negro Press" since they were the "worst enemy" of them all.[124]

Part of what drove the ANP—and Barnett—to the left were rumblings from the base, where periodicals such as the *Eagle* and Roscoe Dunjee's *Oklahoma City Black Dispatch* were firmly in the grasp of publishers who were favorable to emerging radicalism. Ultimately, Barnett arranged for the leading black pilot, John Robinson, to travel to Addis Ababa to organize the fledgling air force there and file stories besides,[125] a decision prompted by sentiment emerging from the Negro masses.

Even before then, Barnett saluted lavishly the man who may have been the most radical black novelist—before or since: Sutton Griggs, the Texan and author of *Imperium in Imperio*,[126] had more than a modicum of Negro readers, which was a clear indication of the direction of political winds.

Barnett remained a Republican, but as the political spectrum among his base of readers and writers shifted leftward, so did he. "In politics this year I expect to stay in the middle of the road," he announced in early 1936. "As a matter of fact,"

The ANP also created lengthy features such as this one on the New Deal for its Negro press clients. Courtesy of the Chicago History Museum.

he said inaccurately, "ANP has never been in politics"—though this revision of history was a way to distance the agency from its Republican origins. "I, a staunch Republican," he told Fay Jackson "will be thinking that Roosevelt is doing a much fairer job for the Negroes than my own party ever did."[127]

At that juncture, in the 1930s, Bass and Barnett were of like minds politically but, as time passed, the ANP chose to place some distance between itself and the Communists in a manner that the *Eagle* abjured. Ultimately, both the ANP and the *Eagle* perished nonetheless, while as of today the *Sentinel* is still chugging along, the premier black newspaper west of the Mississippi River. In some ways, Barnett was flexible ideologically to the point of opportunism. When the ANP chose to emphasize global press coverage, with an emphasis on Pan-Africanism and consorting with the likes of Kwame Nkrumah, it inevitably would spell difficulty in breaking with the left in order to fit extant Cold War norms: this dynamic pointed ultimately to the demise of the ANP.

CHAPTER 3

World War Looms

In the 1930s Barnett, then approaching middle age, had adopted a noticeable interest in one of Los Angeles's major earners, the entertainment industry, not least since he had married a bona fide Negro star in 1934, Etta Moten. Her viability as a performer depended heavily on being au courant with dominant political trends, which made it difficult for the couple to follow the left-wing Basses of the *Eagle* or even the *Oklahoma City Black Dispatch* in lockstep. On the other hand, Moten's demonstrable difficulty in obtaining suitable employment in the United States drove her to seek work abroad. This reinforced Barnett's preexisting interest in global affairs and put him in touch with others similarly oriented, which had the impact of driving him leftward nonetheless.

Born in Texas in 1901 to an African Methodist Episcopal pastor, Rev. Freeman F. Moten, and Ira Norman Moten, a teacher, both of Weimar, Texas, Etta Moten was educated at Paul Quinn College's secondary school in Waco. In 1914 her family moved to Los Angeles, then to Kansas City, Kansas, and she attended high school in nearby Quindaro. As Barnett was launching the ANP in 1918, she was marrying Curtis Brooks and moving with him to Oklahoma. In rapid succession she gave birth to three daughters—Sue, Gladys, and Etta Vee—but then divorced Curtis and returned home to attend the University of Kansas. In 1931 she received a Bachelor of Arts degree and then entered the world of entertainment, rapidly gaining prominence when she performed in Zora Neale Hurston's musical revue "Fast and Furious."[1]

She too came from an activist and internationalist milieu. She was multilingual, as was her father: He spoke German, as did she (and other languages besides). The Los Angeles branch of the NAACP was formed in the back of her father's church. She may have been related to a prominent family of Motons associated with Tuskegee. One of Robert R. Moton's daughters, said Ms. Moten, "looks like me." In fact, it was at the Virginia summer home of Tuskegee's Moton that Barnett swept her off her feet and convinced her to get married on the spot. "I said I hadn't told my family," said the prospective bride. "He said tell them later. So

[Moton] gave me away and [we] were married on the lawn." This was 1934, and they had met in 1931. "He was most supportive of my career," she recalled, which was quite true. Because of his avid promotion of her talents, she said, "there's almost as much stuff out there about me and my career as it is about his Associated Negro Press."[2] They were a partnership in power, with part of the value she brought to their team being her effortless multilingual capability, an asset for an ANP with global ambitions. "The study of language when I did come to it," she said modestly, "was never hard for me."[3]

Enoch Waters of the ANP was among those impressed with her "regal carriage and impeccable manners" and her exquisite "taste in clothes." Speculating from close observation, he averred that "I imagine" that "as a wife" she was "complete in all respects . . . she was Claude's greatest asset" and "he stabilized, directed and elevated her." This mutuality was reinforced, said Waters, by her "exceptional charm" and their "smoldering passion."[4]

The magnetism of this couple also attracted the attention of Zora Neale Hurston. She too appreciated the "seductive Etta," telling Barnett, "some day I want you to write for me your emotions when you first saw Etta Moten. What part of you responded first? Your eye, ear or, shall we say your libido?" Perhaps "an article by The Etta herself" could help unravel what Hurston termed emphatically "a famous love affair."[5]

That it was. The tireless Barnett began almost immediately upon their liaison to promote his talented spouse. In January 1934, when their relationship was just blooming, Barnett—an audacious Republican—informed President Roosevelt, a Democrat, about Moten, a "young colored woman, who is idolized by the colored women of the country"; she happened to be "in Washington this week. If you could invite her to serve you during the afternoon or evening, I feel confident you will be most pleased at the result" because she "possesses a beautiful voice." Besides, "Colored people the country over are proud of Miss Moten." As an added touch, he enclosed a pro-FDR article by the ANP.[6] Then he informed a British impresario that she "can sing in French, Spanish, Italian and German, having studied all these languages" and "can take speaking parts [in films] in these languages" too.[7] Eslanda Robeson, then deftly managing the career of her spouse, Paul, and who was to become an ANP correspondent too, recommended his agent to her.[8]

It could not hurt her career when Barnett also began to schmooze with Hollywood bigwig Will Hays, once regarded as the industry "censor." He too was a major donor to the Republican Party. Paul Williams, an African American who designed many of the plushest mansions in Southern California,[9] was part of this circle: Barnett hailed Hays for "giving Mr. Williams the privilege of building your home."[10] Then he got down to business, which was probing Hays about the present and future of blacks in Hollywood, a worthy probe certainly, but also of benefit to his spouse. He was more direct in seeking to place Moten in the forthcoming film "Goldwyn's Follies"[11] and was disappointed to find that that though things looked "encouraging" for her to land a role in "Gone with the Wind,"[12] she was rejected. Undaunted, Barnett informed the studio, who may not have known of his relationship to her, that "Miss Moten is very definitely interested" in this blockbuster. "She has read the book and feels that the stolid Indian-like girl 'Dilcey' presents a role which she could do particularly well with," adding that "Etta is in splendid health."[13]

Moten, said Barnett, "does not have to do a straight Negro part though she prefers to do so," because she "would photograph light enough to do a really effective South Sea Islander or a Mexican or Spanish type."[14] Ed Sullivan, a future power in television, was told that Moten possessed "one of the most beautiful singing voices in the country." She had been slated to act alongside the bona fide star Jean Harlow in "Blonde Bombshell," but the director, Victor Fleming, objected on the premise that she "will make the audience forget Miss Harlow is on the stage." So they voided the contract, paid her a fee, and hired Louise Beavers, viewed by Fleming as not as alluring and diverting as Moten. In fact, said Barnett, she was "so stout that instead of wearing Miss Harlow's clothes," as Moten could have done, "all Beavers could do was hold them up to her neck and wonder what she could do with them."[15]

He hailed "Imitation of Life," a movie for which Barnett had "appreciation," though he thought Dixie would feel otherwise about this drama about racial "passing." In any case, his recommendation to Hollywood was that the popular screenwriter Anita Loos develop a script of a similar type for Moten.[16] Barnett also befriended the rising Negro actor Clarence Muse, whom he considered to be "a good friend" and, inexorably, of value to his spouse's career.[17]

Barnett worked strenuously on behalf of his spouse but often was frustrated. "Hollywood is difficult for Negro performers" was Barnett's euphemistic conclusion in the midst of his mostly unsuccessful campaigns for roles for his spouse.[18]

With the difficulties she faced in pursuing her craft in Hollywood, by 1936 Moten was looking southward. "I was in New York," Barnett told Pickens, "to see Etta off for South America where she goes on a three month engagement"[19] to perform in Brazil and Argentina. "She has met with marvelous success both in her work in the theatre and in broadcasting," said Barnett of Buenos Aires; "the papers have been full of her pictures and she is on billboards everywhere," which was a prelude to a similar welcome in Rio de Janeiro.[20] It may have been because of her performances in Buenos Aires, known for its sizable population of Italian descent, that Barnett was informed that the Casino Municipale in San Remo, Italy, wanted to host Moten.[21] It is not surprising that the ANP correspondent in London reported in 1937 that "Etta would do well here."[22]

Barnett did not have to be prodded to seek opportunities for his spouse, asserting that she possessed "one of the finest voices in all America": "it is truly lovely." And after her recent foreign concerts, she was now capable of rendering "South American Sambas, which are much like our Negro folk songs."[23]

The noted bibliophile Arturo Schomburg was then "reading in the African newspapers the very lovely experience your better half is receiving in the various cities of South America."[24] Moten was contracted to spend eight weeks in Argentina and was expected to be in Brazil even longer, providing Schomburg with many more opportunities to read of her performing feats.[25]

Perhaps inspired by the warm response to Moten, the Fisk Jubilee Singers, already renowned for their globetrotting, expressed a "wish to go to South America,"[26] which Barnett sought to actualize.[27]

Moten's journey to Brazil was accompanied by ANP coverage of Brazilian Negroes who opposed the "fascist dictatorship," pushing the nation to the verge of civil war.[28] The same held true for Argentina; for example, there was the ANP story about ninety-six-year-old Lee Moore, who was "shanghaied into slavery at 15" from the streets of this South American nation and then "sold into slavery in West Virginia."[29] The diligent Barnett began to collect material on racial problems in South America.[30]

It was at this point that Barnett and the ANP assumed more forcefully the role of the Negro's State Department, inquiring persistently about barriers strewn in the path of African Americans who sought to travel abroad. The ANP contacted the Brazilian embassy in Washington about the alleged barring of U.S. Negroes, though their charges were met with denials and, instead, the envoy expressed "amazement" at the intensity of Jim Crow in the United States.[31] The Brazilian embassy in Washington reassured the ANP, stating "we would like to welcome more American settlers."[32]

Nancy Cunard, ANP correspondent, substantiated the embassy's viewpoint in asserting that "even two hours in Brazil will show how . . . this must be the best country of all for people of color!"[33] Later the eminent sociologist E. Franklin Frazier agreed when he proclaimed that there was "no color line in Brazil."[34]

Barnett reconciled this conflict of opinions by pointing the finger back at his nemesis: Hollywood. The man with whom he had shared confidences, Will Hays, "President of the Motion Picture Producers Association of America has recently issued an order that Negroes are not to [be used] . . . as actors" in "depicting . . . people of Brazil." He referred to a recent "Technicolor short in which Katherine Dunham," the acclaimed African-American choreographer, "appeared in a Brazilian dance" despite stern objection. This objection, thought Barnett, was outrageous because "the Negroes of America feel an especial kinship with the people of Brazil. I plan immediately," said the ANP chief, "to broadcast the above fact to all of the newspaper[s] in Brazil."[35]

Again, the Brazilian embassy found this allegation about their objection to be "awfully wrong. Nothing like this ever came through the Embassy," the ambassador said with a huff. "We have never made any representation to the Will Hays office."[36] Barnett was impressed by the intensity of the ambassador's denial.[37] An irate Barnett then recounted all this to the relevant casting director, Bill Grady of the MGM studio.[38]

The ANP did not necessarily come to this issue with clean hands, for it could be accused easily of falling victim to nativist bias in objecting to Latin American migration to the United States, as it demanded an open door for African Americans to enter other nations. The agency "warmly congratulated" Senator Hiram Johnson of California when he sought "to place Mexico upon the quota list and thereby subject its prospective immigrants to the same rigid but reasonable rules as apply to the immigrants coming from continental Europe and other foreign countries" because "they have displaced from jobs both white and black natives. . . . Negroes have suffered especially from the underbidding proclivities of Mexican labor." This was compounded, it was said with disgust, by the "latest and most bitter insult of all," as Mexico was now trying to "restrict ALL PERSONS OF THE NEGRO RACE from immigrating [there]."[39]

"Thousands upon thousands of swarthy Mexicans low in their standards of living and wage cutters to a startling degree, have been steadily crossing the border in to America," the ANP reported anxiously in late 1928, displacing Negro labor supposedly. All the while, it was said accusingly, "their home government in Mexico City bars Negroes from entering Mexico."[40] In Los Angeles, claimed the ANP, "Mexicans and Filipinos cause Negro unemployment."[41]

The Mexican government irritably denied that it barred African Americans from arriving south of the border,[42] after being accused thusly by Barnett.[43] Thyra Edwards, whom Barnett knew well, was then in Mexico City, assisting the settlement of Spanish refugees from the civil war and would have been in a position to confirm—or deny—this point.[44]

William Pickens explained that there was "no race discrimination in Mexico," but consuls and emissaries in the United States often were unduly influenced by their posting and violated government policy freely.[45] It was reported by the ANP in 1936 that "whites [are] admitted to Mexico free; Negroes must pay $150."[46] This allegation was based on information provided by an esteemed delegation that included Dr. R. C. Barbour, a leader of Negro Baptists, and Dr. H. M. Smith, dean of the School of Religion at Bishop College in Marshall, Texas. They had taken a train from Mexico to Laredo, Texas, and it was in planning this journey that they applied to consuls in Galveston, Houston, and San Antonio "with absolutely identical results: as soon as they discovered we were Negroes they refused to grant us the tourist identification cards which white Americans receive as a mere formality in 2 or 3 minutes." They journeyed to the border anyway and "the police who were in charge being Indians" admitted them to Mexico.[47]

Edwin Embree of the Rosenwald Fund affirmed the ANP supposition that Mexican consuls tended to capitulate to rancid Dixie attitudes in handling tourism and migration.[48] The coda was left to the painter, Aaron Douglas, who declared, "the Negro sheds his color when he crosses the Mexican border and replaces it when he returns."[49]

Nevertheless, when a Mexican of African descent was lynched in Mexico in 1930, the ANP was hard pressed to blame Dixie for this reported outrage.[50]

The ampler point was that—again—the ANP perception that Jim Crow abroad was driven by Dixie was reinforced by this skein of events.

Unfortunately, it was not just Mexico where the Jim Crow problem arose.[51] The ANP was likewise perturbed to find "no Black officials" in neighboring Costa Rica. "Black engineers, firemen and conductors cannot drive or conduct a train from any part of the country to the capital," and "even mulattoes" faced "rampant" bias.[52] Repeatedly, the ANP reported on African Americans—including Raymond Pace Alexander, Robert Vann, Joseph Rainey, and William Pickens—and their shock and disgust at the flowering of racism in the Panama Canal Zone, where the United States held sway.[53]

Dutifully, the ANP reported that "American Negroes should take more interest in Spanish America" because "there are opportunities for engineers, tractor drivers, mechanics, architects, electricians" and other skilled personnel. Expatriation should be considered because "chances to succeed in those fields are almost completely closed to us in the states."[54] Presumably this optimism about "Spanish America" did not include the Dominican Republic, which had a deserved reputation of discrimination against the darker-skinned. With skepticism, Barnett wanted his Washington correspondent, Alvin White, to interview the Dominican president in order to "know how many blacks there are in his republic, their status economically and socially" and "his knowledge regarding American Negroes, his opinion of them and his color line opinions."[55]

*   *   *

Bolstering the view that the United States was a site to abandon was the ANP account of the experience of Caterina Jarboro, the "world renowned soprano," who had been residing in Europe since the year of Barnett's marriage, 1934. She was "said to be the greatest operatic singer in the race"; yet she was of the view that on the old continent "there is no color line. I was recognized everywhere as an artist and treated as [if] I [were] white. It was only arriving in the U.S.," she said dolefully, "that I was insulted."[56] "Being over here," she said of Europe, "is much better than being in America" because "over here, life is very nice and gay." As Moten performed in South America, Jarboro told Barnett that she had just traveled from Paris to Warsaw and from there to Łódź, then to Poznań, then Riga, then Estonia. She wound up in Monte Carlo, of which she said, "I plan to stay as long as they give me work," which was likely to be the case because "packed houses" greeted her during her serpentine tour. "Claude," she said familiarly, "you don't mind my saying so but my dear, your wife would just walk away over here and most of all in Paris and London." She had "been talking quite a bit about her to an agent," said the popular singer, who recalled that "the President of Latvia came [to] my opening in Riga" and the audience was so supportive that she was "so happy like a fool I cried."[57]

The ascending diva Marian Anderson did little to dispel Jarboro's favorable perception of Europe, when near the same time she spoke of the "enthusiastic way in which the Swedish public accepted [my] performances."[58] A Moscow periodical praised her "brilliant . . . concert,"[59] and on cue the ANP was full of "praises" of "Soviet theatre and audiences."[60] With exuberance, she told Barnett of her "two and a half months" in Russia and the "summer concerts" where "Salzburg was of course, the high point. And [Arturo] Toscanini's attendance or rather presence gave it an extra importance." It was "thrilling to [talk] with" this important conductor. Signaling how her absence from the United States did not signal her absence from the Pan-African ramparts, she was "preparing to give a concert" for "the benefit of the Red Cross ambulance to be sent to Abyssinia," then confronting Italian fascist invaders.[61] This activism solidified her role as an ANP favorite.[62]

As war crept closer to Europe, threatening to disrupt the haven so many African Americans had found there, Barnett sent ANP's Los Angeles correspondent, Fay Jackson, to London and Paris. She was tasked with "paying particular attention to world color problem[s]" and colonial administration.[63] Like Rudolph Dunbar, another ANP correspondent in Western Europe, she was pleased with her treatment. "There are 300 correspondents in London" and "only 10 seats for them in Commons. Thursday, I had one of these 10 seats in Row One!" Hence, she was doing fine "socially and professionally" but, like most who toiled for the ANP, "financially, not so swell." It seemed that other than male supremacy, Jackson was

Fay Jackson, no date, circa 1930s: The ANP relied heavily on women journalists such as Jackson, who covered tumultuous events in Europe in the 1930s. Courtesy of the Chicago History Museum.

doing quite well in London,[64] though she complained of "loneliness." Yet London had been so apparently accommodating to African Americans that Father Divine, the notable man of the cloth from Harlem, developed "plans to open a kingdom in London" because "there is one already in Finland!" said an amazed Jackson.[65]

This roseate view of Europe also influenced retrospective analysis. William Pickens argued that "the working people of Great Britain, the masses of Englishmen, Welsh and Scotsmen are as much to be credited with the emancipation of slaves in America as is Abraham Lincoln." Disconsolately, he concluded that "many Negroes have forgotten this. Most Negroes have never even found it out."[66]

*   *   *

The conflict in Europe, said the ANP's Fay Jackson in 1937, was "definitely over who shall rule and who shall rule the Blacks."[67] Berlin, she declared, desired African colonies now held by Paris and London and this was driving the push toward war.[68] In that, she echoed the opinions of W. E. B. DuBois, often acknowledged as the "Father of Pan-Africanism."[69]

The ANP was enmeshed in reporting on European conflicts but, unlike the mainstream press, this agency—particularly when contemplating Berlin's challenge—saw Africa as the heart of the matter.

The point was that the ANP was an indispensable source for news from the Pan-African world, Africa not least, Barnett's own self-interested dealings aside. Because of this, the ANP became the hub of a network of informants who sought to reach a larger African American and Pan-African audience by passing on news items to the ANP. Thus, in 1935 Noah Williams managed to get an item to Barnett about Damascus—"where the Apostle Paul received his sight" and "the French have a mandate"—concerning the fact that "most of [the French] soldiers here are from Senegal" and "very black" besides. Williams's point was also that "there is so much of the greatest things in our civilization that have their roots in the races of Ham and Shem," meaning that "no one should be ashamed of being a Negro or a Jew," an uncommon feeling at the time.[70]

Still, the ANP was not immune to the seductiveness of Paris, which over the years was to ensnare numerous African Americans, including the agency's own Richard Wright.[71] Reaching Barnett from his Brooklyn residence, the growingly popular writer was then "thinking seriously of trying my hand at something new," working as "a sort of foreign correspondent job for the Negro press. I'd awfully like to go to Russia, China and India and report the war for a three month period, because of my intense interest in colonial and subject people." Why? "Since this war began," said the farsighted Wright, "I've had the feeling that the center of gravity of Western Civilization has shifted from Europe to the Americas and Asia." His peer, Ernest Hemingway, had just left for China on a similar assignment, but Wright saw his mission as being different. Wright was "not expecting any organization to defray the whole of my expenses while on such a trip. (If the

ANP were the AP, I'd quote you a stiff price!)," even though his recent spate of fame meant that he was "beginning to feel almost *respectable*! I thought I was radical," he mused, "but the public is catching up with me." Even "some of the white folks are waking up, but I don't know how far they are willing to go in correcting things in relation to the Negro in America." He signed off with "best wishes" to both Barnett and his good friend, Frank Marshall Davis.[72]

Barnett replied encouragingly since Wright's proposal was closely akin to "our whole ideal for [the] ANP," which was "to give a broad picture of what is happening to black people—both domestically and away." Barnett pledged, "I will do my best to get it accomplished,"[73] and he tried to do so. "If the State Department should happen to call," he told his Washington correspondent, "and inquire whether Richard Wright is on our staff and was going to Moscow, China, Japan and the Far East, merely say yes. They will be making inquiry regarding his passport. If they ask how long, merely say that you do not know. He was associated with us in his embryonic days as a writer, which is true."[74] But for various reasons—Wright's growing fame, logistical issues, and so on—the idea was stillborn, though the ANP sought to convince Secretary of State Cordell Hull otherwise.[75]

Wright's occasional sparring partner, Zora Neale Hurston, was thinking along parallel lines. She found it "curious that I am so much better known among the whites than among my own people," which may have driven her to the major point she conveyed, which was that she was "getting very keen about the English." "My last book, 'Their Eyes Were Watching God' was published by them and it went very well indeed in England, so I am asked over there for a speaking tour" and, she added zestfully, "if my present enthusiasm for the English keeps up, I will stay a long time," particularly since "I get such lovely letters from all over England."[76] Barnett was a logical party to discuss this proposal because the ANP did not hesitate to tout her popularity in London[77] and publicize Hurston's work by various means.[78]

Wright also was seduced by the charms of Western Europe and though he did not mention his future home—France—in his proposed itinerary, the hexagonal republic had long been a preoccupation of his fellow Negroes. Paris was no utopia, said the future U.S. ambassador to independent Senegal and Gambia, Mercer Cook. This African-American man of letters—like so many others—blamed the occasional difficult experiences encountered by those like himself to the "influence of white Americans" which was "keenly felt" in France. "Nor has Hollywood helped," he said, "by portraying the Negro as either a clown or coward." In fact, in France he found "more prejudice against Jews than against the black man."[79]

By 1937, ANP correspondent Fay Jackson was lollygagging in a sidewalk café in Paris, sipping a specialty coffee and, as she put it, "drawing a dull puff on my last American Lucky, looking wistfully out at the rain," when she spotted "this giant magnificent black man." They chatted and he asked about the Scottsboro 9. Yes, said Jackson, "we look upon France as the black man's dream of a perfect

Nirvana of freedom from all the ills and injustices we suffer in America"—but this was exaggerated at best, she said. Like others then she too stressed that "WITH-OUT COLONIALS—OR NEGROES—FRANCE CANNOT DEFEND HERSELF AGAINST GERMANY."[80]

Colonials also were essential in the defense of London and the British Empire; though as war stalked Europe, much of the U.S. press portrayed this urban node as a capital of freedom, the ANP adopted a different stance (while continuing to portray Britain as being more advanced on the "race" front than the United States).[81] An ANP columnist, the moderate Gordon Hancock, went as far as asserting that during a 1938 journey to Europe, he was "treated better in Germany than in England." In the former nation "the Negro is outlawed as a man but they treat him as a man; in England ever so much is said about 'equality.' . . . but the treatment of the Negro is far from ideal." In fact, he said, "the center of this racialism that proscribes the Negro is in England."[82]

A few months later, Hancock seemed to suggest that the "center of this racialism" had migrated across the Atlantic. Fascism "can happen here," he said, speaking of the United States. "In fact, it would have already happened had it not been for the Klan's colossal mistake of including Catholics and Jews within the orbit of its persecution. Had it concentrated on the Negro as did the original Klan, the Negroes in this country would have suffered tribulations comparable to those being suffered by the Jews in Germany."[83]

Loren Miller, presumed to be a member of the Communist Party, tended to feel differently. This ANP correspondent was headed from Russia to Germany in the late 1930s and saw a "colored heavyweight fighter" who was "getting the best of a German in a match in Berlin. The police slipped into the ring, stopped the fight and arrested the colored contestant. Then, following their custom of sterilizing criminals, he was immediately taken to a hospital and operated upon. Nothing was learned of his final fate in the hands of these 'Aryans.'"[84] As the contrast between Hancock and Miller suggested, for the most part ANP radicals, more than moderates, were taking the hardest line against an ascending fascism.

But even the moderate Hancock mirrored radical viewpoints, when he was not overly ruffled by the Berlin–Moscow nonaggression pact of 1939, which set the stage for Europe plunging into world war. Moscow had pulled off "one of the masterly strokes of diplomacy history has known," said the bedazzled columnist. It "marks the downfall of the English hegemony on the earth," he said with foresight. "England and France are getting their just desserts. They will soon be sitting where Ethiopia was sitting a few months ago,"[85] he said, without a hint of mourning. The skeptical London correspondent of the ANP, Rudolph Dunbar, continued to back London against Berlin "despite her faults."[86] Pickens sternly disagreed with the import of the Molotov–Ribbentrop pact and condemned Stalin and Moscow, the position that was to hold sway for decades subsequently in the United States.[87]

* * *

"There may be something to Lothrop Stoddard's [imminent] terror of the 'Rising Tide of Color,'" said the ANP, referring to this racial theorist's ill-famed tome; for his nightmare was "becoming increasingly apparent" in India where "many billion dollars of English and American capital are tied up."[88] Thus, the agency gave maximal attention to the anticolonial activities in London of Paul Robeson, a dear friend of anticolonial India and even then regarded as a friend of Moscow. A "huge crowd" greeted this performer and activist in July 1938 when he appeared alongside Jawaharlal Nehru at a massive London rally. Robeson, it was reported, "delivered a magnificent speech" and "received an overwhelming and spontaneous reception, even greater than Nehru['s]." Robeson, it was said, was "now hailed as a national hero in England."[89] Reportedly, Robeson was writing a play about Mohandas K. Gandhi.[90]

At the same time, the ANP reported that though the blood of U.S. Negroes was segregated for transfusions in the United States, Dr. Charles Drew of Howard University Medical School pointed out that "all of the blood sent to England has been used"—that is, "there was no segregation of the donors of their blood." Dr. Drew condemned the U.S. Red Cross for "obviously" pursuing a "rotten policy."[91] Barnett, a leader in this fight, was irate, remonstrating the "white folks of the south" who were "up in arms about Negro blood being filtered into those anemic crackers." Well, he sputtered, "if they did not want good, rich Negro blood, then don't take it"![92]

This ambivalence toward London left the ANP and Barnett uneasy. In mid-1941 London correspondent Rudolph Dunbar told Barnett that he sensed that the nervous authorities there were seeking to lobby him, so as to influence U.S. Negroes and, through them, the United States itself. London was reputedly concerned with the attacks by the U.S. Negro press on the empire's oldest colonies, those of the Caribbean.[93] That helped Dunbar to realize that "our newspapers can wield untold power in America" and "our common cause can advance more in one year of war than in 20 years of peace" as a direct result. Why tail after tired colonial powers, he asked, when "the Negro Press can represent effectively the interests of the coloured people of the British Empire and the Free French Territory in Africa and the Belgian Congo." But for this to be done, the ANP would have to pay more, because "a hundred good journalistic scoops have been lost through lack of funds."[94]

Nonetheless, criticisms of Paris and London aside, it was Berlin that was the major worry for the ANP and its readers. It was the prism through which Jim Crow was viewed—and magnified. Barnett, chairman of the board of Provident

Hospital in Chicago, denounced Morris Fishbein of the *Journal of the American Medical Association* after he said in 1938 that U.S. medical care was superb—"with the exception of Negroes." The "implication," said Barnett, was that Negroes "were so unimportant in American life that the situation surrounding them was inconsequential and demanded no remedy." Then the ANP chief got personal, reminding Fishbein that "as a Jew, you would be expected to have an acute understanding and sympathy for minority causes. You must be acquainted with the problem of the Jew in Germany" and wondered how he would react if such reasoning as his were to be applied in Berlin.[95]

The perception within the ANP—and within Black America generally—was widespread that Nazism was simply a close cousin of Jim Crow and if the former prevailed, the latter would get a new lease on life.[96] Ineluctably, the ANP hailed Joe Louis's victory in the boxing ring over the German Max Schmeling and was sufficiently bold to add that it "suits Russia" too.[97] Moreover, said an agency reporter, after the match "the happiest people I saw at this fight were not the Negroes but the Jews."[98]

Pickens pointed out that Jim Crow eroded the efficacy of U.S. criticisms of Germany and said if a 1923 treaty between the two giants had mandated no bias "based on race, color, creed, religion, etc.," this would have aided German Jewry—but would have harmed prevailing mores in Dixie.[99] Ben Carruthers, a Negro intellectual who—like Pickens—was multilingual, agreed that the "foreign policy" of the United States was "handicapped by American prejudice against Negroes." This was "not unknown in the German embassy in Washington" and "constant mention [of this] is made in the Nazi press under the pressure of the efficient Minister of Propaganda, Paul [sic] Goebbels."[100]

Thus, the Hollywood Anti-Nazi League had a "pretty large" black membership, said the ANP, evidenced by fights between the group and their opponents, where Negroes "played an active part," including tossing "rotten eggs, decayed vegetables, brickbats and clubs" at pro-Nazi forces "carrying swastika flags." This left "practically every window in the building" of Deutsche Haus "smashed."[101] Of course, Loren Miller was in the vanguard of these protests.[102] When antifascists in Hollywood praised the movie *Confessions of a Nazi Spy*, the ANP opined that it opened the way for anti–Jim Crow films in the United States.[103]

There was a National Negro Stop Hitler Committee in Black Chicago, and Du Sable High School in November 1941 was addressed by the eminent lawyer William Hastie and Canada Lee, the boxer and actor, who offered a discordant note.[104]

All wings of the ANP—and most of Black America—were outraged when the perceived idyll that was France was marred by the Nazi occupation. Their sorrow was symbolized by their reporting on the case of Arabelle Middleton of Washington, D.C., a Negro woman who fled Paris so hurriedly in the face of terror in early 1941 that somehow she was forced to leave her ten-year-old son behind.[105]

Thus, when the inevitable happened and Germany invaded Russia in June 1941, Hancock, Pickens, and Miller—in effect, all wings of the ANP led by Barnett—united in angry opposition to fascism. This was not a great leap for the agency in that already it had shown more than a willingness to overlook Moscow's manifest flaws, possibly because of the Soviets' stiff opposition to Jim Crow. Thus, shortly after the launch of Operation Barbarossa, Pickens congratulated Prime Minister Winston Churchill for choosing Stalin over Hitler.[106] Yes, he conceded with a sigh, "there are criticisms which we could make against Russia, but why make them at this moment," particularly since "in this fight we are pro-Russian."[107]

Hancock concurred, asserting that "as many lies have been told on Russians as have been told on the hapless Negro race, and yet today, Russia is fighting on the side of those who have maligned her."[108] "Much has been made of the bloody purges in Russia; but what nation has not had its bloody purge? Could the War of Secession" in the United States "be called anything else. . . . what about England's purges in Ireland and India" and, of course, "the French Revolution was a bloody purge." By October 1941 he was carping because "Russia is being left to the destruction of the German armies because the democracies fear what may happen if communistic Russia survives. We are asking questions about Russia" as "if it were our business. Russia could with equal propriety ask us questions," especially "in regard to the Negro."[109] Escalating its already prevalent bias toward Moscow, the ANP recalled the embrace of the great Negro tragedian, Ira Aldridge, who toured Russia "nine times" and thought of this nation as his "second Fatherland" because "his greatest success he found in distant Russia."[110]

CHAPTER 4

War Changes

The U.S. entry into World War II marked a watershed for both the Negro press generally and the ANP specifically. The "Double V" campaign among African Americans targeting fascism abroad and Jim Crow at home was a simple continuation and escalation of ANP prewar policy. A wartime cartoon in the *Atlanta Daily World* neatly linked the two ogres as it showed Hitler being embraced by Dixiecrats, including "Herr" Congressman James Eastland, "Fuehrer" Senator Theodore Bilbo, and Congressman John "Von" Rankin.[1] Despite the racial progress propelled by the antifascist war, there were contrary disquieting notes that did not escape the gaze of Claude Barnett.[2]

The Negro press could hardly ignore the ambivalence, if not outright support, within their constituency for Tokyo. This factor helped to further propel black militancy at a moment when Washington was demanding stolid acquiescence in the face of the external threat.[3]

This widespread sentiment had led the FBI's bulldog leader, J. Edgar Hoover, to demand Espionage Act indictments of certain Negro papers.[4] It is possible that the FBI had opened the letter Barnett sent in early 1942 to a friend in California in which he did not seem terribly upset in asking tranquilly, "[I] hope that [Japanese] submarines off Santa Barbara did not disturb your peace of mind."[5] Then there was a resonant isolationist sentiment in Black America grounded in no small measure in disappointment with the results of World War I. A number of influential African Americans were supportive of the America First Committee, which included figures as diverse as aviator Charles Lindbergh and future U.S. president Gerald Ford.[6]

*   *   *

It was with enthusiasm that Barnett proclaimed in early 1942 that "the Negro newspapers have never reached more people than they [do] today. They are literally the eyes and ears of the group."[7] Undoubtedly, Gunnar Myrdal had the war in mind when he found the Negro press to be "the greatest single power in the Negro race."[8] A. T. Spaulding, the affluent leader of the National Negro Insurance Association concurred and noted that "without doubt the Negro Press is our greatest offensive and defensive weapon."[9]

An antifascist war was not conducive to the perpetuation of Jim Crow, since it was possible for antagonists to underscore the taproot it shared with the enemy in Berlin and, doubtlessly, this too buoyed the ANP.[10]

William Pickens was among those who before the war praised the role of Jewish Americans within the National Association for the Advancement of Colored People (NAACP) and, thus, were well placed to denounce Europe's unfolding tragedy.[11] It was Pickens who upbraided Lord Lothian at the British embassy in Washington in late 1940 for the colonizer's "barring admission of homeless Jews to Palestine," who had been "driven like animals or criminals from their homes."[12]

Thus, during wartime, the United States—racially—had one foot in the past and another in the future with both striding furiously in opposing directions: combating pestiferous bigotry and countenancing it too. Thus, the illustrious Negro composer William Grant Still was contracted to work on the Hollywood cinematic extravaganza "Stormy Weather," but his contribution was discarded in favor of stereotypes. Yet, as he told Barnett, "ironically enough all this happened just as I received word from my publishers in New York that the OWI [Office of War Information]" sent this work "to Russia and other parts of Europe for performances for official government propaganda purposes."[13] In short, his work was too advanced for domestic consumption but just right for foreign purposes; in coming years, the former would seek to catch up with the latter.

In yet another of a plethora of contradictory events during the war, four thousand persons crowded into a theater to view the Hollywood film "Mission to Moscow," a pro-Soviet blockbuster, since denounced as an apologia for Stalinism. Yet, lamented the ANP, "Negro newspaper men were excluded from the showing"[14] as a Jim Crow audience gathered to provide obeisance to the socialism of Josef Stalin. Ideologically, William Pickens was denounced during the war by right-wing congressman Martin Dies as a "stooge for Stalin" while moderate Negro leadership considered him to be an Uncle Tom.[15] All this was part of the contradictory chain of events that ultimately was to lead to the erosion of Jim Crow.

Barnett, who was as informed about global trends as any, had detected monumental changes internationally that he discussed with C[ornelius] A. Scott of the *Atlanta Daily World* in early 1942, suggesting that sending U.S. Negro troops to Africa would unleash Copernican changes on the continent with redounding benefit to the United States itself. A similar letter was sent to other editors with a plea to combine resources in order to gain insight into the herculean changes at play.[16] P. B. Young of the *Norfolk Journal and Guide,* sited in a citadel of naval strength, was a noticeable target for Barnett.[17]

Barnett's critics on the left thought that his rhetoric exceeded his actions. ANP correspondent and activist Thyra Edwards was disappointed when the agency did not cover an important gathering of the International Labor Organization,[18] an important global agency to target in light of Africans' worldwide role as cheap labor.

Nevertheless, Barnett's grand ambition—and rhetoric—was driven not only by the capacious scope of the global changes unfolding; for even then, Barnett sensed that "the white press services" already were encroaching and seeking a "monopoly on a type of news which ought to be the privilege of our own papers."[19] He knew that "circulations will grow in proportion as we can give adequate coverage"[20] during the war, but even this scenario could be compromised by mainstream encroachment. But if anticolonialism and anti–Jim Crow measures proceeded, wouldn't that erode logically the ANP's monopoly on a type of news?[21]

At that point, the ANP considered a merger with those with which it had been jousting, for example, the *Chicago Defender* and those grouped within the Negro Newspapers Publishers Association (NNPA): "we are all for closer cooperation," said Barnett,[22] a point of view shared by the ANP staff.[23]

Ira Lewis of the *Pittsburgh Courier* and the NNPA was not as sanguine. "To get down to the point, Claude," he said brashly, "the publishers were somewhat riled up as a whole with the present ANP, which you say is a non-profit proposition." Their idea was that "like the white papers, we form our own Associated Press" and evade Barnett's ANP altogether.[24]

"We are willing," Barnett conceded in reply, "that the ANP become an organization under the general control of the NNPA as a subsidiary,"[25] which would have strengthened both but did not materialize. The competitive pressure being placed on the ANP and the NNPA as the mainstream press began to contemplate hiring more Negro writers and adjust its coverage accordingly—born of antifascist progressivism driven by war—in turn drove the two to contemplate merging.

*   *   *

Typically, the ANP did not ignore the importance of Africa in its calculations, as the New York correspondent Ernest Johnson observed in mid-1943: then the president-elect of Liberia was in the United States and was "very much interested in 'selling' Liberia to American Negroes as an 'asylum,'" a potentially transformative proposal.[26]

Exemplifying the transformative potential of Pan-Africanism, Johnson instructed William Hassett at the White House that, when the Liberian leader visited, "five Negro correspondents [be] given temporary credentials" to cover his visit. "[T]his was the first and last time to my knowledge that such has happened,"[27] Johnson said, as the dynamics of antifascist war in which Africans played a prominent role ensured that this archaic policy would erode. When President Elie Lescot of Haiti arrived in Washington weeks later, the ANP continued to push for an enlightened policy on press credentialing, particularly since this leader, said Johnson, "is a very friendly sort of person and very definitely speaks of 'we Negroes.'"[28] The Haitian authorities, whom ANP had previously portrayed as being indifferent or even hostile to Pan-African solidarity, were depicted differently during the war. In early 1942, it was reported that M. Abel Leger, the Haitian emissary in France, demanded and obtained an apology from a German general whom he had challenged to a duel. The envoy, it was said, was "willing to fight the general and be killed for the honor of his race."[29]

Similarly, Johnson then met Yilma Deressa, chairman of the Ethiopian delegation, at a conference at the White House and discussed a visit to Addis Ababa to work on a book with the hosts subsidizing costs. Like his supervisor, Barnett, Johnson too sensed the monetary potential of a sovereign Africa and had also bruited about this proposal with his Monrovian friends.[30] Later the innovative Johnson "managed to wangle myself into the [Liberian] President's party" and "discovered the real goal of the visit [to the United States] by reading carbon paper I had lent" to one of his party "aboard a Buffalo-bound train, along with my typewriter, in order that he could prepare an official memorandum on their negotiations." His awareness of the Liberians' thinking was enhanced further when the president "entertained Mrs. Johnson and me at a private dinner."[31]

This report was part of an ANP trend that flowered during the war, ties of singular intimacy between Africans and African Americans, perhaps the most direct expression of Pan-Africanism.[32] Overall, the ANP spotlighted Pan-African solidarity, which was sufficiently elastic to be stretched to encompass the indigenes of the South Pacific. The ANP provided ample publicity on the tour of Reverend W. H. Jernagin, who in 1945 visited what were called "Negro military installations in the Western Pacific area," which included stops in Hawaii, Manila, Noumea, Saipan, Guam, and Iwo Jima.[33]

This initiative also impelled ANP to underline what the Harlem bard Langston Hughes had been saying all along, which is that many writers in Latin America considered to be "white" would be defined as "black" if in the United States, which too expanded the boundaries of Pan-Africanism.[34] By the same token, the ANP reported how a "stomp band" composed of Negro soldiers in India had influenced "Indian Nagas" who took "to the beat of a boogie-woogie band like a bee takes to honey."[35]

Barnett sought to deploy a Pan-African approach when "visiting correspondents from South America" arrived in the United States. "Why were Negro newspapers not given an opportunity to interview them,"[36] Barnett asked plaintively, though he intuitively knew the answer.[37]

Of course, there were other bumps in the road. In a confidential message, Barnett was told that Ethiopia "opened a ministry in Washington" but was difficult to reach. He consulted William Leo Hansberry of Howard University, the respected scholar of Africa, who told him that Addis Ababa was "trying to accomplish something [that] is extremely important to Ethiopia, to Africa and to black people" generally by "opening a legation" and certain "elements sense[d] and want[ed] to interfere." Thus, an "attack [was] being made by certain British elements against an independent Ethiopia," along with "skullduggery" by "persons of like mind here in America." London "consider[ed]" an independent Ethiopia to be "a bad example for the rest of Africa" and, thus, John Bull was accused of "making a deal with the Italian government to defeat the Ethiopians" as a result.[38] The legation had hunkered down, reluctant to provide ammunition to their foes by aligning more openly with African Americans.

Part of the paradox of Jim Crow was that as soon as Barnett and his allies sensed that monumental changes were eroding the innards of this system of iniquity, those who had been in the forefront of bringing the erosion on began to sense impending extinction. That is, as mainstream news outlets sensed that a "new world was coming," they began to adjust by recruiting Negro journalists who theretofore had been ignored and by covering the Pan-African world more judiciously where theretofore it had been ignored or defamed. This shift tended to dissipate the ANP's competitive advantage in the marketplace. Barnett found it "discouraging to always run into the statement that Negro newspapers are loose in their journalistic practices," a charge that mounted as the challenge to their very existence ascended.[39]

By June 1945 Johnson had been considered—then rejected—for a post with the *New York Post*,[40] but this rejection augured what was to come when writers with few options suddenly found many more. Even Turner Catledge of the august *New York Times* contacted "Dear Claude" in a missive marked "personal-confidential," requesting that he "suggest any other young Negroes who . . . might be fitted in as good general reporters."[41] The opportunity for talented Negro writers to defect to the mainstream at once diluted an advantage the ANP had and also subjected these writers to the ideological influence of the U.S. ruling elite, making it more difficult to provide an accurate picture of the Pan-African world.[42]

Barnett's seemingly naïve response to this overture was also revelatory. He told Catledge, "I should have included Mason Roberson in the list" of potential recruits; he was then "on the staff of the *People's World*," which "has some exceedingly good people on the staff." Roberson "some years ago" had "worked briefly for us,"[43] that is, the ANP. What Barnett did not mention was that the *People's World* was a Communist Party periodical and, though the ANP was open to collaborating with these forces, the *Times* definitely was not and Barnett could have been deemed to be a provocateur to assume as much. Catledge may have noticed that in the important ANP role of covering the San Francisco conference that led to the founding of the United Nations were two Communist journalists,[44] Mason Roberson and John Pittman.[45]

Similarly, it was during the war precisely when opportunities were opening as rarely before for African Americans, Barnett audaciously recommended Frank Marshall Davis for a strategic post in Washington, terming him to be "exceptional in ability, in experience and in character." As feature editor of the ANP, Davis was "one of the outstanding men in Negro journalism today."[46] Also unmentioned were the reputed Communist ties of this future Hawaiian.

When the collaboration between the Communist Party and the ANP was collapsing, as the latter's advantages were being ceded and the former was under assault, the ultimate sufferers were those who craved accurate and balanced coverage of the Pan-African world. Ultimately, the *Times* hired George Streator, whom Barnett found to be "rather unpopular in some circles and I doubt if I would have presented his name," which also was telling in terms of future coverage.[47]

The mainstream press deigned to notice even Barnett himself for it was in early 1942 that he made a rare appearance on national radio discussing the usually neglected Negro press.[48] A stunned Barnett was surprised by his sudden popularity among those who typically had ignored him.[49]

Johnson was not the only ANP correspondent on the verge of leaving. Rudolph Dunbar in London was now being considered for his original occupation: orchestra conductor. As the war was winding down, the talented writer was wielding a baton on behalf of the London Philharmonic and its French counterpart in Paris; he was, said Barnett, "the best known authority in England on jazz. A master of the clarinet" who previously had "conducted an orchestra" in Manhattan and now, paradoxically, as opportunities were opening for him, contributed to the depletion of the ANP.[50]

In late 1944, one of Barnett's chief allies, the Negro publisher Roscoe Dunjee, reported on a delegation of the National Negro Business League to Africa at Washington's expense. Apparently, these delegates were seen by U.S. elites as being useful in their ability to create an open door for further penetration by Washington, as against the "imperial preference" of the European colonizers. The trip was scheduled to take three months, and from the delegates' viewpoint they would return with "valuable information respecting the economic possibilities of Africa." Following up, the delegates met in Birmingham, Alabama, with two African guests who, said Dunjee, "presented a sound business proposition to the League," though "few were inclined to have anything to do with the plan of financing the shipment of raw materials from the African continent." They did, however, want Washington to send them on a similar journey to "South America, the Caribbean and [to] Russia" for similar mutually beneficial reasons. Yet it seemed a tad naïve to think that the government would "send a mission of Negro citizens on an extended visit to foreign countries so that Negroes may develop an independent philosophy respecting fundamental social-economic changes." It was unclear why Washington would want to strengthen Negroes' global ties so they could better challenge Washington, particularly since—as Dunjee noted— "already the purchasing power of Negroes is greater than the foreign trade of America with any single nation."[51]

So moved, the ANP increased its coverage of the news, particularly global coverage. By 1944, its reports were so valued that those not directly involved in newspapers—a Los Angeles radio broadcaster, for example—sought them. "We deliver ten times as much news," said Barnett, as their local affiliate there "can absorb."[52]

"Back in World War I," said Barnett, "no [Negro] newspaper sent a correspondent to the front," and it was not until September 1918 that a sole correspondent, Richard Tyler, arrived in Paris. But during this war, the *Courier*, the *Afro-American*, and the *Journal and Guide* all had sent reporters to Britain, Australia, and North Africa, for example. One major difference between the two titanic conflicts, said Barnett, sparking more coverage, was there was more Negro sedition during World War II and "unlike the earlier conflict, this war has a definite racial angle," a muted reference to the role of Tokyo.[53]

It took the ANP a while to gain the scale of operations the war demanded. During the early stages of the war, Albert G. Barnett of the ANP counted seventy newspapers as being part of the ANP with their top writer, William Pickens, having a "reading public estimated at 1,000,000 weekly."[54] By January 1945, Claude Barnett said his agency now included "78 member papers."[55]

Though it was not well recognized at the time, the ANP had easier access to certain critical sources than its mainstream competitors. There was Arthur Prettyman, for example, an African American who served as Roosevelt's valet and accompanied him on his meeting at sea with Churchill that culminated in the Atlantic Charter and the president's trip to Liberia, Brazil, and North Africa. Prettyman spoke with Ollie Stewart of the *Afro-American* in Rabat and again in Casablanca, where the reporter chatted with Roosevelt.[56] The ANP also had a direct pipeline to the National Maritime Union, which during the war had a Jamaican-born Communist—Ferdinand Smith—as the number two leader and, through him, Barnett sought to reach ship stewards, disproportionately Negro, who sailed in and out of ports globally.[57]

In 1945 Barnett's good friend Jesse Thomas "arrived in Paris after 25 hours by plane," all the while in "high and diplomatic Company," including "this Russian Diplomat. As you watched him behave, one thought of Commissar Molotov. He really was the dominating personality in the plane," and Thomas interacted with him for hours on end.[58] In November 1944, Dunbar "was talking to a French man" in Paris who "told me" that when France was "liberated his wife told him that she must kiss an American. He told her that he would agree to her request under one condition," which was that "she must kiss an American Negro soldier because he is the only true American."[59]

In liberated France, said Ernestine Hughes, both U.S. female personnel and Frenchwomen tended to "prefer the association of the brown American Yanks," while in Britain, "they thought Negroes were unintelligent" before meeting them because of what "they had seen in the movies." Thus, clubs for U.S. personnel in Liverpool were segregated.[60] Barnett was told further that the police in Britain were "polite," in contrast to their U.S. peers and the American MPs, who "act like bullies."[61]

Jesse Thomas told Barnett that notwithstanding the odiousness in Europe, "universally the Negro soldier here has a better rating with the civilian population in every place I have visited in France and in Italy," in contrast to "the average white American soldier," who saw himself as "the top man in the world." The latter felt that "whatever he wants, people ought to be able to give it to him," as the "majority of them seem to feel that it would be admitting certain inferiority if they submit to the French and Italian people teaching them anything." This also "explains why the average Negro solider has developed a much larger vocabulary in foreign languages and speaks more fluently the language of the natives." Europeans saw the "white [American] as the conqueror, as the man who is his overlord" and saw "the Negro as a humanitarian and friend."[62]

An emblem of this unique intimacy was what the League of Coloured Peoples in London referred to as "the illegitimate children born in Britain of English mothers and Coloured Americans."[63]

These sorts of access did not automatically translate into better coverage. Six months after Pearl Harbor, Barnett was upset because ANP newspaper affiliates had not cooperated by submitting pieces that would be shared by other papers. "Don't think that the fact that we [do] not have an adequate foreign service is due to lack of vision on our part," he advised. "[T]his is why we carry all of the African material we can get," because that beleaguered continent was "the real prize of the war." At that juncture, the ANP had a "voluntary correspondent in Panama, another in the Bahamas, another in Hawaii," but "we can't offer them adequate postage." Rudolph Dunbar in London "works from hand to mouth," he moaned, "cusses us out for our inability to pay but works on like the true patriot he is." And under similar circumstances, "well written features come to us from Paris, Africa and the West Indies by Nancy Cunard." Richard Wright's proposal to globetrot did not gain altitude, though he had the brilliant idea "that the real causes behind this war and the implications to darker peoples all over the world would be found, not in America," but in "Russia, Japan and China."[64]

But soon the ANP had upped the number of foreign correspondents on its roster too. As of 1943 Barnett ascertained that there were "over 100,000 Negro troops overseas"[65] and by 1944 the ANP had correspondents listed in London,

Lagos, the Panama Canal Zone, the Southwest Pacific, Johannesburg, Honolulu, Moscow, and Teheran.[66] By 1944 the ANP also had added correspondents in India and three others listed "somewhere in [the]South Pacific," another listed as "somewhere in Africa," and yet another listed simply as embedded with the U.S. Navy. They faced stiff competition from the *Defender*, the *Courier*, the *Journal and Guide*, and other Negro press organs that too had managed to employ foreign correspondents. There was official resistance to providing credentials to ANP and these other correspondents because of the perception of the Negro press as potentially seditious; thus, when Barnett reported these additional correspondents, he mentioned that "the army is capitulating" and granting them credentials after pressure was placed upon them.[67]

By April 1945 the ANP's London correspondent was boasting of a "bid for world wide news coverage" that "will be made by the Negro press of the world after the war." There were "143 Negro newspapers" in the United States alone and there were now "Negro news correspondents in all theatres of war."[68] The ANP's Enoch Waters, who later sought to expand the agency's operations into the heart of Africa, by 1946 had spent "three years in the Pacific theatre of war as a war correspondent beginning on June 3, 1943."[69]

But capitulating, which Washington purportedly did, hardly meant surrender. The ANP had to handle being upbraided more than once by the Office of Censorship of the United States.[70] This led to Barnett negotiating with the authorities about what ANP dispatches could pass muster.[71] Rudolph Dunbar, the ANP correspondent in London, groused to Barnett in 1944 that "we have a colossal fight with censor intervention"—words followed in his message by a snipped sentence.[72]

Barnett complained to Attorney General Francis Biddle that "the Special War Policies Unit of the [Department of Justice] is evidently interfering with the mail address[ed] to" the ANP. "Our mail has been delayed," he grumbled, noting sarcastically that he did not mind if his mail was opened as long as it was delivered in a timely fashion.[73] Rumors persisted in Chicago that the postal authorities were scrutinizing every letter coming to the ANP from Alabama, Georgia, and several other states where it was thought that Negroes might have good reason to be disgruntled, and perhaps seditious.[74]

J. Edgar Hoover, choosing his words carefully, informed Barnett that his FBI denied the rumors that the government was "opening, examining and copying letters originating in the South and directed" to ANP.[75] Hoover was "unable to verify" the allegation that "the letters were inspected by the FBI and then sent on," though he advised that there was "absolutely no foundation in fact for the implication that this Bureau has engaged in activity as referred to." Besides, he concluded ominously, Barnett was acting "maliciously" in making such charges.[76]

There was vitriolic rancor directed at the Negro press because of the perception that they were stoking sedition. Oswald Garrison Villard, thought to be a friend of the Negro because of his roots in abolitionism, said the Negro press was too sharp in "their unbridled attacks."[77] In that vein, the burghers of Henderson, Texas, sought to ban the *Pittsburgh Courier* and the *Kansas City Call*.[78]

Walter White of the NAACP told his comrade Barnett that the "attacks on the Negro press add up" to "create an impression that the 'racial tension' is caused by Negroes themselves and in particular the Negro press."[79] The situation had become so serious that during the height of the war, a number of editors of the Negro press were summoned to Washington, where they were shown reports that indicated that the only soldier thus far found guilty of sedition was a Negro—and the press was blamed for it.[80] It was at that point that Thurman Arnold of the Department of Justice sent the ANP a curious letter, declaring that his agency was ending an antitrust lawsuit "against the Associated Press" and demanding detail on ANP operations as if his next target would be Barnett's creation.[81] An alarmed W. E. B. DuBois was taken aback by this venomous attention to the Negro press.[82]

The authorities, bent on enforcing strict solidarity, also may have been displeased by ANP stories about those Negroes—for example, the future scholar St. Clair Drake and future St. Louis labor leader, Ernest Calloway—who were among those who declared they would not serve "as long as Jim Crow persists in the military."[83] The ANP gave special attention to pro-Tokyo Negroes such as Leonard Robert Jordan of New York, who told the FBI that Walter White and Adam Clayton Powell were among the "Dumb American Negroes" who were slated "to be beheaded" when Japan won the war. An agent of the FBI, said the FBI, attended a party in the home of one of Jordan's comrades "where the guests cheered radio reports of Jap [*sic*] victories."[84] Likewise, there was probably disapproval in official circles of an ANP report from Senegal, discussing how women there "have tried to kill American soldiers by throwing their arms around them and attempting to slit the man's throat during the embrace," a militant action attributed either to the influence of enemy propaganda—or the misdeeds of these men.[85]

The authorities may have thought that the ANP particularly took too seriously the wartime alliance with Moscow, instead of seeing it as merely a matter of pragmatic convenience. The ANP asserted that "Russia was the only country without Jim Crow," and Mordecai Johnson of Howard University, according to the ANP, thought that it was "the only great nation to have eliminated race prejudice."[86] ANP correspondent Chatwood Hall made a special effort to stress the linkages between Moscow and Black America, invoking Ira Aldridge and Alexander Pushkin.[87] Hall immortalized Pushkin, recounting to ANP readers how he "fell mortally wounded in a famed duel" and how Hall had "stood on the exact spot where Pushkin was murdered."[88] Thus, a typical ANP headline from this era illustrated what they chose to foreground: "Reds re-capture Aldridge's burial place [i.e.] Łódź, Poland."[89] A typical report from fascist Rome told of how African-American singer Roland Hayes was beaten there by "three husky city police."[90] Paradigmatically, the ANP reported from Iran in 1944 that "Negro GIs, Red soldiers get along wonderfully."[91]

It was the African Abram Hannibal, said Hall, who centuries earlier "helped build and arm the great Kronstadt fortress at the head of the Gulf of Finland which served to prevent the Germans from reaching Leningrad by sea in this war" in a battle that rivaled Stalingrad in its ferocity and intensity.[92] The ANP played up the role of the African-American woman they called "Mrs. William Burroughs," whose "radio name" was "Omma Percy." She had taught school for fifteen years in New York City but, like so many U.S. Negroes, had chosen exile in the Soviet Union, by 1935 in her case, and was now broadcasting in English via shortwave from there. Her fellow broadcaster, Lloyd Patterson, also was an African American, a graduate of Booker T. Washington's alma mater, Hampton Institute; unfortunately, he died during the bitter winter of 1942.[93]

When Kiev was pummeled during the war, Hall illuminated his story by discussing the Hotel Continental, "which housed many Negro tourists in the past" but was now "a pile of brick, stone and steel."[94] Dramatically, Hall was writing his dispatch "in gloves and overcoat" accompanied by a "feebly smoking candle" near the "charred and smoking ruins of ancient Kiev University where Ira Aldridge was once a guest."[95] "Jim Crow ran rampant in the besieged city of Kiev before its recapture by the Red Army," said Hall, as he equated Nazism with its U.S. relative.[96]

When the "crack 416th rifle division of the Red Army . . . slaughtered whole divisions of the Nazis," Hall was quick to note that the triggers were pulled by "tawny colored Azerbaijanis."[97] Hall continued his prewar reporting on Abkhazia, where "Caucasian Negroes [*sic*] enjoyed first class citizenship."[98] It was the "Russian Negro troops," claimed the ANP that "blocked Hitler in [the] Caucasus."[99] The ANP correspondent in neighboring Iran provided some of the most comprehensive journalism in the United States about this nation that, after all, was the site of a profoundly important summit of the allies in Teheran. An African Methodist Episcopal bishop had visited there in January 1944, which was the occasion for the ANP to present a harrowing slice of life there.[100]

But Iran notwithstanding, it was the ANP coverage from the all-important Soviet front that proved to be immortal. Hall was billed as the "only Negro War Correspondent in Russia," though he also filed reports from the vicinity, for example, Dachau.[101] Hall stumbled at times[102] but, generally, his reporting from the decisive Eastern Front was eye-opening.

German depredations also were emphasized, though often the angle was on how Berlin's forces massacred Africans,[103] just as their reportage on concentration camps often emphasized how Africans were ensnared. When police officers ran amok in black neighborhoods in the United States in 1944, the ANP called them the "White Gestapo," analogous to the "feared German Gestapo."[104]

The agency trumpeted the words of Edwin Embree of the Rosenwald Foundation, who called the U.S. demand that Berlin renounce racism "ironic."[105] The contradiction between U.S. condemnation of German racism and acquiescence to Jim Crow was highlighted to the detriment of the latter. For example, the ANP's Chatwood Hall compared German "slaveholders" to "contemporary Simon Legrees,"[106] and at a hearing of the Fair Employment Practices Committee on Jim Crow in railroad travel and employment, attorney Bartley Crum commented that Berlin pointed to Jim Crow as evidence that the United States was ill placed to critique Nazi policies. Berlin, he said, also sought to manipulate Negro "discontent and possible revolutionary elements" in the United States.[107]

Assuredly, ANP was in the vanguard of those who directed antifascist fervor adroitly and successfully with the aim of destabilizing Jim Crow. It was unsurprising to regular readers when in August 1945 the ANP reported that Negro soldiers in occupied Germany encountered "little prejudice except that from fellow Americans."[108] As was to be portrayed dramatically and decisively in the postwar era, Jim Crow was depicted as at odds with national security, a contradiction that was underscored when Brazilian troops en route to Italy on U.S. vessels were subjected to Jim Crow.[109]

Naturally, the ANP focused on the triumphs and travails of African-American soldiers and sailors abroad. Barnett was told, for example, that "the boys operating those 'ducks' in the beach-head landings at Normandy were all black."[110] The well-informed Barnett intelligently directed the news coverage in various theaters of conflict. In early 1943 he directed his New York correspondent to "contact the Free French embassy," which Barnett had reached earlier. "[T]hey have a smart group there. They admitted that the Free French Army coming up from Lake Chad to aid the British and Americans in North Africa was 95 percent black but would not give exact figures because 'they did not wish to make the whites look bad.'" Despite this heavy reliance on African troops, Barnett did not notice "a picture of [Félix] Éboué or any other black soldier [or leader] among the many in their front office," an indication that despite the agony of war, Paris intended the continuation of colonialism. This was occurring, said Barnett, though "the only armies of [Charles] De Gaulle were black armies. Black Frenchmen really carried on the ideals of France," though they were slated for a secondary postwar role.

"Finally," said Barnett, "they admitted that coming to America (most of them could scarcely speak English) and finding such appalling prejudice against Jews and Negroes, they regarded it as the sensible thing to take a middle of the road path and prosecute their main business and not get involved in controversial affairs."[111] The ANP's Ernest Johnson challenged Barnett's figures—but not his political analysis,[112] as the ANP continued to stress the importance of "Governor General Éboué of the Free French, in charge of the most strategic section of Africa and a power."[113]

The ANP kept a close eye on the Free French, reporting on their activity from Madagascar to Senegal and further north.[114] As early as 1933, Cameroonian leadership had contacted the ANP in search of regular copies of Negro newspapers.[115] During that same year, Barnett had contacted Éboué in his capacity as governor general of Guadeloupe,[116] and Éboué responded at length.[117] After the German occupation of France, Barnett told him that "we here in America . . . have been filled with pride as we observed your exploits and success." He reminded Éboué that "due to the story which we used about you in 1938 while you were still in Martinique, Negroes in the United States are somewhat familiar with your career."[118]

There also was the gnawing perception that black personnel were disproportionately subjected to court-martial and other forms of harsh discipline, leading those so treated to contact the ANP, just as some would have contacted the NAACP.[119] "Many things in the army are rotten as far as Negro soldiers are concerned," Barnett concluded.[120] As ever, the ANP was as much the organization to contact as the NAACP in cases of racist injustice. Dorothy Porter, the revered Howard University librarian, briefed Barnett about an incident at "Camp Devon, Massachusetts," and inquired whether there was "any way in which the facts could be published without revealing the source," that is to say, herself. What happened was that a "white captain . . . beat a Negro over the head until he bled with the but[t] end of his rifle," just "because the soldier refused to shave his beard which was against his religion."[121]

Many of these charges were scrutinized by ANP correspondents, who were not only the "eyes and ears" of black America but of Washington too. Such was the case when Frank Marshall Davis told Truman K. Gibson that "quite a few stewards on the Santa Fe Line are of German nativity" and "prior to Pearl Harbor, many were loudly and belligerently pro-Axis." And though their routes took them past "troop stations and munition dumps," there seemed to be little concern about their presence. "Perhaps Negroes associated with the FBI should be 'placed' in the dining car crews on different trains" was this presumed Communist's helpful advice.[122] As Germany was occupying France, the ANP raised suspicions in Washington, DC, about the "passing of Negroes from the hotel scene" and "their replacement with German and Italian workers in many of the largest hotels and clubs"; there too "even railroads" were "turning" in their direction.[123] When a racist riot erupted in Beaumont, Texas, in June 1943, as "Negro homes and businesses were destroyed," the ANP blamed not only "resentment by low class whites" but pointed to the allegation that "in and about the city are many people of German birth and origin" who were suspected of engaging in "organized sabotage" under the cover of routine racism. Perhaps, the ANP implied, that was the reason that "for the first time in the South, Negroes have been protected by authorities."[124]

*   *   *

The war drove change, to be sure. But, as if desperate to regain lost ground, the antagonists of the ANP and their erstwhile Communist allies strained to reverse many of these changes even as this titanic conflict was grinding to a conclusion.

CHAPTER 5

Red Scare Rising

Above all, Barnett was a skilled businessman, ever ready to capitalize on opportunities, and his trait was exemplified as the guns of war were roaring, when in 1942 he took a position as a kind of consultant with the U.S. Department of Agriculture (USDA) in Washington. At once the position brought him into closer contact with policymakers at a fraught moment and exposed him to a business—agriculture—that was ubiquitous globally. Moreover, part of his portfolio was arranging for the importation of labor from the Caribbean to plantations in Florida, which provided him with more contacts in a region where he already had established a toehold, specifically in Haiti. This then created a further opening for him to continue his own unique brand of Pan-Africanism, which had involved accumulating up-to-date intelligence (and news) and relentless networking.

The succeeding years stretching until 1947 were to witness the expansion of the ANP and, concomitantly, Barnett's ever-lengthening list of business interests. This success, however, had been based and premised on circumstances—for example, entente with radicals like Frank Marshall Davis and Robeson—that were to erode, most notably with conclusion of the Pacific War.

Thus, by 1947 he and his spouse, Etta Moten, departed on his first journey to Africa, which proved to be bountifully profitable to his investment portfolio while having the added benefit of enhancing his newsgathering operation. The changing circumstances notwithstanding, this Republican adapted smoothly to the postwar eruption of anticommunism in a manner that left him with valuable contacts. Those under siege, such as his editor, Davis, in 1948 fled to the more hospitable clime that was Honolulu.

*   *   *

Barnett had been angling for a post within the USDA for some time. It was in early 1937 that Charles Johnson of Fisk University lamented the "lack of a Negro writer or journalist" there who could "interpret some of the rich mass of information and service possibilities to Negro farmers." Barnett "might be consulted," he said presciently, while dangling the point that "probably as a sideline you could put one of your aces on the Department staff and thus insure for the ANP a Washington correspondent without excessive cost" since "you need a Washington office of the ANP anyhow, I should think."[1]

An ANP correspondent in the capital did materialize, but it was Barnett who positioned himself there to take full advantage. For the wise entrepreneur realized then that "the lives of more Negroes are touched by this department than any other government agency."[2] In fact, he said, this department was supporting "about three fifths of all the Negroes in this country," which necessitated taking "full advantage" of a "psychological time" to "push the interests of Negroes forward"[3]—not to mention his own interests. By "Negroes," as usual, Barnett did not simply mean just those from the United States. By 1941, in part because of his lobbying, the sugar quotas for Haiti and the Dominican Republic had been raised so that ninety-five thousand more tons of this commodity could be exported in 1941 than in 1940.[4]

There were others with whom Barnett was in contact, who thought that during wartime it was prudent for U.S. Negroes to remain on farms and abandon cities because, if "the enemy should rain down bombs" as was then occurring in Europe, it was more likely to occur in urban areas. Thus, Julius Pettigrew of "The Back to the Soil Movement among the Negroes of America" told President Roosevelt that the "great and helpless mass of my people would be unavoidably slaughtered and blown to pieces," eliminating a "major percent of the whole race."[5] Barnett in contrast sailed in an opposite direction, to his benefit.

Thus, in early 1942, as the fate of the war hung in the balance, Secretary of Agriculture Claude Wickard, while gratuitously and nervously asserting that "I have no doubt about the loyalty and devotion" of Negroes to the United States, offered Barnett a "position in my immediate office as Special Assistant to the Secretary" as "Consultant and Adviser on Negro Affairs." Travel and per diem costs were included in the package.[6]

Secretary Wickard may have known, as Barnett did, about recent events in rural Missouri that were not propitious for wartime cohesion. As Barnett was signing his contract, he had followed a racist eruption in Sikeston, Missouri, where, he said, "poor whites were envious and that poor whites and landlords joined hands to crush Negroes."[7] In confronting another eruption, Barnett also tried to make sure that it was Negroes—not Mexicans—who replaced interned Japanese and Japanese Americans in California.[8]

The progressivism delivered by the antifascist war influenced many in rural areas to not be as accepting of exploitation. A Negro leader in East Texas told Barnett in 1944 that "racial tension is very high," though he hoped that Barnett would "refrain from publicizing" the conditions.[9]

Restraint was a must since in the early postwar period, a USDA official declared that in "certain counties of the country" it was "dangerous for the Negro farmers to make inquiries regarding their inability to purchase certain farm implements and especially tractors."[10] One of Barnett's confidantes, Horace Mann Bond, then president of Fort Valley State College in Georgia, provided Barnett with a firsthand view of the danger that lurked in rural areas where Negro farmers resided.[11]

In short, the USDA had good reason to consult one with Barnett's experience, because it appeared that all-important rural areas were coming apart at the seams at a time of war: though the antifascist war was pulling in a progressive direction, in rural areas such as Sikeston, it appeared that the racism embedded in the Pacific War was operating in an opposing direction.

The tensions also were to be found due east. Barnett was instrumental when during the war Jamaicans and Bahamians arrived in Florida to harvest what were described to him as "vital war crops."[12] The problem there was that these migrant workers were not necessarily acclimated to the peculiar racial folkways of Dixie, which led to uprisings by October 1943. "We have 1700 Jamaicans in the state harvesting something like 33,000 acres of sugar cane," Barnett was told. So many migrant workers were needed, it was said, because "very few domestics are working for the United States Sugar Corporation due to the terrible name they have carried in the past—peonage." Thus, without the Jamaicans, the sugar crop would have rotted in the field.[13]

By early 1944 Barnett was in the Everglades conferring with hundreds of unhappy workers. Despite the uproar, the United States then saw no alternative to importing hundreds more to toil in the fields.[14] Barnett himself was probably the source—if not the writer—of the ANP release, which referred to those who were "unyielding in their demands to receive the going wage and who refused to submit to discrimination" and, thus, "are not going to be brought back this year." The department would now look to "other West India islands" for toilers. Also noted was the "oral agreement" between the United States and United Kingdom indicating that the notoriously rebellious Jamaicans "would not be required to work beneath the Mason and Dixon Line and that they would not be subject to discrimination."[15]

Thoroughly dissatisfied, hundreds of Jamaicans headed home disgustedly by November 1943 after refusing abjectly to work in states where Jim Crow reigned.[16]

Nonetheless, a postwar analysis shared with Barnett observed that "Jamaican workers contributed to larger production on American farms" and, along with their Bahamian counterparts, their presence and productivity "meant better wages and working conditions for domestic workers." This analysis suggested that after the war somehow more of these workers would have to be imported, which meant easing the Jim Crow conditions that had caused them to fight or flee, a trend that was to the benefit of their African American peers.[17] In sum, Barnett and his ANP had received yet another lesson in the benefit of paying careful attention to developments beyond the borders of the United States, when it was revealed that even the presence of poorly paid Caribbean workers on these shores could be quite helpful in alleviating the sorry plight of African Americans.

*   *   *

What was exacerbating Barnett's tumultuous experience with the USDA was a larger historical trend unleashed by the war: Washington was replacing London in many of the latter's colonies, which required a severe adjustment. Hence, it was also in 1944 that Jamaicans were protesting vigorously the implantation of Jim Crow that accompanied U.S. encroachment on the island. In neighboring Antigua, U.S. personnel were seeking to impose Jim Crow on buses, for example,[18] already in place on the military base served by public transportation.[19] In Trinidad there were clashes between U.S. troops and residents.[20] Nerves were not soothed when reports emerged that suggested that these colonies might be transferred to permanent U.S. control, with the stultifying experience of the U.S. Virgin Islands as a negative example.[21]

Barnett became more familiar with the tumultuous Caribbean as a result of his USDA post, which redounded to the benefit of the ANP. By 1945 he was subscribing to "a daily [newspaper] in Jamaica" though it "takes 30 days to get here."[22]

Already Barnett had evinced interest in events in Mexico, Brazil, and the hemisphere generally and now—spurred by his Caribbean experience—he embarked on a more concerted effort to bring these diverse colonies and countries within the ambit of the ANP. It was in October 1941 that he sent a series of letters seeking ties to newspapers in Bermuda, Barbados, Trinidad and Tobago, St. Lucia, Antigua, Dominican Republic, and so on.[23] Utilizing his experience with migrant laborers, he arranged to send stories on various topics throughout the chain of islands within hailing distance of Florida.[24]

By 1943, he had expanded his interest to include the Spanish-speaking nations (and Brazil). For example, he asked Vicente Machado Valle, editor of *La Epoca* of Tegucigalpa, Honduras, "Please tell us something about *the people of your country*," he inquired, "who may have been of African descent."[25] A similar letter was sent to scores of periodicals, as Barnett quite ambitiously was seeking to build an unparalleled communications network.

Simultaneously, the ANP began to send articles southward detailing racism in the United States, a maneuver that was embarrassing to Washington as it sought to spotlight the grave weaknesses of Berlin in the same realm. These words also served as a lever to change the United States.[26] The desired result was attained when Luis Esteban Rey in Caracas was moved to "know more deeply the race problem in the United States to the end of being able to collaborate," that is, "democratic sectors in Venezuela might be interested in creating a movement of public opinion favorable to the just aspirations of the North American Negro population." Like others, he expected reciprocity: "Oh that something similar might be done in all the other South American countries!" he cried.[27] As things evolved, the ANP initiative was a prelude to a resuscitation of the prewar campaign to knock down laws and practices that barred U.S. Negro migration and immigration southward.

*   *   *

ANP's internationalism had long been congruent with that of the Communist Party, which styled itself as part of a global phalanx. The ANP was not adverse to hiring real or imagined Communists, as the example of staffer Frank Marshall Davis demonstrated and as the publishing of Richard Wright during his Communist phase also showed.[28] It was not unusual when the well-regarded Harlem librarian, Jean Blackwell Hutson, visited Moscow in 1937, the ANP provided amply respectful coverage.[29] In early 1939, the ANP seemed repulsed when the National Labor Relations Board ruled that it was a violation to call a worker a Communist but no insult was to be found in calling a worker a "n-gger": The message, it was said with revulsion, was "be careful what you call a white man."[30]

Actually, it was deeper than that. The wider point was that racism was acceptable but radicalism was not. Moreover, though the ANP in the U.S. pattern kowtowed generally to organized religion, with the comfort of distance, their Teheran correspondent questioned the saliency of Islam, arguing in 1943 that "to some extent I believe it is their religion that keeps them [down], together with tradition. They will stop anywhere and pray to Allah. Their prayers are usually very long."[31]

World War II, which involved an alliance between Washington and Moscow, facilitated the trend. But the end of this titanic conflict inaugurated a new stage—the Cold War—which, from the U.S. standpoint, placed real and imagined Communists in the crosshairs. ANP's internationalism proceeded but could no longer overtly rely upon the counsel and contacts of those now demonized by Washington. This made for a weakened internationalism and, ultimately, a weakened ANP that set the stage for its eventual demise. For the equation then was that resemblances to Communists in effect meant you were one; so, if Communists manifested internationalism and you did too, like an associative law of mathematics, this meant that you were as red as Santa Claus's outfit.

Just before the onset of war in Europe in 1939, William Pickens addressed a gathering of the American Youth Congress, where Communists were thought to nest. There he issued a portentous declaration that did not materialize. As a replica of "the Thirty Years War of the religious sects," he asserted, "we do not want to substitute a hundreds [years] war of Democrats, Republicans, New Dealers, Townsendites, Communists, Socialists and Independents." But even then Pickens noticed this trend unfolding, which he then saw as harmful. "It was not comforting," he said, "that so many of the Jewish members of the Congress, when they began to debate . . . found it necessary to remark, 'I am not a Communist.'"[32]

But this rhetorical ritual was to become de rigueur for those who did not want to be tainted with a red brush, particularly if they wandered into the minefield of internationalism.

Early on, even when communicating privately, ANP was not particularly censorious about radicalism. It was also in 1939 that the agency's Washington correspondent was telling Barnett about a meeting featuring Trinidadian intellectual C. L. R. James that was sponsored by intellectuals like Abram Hill and future

Nobel laureate then Howard professor Ralph Bunche: "They call themselves the 'Trotskyites.' Rather a significant name don't you think?" The writer, Alvin White, knew Hill for "many years" and knew he was "filled with radical ideas and such—a sort of parlor pink,"[33] which was the harshest phrase he used. A few years later, White had "been busy . . . all day" working alongside the Southern Negro Youth Congress, thought to be led by Communists. "They did a swell job," he confided privately to Barnett. Their leaders, Edward Strong and Louis Burnham, read his account of their busyness and was "pleased with it" to the point where they sought to join the ANP as "associate members and subscribe to the service."[34]

Still, White wrongly accused Ted Poston, a Negro journalist who was part of the mainstream, of being "an out and out Commy" simply because he had traveled to Moscow with the ANP's own Loren Miller in 1932—and eventual NAACP leader Henry Moon—"to film that picture that was never released, or made for that part," a reference to an attempt to produce an antiracist movie.[35]

A problem for Barnett and the ANP as the nation moved rightward was their friendliness toward Iowan Henry A. Wallace, a U.S. vice president, then the leader of the Progressive Party, which in 1948 quite famously rejected anticommunism and, thus, was seen as a stalking horse for Reds or dangerously deluded. Barnett's

Former U.S. vice president Henry A. Wallace (center) joints Barnett (right) in Tuskegee in 1946: The two once collaborated closely, but as the Red Scare dawned and Wallace led the Progressive Party to defeat in the 1948 presidential election, Barnett—who had been close to the Republican Party—moved away as well from his former ties to the organized left. Courtesy of the Chicago History Museum.

association with the USDA, which Wallace had headed, did little to dissuade their enthusiasm for him. Wallace, said Barnett in 1939, was "one of the finest men in public life" and, quite rarely for the times, was "absolutely fair as far as Negroes are concerned"[36] and, quite unusually, had "surrounded himself with a group of men who appear to have no color bias."[37]

On the verge of his becoming vice president, the ANP chose to "predict Big Negro Support" for him since "he is no stranger to the Negro and probably knows more of the problems of the Negro in the middle hard working class than any other man in the present set-up, including the president himself."[38] In July 1944, when Wallace was dislodged as the vice presidential nominee of the Democrats, the ANP remarked that "Negro voters here as everywhere were almost solidly for Henry A. Wallace to be re-nominated for the post he now holds." Further, "the fact that the South plumped" energetically for his replacement, Harry S. Truman, was thought to be "disquieting."[39] ANP columnist, Gordon Hancock, chimed in, denouncing the "political strangulation" of Wallace.[40] Hancock, no radical, found Wallace to be "without doubt one of the majestic figures of this generation."[41] One African American thought so highly of Wallace that after his being ousted as vice president, he asked FDR to somehow arrange his appointment as governor general of the Belgian Congo.[42]

Barnett was similarly effusive about card-carrying Communists, such as Ben Davis, elected to the New York City Council in 1943.[43] That year, a prior engagement barred Barnett from attending a reception in Chicago for Davis, though he admitted candidly, "I would enjoy being present" since "not many men raised with a golden spoon to their mouths and Ben's was silver, if it was not golden, would espouse the cause which he has" (Davis emerged from an affluent Atlanta family).[44]

Davis was also a favorite of his namesake, Frank Marshall Davis. He too was pleased to know that the former Atlantan "renounced easy gold for manhood," which suggested "we ought to get more savvy about the Communists." Please note, he said, that "practically every social advance" made under the Roosevelt regime has been labeled "Red," and do not forget that "race prejudice is outlawed among Communists. Have either the Republicans or Democrats, also political parties like the hated Reds, ever taken such a stand?" he asked rhetorically.[45]

The ANP seemed as alarmed as the Communist press when in Los Angeles in 1942 there was a rumor about a potential "mass lynching to include Paul Robeson" and local Communist leader Pettis Perry launched by ultra-rightists outraged about possible desegregation of blood banks.[46] Naturally, a Haitian journal joined this chorus, condemning lynching, urging "Negro unity" and praising Robeson's repudiation of President Truman for his timidity on this issue.[47]

Robeson in this era became a symbol of resistance in the pages of the ANP, which was a duplicate of what was occurring in India—again—where the biggest newspaper there condemned the crucifixion of this talented actor and activist.[48]

As late as October 1946, Barnett demurred when he was importuned to join a group that would challenge Robeson's Council on African Affairs.[49]

At the same time, the ANP was often critical of the anticommunist detractors of Davis and Robeson, A. Philip Randolph in the first place. Just before raising an alarm about possible harm to befall Robeson, the agency's New York correspondent was reproving the labor leader directly, lampooning what were perceived as his needless pretensions to authority.[50] P. L. Prattis, known to be close to Barnett though he had departed the ANP staff years earlier, pointed out that his present employer, the *Pittsburgh Courier,* was strongly opposed to Randolph's signature effort, a proposed march on Washington designed to pressure the White House, albeit with anticommunist earmarks.[51]

Then as political lines were drawn sharply, George McCray, who was to join Randolph in the anticommunist pantheon, then termed him "particularly stupid" for shunning the World Federation of Trade Unions (WFTU), thought to be dominated by Communists. This error was magnified by the ample representation of "colonial labor" in the WFTU, with which African Americans shared numerous commonalities.[52] It was McCray who found the WFTU to be "pro-Negro" and pointed out that both the *Courier* and *Defender* provided favorable coverage to the group's founding in 1945.[53] It was McCray who later found that "in the minds of most Negroes there is a small spot for Russia because most of us believe the Russians do not believe in nor practice racial discrimination."[54]

Yet even then there were signals of a change that was to come. During the war, the ANP had syndicated the riveting journalism of Chatwood Hall from the Soviet front but found even in the midst of wartime fervor that "some of it" was "so far off the beam as far as Negro interest is concerned that we have not been able to make use of it."[55] When the FBI interviewed Chester Arthur Franklin of the *Kansas City Call,* they got a glimpse of why the Negro press was so open to Communists. He was asked why "he published Communistic news . . . on the front page of the paper," and Franklin replied, "Such news is important to my people, that is why it goes on the front page." He stated further, "[I]s it any wonder that my people are interested in Communistic news or are members of the Communist Party" because of "the way the white people are continually suppressing and oppressing the Negroes. At least in Russia everyone is equal according to their philosophy. When the white people accept the Negro race as equal to them you will find no Communists among my people."[56]

Concurring, George McCray, argued, "The South" of the United States was "the secret of Russia's strength."[57] Gordon Hancock informed ANP readers that "Communism threatens White Supremacy," "[A]nyway," he continued, "Hitler was never more bent on white supremacy than Churchill and Bilbo and Rankin and their subtle devotees." The only difference was that the "fascists were caught" and, like Hitler, were "dead" physically or otherwise, and this meant the "only threat to white supremacy ideology is the Communistic ideology," hence the Cold War.[58]

Barnett probably agreed with a 1945 newsletter he filed that chided Secretary of State James Byrnes, born in South Carolina. Moscow, it was said, "was given reason to laugh" at this U.S. official's "pompous memorandum to Bulgaria" on the USSR's "attitude toward elections" in Sofia. "Russia is not unaware," it was stated briskly, "of the un-democratic election procedures in Secretary Byrnes' own state—and in six other poll tax states."[59]

But then confusing political conditions arose as the tectonic plates of politics were shifting suddenly toward anticommunism. Barnett, who was connected organically to movements and individuals abroad who—like U.S. Negroes—were not as taken with the new anticommunist impulse, was less prone to adhere to the newly enshrined political line. Thus, reaching George Padmore, the former Communist who was to become a key advisor to Kwame Nkrumah in the Gold Coast, Barnett enthused that it was "fulfillment of a long anticipated pleasure when [I] met you." Like a dumbstruck fan he enthused, "I always wondered what the real George Padmore was like."[60] Padmore, put sufficiently at ease by this fandom, asked that Barnett "pay for me a subscription to *Negro Digest* and *Ebony*," the recently launched periodicals by Chicago's John H. Johnson, who was to become a major competitor of Barnett's.[61]

But unlike Padmore, who was in London, Frank Marshall Davis remained under the jurisdiction of the United States and, as Barnett was effusing, his staffer was under siege,[62] threatened by the hard-charging House Committee on Un-American Activities.

As matters turned out, it was Davis's supervisor who was subjected to the most extensive investigation because the "FBI had prepared a report on me as editor of ANP," said Barnett, "which was pages long. They had me attending meetings and being at places which were Communistic," he said with derision, then told him "that it was my close association over a period of years with a person suspected of being a Communist" that alerted them—a possible reference to Davis. "They really asked everybody and his brother" about him, which was "really laughable. Here I have the reputation of being a conservative," being a Republican, yet "they seemed serious," he averred, seemingly perplexed.[63]

Years later, P. L. Prattis, who worked alongside Barnett from 1923 to 1935, also was dismissive of the notion that ANP was a kind of Communist Front, stressing the agency's Republican ties.[64]

Yet Prattis too was facing accusations about his "loyalty," and it all related to his ties to a now suspect ANP.[65] This was in the context of the rise in deployment of the notorious "loyalty oath," wherein those taking positions hostile to the status quo—such as opposition to Jim Crow—were thought to be "disloyal" to the nation. If there was any consolation, John H. Johnson, Barnett's fellow press mogul from

Chicago, also was being accused of Communist links, as the allegation was that his periodicals were "Communist initiated and controlled or so strongly influenced as to be in the Stalin solar system."[66] In response, the popular songwriter Andy Razaf wrote a ditty lampooning the loyalty oath, but his was a voice that was being ignored.[67] What was at issue was that these press moguls found it useful to employ perceptive Communist writers like Frank Marshall Davis, providing these activists with income, part of which was transmuted into party dues. And then there was the stubborn internationalism of the ANP that did not see anticommunism as a pressing priority.

Barnett was under siege, investigated by the FBI pursuant to Executive Order 9835 with suspicion cast on his decision—now viewed suspiciously—to work with the USDA. When asked to fill out a "personal and confidential" form from this department, to deflect attention from his own presumed misdeeds he pointed to the then besieged "Council on African Affairs," observing archly that "some of [their] officers are reputedly Communists [who] attacked me. . . . I understand they regard me as capitalistic or reactionary."[68]

Frank Marshall Davis "got a tremendous kick" out of this brouhaha. "Imagine anybody calling you a Communist! And yet," the astute analyst continued, "it points up what I said before about the Truman loyalty order and with which you disagreed," that it was "used to violate the civil rights of individuals. You are not classed as even a militant, yet you are accused of communism"; he pointed out "how defenseless is an accused person without your connections."[69]

A friend of Barnett's, Sam Bledsoe, told him that he had reason to be worried since "an FBI agent came to me the other day to check on your 'loyalty' and patriotism," questions raised by what was seen as a curious decision to take a position with the USDA.[70] Bledsoe thought correctly that the "case seemed conclusive that you are neither subversive, radical or irresponsible."[71] This was obvious but not the point. The point was that Barnett and those like him were being softened up. He and those like him were to be accorded anti–Jim Crow concessions but in return were expected to concede no more solidarity with Robeson or praise of Ben Davis or favorable press reports from Moscow.[72]

Rather crudely though not inaccurately, Bledsoe summarized adeptly why Barnett and so many others had to reverse field and, minimally, acquiesce to the ascending anticommunism. "Any seizure of power in the United States by any group," said Bledsoe, "would come from the right"; hence, "if we are to have Fascism—. . . God forbid!—let us try to extract from it the fangs of racial reform. There will be enough fangs remaining."[73]

Fundamentally, this is a description of the postwar era. The "fangs of racial reform" were extracted as the radical left shrank—and, predictably, there were mighty "fangs remaining." The further problem was that this mighty concession that was racial reform occurred in part because of apprehension about how Jim

Crow weakened the United States in the confrontation with Moscow. But what was to occur if the Soviet "threat" disappeared? That too was part of the paradox of Jim Crow.

In any case, if the USDA had read a FBI report from 1945 they would have gathered that Barnett was not a Communist "nor actively controlled" by them but that Frank Marshall Davis, then executive editor of the ANP, was a party member and so was Luther Townsley, another ANP staffer. The latter had the key role in the agency: His job was to read "the papers from all over the United States and make rewrites on the news" for ANP distribution. "On one occasion," in what was seen as a devastating admission, "Townsley stated that whenever he reads an article in a so-called reactionary Southern newspaper, he merely takes the facts and turns them around to the exact opposite to what they are as set forth in the Southern newspaper."

Also subjected to scrutiny by the FBI was Chatwood Hall, the nom de plume of Homer Smith, the ANP's Moscow correspondent. With roots in Natchez, Mississippi, he had worked in the post office, where his coworkers remembered him for his extolling the benefits of socialism, before becoming an exile in the USSR by 1932. He worked for the post office there and reputedly established the first special delivery service in Russia. The diminutive Smith then morphed into a writer with a Russian wife. This matter of Russian women caught the eye of the FBI because Townsley too was "keeping company with a Russian woman, white" in Chicago, who was "supposed to be interested in the psychological aspects of American jazz." The FBI thought she was associating with him "for the purpose of either obtaining some type of information or furnishing material of a propaganda nature to Townsley" to be smuggled into ANP releases.[74]

Nevertheless, it was Hall/Smith who seemed to be the main object of scrutiny by the FBI. Born in 1899 in Quitman, Mississippi, he repudiated his U.S. nationality by 1939 and became a Soviet national.[75] He was accused of using the ANP to "disseminate Russian propaganda in the form of protests against alleged racial discrimination and inequality in America."[76] Cited at length was an article Hall placed in the *Chicago Defender* that posited common interests between the Coptic Church in Ethiopia and Christianity in Russia.[77]

FBI reports did not cite but probably knew about an ANP dispatch quoting black Communist Esther Cooper Jackson, who said, "I travelled in England, France and other countries" but "the Soviet Union was the sole country where a Negro felt a complete absence of discrimination,"[78] a viewpoint that mirrored Hall's and reflected his pervasive influence. It was Hall too who "read recently that Negro newspapermen are not allowed to sit in the press boxes of the U.S. Congress. Russia invites all" to its equivalent,[79] by way of contrast. "Alone among the great organizations of human society," said the ANP, "Islam and the USSR have practiced what they preached in relation to race and color discrimination," while "Christians preach it and their founder was himself a colored man but" they countenanced racism, not least in the United States.[80]

Everett Moore, ANP's Teheran correspondent, in discussing Negro units sent to Persia to build roads leading to Russia, added that as long as the war hung in the balance, there was interracial comity—but as the war wound down and it was clear that the U.S. side was prevailing, "Iran was fast becoming a Mecca of hate" and soon even Persians were using racist slurs against blacks they learned from Euro Americans.[81]

In other words, the FBI had reason to question the agency's anticommunist credentials. Richard Wright had been part of the ANP but soared to fame on the wings of his novelistic talent. But by 1944 an ANP writer was reprimanding him because of his anticommunist writings.[82] Piling on, his closest friend within the ANP, Frank Marshall Davis, accused him of being "out of step with the war torn world" and pronounced that he was "disturbed with Wright's preoccupation with pornography."[83]

At the same time, the ANP was complimenting Sergeant Walter Garland, who was studying music in France in 1938 when he decided to go fight in Spain. There he encountered Serbs and Croats and wound up in command of a machine gun company and was wounded thrice while fighting alongside Socialist Yugoslavia's eventual premier leader, Joseph Broz Tito, during the world war, whom he praised fulsomely.[84]

Another factor in the tug of war for Barnett and the ANP was the growing perception that anti–Jim Crow concessions would flow if only African Americans would distance themselves from Communists. This factor combined with the bright vistas opening for Barnett, as British colonialism retreated overseas and as U.S. neocolonialism advanced, all of which helped to push him toward acquiescence to the newly minted status quo. "What has happened to that estimable lady, I don't know," said Barnett of Charlotta Bass, his one-time comrade, who was the publisher of the *California Eagle*. But now he derided her because "apparently she has been taken over lock, stock and barrel by those of Communist persuasion. A few years ago," he said of a woman who, unlike him, did not deviate, "she was the head of the Negro Bureau for the Republican National Committee during one of the national campaigns."[85]

Despite his dismissal of Bass, her Los Angeles competitor—according to the ANP correspondent in this growing metropolis—had no loyalty to the ANP and had the temerity to "gleefully" predict "the end of ANP."[86] This was occurring as postwar racial changes in Los Angeles were reputedly proceeding with more speed than elsewhere, creating the possibility for a wider market for Barnett's wares.[87]

Claude Barnett had been living a charmed existence, propelling the ANP from a kind of Republican Party appendage to a worldwide instrument of influence. He had lived a contradictory existence, comfortable with U.S. elites as befitting

Like many of their correspondents, Harry Levette of the ANP did not rely solely on a check from the agency in order to make a living. The ANP did not neglect popular culture; their correspondent in Los Angeles also covered the growth of what came to be one of the more substantial African-American communities. Courtesy of the Chicago History Museum.

a Republican backer but also comfortable in diverse African American circles, including those of the radical left. But now contradictory winds were blowing that would lead to his garnering lucrative investment opportunities in Africa though, simultaneously, there were already indications that his firm grip on news and contacts in the Pan-African world would be challenged as anticolonialism gained strength.

In 1947 Frank Marshall Davis warned that capitulating to surging anticommunism would be perilous.[88] What Davis warned against was what occurred: a rupture between left and center that led to the bludgeoning of the former and the inexorable weakening of the latter as a direct result. As left-led unions were weakened in particular, African Americans were to find that they now had the right to check into hotels—but insufficient funds to pay the bill. Writing from balmy Honolulu during the winter, Davis commented, "I can assure you that I will not miss the ice and snow of Chicago," though he could just as well have referred to the icy political climate that was descending on the mainland.[89]

* * *

For years Barnett had been smoothly navigating a rutty road, able to satisfy Communists and Republicans alike, but with the war's end, his options were narrowing. His sentiments were firmly with the Republican Party, though some of his more formidable detractors thought otherwise. The point was that the business model of the ANP was also undergoing challenge, while his ability to exploit the talented labor of Communists like Frank Marshall Davis was under similar assault. As Republicans rose in Washington and statehouses alike, as the New Deal—then the Fair Deal—were whacked, opportunities did arise abroad for him as European colonizers nursed the severe wounds they had absorbed during the war. The paradox was this: As his ANP business was encountering headwinds, his investment opportunities were propelled by gusty tailwinds.

Inevitably, Barnett the entrepreneur would win out over Barnett the activist. When Congressman Adam Clayton Powell Jr., who was caught in a similar dilemma, spearheaded the attempt to purge his Harlem newspaper of presumed Communists, Alvin White found it wise that the politico was "trying to get rid of the party liners," particularly Doxey Wilkerson and Marvel Cooke.[90] The ANP evinced no particular distress when Robeson's Council on African Affairs erupted in fisticuffs. Wilkerson was arrested, amid charges of "armed guards" unable to prevent broken spectacles and ripped clothing, as the group split on a right-left axis.[91]

White, who had assumed the role of a kind of ANP commissar, found the future Harvard professor Ewart Guinier to be "as red as Joe Stalin," for "his rep is tainted and I don't know how we could profitably deal with him."[92] In a like vein, the doyenne of the anti–Jim Crow struggle, Mary Church Terrell, canceled a trip to the World Peace Congress in Paris because, said the ANP, it was "branded as 'Red.'"[93] In a sign of the times, a historically black university asked Barnett to join in a "Round-the-World Travel Project, a Crusade Against Communism."[94]

Barnett also was a self-styled expert in public relations and listened carefully to other practitioners of this dark art, particularly Sam Bledsoe, based in Washington. In 1948 the Washingtonian "noticed that quite a few very able Negroes and this is particularly true of the younger ones, are quite radical in their viewpoints. A few, notably Paul Robeson, are generally regarded as Communists or Communist sympathizers. Others are merely Left Wingers" and "rightly or wrongly, the capitalistic system becomes associated in their minds with discrimination because of color"; moreover, "the conservatives generally are regarded as leaning in a sub-conscious sort of way towards Fascism, with its violent racial prejudices, and away from Communism." In addition, "the Negroes who have done outstanding things have received much more recognition from the liberals and Left Wing Groups than from the conservatives." He worried that "the great bulk of the Negro vote is likely to go more and more to the liberal and Left Wing forces unless counter-forces are established." The "world situation" was "even more important" in terms of the "implications of racial discrimination" since "we today are engaged in a struggle for world mastery with Soviet Russia." But "Russia has one asset which we too often overlook. In theory, at least, Russia does not practice or countenance racial discrimination" while "we systematically practice racial discrimination in the United States." The problem was this: "[H]ow can we hope to make the colored races, which vastly outnumber the white race, our steadfast allies"? He opined that "the primary reason for Hitler's downfall was that he turned the Jews and colored races against him" and this, in turn, carried a sobering lesson for Washington.[95]

Bledsoe's admonition placed Barnett and other Negro leaders in a bind when their erstwhile friend, Henry Wallace, challenged President Truman from the left. Barnett and his colleagues responded by rejecting Wallace and, thus, evading charges of disloyalty to the status quo and, instead, embraced the incumbent. Channing Tobias, who had grown increasingly close to Barnett as an outcome of their investments in Liberia, told the ANP leader that "the way the Negro press chimed in with the press of the country in waging a subtle wishful thinking against President Truman was very discouraging and disappointing." Tobias bumped into P. L. Prattis and lectured him about the *Courier*, which—said Tobias—"played its usual game of going into moral eclipse just before the election."[96]

In embracing Truman, Barnett and Tobias turned their backs on what the ANP itself was describing: "Haitians applaud Wallace and Robeson," it was reported, and their cry for "more equitable and democratic status" for those of African descent, at home and abroad, and not just allocating concessions to a thin sliver of black investors.[97] Haitians, if the ANP is to be believed, were as anxious about lynching in Florida—well aware of how pestilence could spread—as black Floridians themselves:[98] a scenario that raised broad questions about Washington's hemispheric policy.[99]

Even the NAACP was sufficiently shaken to protest Panama's ban on visiting African Americans and the complementary policy that segregated favored "gold" and disfavored "silver" workers on the basis of racism and color.[100] Even Robeson, said the ANP, needed "special permission to visit Panama" because of a ban against English-speaking African Americans, deemed to be a "prohibitive race."[101] As a result, the Chamber of Deputies in Haiti adopted a resolution calling for "an international conference of Negroes" with a central purpose being "aiding American Negroes":[102] those opposed were accused of "psychological treason."[103]

The Haitian leadership was "incensed," said the ANP, when their minister of agriculture was confronted with "insults" in Biloxi, Mississippi, as certain locals probably confused him with a degraded U.S. Negro. "A man of color [is] in peril" in the United States was the sober conclusion of a Haitian editorialist.[104] This Haitians knew because so many of their leaders, for example, Elie Lescot, who served as both ambassador in Washington and president of Haiti, were quite familiar with Dixie and the desperate plight of African Americans. His sons were "educated at colored colleges" in the United States. Like other Haitians he had bitter memories of disrespect such as when one of their leaders departed New York City and the military band proceeded to play "Bye Bye, Blackbird," which—said the ANP reproachfully—"nearly precipitated an international incident."[105]

Retrospectively, there may be a connection between the surge of race consciousness in the United States and that which unwound simultaneously on the island—though it also is true that this consciousness rose in the United States as class consciousness retreated in the face of hammer blows inflicted by the Cold War and Red Scare.[106]

Such reactions and non-U.S. initiatives helped to drive an anti–Jim Crow mandate, but the question was evident: How meaningful could this be in the long run absent the forces arrayed behind Robeson and Wallace who had driven this policy in the first instance?

Barnett and those of his kind only realized dimly the consequences of their postwar bargain, a reality that hit with a thunderclap in one of the most disgraceful episodes in African American history, when allies of Barnett and Tobias picketed Truman's opponent, Henry Wallace, when he appeared in Birmingham, Alabama. These Tuskegee students were joined by men described as "hoodlums" who chanted "Down with FEPC," a critical anti–Jim Crow measure.[107] Barnett's friend, the institute's leader, Frederick D. Patterson, found all this "deeply regrettable,"[108] which was an appropriate response because it was troubling when those opposed to bigotry were targeted by black students.

Barnett, in any case, was unimpressed with Wallace's Progressive Party. Their convention, he said, "convinced me more than ever that Negroes cannot afford

Rufus Johnson, pictured in this undated photograph, was typical of editors and journalists in the Negro press, who relied heavily on articles from the ANP—the *Weekly Review* in the heart of the Black Belt in Alabama in his case. Courtesy of the Chicago History Museum.

to do other than support Mr. Truman." Reversing field, he said, yes, Wallace was a "nice man personally" but warned that "his championship of many angles affecting the race are of recent origin. He was always sound, always admired by Dr. [George Washington] Carver, always was helpful but he was no crusader in past days, not as his present picture would indicate. I'm a New Deal Republican now," he proclaimed. "I'm for Truman with all my heart. If he loses, I am still with him."[109]

Yet the ANP itself, if it were not to become irrelevant, had to express a broader sentiment, which it did by reporting that Wallace's "[third party] candidacy appeals to Negroes," although "liberal Negroes" courageous enough to back him openly were "labeled 'pink.'" Yet, said the reporter, there was "no question . . . but that Mr. Wallace stands high with Negroes all over the nation" because he was a "bitter foe of racial segregation."[110] Still, according to the ANP, in an indication of Barnett's own devolving thinking, eminent Negro attorney William Hastie derided Wallace's Progressive Party as a mere "puppet" of the Communists.[111]

Even those who were also pro-Truman, such as the NAACP's Walter White, were deemed by a key ANP operative to be insufficiently supportive of the Missourian, as the potential victors squabbled about the future allocation of the spoils.[112]

Nevertheless, this stampede toward Truman and its corresponding movement away from Wallace, Robeson and those to Truman's left, was to produce grave consequences for African Americans as a whole, including Barnett's ANP.

CHAPTER 6

Back to Africa

The postwar scenario seemed to be bright for Barnett, then in his fifties, and the ANP, but a closer inspection revealed a more complicated portrait. By 1945 the leading newspapers—the *Afro-American, Defender, Courier,* and *New York Amsterdam New*s—buoyed by their aggressive wartime reporting, each had a circulation well over 65,000, with the *Pittsburgh Courier* leading the pack with readers in the hundreds of thousands. The healthiness of the market was revealed by the fact that in 1930, 51 new Negro newspapers were started, then 58 more in 1936, but—in a telling sign—by 1949, only one.[1] The Negro press was shielded to a degree from the ravages of the Great Depression because it was not as dependent on advertising as their mainstream counterparts.

Still, this postwar decline in startups could be seen as a product of market saturation—or it could be seen as a reflection of flagging interest in the target audience, now sensing that a new era was coming where mainstream periodicals broadened their coverage to include those traditionally ignored or defamed. Moreover, the four largest journals, organized into the Negro Newspaper Publishers Association (NNPA), continued to see the ANP not as a resource but as a competitor, constraining Barnett further. Moreover, the entire realm—ANP and NNPA alike—both suffered decline in the 1950s, suggesting that cooperation may have been a more profitable recourse to pursue.[2]

In December 1949, the NNPA closed every bureau, except the one in Washington. Their New York correspondent, James Hicks, then defected to the *Afro-American*. The ANP's D.C. correspondent was unsure whether the bell was not tolling for her too, as she didn't "know whether their closing will mean more business for us or whether it means that [all] the papers are going broke."[3]

Just before that, it was reported that a pillar of the Negro press, the *New York Age*, was purchased by a "white Englishman" who was "married to a Negro" and "for the first time in the paper's history, it will hire white staff members."[4]

In any case, in the early postwar era, both the ANP and the NNPA had competitors beyond the mainstream, among them the United Negro Press in Durham, North Carolina, and 13 others of the same caliber. Thus, by January 1948, the NNPA agency distributed news to 33 newspapers with a circulation of eight hundred thousand, but in a year the number had dropped to 20, and by 1960 the agency was defunct. The ANP, on the other hand—according to one account—had about 80 subscribers in the 1920s and 112 by 1945, then 60 by 1955 but 101 by 1964.[5]

This latter soaring was misleading in that it represented growth in Africa that was soon to be challenged by indigenous and mainstream competitors—not to mention Barnett's declining health. In response, the ANP sought to centralize, requesting that certain sources forward information solely to their Chicago office, rather than affiliates.[6] Despite Barnett's ramifying interests in Africa and the Caribbean, the ANP still found it difficult to pay writers decent fees, even those involved in the life-and-death work of investigating the Ku Klux Klan.[7]

Nevertheless, it was evident that opportunities for ANP expansion were delimited: hence Barnett's tendency to look abroad increasingly for investments.

*   *   *

This tendency to look abroad was complemented by the ANP continuing to report aggressively on global affairs, including—but not limited to—Africa.[8] This trend was complemented by sectors of Negro leadership—at least initially—as when Lester Granger of the National Urban League speaking at Kentucky State University declared that the "hope of Negroes rests [in the] U.S. desire for world respect."[9] As the British Empire weakened, notably in the jewel that was India, it did appear that more full-throated denunciations of Jim Crow emerged by leaders of this Asian giant.[10]

As India surged to freedom, it surged to the forefront of concern for both the ANP and Barnett. Months before this nation's epochal independence in 1947, Barnett was contacted by Dr. Lanka Sundaram, a high-level Indian official who had pressed at the nascent United Nations for what was termed an "antisegregation resolution" and was told further that "Nehru is calling a conference to plan next steps in the fight against racial segregation" and "is suggesting that one or two American Negroes be invited," including the ANP chief himself.[11] "We have a representative at New Delhi and will see what he can do," Barnett replied.[12]

In 1949 Barnett met with Nehru in Manhattan. Barnett wanted to probe his "thought about the world of color," but the Indian leader "set the terms of reference early" and wanted to concentrate on "Negro life in the United States."[13] It was likely that Barnett was following up on an ANP dispatch from New Delhi, which in April 1947 asserted that "for the first time in history, the colored peoples of the world will have an organization of their own,"[14] which would have included U.S. Negroes. Cedric Dover, who had close ties to both London and Delhi, praised Barnett for fostering "close relations between American Negroes and the rising Afro-Asian" bloc; he went on to introduce Barnett to Ramesh Sanhari of *Blitz,* a leftist periodical in Bombay that regularly blasted Jim Crow.[15]

Not shy about brandishing his ties to Delhi, Barnett told a British colonial official in Ibadan that Nehru and "his sister, the Indian Ambassador to the United States," are "very close to colored people." The envoy "liked Etta" in particular, he confided.[16]

This beehive of activity seemed to create an environment that allowed others to raise their voices, a growing list that included Swedes,[17] a movement that was bolstered further when the Swedish star actor, Ingrid Bergman, denounced the "Jim Crow policy" in Washington's National Theater.[18] There were only "18 or 20 Negroes" in Stockholm, said the ANP, who were "mostly musicians and artists"; yet, unlike the United States, "the colored citizen of Sweden is treated as the equal of his Swedish brother."[19]

Paris too continued to be a haven for arriving U.S. Negroes, as was Moscow.[20] In the latter city, the director of the State Jazz band had audiences laughing and crying in a show that featured the United States. Lynching was a critical component of the production.[21] Those who were excoriated routinely in the United States, like boxer Jack Johnson, were greeted like royalty by royalty in Europe, said the ANP.[22]

The global coverage of the ANP reinforced the message that it was the United States that was the outlier and miscreant when it came to Jim Crow. This news helped to sustain African Americans during their darkest days and supported the idea that they were far from being alone.

A similar pattern, in short, was unfolding in increasingly Communist-dominated Eastern Europe, according to John Pittman, billed by the ANP as an "outstanding young labor figure [and] journalist" (who was also a member of the U.S. Communist Party): He reported that "one of the most highly respected citizens in Warsaw" was a Negro, while "in Rumania" he met "the old familiar Jim Crow brought there by American officials."[23] This shrouding of Pittman's party membership may have been accidental, for even Gordon Hancock then was stoutly assailing anticommunists and proclaiming "Negroes and Communists" as "Co-Scapegoats."[24] Meanwhile, per Pittman, the Jim Crow encountered by visiting U.S. Negroes in London was ascribed to U.S. influence, as the Labour Party warned hotels would lose their license to operate if they continued such a practice.[25]

The ANP continued to publicize the point that numerous African Americans—and their progeny—were doing quite well abroad and had escaped Jim Crow terror, particularly by relocating to Africa, Ethiopia notably, where opportunities were said to abound. At the same time, Africans visiting the United States solicited aid from African Americans.[26]

The value of the ANP was that a close reader of their dispatches then could gain a reasonable grasp of the global balance of forces, which over the centuries had been profoundly important in allowing African Americans to develop a sound strategy to combat bigotry.[27] Not only were the gains in Paris reported but, as well, the massacres of hundreds of thousands of Africans at the hands of French colonizers in Madagascar.[28] As Barnett gathered the facts on these outrages, he was at the same time pressuring Paris in that the very act of demanding facts made France aware that a spotlight had been placed on their misdeeds.[29]

This was an aspect of a larger story: why "denazification" in Germany was failing to the point, said the ANP, that "Nazis are re-educating the Americans,"[30] a point confirmed by Bishop William J. Walls of the African Methodist Episcopal Zion (AMEZ) denomination, who found that in Berlin the barracks' swimming pool was "drained after colored troops use it."[31] Predictably, Lieutenant Colonel Marcus Ray of the U.S. European Command told Barnett that he had "received many queries from Negro soldiers serving in Europe who are interested in finding a country in which to settle other than the land of their birth. Many are interested in Liberia."[32]

Finally, bowing to unremitting pressure, President Truman, as reported in an ANP exclusive, announced the U.S. intention to attain the "complete end of Jim Crow" in the armed forces.[33] Immediately, Shirley Graham mounted the rostrum at Howard University and declared that the petition to the United Nations protesting the plight of U.S. Negroes, drafted by her future spouse, W. E. B. DuBois, was the proximate cause of the White House's dramatic announcement. It was a "remarkable sign of the times," she said, emphasizing that "one week" after DuBois filed his petition, "we were reading the report of the President's Committee on Civil Rights."[34] Consistent with his lengthy praxis, DuBois had asserted that "the American Negro is part of a world situation" and, thus, were "in a Quasi-Colonial Status. They belong to the lower classes of the world."[35]

Those who agreed with him—and her—would have gained the lesson that the global pressure that Barnett and the ANP specialized in was a winning weapon. Graham also would have agreed that when Truman hastened to appoint Barnett's friend Charles Johnson of Fisk University as a delegate to the initial meeting of UNESCO,[36] then added Howard Thurman and his spouse (prominent black theologians *both*),[37] he was heeding the insistent pressure in the global arena of African Americans.

In some ways, Barnett and the ANP were like a rider seeking to ride two horses going in opposite directions at the same time. On the one hand, the old-time religion was being preached of militant attacks against Jim Crow and colonialism, a reluctance to join the baying against actual and supposed communists, and the like. On the other hand, lush opportunities were opening up for Barnett abroad—as his 1947 journey to West Africa showed—and those in London and Washington who smoothed the path for this trip were not to be found in the pews where the old-time religion was preached. Thus, although he was sure to remind Washington of how Jim Crow protests were being received in Lagos, he also informed Charles Ross of the White House staff that "you and perhaps Mr. Truman will be interested in seeing how [the Lagos press] played up his address before the NAACP which we syndicate to them."[38]

It also was in 1947 that a high-powered delegation of one of Booker T. Washington's creations, the National Negro Business League (NNBL), made a tour of Cuba, Jamaica, and Haiti, and on the agenda was not militant solidarity but business deals. The delegates were all comrades of Barnett's but, unlike him, they were less interested in even pro forma bowing to solidarity.

Of course, there were aspects of this delegation that demonstrated that even the NNBL was not altogether supportive of Washington's agenda. A. G. Gaston, an affluent resident of Black Birmingham who played a critical role in the epic desegregation battles of 1963, was thrilled to find that in Haiti, "white people cannot buy land," and was disappointed to find that "Jews and Assyrians . . . are doing most of the business." His Haitian interlocutors apparently were not terribly upset with his words because they pledged to send a delegation to the NNBL meeting of 1948. In Havana, Gaston was given an elaborate welcome and was elected an honorary member of an elite club of Afro-Cubans.[39]

The NNBL junket was a kind of Pan-Africanism that the ANP endorsed. The news agency splashed the news when Mary McLeod Bethune, an ally of the late president Franklin D. Roosevelt, was awarded the honor of "Grand Officer of Honor and Merit" of Haiti and accorded a "full schedule of conferences with government officials and leaders in civic affairs." At a festive reception for her, she was hosted by the president and his spouse and, not coincidentally, was feted at the U.S. Embassy. To her credit, she urged "extension of the franchise to the women of Haiti."[40]

The Atlanta University scholar J. Max Bond—related to Barnett's friend Horace M. Bond—who admitted to having a "fluent command of French," asked the ANP leader to lobby so that he could be "appointed Ambassador to Haiti."[41] The shrewd Barnett, acutely aware of the politics on all sides, advised him not to lobby Congressman William Dawson, the Negro legislator from Chicago who—if he knew the post was about to open—would grab it for a crony in Chicago; instead, Barnett counseled "sell a bill of goods" to a Georgia senator by stressing that "Northern Democrats are gunning" for this plum and bank on the Georgian's negative reaction.[42]

When Barnett's fellow influential Chicagoan, the attorney Earl Dickerson, traveled to Jamaica, one of the island's key leaders pledged to "look out for these important visitors and will be sure to do all we can to make their stay in Jamaica an enjoyable one."[43] A similarly powerful Haitian promised to do the same for Dickerson in Port-au-Prince,[44] and the Chicagoan departed "greatly impressed" with the republic's president.[45] But the wider message conveyed by the cases of Bethune and Bond (and Dickerson too) was the idea that, increasingly, African Americans were coming into their own, becoming an entering wedge into the Pan-African world on behalf of Washington.

*   *   *

Barnett made his first trip to Africa in 1947, a replica of the Caribbean journey. Previously, colonizing powers there were not disposed to provide visas to African Americans, suspecting that their very presence provided a negative example for the colonized.[46] With the Cold War challenge from Moscow, however, the inclination was to deploy African Americans as a kind of Trojan Horse in the Pan-African world.

This was a turnabout. There was "widespread knowledge," Barnett informed London in 1947, "that Negroes have great difficulty in securing visas to visit" their ostensible homeland. "Missionary groups, even those from the United States, have never used Afro-Americans in their missionary work" as a direct result, he charged.[47]

Sensing the direction of prevailing winds, in 1946 Barnett advised the U.S. State Department that "if some definite commercial tie-up could be effected between a group of influential Negro citizens of the United States and Liberia, it could go far to cement relationships between the peoples of the two countries."[48] Barnett was in touch with the desk officer at the State Department for Liberia about "tests being made on piassava," a fiber used for brooms, because he was interested in importing it.[49] Already, he was "doing some small importing" from "parts of Africa," particularly carvings, in league with Lloyd Kerford, an affluent Negro businessman "who is making lots of money and is an old friend," he said. Barnett had visited executives of Firestone, whose interests in Liberia were legion, to confer. He already knew of "active competition" from "the Dutch, French, and Lever Brothers, to say nothing of Firestone's trading company and the Syrian merchants" who "infest" West Africa.[50] Barnett was then "thinking of starting a small trading corporation to do some business in Liberia."[51]

Barnett was also eager to widen news coverage of the exploited continent but found that his affiliates were unwilling to subsidize this mutually beneficial venture, which pushed him further into generating income through nonjournalistic efforts.[52]

Washington was willing to lend an ear to Barnett's proposal because it dovetailed with a desire to gain a foothold in the resource-rich continent so as to weaken further colonizing powers that had been debilitated by the war in any case. At the same time, Barnett, whose acumen in public relations already had established him as a hub for black business generally, had contacted then secretary of commerce Henry A. Wallace about expanding overseas ventures. It also was in 1946 that the secretary's adviser on Negro affairs approved Barnett's proposal for a "conference on the Negro in Business," an approval driven "in response to numerous inquiries from Negroes in Africa, Cuba and South America." The idea was to invite "Negro businessmen from foreign countries" for this confab on "Foreign Trade and the Negro in Business."[53]

This was a prelude to Barnett and Moten journeying to Liberia in 1947, a nation to which he long had devoted attention. It was in 1945, illustrating the advantage of controlling a news agency, that he was asked to investigate why a U.S. firm in Liberia was building a harbor but drew "the color line on employment of skilled Afro-American help while flying in . . . non-African stock for skilled work."[54] Following his usual pattern, Barnett could follow up on this tidbit of information and either publicize it—or pledge not to do so in return for a public-relations contract.

By March 1947 Barnett was happily informing the chairman of the board of Tuskegee Institute that "I am going to Liberia especially to visit the Booker T. Washington Institute of Kakata of which I am a trustee. It is a small replica of our school," he said referring to his alma mater, "fashioned after Tuskegee."[55] Barnett and Moten arrived in West Africa with a fair knowledge of conditions there, based in part on briefings with African Americans who had ties there.[56]

For example, the uncle of the ANP's Enoch Waters taught in Liberia for years.[57] Barnett's friend Jacob Reddix, president of Jackson State University in Mississippi, told Barnett "you are interested in the same thing in which I am interested" in that "my two brothers have had over thirty years experience in owning and operating a sawmill" and wanted to replicate this business in Liberia.[58]

Barnett, in sum, was well briefed before departing. Black Chicago's Sidney Williams told Barnett about his sojourn in Casablanca during the war and gave him names of friends to consult, for example, "Dr. Du Bois Robert of Rabat" who "operated on Josephine Baker," the Franco-American performer; then there was "my good friend, Sidi Mohammed Menabhi of Marrakesh," a multimillionaire who "looks just like [a] brown skinned American Negro man. His family rules the southern half of Morocco. All you need to do," Williams advised confidently, "is to let him know that you know me and Josephine Baker."[59] The ANP reported that when Nazi persecutors placed Baker's name high on the list of those to be put before a firing squad, she found "refuge in the court of Pasha El Giaoui in Marrakesh" in a dramatic display of antifascist Pan-Africanism.[60]

Wall Street's George Burchum appreciated the conversation he and Barnett had shared about Liberian lumber but found in his elite circle a "complete lack of interest in the furnishing of risk capital at this time," which then was thought to put a premium on African-American capital.[61] Barnett realized that Africa presented a vast, untapped market, subject to exploitation on various levels. Before departing, he contacted Eli Oberstein of Radio Corporation of America (RCA), the recording company in Manhattan, reminding him that his spouse "can put more into a song than most folk"; thus, he asked, "would a wire recording of African songs and music on a comparative basis have any interest" for him, because "Mrs. Barnett plans to do some studies in African music."[62]

Thus, Barnett knew well Lester Walton, a U.S. Negro who held the quota envoy position that consigned those like him to Monrovia and few other sites. As early as 1935, Walton, writing on the stationery of the U.S. legation in Monrovia, told Barnett "confidentially, the most cordial and confidential relations exist between President [Edwin] Barclay and me." He was able to "drop in" to Barclay's palatial abode at his leisure; their intimacy was exposed when Walton prepared a Thanksgiving dinner for him.[63]

Still, Walton's parlous position at home was symbolized dramatically when, at a groundbreaking ceremony in Washington, he collapsed and fell into the waiting arms of several powerful white men seated on the platform.[64] Thus, by 1945 Walton was said to have been sidelined by President Truman because of protests by African-American soldiers in Liberia of his avid support of the local elite against the strivings of the masses,[65] a story that Walton found "libelous."[66]

In truth, he told Barnett, he was so well received in Monrovia that there was "quite a popular demand that I may be Liberian Minister" to the United States.[67] He was not far wrong in that relations between African Americans and Liberians were often warm: Monrovia was inviting, said the ANP, "immigration of American Negroes."[68] There were nettlesome conflicts too, calling upon Barnett's immense diplomatic skills once he arrived.[69]

Barnett did not meet a key Founding Father of Nigeria—Nnamdi Azikiwe—until he arrived in Africa, but this prolific writer, said Barnett, "has been on our staff for the past 10 years, in fact he joined us [when] he was in Accra," working as an editor.[70] Barnett told Azikiwe directly that he appreciated the "wealth of knowledge and information which we glean from the newspapers which you publish." The ANP had "our own correspondent in Liberia" and, perhaps, there could be collaboration in Nigeria to their mutual benefit.[71] Yet Barnett continued to feel a class tug and told one of Azikiwe's Nigerian colleagues that this founding father was one of the "leaders of a certain unrepresentative movement in Nigeria,"[72] a reflection of his warming ties with London.

By September 1947 Barnett and Moten were reporting enthusiastically on their West African journey, giving profuse thanks to two principal parties: the Phelps-Stokes Fund—the well-endowed foundation—and the U.S. State Department. "We were guests of both the Governor of Dahomey and the Governor of French Togoland," he said. In Nigeria "we were guests for five days in the palace of one governor, having all our meals, except breakfast, which was served in state in our suite, a complete wing of the government house in Lagos." He also pointed out intriguingly that "the Africans in meetings and in person, often ask about lynchings, segregation and other practices which they heard abound in the United States," often reported on the British Broadcasting Company. This radio network was "heard all days and part of the night in West Africa and every lynching or racial disturbance in the United States is played up."[73]

While in Achimota, Barnett told Channing Tobias that the "pace which we have been keeping has been most difficult," which included "a tea with the Shacklefords, West Indian bakers," then a "broadcast by Mrs. Barnett," then "cocktails with the governor," then "Mrs. Barnett's concert at King George Hall in Accra," which was "sold out three days before the event" as "there were as many people outside as in."[74]

Kano "lives up to its reputation" said Barnett about the city in northern Nigeria. It was "almost totally Mohammedan, the men all wear white robes and some" with a "fez. . . . [M]et the Emir this morning," a "very conservative" man. The "governor gave a luncheon for us."[75] He also met Georges Apedo-Amah, a "young African" and "secretary to the Governor of French Togoland. We were guests of the governor at cocktails while in Lomé and the government put us up during our stay there," he wrote to Dale Cox of International Harvester, a major U.S. manufacturer of agricultural machinery. Nigeria had "considerable plans for development" and, of course, Barnett was more than willing to be a middleman to discuss how a sale could be brought about.[76]

Turning to Apedo-Amah, he informed him of International Harvester, which supplied "the largest farm machinery and dirt moving equipment" extant. "Some of its officers I know well," for "they employ many Negro people." The point was, said Barnett, "if you could see to it that those governmental orders went to [International Harvester] I believe that the Negro mechanics you desire would be sent with them to teach your people how to operate them."[77] "Our Foreign Operations Division has taken much interest in this matter," the impressed Cox assured Barnett.[78]

By their very presence, the intelligent and well-appointed Barnett and Moten served to question easy ideas about subjugated U.S. Negroes. They also were the thin wedge of a U.S. offensive to influence vast territories that had languished under colonial rule. In the bargain, investment opportunities were presented to Barnett and Moten. Apparently, the couple left a positive impression. A London official told Barnett in October 1947 that "Ivor Cummins, who is at the Colonial Office, has just come back from a trip to West Africa" and "says the whole of West Africa is talking about you and Etta" in that "everybody you met is tremendously impressed with enlightened Americans, exemplified by yourselves."[79]

Cummins probably heard of the positive reviews of the benefit concert rendered by Moten on behalf of the Red Cross. "It was packed," said a thrilled Barnett. "In fact she gave concerts for charity causes in Accra, Gold Coast, Freetown, Sierra Leone and Monrovia."[80]

Understandably, London was pleased with Barnett's arrival, though he represented a competing power, because he was said to propose "recruiting American Negro staff for services in West Africa," a project in which the Colonial Office was "extremely interested." The project would involve, for example, "teachers in secondary schools" and "training teachers in agricultural education in Nigeria" and various "scientists" too.[81] Barnett had made it clear before his departure that he would be soliciting opportunities for "skilled American Negro workers in such trades as carpentry, brick masonry, electricians" and "Negro businessmen with capital to invest."[82]

London may have been pleased with Barnett's visit because he sought to propagandize Africans about the alleged successes of U.S. Negroes, which assuredly may have put the U.S. competitor in a less than harsh light but, more to the point, bolstered the anticommunist power then seen as necessary to the perpetuation of colonialism, in light of the British Empire's known debilities.[83] Barnett sought to bring "a couple of films" to show "the natives" in order to "give a graphic picture of life among the Negroes in the United States and especially in the schools and agriculture."[84]

Barnett the businessman also was expanding into the field of film. He shipped containers of 16mm film of his journey back home that he shot in the principal countries he visited: Liberia, the Gold Coast, and Nigeria.[85] Etta Moten exhibited these movies in Beaumont and Prairie View, Texas, which featured the Booker T. Washington Institute in Liberia, which meant that Barnett was playing a useful transatlantic role of propagandizing—or, perhaps, educating—Africans about African Americans and vice versa.[86]

This closeness to colonizers could have compromised Barnett's bid to build bridges to Africans, which arguably was in his long-term interests and Washington's too. Upon his return, he got wind of "troubles" in the Gold Coast. "Isolationist daily papers have seized upon the incident to the disadvantage of Great Britain," he candidly told a leading British official in Ibadan.[87] Official London felt sufficiently comfortable with Barnett to inquire about Kwame Nkrumah who, it was said, held a Communist Party "card."[88]

Barnett had to tread carefully. He was told about an acquaintance just back from the Cameroons where "one of the French officials noticed the [insignia of the] U.S. Department of Agriculture on his briefcase and they were a little bothered for fear he might be spying" for "the U.S. Government in some secret capacity." Those he visited in French Togoland might have looked at Barnett with more suspicion if they had known of his association with this department.[89]

Barnett also told London that "most Negroes have felt they would not even be permitted to visit or settle in West Africa," but times were changing.[90] After

Barnett's return home, he was told about "various African students" who were "requesting your assistance in their plans to come to the United States for further education."[91] "Our African friends have no hesitancy in making requests," said Barnett; one had written him asking him to "buy $2000 worth of his new book."[92]

Recruiting African Americans to bolster the British Empire in Africa also was a signal of a colonial system in distress. It also created an opening for Barnett. His London correspondent then informed him about the paradox of anticolonialism in that "years ago" Rudolph Dunbar had told Barnett that "because of the pre-eminence the Negro press would play after the war," the ANP should set up shop in Africa. "You paid [no] attention to this advice," he said remonstratively. But now "Lord Rothermere (the *Daily Mail* and Sunday Dispatch Group) is going to establish the biggest chain of newspapers in West Africa. They have approached me to work with them," he advised.[93] That is, just as wide and rich new vistas seemed to be opening for the ANP, what was actually happening was an adjustment that would undermine its business model.

Still, not all the news was gloomy, for Barnett's account spurred Richard Wright, then residing in Paris. "I too plan a trip to Africa," said the novelist, and "your word in that direction made up my mind." This was so though France had "claimed my heart"—"did you know that the President of the French Senate is a Negro named Monnerville" he asked with wonder.[94] Just in case Wright followed his peripatetic instinct, Barnett, rarely capable of passing up an opportunity, verified that Wright would continue to be an ANP correspondent.[95]

Barnett returned home with an overflowing basket of investment opportunities. That was not all. "When I was there," he informed the district magistrate in Kumasi, Gold Coast, "I ordered a mahogany bed, several tables from elephant bases and some stools."[96] He also added to his growing collection of African art.[97]

The gushingly favorable publicity he received was emblematic of his growing role[98] as the U.S. Negro most clearly identified with Africa, a view enhanced when the competitors for this honored role, for example, DuBois and Robeson, were undermined. While the passports of the latter were in the process of being confiscated, Barnett and Moten were traveling twenty-one thousand miles over a period of many weeks through Africa—and they did not hesitate to thank the State Department and the Colonial Office in London for their ample aid in doing so.[99]

Upon Barnett's return home, he sat alongside a former U.S. secretary of state, Edward Stettinius, the Liberian leader Gabriel Dennis, and the NAACP leader Channing Tobias as they convened at the plush Savoy Plaza Hotel in Manhattan in the maiden meeting of the Liberia Company. Stettinius was chairman of the board,[100] as he and his colleagues contemplated substantial investments in the nation's "gold, tin, manganese, cocoa, timber, palm kernels, kola nuts"—and more. "A new day is here," chortled Barnett, as the nation proved to be "eager . . . to have American Negro businessmen"; on a more sober note, he admitted, "never have

I observed such poverty and such low standards of living as I saw in primitive West Africa," but in an upbeat moment he knew that "they represent one of the greatest future markets in the world."[101] Still, he remained steadfastly optimistic since the United States was now "pouring billions of dollars" into coffers "all over the world, trying to stem the tide of Communism."[102]

A kind of Pan-Africanism was accelerating that envisioned African Americans as an advance wave on behalf of wider U.S. interests in Africa. "At the request of Mr. John D. Rockefeller, 3rd," said a seemingly startled Tobias, "I had [a] luncheon with him" to prepare him for his own African journey; "at his insistence," Tobias "wrote letters of introduction for him. (Imagine that!)"[103] Barnett's Liberia Company then joined delegates from Nigeria and Haiti in a conference sponsored by Washington on the theme "The Negro in Business," addressed by the influential diplomat, investor, and future governor of New York, W. Averill Harriman.[104]

Barnett also played up his access to widening circles, accentuating his ties to Stettinius. He gave *Ebony*, the growing monthly founded by fellow Chicagoan John H. Johnson, "the first opportunity to use" photos of the former Secretary of State traipsing around Liberia."[105] An executive with the Liberia Company liked the magazine's feature on Stettinius "very much," telling Barnett that "your active interest was certainly a great help." He prodded Barnett to press Azikiwe to "establish a magazine in the interests of Liberia,"[106] which was all well and good, though it was unclear how buttressing the businesses of Johnson and Azikiwe aided Barnett's own.

Nevertheless, Barnett was pleased. "Years ago when I was active as a Republican," he replied to Tobias, "I sought to sell the idea of Big Business giving adequate advertising to Negro newspapers—opening up new accounts, etc., for political support," since "back in those days all our newspapers were Republican." But now, he said in late 1948, "I have a notion some of those efforts have just now come to fruition."[107] Barnett apparently did not grasp the dynamics at play or realize that by letting loose the likes of Rockefeller on Africa, they were simply closing off space for their own expansion, thereby illustrating the paradox of Jim Crow. As efforts at integration proceeded apace, Negro institutions that had survived apartheid began to crumble.

*   *   *

After his return home from Africa, Barnett heard from "two young African photographers in New York" who "came to the U.S. at their own expense" with the aim of capturing "pictures of Negro life in America to show to West African audiences," a reflection of the interest in the United States that he had stirred in Africa.[108] Poignantly, Jacob Dosoo Amenyah of the Gold Coast requested ANP help "for a trace of my great-grandfather in America" who was kidnapped by "both European and Africans" decades earlier.[109]

This was not the only African interest that had been stirred by Barnett's and Moten's journey. F. D. Patterson, the leader of Tuskegee, had to caution Barnett that "frankly we have taken on so many African students that I don't see how I can commit our limited budget for any more just now," though demand had risen sharply.[110]

Barnett had good reason beyond the altruistic to continue aiding Africans, for he had returned from Africa wealthier. He purchased a considerable amount of African art, whose value was bound to appreciate. He intended to mount an exhibition of this art in the United States, which he thought would be "one of the most effective means ever proposed for educating American people on what Africa is like" and to demonstrate "what Africans can do in craftsmanship or art."[111] This art also brought—at least—aesthetic benefit to him. "The marvelous Art Collection you and Mrs. Barnett acquired from Africa" impressed the librarian Dorothy Porter, who thought that "your home must now be a veritable museum of African Art."[112]

Soon Etta Moten and "two friends," said Barnett, "set up a gift shop in New York, the Afro-Arts Bazaar" and began "selling curios from Africa and bags and leather work from Mexico." It was "doing remarkably well. They have material from Lagos and Benin City especially," indicative of the success of the West African voyage. This journey also reacquainted Barnett and Moten with Nelson Eddy, the Hollywood singer and actor, who was with U.S. troops in the Gold Coast during the war and had created a bust for Etta during that time. Upon their return home, they supped with him, then dined with Roland Hayes,[113] yet another celebrated singer, as their social quotient soared, which could mean only more lucrative opportunities.

Barnett continued to aid newspapers in Nigeria as they sought to publicize news about African Americans.[114] Again, this was not altruism, because solidarity is a two-way street. Thus, writing from London, Joseph Emmanuel Appiah, secretary of the West African Students Union, pressured the governor of Missouri, viewing with "great concern the dark prospects of the two Negro boys" slated to be "electrocuted."[115]

Then Barnett visited Oscar Chapman, the undersecretary of the interior, and quizzed him about how a flap about the desegregation of a local swimming pool was reported abroad, reminding him that "there are four daily papers published in Lagos" alone and the "*West African Pilot* is one of them," with which he happened to have close relations.[116] "Never having seen an African newspaper before," Chapman was impressed.[117]

To remain current, for years Barnett received a "regular service of news cuttings from the West African press."[118] "We have been able to keep up with the news fairly well," he said in early 1948, referring to an outburst of unrest in that vast region, since "we get most of the newspapers from Lagos and even the *Southern Nigerian Defender* from Ibadan."[119]

Barnett fretted that this unrest would have a negative impact on his Liberian holdings.[120] Irked, Barnett disparaged the now deceased Marcus Garvey and various repatriation movements to Liberia led by U.S. Negroes as being disreputable causes of turbulence.[121]

In short, in order to combat a long-term shrinkage of the Negro press, Barnett heightened his focus on Africa. "Working with the British Information Services," he announced in December 1948, "we have been sending a number of interesting photos from Africa to the papers we serve. I would say that African items have increased 150 to 200 percent since we returned" from West Africa. In doing so, Barnett gave a shot in the arm to Pan-Africanism nationally. He did so—by his own admission—by "working with British Information Services," which deluged ANP with "interesting photos from Africa to the papers we serve,"[122] designed not to place colonialism in an unfavorable light. Barnett also knew that prior to his visit, by one account there were only 10 U.S. Negro newspapers "effectively reporting news on Africa," which provided a bounteous opportunity for the ANP[123] that ultimately was unrealized.

"I was favorably impressed on the whole," Barnett said subsequently, "by the efforts and very evident sincerity of British colonial administrative and agricultural officers to improve the lot of the African and to raise his standard of living."[124] Anticolonial stalwarts, some of whom Barnett knew, would have disagreed. But continuing his contradictory pattern, Barnett—who had not visited East Africa and southern Africa up to this point—raised searching questions about colonialism there.[125]

*   *   *

As noted, Barnett—as well as many other African Americans—thought highly of Henry A. Wallace. Like many others, however, Barnett did not support Wallace's campaign for the White House in 1948. Instead he found Truman's victory to be "totally a just result," though he remained a titular Republican. "I worked for him quietly but with all of my might," he confessed.[126] Other Negro editors and publishers were less guarded in their support for Truman.[127]

Barnett's evolution from a staunch Republican to a stauncher still defender of a Democrat mirrored a larger transition that encompassed African Americans on a similar journey. This evolution was part and parcel of a devolution, which was the sidelining of a once vibrant political force to the left of both major parties that had received more than a modicum of support from African Americans. This was the price of the ticket of admission—for some—into the higher ranks of the nation.

CHAPTER 7

Cold War Coming

Alice Dunnigan was overwhelmed.

It was October 1949 and this ANP correspondent was surrounded by reporters from India in her home base of Washington, D.C., as they bombarded her with pointed questions. They stated that she was the first Negro reporter they had seen since their recent arrival in Washington to cover the heralded visit of their leader, Jawaharlal Nehru. Querulously, they questioned why no Negroes had been at the other gatherings to which they had been escorted in a capital city still marked by Jim Crow. To that point, she said, they had not "seen a single Negro American" at various functions to which they had been shepherded. They had spoken to Walter White, the leader of the National Association for Advancement of Colored People (NAACP), when he had passed through India but, said Dunnigan, "he attempted to convince them that there was no such problem existing," in other words, that Jim Crow was in its death throes. Unlike White, these scribes insisted on discussing Paul Robeson, then under siege by his government.[1] Back in Madras, for example, ANP correspondent Lawrence Burr reported that "India eagerly awaits Paul Robeson's visit."[2]

It was Burr who reported that "today many Indian leaders are asking why intelligent Negroes remain in a religion"—Christianity—"that has as one of its goals the continued subjugation of non-whites."[3] It was also Burr from his perch in Madras who found in 1949 that "national freedom achieved by Asiatic nations results in increasing interest in problems of the Negro."[4] "Sooner or later," said the ANP, "every traveling American will be asked to justify his position on the race question in the United States."[5]

This was a telling trend abroad. At home Barnett, along with many other Negro leaders, had exerted his influence to make sure that President Truman was re-elected though they had undercut the anti–Jim Crow movement by scorning the most resolute, including the defeated Henry Wallace and Robeson. They also undercut their previous esteemed position with rising powers, for example, recently independent India, by seeming to oppose those that Delhi appreciated, for example, Robeson. Personally, Barnett's wide array of investments continued to generate profit, but the process of "integration" combined with positions diverging from those of the planet's majority, which was the price of admission, served also to undermine the centerpiece of his business universe: the ANP. Thus, instead of highlighting Robeson's anticolonial and antilynching crusades, the ANP shifted subtly to trivia designed to demean this leader, providing reports about a new black group that denounced the performer, not least for the alleged sartorial confusion he helped to create.[6]

*   *   *

Dunnigan, one of the first women to be hired by the ANP as a correspondent, also proved to be a feminist prod, pressing Barnett and others on missteps. "I have never been able to get through my mind, how we as a Negro race, particularly newspaper people can raise so much cain when we are segregated," yet "within our own group we practice the most vicious type of segregation." That is, when "one of our own group says he is skeptical about hiring a woman because she may not be able to fill the needs, that is alright"—but, she insisted, "segregation is segregation." The "NNPA has a staff of two men and two women," she said in early 1948, "as compared with ANP's one person" in Washington. James Hicks, her NNPA counterpart had "his own car while I [roam] around on a street car." Because of Barnett's penuriousness, Dunnigan averred, "I am in far worse shape [financially] now than I was when I began the work." Such was the case, though she had "a child and two aged parents" and despite "how much the cost of living has increased since January 1947 when I began working" for ANP. She was being exploited shamelessly, though—Dunnigan contended—an article in "the Negro History Journal on women of achievement from 1940 carried a paragraph about me."[7]

"Just yesterday," she told Barnett before Truman's reelection, "I met one of my female fellow-workers on the street and she reminded me that she had been informed that ANP had been trying to find a man to take my place in Washington. She also told me that one man under consideration from New York had been offered $50 a week but refused to accept the job for less than $75. That is the second person," she complained bitterly, "who [has] called [to] my attention that you had offered a man $60 a week for the place which I am filling for $25."[8]

As if to warn her boss, she told Barnett that "I joined the labor union . . . as soon as I discovered that there was one in the government" and preempted any attempt to charge her with racial disloyalty because it was in her first job that she "learned to work without thought of race."[9] This pro-union proclivity and the prevailing political climate induced Barnett to ask his star reporter whether she had "Communistic leanings." Without skipping a beat, Dunnigan replied emphatically, "The answer is definitely *NO*," while adding ingenuously, "I don't really know what the word means." But her addendum—"I am a strong advocate of organized labor"—may have been just as unsettling for her businessman boss. Cavalierly disregarding his concern, she said, "If a believer in the common man, and a fighter for the underprivileged person is a Communist, then I guess I am one."[10]

When W. E. B. DuBois was tried in federal court for being the agent of an unnamed foreign power, presumed to be Moscow, Dunnigan excoriated bias directed against black women journalists at the trial. Presciently, she commented that "when this fight is won," meaning propelling recognition of Negro newspaper reporters as first-class citizens, then the "women of the Fourth Estate must then fortify themselves for 'the battle of the sexes'"; there was simultaneity of this fight too because women "in this business often find themselves attacked on two fronts—that of race and sex."[11]

Yet as Dunnigan mounted her soapbox, the Jim Crow paradox already was atrophying the sinews of black feminism, emitting a loud signal to the ANP itself. Months after U.S. troops were in combat in Korea, the National Association of Graduate Nurses—Negro medics—disbanded because it was deemed that this group was now "well integrated into nurses' work." It had been founded in the early part of the twentieth century but now was thought to be "the first Negro organization on the national level to disband because its activities were no longer necessary."[12] Barnett continued to seek out news of interest to Negro nurses but the demise of the association undermined his effort.[13]

But even Dunnigan, as a feminist, rarely stopped to ponder the overarching reasons why her boss was so unenlightened about matters of gender. For Barnett was now a full-fledged defender of the president and thus blamed "Copperhead [Robert] Taft," a leading Republican "for stirring up trouble" in Asia because "Truman did not want to get involved in China."[14] Barnett rarely stopped to think about the larger implications of his support of Truman's anticommunism and bellicosity in Korea and Asia in the context of growing McCarthyism and attacks on those like Robeson whose strength had buoyed those like Barnett himself.

Repeatedly, Dunnigan—on the other hand—railed against Barnett because of his various transgressions, which she thought were driven by sexism. "I enjoy being the only woman sports writer at the ringside at fights or in the press box at football and baseball games" and "I am doing a much better job than those who are continuously taking potshots at me."[15] Barnett demeaned her in private conversations with third parties, she charged angrily.[16] "There is no excuse for you flying off the handle," Barnett replied. He insisted, "don't go around getting an inflated ego," since "your chronic complaining gives me a pain."[17]

This dispute was an old-fashioned one: labor objecting to management high-handedness, generated in a nation where progressive unions were writhing in misfortune weakening workers nationally. This was then buttressed by the reality that women workers, especially those who were black, had few options and little leverage. When Barnett and fellow leaders turned their backs on Wallace and Robeson, it was inevitable that those employed by him would suffer. "I no longer have any telephone service due to failure to pay the bill," Dunnigan then groused, "since I have no allowance for transportation or other expenses and now no telephone service."

"I am not paid sufficiently," she charged: "I have no tools with which to work," since—as she told Barnett—"you supply no typewriter, no telephone service" and "no file cabinets" and "no paper, no carbon, no paper clips, no staples, no notebooks, no pencils, no ink or anything else." Adding insult to injury was her "starvation wage." When she considered joining ANP, she was told that the agency did "have the name of not paying their people but it also [had] the name of heckling its reporters" all the time and her maltreatment vindicated this allegation. With steely resolve, she said, "my entire life has been filled with rough breaks, that is why I am as hard as nails and as bitter as gall," which is why she was able to say "people look upon you as 'something,' 'that woman is a White House Reporter,'" but then she went home and had to eat "pig-ears and turnips." She was forced to explore other options, even "if it is nothing but a maid or messenger in the government, they make around $2000 a year, which is more than I make as a so-called 'White House' or 'Capitol' reporter," she said in a huff.

"I can't live any cheaper," Dunnigan added carpingly. "I am now housed in a one room basement and that costs $50 a month plus lights and gas and telephone." Besides, "I have to look half way presentable," meaning spending on a wardrobe. "I work seven days a week around the clock for ANP" and, she exclaimed reprovingly, "I wonder how it feels to an employer who keeps his wages so far below the prevailing wage rates of other people in the same business and still expect the same efficiency in the work of the employees."[18]

Eventually, Dunnigan was to abandon ANP because integration also created opportunities for her, and when this valuable employee abandoned ship, it was one more signal that the agency was highly perishable. In 1948 Barnett evidently had fired her,[19] but they reconciled before she departed for good a few years later.

*   *   *

Meanwhile, the ANP in some ways was vitiating the anticommunist consensus it had helped to create by continuing to uncover stories that did not necessarily place Washington in the most favorable light. Part of this was unavoidable in that the ANP continued to speak to an audience—U.S. Negroes—with numerous unresolved grievances who, thus, were eager to hear news that placed on the defensive a government that countenanced the causes of those grievances. Moreover, a major news story that was hard to ignore was the U.S. attempt to point the finger of accusation at human-rights violations in Moscow, which automatically opened the door for flyspecking its own record.[20]

What was remarkable about Barnett was that he was as well informed as any executive who had a small army of correspondents filing reports globally about all manner of news, and he too was a clever politico. This rare quality in the postwar era seemed to be overwhelmed, however, by a more common instinct, the desire to take economic advantage as doors that had been shut to Negroes were opened. The attractions of such opportunities overwhelmed any desire to help plot a political strategy to take advantage of what he knew, which—to be fair—would have been difficult in any case because his partner in such a venture, the NAACP, was not up to the task either.[21]

Barnett's own ANP reported that at a United Nations debate in Geneva, Moscow rapped the U.S. ban on interracial marriage as being "reminiscent of Hitlerite Germany,"[22] and in protest against Jim Crow, Communists in Poland demanded that the UN headquarters be moved from Manhattan.[23] In western Germany, said the ANP, "Negroes [and] Russians" had become the "new victims of German hate theories."[24] Barnett knew that in Stockholm "a Negro in the eyes of the Swede is quite different from the Negro as seen through the eyes of an American, according to Kosto Kilroy colored concert pianist now" residing there; whatever negative attitudes that were held by Swedes were said to be driven and "guided by American movies."[25] The ANP reported in 1949 that heavyweight boxer Jersey Joe Walcott, a Negro, was the "most popular man in Sweden today" and that "Swedish children are crazy about Joe."[26]

More than most, Barnett knew that the postwar scrambling of the global deck created new vistas for African Americans to explore and exploit. A number of African Americans volunteered to fight for the creation of Israel,[27] just as George Harris, formerly of the New York Police Department, was one of two Negroes assigned to provide security for the soon to be assassinated Swedish diplomat, Count Folke Bernadotte, the UN mediator in Palestine. Harris, said the ANP, had "working knowledge of some eight languages, including Russian and Chinese."[28]

As the second half of the twentieth century unwound, Barnett was in a position with which he had grown comfortable: at the center of a web of reporters in far-flung outposts, disseminating news and taking advantage of investment opportunities. He was moving into more commodious offices in a building he had purchased, this after the ANP had been residing at 3507 South Parkway in Chicago in an edifice owned by the Supreme Liberty Life Insurance Company.[29]

But Barnett was constrained in his ability to take advantage of the shuffling of the global deck. This period also featured an escalation of anticommunism, an outgrowth of war in Korea, and that conflict too placed a good deal of the Negro leadership on the defensive in that so many of them—like a good deal of the nation—had not been enthusiastic anticommunists in the previous decade.[30]

Once again,[31] the conservative columnist Westbrook Pegler, who had pilloried the Negro leadership during World War II, was doing the same, except the ostensible grounds had changed.[32] What was unmentioned generally was what the ANP correspondent in Los Angeles noticed. Harry Levette "had just [intervened] on behalf of wealthy retired dentist Dr. C. W. Hill, who was preparing to start importing from Korea to the United States in 1950 just before hostilities broke out."[33] As activists like Robeson were forced to retrench, investors like Hill advanced, and Barnett felt compelled to follow the latter.

This anticommunism hampered the ability of Barnett and Channing Tobias to maneuver abroad because Africa particularly was not as enthusiastic about this ideology as the United States. Barnett told the NAACP leader that what was taking place in East Africa was "especially dangerous" where a political formation was developing "under the domination of South Africa." Yet what really concerned him was the influence of the former Communist George Padmore, who was "very left wing" and, nonetheless, "has his articles especially in Azikiwe's papers and those controlled by Nkrumah's party and Wallace Johnson['s] up in Sierra Leone."[34]

Incendiary charges of being sympathetic to Reds leveled against Tobias did not bar his receiving an appointment to his nation's United Nations delegation. Helpfully, Barnett provided tips on how to navigate Paris, including how to reach Leopold Senghor, founding father of independent Senegal, whose neocolonial bent mirrored the thrust of Barnett and Tobias. "[H]is secretary," said the ANP chief, was "a good friend, speaks good English."[35] If Tobias cared to peruse ANP reports, he would have noticed that ANP continued its historic mission of publicizing "beauty culture" and hair straighteners, but now with an emphasis on Paris and the French-speaking world.[36] If Tobias paid attention to ANP reports, he would have noticed also that—in consideration of the interests of readers—it continued to cover contentious political matters, but increasingly frothy matters were to be found too. Thus, B. T. Bradshaw, president of the Virginia Mutual Benefit Life Insurance, thought it was "most kind" of Barnett to convert his routine trip to Paris into a news item,[37] a favor that Barnett probably thought could pay dividends down the road.

Thus, upon his arrival to serve as a delegate to the General Assembly in Paris, where he sought to block the Robeson initiative to petition the assembly on behalf of justice for African Americans,[38] Tobias proved helpful in trying to ensure that "Etta be given an opportunity to sing under U.S.A. auspices here in Paris."[39]

His support for Tobias in his Paris post paid off further when the French president, Pierre Mendès France, as Indochina was slipping from his colonial grasp, announced—said Barnett—a "bold and important new program for the African colonies." An unnamed "African deputy" in Paris—a "friend of mine," Barnett admitted freely—"confide[d] to me that Mendès-France would like nothing better than to sit down with a group of American Negro newspaper men and explain his whole program."[40]

Despite this fondness for Paris, Barnett railed against the French in Africa: They were "ruthless exploiters," he told the U.S. State Department, and "if communism progressed it would be in French areas I would think." It was unclear what the implication was of his statement that "much nationalist talk merely sounds like

Red lingo."[41] Was this an endorsement of the central anticommunist allegation or a warning against phrasing that supposedly echoed Communist statements? With Barnett during this era one could not be too sure. One could also surmise that his critique of Paris was an endorsement of Washington's immediate goal of replacing European colonialism with U.S. neocolonialism. As to London, he was clearer, denying he was a "defender of British Colonial Officialdom" but finding them to be "infinitely superior to what I say of the French" whose "old type colonial rule" was "on the run in Africa today."[42]

It was not so long ago that Barnett was thought to be sympathetic to the radicalism still expressed by Robeson. Now he advised that DuBois and "Paul [should] watch their steps and their company."[43]

Similarly, George McCray once had expressed sympathy for left-wing unions with which Robeson was associated but was now sharing intelligence with Barnett on their decline. Barnett found the United Electrical, Radio and Machine Workers "now totally on the 'Party Line,'" which he did not tie to his wider point that the union "got so many Negroes in it."[44]

Yet Barnett and the ANP could not be wholly enthusiastic about this rightward turn. This became clear when the ANP reported at length on the difficulties of Aaron Bindman, described as a "Jewish labor leader" of a left-led union who boldly "invited Negroes to his home for a social evening"—and then faced foreclosure on his residence as a result. "Attacks on Jews and persons believed to be Jewish Communists" followed, while a common slur for Negroes was uttered promiscuously.[45]

Scrambling to keep up with the fast-moving times, labor, religious, and other leaders in Chicago tried vainly to draw a parallel between the attack on anti–Jim Crow measures and "Communist aggression against South Korea."[46] "Colour bars and colonialism are the two greatest evils on earth,"[47] said an ANP correspondent in 1951; the problem for Barnett was that his agency now had to acknowledge a third C—Communism.

Similarly, Barnett sent red-baiting letters to Liberia, denouncing "Commies" and their alleged allies in Robeson's Council on African Affairs (CAA).[48] "Liberia has been fortunate in escaping inroads of Communism," was his message to the president in Monrovia.[49] But Barnett had a problem that others in his class did not: He was seeking to appeal to an African American community not as moved by anticommunism as others and he was seeking to invest in Africa where a similar progressive sentiment prevailed. Thus, after Nigeria's Azikiwe protested to Truman about the prosecution of DuBois, Barnett felt compelled to admit that he too objected.[50]

Barnett proceeded fitfully since the ANP recognized that the Communist "Party boasts some of the best Negro minds in the country," including "Eugene Holmes, professor of philosophy and regarded as successor to the brilliant Alain Leroy Locke," and Robeson's Council on African Affairs coworker, W. Alpaheus Hunton, recently arrested and "another of the highly educated Negroes identified with the Communists."[51] Actually, said the ANP in 1951, "Negroes in literally every field of activity" were "cited as Communists or Communist sympathizers" by the House Un-American Activities Committee.[52] The list included one of Barnett's business partners in Chicago, the attorney Earl Dickerson, who also was quite friendly with Robeson and had chosen not to break his ties to the National Lawyers Guild after it had been denounced as a "Communist front." Barnett was upset when Dickerson was "eliminated from the board of nominations" of the NAACP in 1952, though he was a "stalwart and active worker." Again, Barnett did not seem to realize that the prevailing political climate, to which he did not object strenuously, was largely responsible for the problem.[53]

Barnett pursued this course though he realized "when issues affecting black people" arose transnationally, "there is [no one] to speak out except the Reds," and, yes, "beyond question" the "activities of my wife and myself," said the ANP leader, "can be credited" too. From the end of the war to the early years after the intervention in Korea, there had been "more interest in Africa than ever occurred before"; yet "Negroes in America are almost totally ignorant of the schemes of their country" there and "their interest in Africa and Africans has been so negligible that they have paid little attention to the schemes."[54] Barnett did not seem to realize that the onslaught against CAA during this period had a lot to do with this weakness he detected.

Nor did Barnett seem to realize that the more CAA was debilitated, the more he found fault with Black America's awareness of Africa. "American Negroes," he said in 1952, "unfortunately have never let their racial consciousness get beyond the shores of the United States." He lamented how "insular and provincial" they supposedly were. "Black Nations on the other hand have rarely raised their voices in behalf of other darker nations" either, he maintained—though a perusal of his own agency's dispatches could provide evidence to the contrary. "Since American Negroes are unable to make their voices felt in the United Nations then we must wait for our African brothers to take up our joint responsibility" was his sighing conclusion, which neatly elided Robeson's project.[55]

Barnett was unable to draw reasonable inferences. It was with "misgiving" that he told Tobias about his unhappiness with "the position of the U.S. delegation on the question of the Trusteeship Council's authority to discuss political matters affecting French-Morocco." Barnett was "dismayed" by the U.S. "refusal to vote affirmative" on an anticolonial matter involving South Africa's questionable role in neighboring Namibia. "We had hoped," he said with naïveté, "that the United States and our mounting influence in international affairs would have gradually gained acceptance," but in a way he could not fathom, "the contrary has happened." Unveiling his new agenda, he asked, "does it not seem that the most effective way to combat Soviet Communism influence in dependent areas is to assure restless, aspiring colonial peoples"? He was surprised to find that

Washington's prime goal seemed to be "to mollify our allies in Western Europe." He was buffaloed because "the President has re-emphasized the issue of Civil Rights here at home" and could not understand why that was not complemented by anticolonialism abroad. "How grand it would be if we could match it with a program of political rights for dependent peoples? What could we lose?" He did not seem to understand that the new short-term strategy involved anti–Jim Crow concessions to U.S. Negroes with no necessary anticolonial complement abroad, particularly when allies were needed in a Korea that the White House could not afford to "lose." Signifying the gravity of this communication, in a rare instance, Barnett first made a handwritten draft before it was typed.[56]

Imperceptibly, Barnett and the ANP had moved from attempting to pressure the U.S. ruling elite alongside radicals like Robeson and mobilized anticolonial forces, notably in Africa and India, to try to influence and wangle favors from these same elites directly. There was a noticeable shift from the attempt to influence policy to an attempt to influence the appointment of personnel, notably appointing more Negro cronies. Barnett and the ANP's new access to power was hardly an improvement over the recent past. Thus, after the war in Korea erupted, Barnett congratulated Truman on "the manner in which the State Department has begun the integration of Negro citizens into various embassies and legations." Secretary of State Dean Acheson, present at the creation of the Cold War, was a "great man," said an admiring Barnett.[57]

He praised Acheson for "placing Negroes in various embassies in Europe and in consulates in Africa"[58] and advised another State Department official that hiring more Negroes "will pay dividends" because of the "rapport" he alleged was held by this minority with those residing in "areas populated by darker peoples."[59] The nimble Barnett was angling for an interview, and so he continued to praise the "considerable warmth of feeling and appreciation" Acheson supposedly generated among "non-white citizens." Acheson, he said, "did not forget the little nations such as Liberia" and Ethiopia.[60]

Barnett did not congratulate Acheson for inviting two U.S. Negroes to be present when the North Atlantic Treaty Organization (NATO) pact was signed,[61] though doing so would have been consistent with his approach. Admittedly, by 1951 Alice Dunnigan was reporting that more African Americans were being employed by the State Department.[62] But this deployment of highly qualified Negro personnel could not compensate for the anticommunist policy they were sworn to uphold, which deprived millions of Africans of self-determination. Change in personnel was the tradeoff for the acceleration of an anticommunist policy.

∗ ∗ ∗

Tactfully, Barnett chose not to mention what the ANP blared: Negro soldiers slain in Korea continued to be buried in segregated cemeteries.[63] It remained true, even as the war plodded on bloodily, that Negro soldiers, according to the ANP, could not be buried in the same U.S. cemeteries as the "white dead."[64] Nor did he echo what the former radical, now UN diplomat, Ralph Bunche mentioned when he spoke at the twenty-fifth anniversary of A. Philip Randolph's union, weeks after hostilities had launched. "Negro soldiers are fighting valiantly so that Koreans may enjoy that freedom and equality which these same Negro GIs have never experienced in full at home."[65]

Barnett had to be told by an editor from one of his competitors—John H. Johnson of the *Ebony–Jet* combine—that "several local Red Cross chapters are segregating Negro and white blood despite a September 1950 nonsegregation directive from national headquarters";[66] this was occurring as Negro soldiers were still making a blood sacrifice.

Perhaps as a result of sharing such inflammatory intelligence, Barnett was forced to vouch for the nonradicalism of Johnson, whom he classified correctly as "a pure capitalist."[67] This wholly unnecessary validation of Johnson came because the Red Cross had considered working with him but was troubled that an official California body said of his *Negro Digest* that it was "Communist initiated and controlled or so strongly influenced as to be in the Stalin solar system."[68]

What was true of Johnson was also true of Barnett, providing a further reason for the latter to reconsider his efforts, for both relied on left-leaning Negro writers and both had evinced previously anticolonialism that could then be misinterpreted as procommunist bias. For during this time Barnett also was told by Charlotte Hawkins Brown that she was being pursued by the same anticommunist bloodhounds, which was "not due to any communistic tendencies that I have," she said balefully, but her "peace" activism. The perspicacious activist grasped the dynamic at play when she concluded, "my greatest hope is that in connection with the fear on the part of the American White Population that Negroes will go the way of Communism is that the American people will lift the bans of discrimination."[69]

For as late as December 1950,[70] Negro entertainers were forced to perform before Jim Crow audiences in Miami Beach and in inferior nonadjacent hotels. Finally, with the arrival and forceful prodding of Josephine Baker from France— an external force despite her birth in the United States—the bar was broken.[71] Yet predictably when the "Counsellor of the Colonial Office in London" headed to Chicago in 1950, it was Barnett who arranged for him to "speak before a group of colored people."[72] Another Londoner was aware that news on the proliferating rebellion in Kenya, just being published in local journals, had appeared in the ANP "5 months previously."[73]

Barnett did collaborate with official London. The British Information Service supplied the ANP with photographs about the counterinsurgency in the colony that was Malaya with propagandistic suggestions for captions.[74] Barnett had the idea of obtaining photos from the British Information Service (BIS) to distribute

Barnett departs Haiti in an undated photograph. Along with Liberia, this island nation was a centerpiece of Barnett's "commercial Pan-Africanism." Courtesy of the Chicago History Museum.

to ANP sources in Africa itself but, in the interests of colonialism, the BIS nixed this proposed Pan-African initiative.[75]

Barnett's collaboration with colonial Britain did not preclude his continued tie with one of the chief victims of colonialism, Haiti, as he acknowledged that "it would help immensely in cementing relations between Negroes in the [U.S.] and Haitians if more [Negroes] were in the [U.S.] legation there," up to and including "The Ambassadorship."[76] The secretary of state thanked him profusely for the fulsome praise he had lavished on Foggy Bottom for its efforts in this realm.[77] Barnett informed Congressman William Dawson that Washington "granted $40,000,000 to Haiti on condition that an American be planted right alongside every Haitian Minister who has anything to do with spending it." He urged his fellow Chicagoan to propose a Negro envoy for Haiti.[78]

And, yes, this ability to both cover and influence the shaping of the news enhanced Barnett's role as powerbroker, able to redeem favors on all sides. J. Max Bond had sought a favor from Barnett in securing the highest diplomatic post in Haiti but by 1954 was merely president of the University of Liberia, from which he thanked the publisher profusely, providing another chip to be cashed in at the right moment.[79]

The sports reporter A. S. "Doc" Young also was "very much interested" in ANP reporting on Haiti. For Young "and two of my friends would like to receive more information, especially on the possibilities in the fields of journalism, radio and business." Was there "a need for live-wire operators in the field of sports?" he asked hopefully.[80] The "opportunities" in Haiti, Barnett replied, were "undeniable;" the island was "so close and the cost of transportation" was "so low." Yet, he admitted, "journalism does not offer much," though "radio might offer possibilities." He put Young in touch with another African American who had done quite well there in recent years.[81] Barnett took the hint in that it did not take long after this for the ANP to have a correspondent on the island.[82]

Yet it was understandable why Young would think of asking Barnett about work abroad, for, as the ANP chief said then, "we [have] definite correspondents in Jamaica, Trinidad, Virgin Islands and the Gold Coast. Our Nigerian and Liberian contacts are good."[83] This Barnett/ANP web was well known, which is why the Panamanian journalist Ernest Jamieson queried Barnett about "emigration" to Liberia after hearing nothing from Monrovia when he inquired for himself.[84]

Barnett had leverage in Haiti because he had lobbied the head of a group of black medics in the United States, urging that they should "make one of their conventions a floating meeting, preferably in the Caribbean or South America, but with even Liberia a possibility," though Haiti was his preference because it was "easy to reach, being only four and a half hours from Miami, including 25 minutes tops in Cuba and Jamaica."[85] Barnett also was in touch with black dentists, whose association was "quite a large body . . . from all sections" of the United States. "I have proposed," he told Haiti's head of tourism, "that they think in terms of inviting their members to extend one of their annual meetings into a trip" to the island.[86]

Barnett continued to see Haiti and Liberia as the keystones of his worldview. Congressman Dawson of Chicago, one of the few Negroes in the U.S. Congress, received the inside story on Haiti from Barnett. As for Monrovia, he was heartened by the "increasing interest of American and American Negroes especially in Liberia [which] suggests that we ought to take advantage of every opportunity governmentally to help the little black republic." He offered to share further insight over a meal.[87]

Barnett was up to date with Haiti because he had just visited there. He was there for the inauguration of the president, along with "diplomats from 32 countries," as he observed in late 1950.[88] There he conferred with "President [Leon] Estime and his charming wife"; Estimé was considered to be the first black—or darker skinned–leader since the end of the occupation in 1934—who was deposed, coincidentally, after his talks with Barnett and Moten. "Mrs. Estime," said Roberta McGuire of Detroit, "particularly delighted us with extensive descriptions of how much your visit and that of your wife's had meant to their country and people. She positively fell in love with you both" and was helpful in establishing ties with the

African-American sorority Delta Sigma Theta.[89] For his part, Barnett promised one Miamian that "all doors can swing open for you" if he headed to the island: the ANP leader had the "thrill of seeing a black man inaugurated president of a black country," which was "too much to overlook."[90]

As doors were opened further for those like Barnett, he felt more comfortable in reporting to the State Department on his far-flung travels: This was the tradeoff. Thus, he told Harold Sims in Foggy Bottom of his "opportunity to talk with President Estime himself" and "he was gracious enough to invite me to go on a cruise on his yacht," which consisted of a "day long cruise down the Gulf of Gonaive [sic]." They "spoke English" as they sailed along and "he said he would be particularly happy to see the United States select well-trained young Negroes as members of the U.S. Embassy staff."[91]

The influential Barnett advised Frederick Douglass Patterson of Tuskegee and his spouse to "call on" a former Haitian president while in Paris because "Etta and I have the highest regard for them," and while in the vicinity, to call on "Whily Tell, who is the general manager of the Folies Bergère," also "a friend of mine," or "Deputy Apithe, another friend. Also Mr. Achilles who is secretary" to Leopold Senghor, "the ablest of the African members of the Assembly" and not to miss the "Liberation legation" where "Senator Cooper who is Minister to France," was also a friend.[92] (Helpfully, Barnett sought to get a book contract for Tell in the United States.)[93] As ever, the ANP tended to blame visiting Euro Americans for problems faced by African Americans in Paris,[94] a tendency that flagged only slightly as the Cold War was launched.

Haiti was just a jumping-off point for a continuing hemispheric project of the ANP. A Negro weekly newspaper in the Canal Zone, which—said the editor—had "the full support of our President Domingo Diaz of Panama," requested Barnett's aid.[95] Even the NAACP assailed Panama's law barring immigration by U.S. Negroes and "stringent requirements designed to discourage them even as tourists."[96] Barnett well knew that the anticommunist wave had washed up on the shores of Panama but did not connect this trend to ensuing racist difficulty.[97]

"Negroes seeking visas at your consulate in Chicago," Barnett brusquely informed Guatemala's foreign minister, "are informed that your visas are not issued to American Negroes." Yet "within the next hour they inform white Americans that special visitor cards will be issued to them." Then "Negroes applying for these cards are told they must contact you or the Foreign Office in Guatemala."[98] Barnett demanded an explanation. A colleague of his met with officialdom and received a partial explanation.[99]

Brazil continued to present problems. The ANP singled out "5000 embittered Southerners" who migrated to South America after the U.S. Civil War as still suggestive of this nation's immigration policy.[100]

Barnett pointed in 1950 to "instances of refusal to admit Negro Americans who desired to emigrate to Brazil," though "the offer of employment there and adequate financial resources have come to our attention."[101] That same year, the celebrated Katherine Dunham was refused service in a São Paulo hotel with even the nation's parliamentarians stirred as a result.[102] As so often happened with Barnett, there was a confluence between "doing good" and "doing well" in that the ANP's interest in Brazil not only facilitated the ability to recruit hemispheric writers at bargain-basement rates, but potential scribes often sought the agency too as a result of the agency's lobbying.[103]

Bishop R. R. Wright Jr. headed an AME church in Brazil's neighbor, the nation soon to be known as Guyana, then on the verge of independence, and he regaled Barnett with how "interesting it is to be in a country where there is no racial discrimination, at least not by law," reminding the Chicagoan that "as you know, there are many more colored people in South America than we have in the United States."[104]

Cheddi Jagan, a founding father of independent Guyana, was quite conversant with Chicago, where he attended a university, met his spouse, and also spent, he recalled fondly, two "memorable years" at Howard University in Washington, though he had distressing experience with the "colour bar."[105] The problem here is that Jagan was a suspected Communist and therefore radioactive as far as many in the United States were concerned. Fenner Brockway, a British parliamentarian—and considered to be part of the anticolonial left—told Barnett that his "first attention" was "devoted to British Guiana,"[106] but in light of the political optics, it was not evident whether the ANP could accept this eminent man's assistance, even if it could have been the site for another pressure point on Brazil.

"Guatemala and Brazil are apparently finding it difficult to let Negroes in," said Barnett during this conflicted era. "The latter does not even want visitors. Think up a group of questions," he instructed Dunnigan, "and ask the ambassadors point blank what was their attitude on Negroes"; provide "proof that their Chicago consuls have refused Negroes and you wish to know why."[107]

Hence, Barnett solicited news and notes from Rio de Janeiro and Buenos Aires particularly in a colloquy with a traveling nurse, and thus, he desired a "report" on "any colored nurses, the tendency to accept nurses of color of foreign countries without question, any resolutions which bear upon equality."[108] The ANP continued to bring attention on racism in South America, including Bolivia.[109]

Finally, as the United States continued to feel pressure to rectify its putrid human rights record, and placed pressure on allies to move in a similar direction, Brazil announced that it would "be more open to more Negro Immigrants."[110]

*　*　*

In short, as the political climate chilled, Barnett and the ANP moved away from critiquing U.S. foreign policy to a demand to be included in its high jinks. "Our Caribbean correspondents report," said Barnett in January 1950, that while "there are troops in the maneuvers there from all over the states," there were "no Negro troops," an absence that demanded an "explanatory note."[111]

Barnett was told that he was "not entirely correct" in his racial description of this "joint Army, Navy and Air Force maneuver" near the colony that was Puerto Rico and Vieques, though few details were rendered, leaving questions hanging.[112] Barnett managed to visit Heidelberg in early 1952 and discovered "segregated units in both Germany and France"; in other words, the "policy of integration" was "not being followed," contributing to a "lack of unity," in supposed contrast to Korea, where "the troops are integrated."[113] Months before he was to be elected, Barnett posed similar inquiries to the supreme commander of the North Atlantic Treaty Organization, Dwight David Eisenhower.[114]

This allegation about Korea was posed though the ANP well knew about the abject difficulty in integrating Negro troops in Korea,[115] a point validated by NAACP attorney Thurgood Marshall when he found that on this battlefield, "32 Negroes and only 2 whites had been convicted by courts martial," with the latter often getting a slap on the wrist while one Negro, Leon Gilbert, got the death penalty.[116] "None of the tan Yanks on the frontlines sang sad songs" when General Douglas MacArthur was sacked, since it was "common knowledge of the existence of segregation in the army in spite" of various mandates from Washington.[117] Segregation was occurring as it seemed that the United States was becoming increasingly dependent on Negro ground forces, comprising about 25 percent of such soldiers, which—said the ANP—"virtually put Negroes in control of the ground force units."[118]

Then there was Africa. Barnett instructed the editor of the *Norfolk Journal & Guide* that he should lobby Liberia for a consul there because of the "shipping especially of mahogany logs" from West Africa there.[119] Barnett and Tobias remained on the board of the Liberia Company, where they were solicited to pay more attention to cocoa and coffee markets. Barnett was also friendly with President William V. S. Tubman in Monrovia and asked whether he could place his portrait on the wall, alongside that of Booker T. Washington's, in his new office in Chicago.[120]

Soon Barnett was heading east to Africa again, this time in early 1952 to Lagos: "twenty-five African nations are to hold a conference in an attempt to chart their future," he told Truman Gibson and "Mrs. Barnett and I will be en route there as you dine."[121] Barnett had to spread his bets because in 1949 the major force behind the Liberia Company, former secretary of state Edward Stettinius, passed away prematurely at the age of forty-nine.[122] His widow told Barnett tearfully that the deceased "felt great admiration for you personally."[123] Within a year, the Liberia Company had shriveled, having "scaled its operations down to principally its agricultural program" and "eliminated all their staff," Barnett concluded mournfully, leaving precious minerals buried in the ground.[124]

Increasingly, as the postwar bloom of radicalism wilted in the face of the Cold War's deep freeze, Barnett—already an expert networker—exercised this skill further. Barnett arranged for the Alabama millionaire A. G. Gaston, to meet President Tubman during his visit to Monrovia. He and his spouse, said Gaston, were "very interesting and cordial" and it was likely that Barnett's various interests in that country benefited as a result.[125]

Gaston too was impressed, which augured well for his varied interests, as he found the neocolonial epigone that was Tubman to be "one of the greatest leaders of our time."[126] At a celebration of his alma mater, Barnett arranged for yet another Liberian leader, C. D. B. King, who also had served as president, to provide the keynote.[127] By 1951, confident in his knowledge of Africa, Barnett was doling out counsel on the peculiarities of certain Nigerian ethnicities, notably the Ibos.[128]

One of Barnett's many missionary friends was pleased with the "very fine reception given us" in Lagos; he also had a "fine conference with the Governor" there, "who also pledged his cooperation" as a plan was hatched to launch "plans for trading with the natives"; almost as an afterthought, Barnett was told that Lagos was "quite tense and ready to fight for freedom," and this had taken a backseat to "plans for trading."[129] Dissents to this newly forged status quo were more remarkable for their rarity.[130] The African Methodist Episcopal Zion church sought to split the difference by honoring both President Truman and India's envoy in the United States.[131]

By 1954, the suspected Communist Kwame Nkrumah held high office in Accra and, thanks to Barnett, Gaston conferred with him in Accra, along with the leader of the Ashanti.[132] After his lengthy journey to the continent, Barnett told Gaston that "Africa will now be in your blood,"[133] though, more accurately, he could have said that now it can become an essential part of your investment portfolio.

Jim Crow meant that African Americans had difficulty in gaining insurance policies, which created an opening for the creation of a black insurance industry, in which Gaston played a prominent role. Barnett had a stake in the Supreme Liberty Life Insurance Company based in Chicago, where he served alongside friends and partners Earl Dickerson and Truman Gibson, among others.[134]

Among the leaders in this industry was C. C. Spaulding of North Carolina Mutual, who received copies of West African newspapers from Barnett, possibly as a prelude to business expansion, which did not occur as Jim Crow crumbled. Yet because of Barnett's own outreach on the continent, by 1950 this Durham resident was receiving "fifty letters from Africa" in a matter of weeks "making requests for donations, scholarships and other types of funds. One letter was addressed to me," he continued, "C.C. Spaulding, United States of America, Multi-Millionaire. Without any other address whatsoever" because of the—supposedly—"erroneous idea the people of Africa seem to have about my wealth."[135] "I am not even one-tenth of a millionaire," he contended, though it was true he headed an enterprise with assets in the tens of millions of dollars.[136] Actually, Spaulding was partially correct in that the new era of "integration" that was opening would erode his captive market and call into question the wealth he had created on the basis of this disappearing reality.

* * *

Barnett remained close to African leadership, particularly Gabriel Dennis, a former secretary of the treasury in Liberia. The ANP leader was kind enough to send photographs of Dennis pictured with "Generalissimo Franco," the Spanish fascist leader, "to a couple of the more prominent papers" in Black America.[137] Bonding further with Dennis, Barnett arranged to send "a newsreel into some 400 theatres patronized by Negroes" depicting the Liberian's arrival at the United Nations.[138] But when he told Dennis to "give both the United States and Great Britain hell" there, he must have known that the balance of forces—a weakened CAA, advancing anticommunism, repressions of anticolonial forces in Africa, and related events—made this prospect quite unlikely.[139]

After the war in Korea erupted, Barnett got a message from UNESCO headquarters in Paris informing him that the Indian ambassador was interested in arranging a "tour of the country lecturing on the life and problems of the American Negro." William Rutherford, an old colleague of Barnett, to whom the invitation was extended, found this to be a "subject of great interest in India and the ambassador (M. Desai) assured me that color discrimination and colonialism are two subjects on which India will never compromise."[140] But times had changed: aligning with Delhi, now a key ally of Moscow in a rigidifying Cold War, was not as easy as it once might have been.

CHAPTER 8

Negroes as Anticommunist Propagandists?

By early 1953, the ANP announced proudly, there were "about 204 commercial Negro newspapers operating in the United States. Two of these are dailies, three biweeklies, and 195 weeklies. . . . Alabama leads the 33 states and the District of Columbia with 19 organs, with Ohio second with 16, Florida third with 13." Though "10 newspapers [were] started during 1952," more telling for the ANP was the fact that "some 10 papers folded during the past year."[1] Within a decade, the ANP was declining precipitously, and within fifteen years it was defunct. This decline was not solely due to the declining health of Claude Barnett. It also was due to the changing community served by the ANP: More options seemed to be opening for black writers over whom Barnett once had the whip hand, and more black radio stations were opening too, challenging from the other end.[2]

*   *   *

In 1955, George Murphy, the left-wing scion of the Afro-American chain, congratulated Alice Dunnigan after she was admitted—finally—to the National Women's Press Club, then hastened to observe that he had "come more and more to see that so-called Integration is a two-way street," in other words, that there was welcome desegregation and unwelcome liquidation of black institutions. Thus, if the ANP and Negro press generally were to survive, they had to "re-evaluate their standard of support to Negro reporters and correspondents," satisfying the likes of Dunnigan, for example, who was now in a position to abandon ship—which she did shortly, wounding the agency. These journalists would "have to be given more help, dignity and better rewards for their new tasks ahead."[3] Similarly, Andy Razaf, composer and frequent ANP contributor, was saddened to note that as African Americans attained more success, they tended to disregard the Negro press, "which often was a great factor in their success" but now was "no longer needed." Some even tended to "boast that they don't read" these journals.[4]

By 1956 P. L. Prattis told Barnett something he probably already knew: "Negro newspapers as such," he lamented, "are running out of gas."[5] "Things are tough all along the line," Barnett confirmed, "except for *Ebony* which keeps expanding."[6] Yet even this apparent good news for John H. Johnson was questionable.[7] Like black baseball, the ANP was part of the collateral damage that accompanied the new era of integration.[8]

It was not as if all this came as a surprise to the ANP, for as early as 1949 W. H. Aiken of the National Builders Association, speaking in Detroit, predicted "if integration comes,"[9] many Negro institutions would fail. He was prescient, though it may have been difficult to convince the ANP chief of this when his agency moved in early 1951 to a commodious new office on 3531 South Parkway in Chicago.[10] The new office was only ten doors down the street from their previous office where they had resided for more than fifteen years; but now they were able to enjoy more space, meaning, it was thought optimistically, an expansion of work. The agency offered writers an invitation to come to Chicago, where "there will be a desk and phone service available for your use," with the ANP finding lodging too.[11]

In any event, even Barnett was aware that a new era was opening for the Negro press and not all the news was positive.[12] It also was Barnett who noticed that, as the drive toward integration was gaining strength, the "decline of Negro drug stores" was likewise gaining speed in that "Washington used to have 25 or 30, Chicago almost as many," but such was no longer the case.[13]

By July 1953 the war in Korea, which had been preeminent in driving the nation in an anticommunist direction, contributing mightily to the marginalizing of those like Robeson, was lurching to an inconclusive end. The ANP praised the new desegregated military that they said had emerged from the fire of war. "Negroes had a full role in execution of the undeclared Korean war," blared the agency proudly,[14] though this was a questionable attainment.[15]

The ANP remained globally minded, though decidedly not as oriented to the left as it had been. Barnett exulted about the amount of "foreign material we now carry," boasting by late 1953 of "correspondents in [the] Gold Coast, Nigeria, London and Pakistan and New Delhi," who "keep us well supplied." The problem was, he said, that "our papers are not internationally minded," calling into question the agency's future viability. Understandably, Barnett took credit for what remained in the Negro press of interest in foreign affairs. It was "certain," he said, "that until we began stressing this type news after visiting Africa, there were not stories at all on Africa and other foreign areas."[16] Whatever the case, by 1955 Barnett was asserting that "we have had so much from Africa especially" sent to affiliates, "that some editors have told us we were surfeiting them."[17]

What Barnett seemed not to realize was that the key recipients of this kind of news, for example, Charlotta Bass of the *California Eagle*, were precisely those who were under siege because of suspected radical ties. In 1949 she was denied a passport as she sought to travel to China in the immediate aftermath of the revolution.[18] By 1950, the ANP itself reported that the paper needed "$20,000 to remain alive" and that Robeson had been recruited to help in raising this sum.[19] "If you know a good newspaperman interested in buying a share in the *California Eagle,*" Bass told Barnett, who is also "sincere, hard-working and one with liberal views politically," he should be sent to her door.[20] Barnett was blunt in reply, professing that "I do not know anyone brave enough to venture into the newspaper game in California. If he must be liberal also, that makes it doubly difficult because none of the liberals who are friends of mine seem to have any money"[21]—a tipoff about why Barnett was moving away from previous political commitments. By 1951, the fanatically anticommunist Los Angeles mayor, Sam Yorty, was praising the paper's new leadership,[22] which—unlike Bass—pledged to oppose communism and racism.[23] Soon the paper's competitor, the *Los Angeles Sentinel,* was querying Barnett to the effect that it merited "exclusive territorial rights" to ANP material,[24] further squeezing the *Eagle,* which was now on the fast track to extinction. The problem was that the *Sentinel* was not as interested in the global news that was the *Eagle's*—and the ANP's—mainstay.

Thus, the ANP also was squeezed, and it appeared that Negroes abroad were not as keen to supply ANP with columns and reports as they once had been, perhaps because eroding Jim Crow gave this mission less urgency;[25] as a result, Barnett consented to supply material to the left-wing *National Guardian,* a decision driven by his preexisting relationship with their staffer, Eugene Gordon.[26]

It is unclear how the ANP responded when a journal in Glasgow, which claimed to "sell quite considerably in the British colonies and in South Africa, India and Pakistan," told Barnett there could be a "good field for some of your features" in their pages.[27] It is clear, however, that Barnett did approach Mark Ethridge of the *Louisville Courier-Journal,* a mainstream journal, about "submitting" a "story on Nigeria." It "is current" he boasted, adding that "our facilities in Nigeria and indeed West Africa are excellent."[28] But why should the mainstream cooperate consistently with a competitor?

From the other shore, the American Red Cross, with whom Barnett had clashed famously over their segregated blood banks, offered Barnett the services of their staff stationed in Tokyo and Stuttgart, who "might be able to turn up material of special interest" to the ANP.[29] Barnett had served on their board, which had been chaired by Ellsworth Bunker, one of the nation's top diplomats and, thus, this overture could also be seen as further evidence of the dividends that the ANP leader's networking provided.[30] It is unclear whether the agency accepted this offer, but the point was that as the political landscape shifted, the ANP was faced with new realities.

As interest in Africa waned in the Negro press, as the promise to curtail Jim Crow materialized, Barnett's options narrowed accordingly. He had developed considerable business interests abroad that a globally minded ANP helped to reinforce. If Negro readers could not be served, however, U.S. interests could be. By 1956 he was in touch with Harold Hochschild of American Metals Climax

(AMAX), a major corporation that he termed "one of the finest influences in the general African situation," especially in sites of bitter conflicts that led to the states now known as Zambia and Zimbabwe. Barnett nonetheless concluded that "Negro public opinion in the United States ought to be serviceable," or bent in AMAX's direction, a questionable goal that he volunteered to help in implementing.[31] Soon the corporate boss was inviting "Dear Claude" and "Etta" to "spend the evening and night" at his plush estate in Princeton.[32] Throughout this era, Barnett continued to press major corporations on their often execrable colonialist and Jim Crow records, but the retreat of forces to his left provided him with less leverage.[33] In any case, it was not easy to press corporations for personal gain and lobby the same for group gains.

This was noticeably so when the overall political orientation was shifting in a different direction, inconsistent with the previous era that had propelled Robeson.[34] In 1956 the Suez crisis erupted with the joint attack by Israel, Britain, and France on Egypt. It was not so long ago there would have been broad denunciation of this attack across the political spectrum in Black America. But now one of the more detectable voices was that of the prominent cleric Gardner Taylor, who said that though this conflict could lead to a "Color War," the "first duty of the American Negro is to his own land," and certainly not to victimized Africans.[35]

* * *

Looking back, Barnett also sought to influence the shaping of the past in a way that would be compatible with an increasingly conservative present. Barnett was disturbed by the less than enthusiastic endorsement accorded his hero, Booker T. Washington, by the historian Rayford Logan.[36] Barnett brought his reverence for this leader to his homestead, Tuskegee Institute, in 1949 where he got an honorary degree and the fanatically anticommunist, Claire Booth Luce, spoke on the presumed virtues of capitalism. The two were joined by Vernon Johns of the soon-to-be-heralded Dexter Avenue Baptist Church in Montgomery, who also hailed Dr. Washington.[37]

Barnett was in the anomalous position of embracing simultaneously "Dr. Washington" while not shunning the reputed Communist Frank Marshall Davis, who had served ANP so well. By 1954 the burly writer had long since decamped to Honolulu, but the U.S. authorities remained concerned about his lingering influence in Chicago. "When Frank Marshall served with us," said Barnett with delicate reassurance, "rumors came regarding some of his political beliefs but early on we had a talk and an understanding" and "never to my knowledge did he use this vehicle in other than an honorable fashion."[38] Others wondered whether those routinely derided as Stalinist could ever operate with honor.

Earlier, Gordon Hancock had argued that the radical left was growing in part because too much effort was put in "holding the Negro down": the inference being that easing Jim Crow would lubricate the path for the ossification of anticommunism and, in a sense, that is what unfolded.[39] "Why is being a Communist so much more damnable," asked Hancock, "in Negroes than in others,"[40] referring to Robeson's suspected affiliations. The new era that had arrived was signaled when Robeson was refused a hotel room in Chicago, not because he was black, but because he was deemed to be a "bad citizen of this country."[41]

More to the point, the ANP's George McCray, now moving rapidly to the right, found that the "heart of the Negro people is stone hard against Communism. The average Negro really doesn't believe in sharing the little he gets with anybody," thus, "it is high time that persons like Paul Robeson thought more of the interests and needs of Negro people and less of the needs of Soviet Russia."[42] Zora Neale Hurston joined the fray when she defended publicly Senator Robert Taft, then viewed as the standard-bearer of the Republican Right.[43]

Walter White of the NAACP would have concurred with McCray. Back from a world tour, he cited instances in Cairo, Istanbul, and New Delhi where there was open discussion of the Negro's maltreatment and that "Nehru told him personally," said the ANP, "that it was a hard job to keep his people from sympathizing with the Russians." Youth in Cairo, said White, preferred higher education in the Soviet Union to that of the United States because "they fear ill treatment in America due to their skin [being] dark."[44] White's own organization, however, then in the throes of an anticommunist purge, was hardly in a position to maintain stout objection to this onrushing trend.[45]

The Egyptian youth that White encountered may have gotten wind of what befell the Nigerian Olusan Awani, described by the ANP as "grandson of the King of Warri in Nigeria" and a college student in Berkeley, who was refused service in a restaurant in Flagstaff and then arrested and fined for disturbing the peace.[46] Then there was the Reverend Joseph Wiwanuka, vicar apostolic of Masaka, Uganda, who had a bitter encounter with Jim Crow during a religious gathering in New Orleans.[47] Even a British parliamentarian demanded a UN probe of "American race prejudice."[48] An ANP writer proclaimed that "Soviet Russia has achieved her gains in Asia almost entirely by exploiting the race problem"; that is, "from the inception of the Cold War . . . the Russians have outsmarted their enemies by showing them up as haters of Negroes."[49]

Yet maunderings about Stalinism aside, the United States still found itself viewed skeptically abroad because of the malignant legalized Jim Crow that it harbored. As the system began to crumble, doors flew open for those like Barnett. To reiterate: The new era meant that the ANP and its allies focused more on personnel—opportunities for Negro diplomats and businessmen—than on opposing anticommunist policy.

Still, it would be one-sided and wrongheaded to portray this new era as wholly replete with a downside. After the high court ruled against Jim Crow, Barnett was happy to see that the Interstate Commerce Commission was "beginning to crumble," because it had sanctioned Jim Crow travel and had been "one of the most difficult agencies for Negroes throughout the years."[50] The gradual erosion of segregated travel was one of the major victories of the movement against Jim Crow. The problem was that the movement was often portrayed as being without complication and complexity, an elision that hardly explained the impending collapse of institutions like the ANP.

*   *   *

By 1954 Barnett was complaining that the U.S. tax authorities had "raised questions regarding" his "gross income" from various sources.[51] He should not have been overly surprised because just before this tax alert was rendered, he had told a paymaster that he had "expected to find the sizeable check you were going to send" but "it had not arrived."[52] Barnett had initiated and accepted a series of projects that proved to be quite remunerative. Via the U.S. embassy in Liberia, he and his spouse received $1,000 for their toil in a propaganda film titled "The Negro in Entertainment."[53]

One of these projects was his work on behalf of Liggett & Myers Tobacco Company, which was interested in expanding its markets, not least to black people at home and abroad. Starring in the commercials produced was Barnett, who was recruited after the chemist Percy Julian—according to a key tobacco executive—proved to be "jealous of the company he keeps" and demurred.[54]

The producer of the Liggett & Myers project, E. M. Glucksman, was involved in another series of films, which ANP touted. Actually, touting the alleged benefits of tobacco was less questionable than these other cinematic creations. Indeed, it may have appeared to Barnett that hailing smoking was a step forward from crowing about the presumed virtues of Jim Crow. That is, these films were designed to stress the alleged positive aspects of Negro life under Jim Crow; Glucksman declared enthusiastically that "one of the dramatic [vignettes] . . . will be a Sabrejet battle with a Russian built MIG over Korean soil."[55]

In one of the Liggett & Myers commercials, Barnett was portrayed casually taking a Chesterfield cigarette from the package, placing the package on a table, and then picking up a lighter and saying in his typically charming fashion, "When I am happy, I light up a Chesterfield."[56]

With his usual thoroughness, Barnett wanted to know whether his tobacco films were to be shown in "Haiti or Jamaica," which he knew turned on whether "Chesterfields are sold there."[57] Barnett, acting as advertising consultant, told Liggett & Myers that the "Caribbean area ought to be a fertile field for Chesterfield. Those better off [buy] American cigarettes I know. The poor can't afford them."[58] After a return from West Africa, Barnett reported promptly on whether "Chesterfields are sold there."[59] Barnett told Liggett & Myers that "American cigarettes are rare . . . because of the British tax and trade barriers"—yet another argument for eroding colonialism. "Tobacco is grown in Nigeria though not of Virginia quality. I believe Liggett & Myers might well think in terms of future

Barnett in the 1950s appeared in a series of lucrative and popular advertisements for cigarette companies that played both in the United States and abroad. Courtesy of the Chicago History Museum.

business there and even of producing cigarettes for wide distribution in West Africa," he advised.[60]

The comradely Barnett also recommended his good friend, William Pickens, for the lucrative job of appearing in movies; yes, he was "a man of years" but he was "quite active. . . . I know him well."[61] The star baseball outfielder Willie Mays appeared alongside Barnett in these ads touting "the cigarettes [tested] and approved by 30 years of scientific tobacco research,"[62] though it was unclear whether Barnett played a role in the outfielder's hiring. Barnett also roped into the venture David Jones, the president of Bennett College in North Carolina. "Chesterfield was so well pleased with their first foray into the Negro field," Barnett said, "that they are doing another picture."[63] The tobacco film was shown in almost "600 Negro theatres all over the United States from Harlem to Los Angeles,"[64] according to Barnett.

Advertising became a profitable sideline for Barnett, which was farsighted as signs emerged of a new dispensation wherein the captive Jim Crow newspaper market might be on the verge of shrinking. He forwarded to a Madison Avenue firm an advertisement for Camels, a best-selling U.S. cigarette, that appeared in a Liberian newspaper. He said, unnecessarily, that the ad "will prove interesting to you." "I have excellent contacts with the papers" in West Africa, he said, "and will, of course, be glad to place them at your disposal."[65] In this vein, Barnett offered to Glucksman a film "shot [by] an ANP reporter interviewing" Nkrumah, along with similar footage obtained in Nigeria.[66]

The ecumenical Barnett also cooperated with London's Colonial Film Unit and the allied International Bank Mission in the vast region of the African holdings of the British Empire that seemed to be destined for independence.[67] Then he asked Ethiopia's UN delegation whether he could arrange the filming of their delegates "talking to Mrs. Frances T. Bolton of the United States delegation and with delegates from Haiti and Liberia. Such a picture would be shown in some 500 theatres catering to Negro audiences," he declared.[68] Barnett gained more than monetary advantage from his star turn. After the mass rollout of the tobacco movie, he encountered three teenage boys skylarking in Kansas City and spontaneously they blurted, "that's Mr. Claude Barnett of Chesterfield." A similar occurrence took place when he attended a church service: "these films are sinking home more than we think," he informed Glucksman in what may have been a typically self-serving reflection.[69]

For a related U.S. propaganda film, Barnett solicited the munificent Ford Foundation for a contribution and was told that a contribution would be more likely if "its funds are to be used for purposes abroad only."[70] Thus, Barnett approached the well-endowed donor in seeking support of "a project to implement current efforts of the United States government to defeat Soviet propaganda about American minorities." He recalled Edith Sampson's Copenhagen visit: "everywhere she appeared," he said, speaking of this African American representative of U.S. foreign policy, "they concentrated their attack upon her" as a symbol of a minority perceived abroad to be downtrodden. "With adequate funds," he reminded, ANP "could increase its service to include foreign newspapers."[71] In short, instead of bringing global news to African Americans, the ANP would begin to bring rosy views of African Americans to the world.

Barnett thought that he was simply adjusting nimbly to a new reality: The swing to the right in the United States was mandated by the 1952 election, he believed. He thought that the Republican victory meant a "sharp reduction in gestures toward European and under-privileged countries." "My suspicion," he said, "is that we are going to see closer cooperation with the imperialistic countries than has been carried on in the past," for example, working "hand in glove with the British in East Africa and the efforts at federation which the Africans oppose and in the plan to unify East Africa with lines of communication leading to South Africa. The plan has our support," presumably speaking of the United States and not the ANP, "because it apparently is a defense measure against Russia with Africa, its raw resources and strategic position as a pawn in the next war. They fail to realize that without attempting to do something to alleviate the distress of the people they are playing Russia's game in more concrete fashion than could otherwise be done."[72]

Barnett also was traversing a wave of anticolonial sentiment in Africa, which both reflected and propelled the compelled retreat of the United States from juridical Jim Crow. In the short term, this trend paradoxically seemed to open markets in Africa for him, as it tended to asphyxiate the ANP. Barnett had a hand in a report that pointed to "the American Negro Market" as being a veritable nation within a nation, with rising income and purchasing power. "This 10 billion dollar market," it was noted rhapsodically, was bound to increase. "When Jackie Robinson came to the Dodgers," African Americans "are reported to have swelled the revenue of the National League by more than a quarter million dollars." Not noted were the fact that inferior white ballplayers were then deprived of unmerited jobs, which was bound to augment their fury at Negroes, or that the inevitable result would be the demise of the Negro baseball league: the Jim Crow paradox largely escaped not only his purview—but to be fair—that of others too.[73]

Matters were now in flux, a point that Barnett himself tacitly acknowledged when he told a potential recruit that "we have access to much which Reuters gives. We do not subscribe" to this news service but had access to a "friendly office which does" and "clips out much material giving us a time advantage."[74] Eventually, even Reuters would be competing with ANP for journalists, and Barnett's ethically questionable use of their reporting would be doubly compromised. "Actually we are the pioneers in offering foreign news," he announced not falsely in 1954. "Papers are using several hundred percent more than when we initiated the idea,"[75] also not an unfair assessment. But this rosy dawn was already eclipsing even as he was engaged in self-praise.

Others besides Barnett joined this lucrative gravy train of producing propaganda. To that end, Tobias and Randolph were sending messages via the U.S.-backed radio station Voice of America (VOA) to those—as the ANP put it—"behind the Iron Curtain."[76] Congressman Adam Clayton Powell Jr. of Harlem aped these leaders when he delivered a speech via VOA to Eastern Europe, though his was transmitted via WLIB radio in New York, a station that was designed to appeal to African Americans.[77] Mary McLeod Bethune joined the bandwagon when she traveled to Switzerland for a summit of the fanatically anticommunist Moral Rearmament movement. Barnett was informed that he should ascertain what this group "might do in our country."[78] Tobias's anticommunist service did not spare his Phelps-Stokes Fund from being red-baited by conservative columnist Westbrook Pegler, which brought instant rebuke from Barnett and Walter White.[79]

What was providing impetus to Barnett's self-aggrandizing proposals were the severe difficulties the United States was encountering abroad because of Jim Crow. When Edith Sampson, a prominent Negro diplomat, appeared in Copenhagen, she was confronted by the visiting African-American journalist William Worthy. The "meeting lasted nearly three hours with Mrs. Sampson on her feet all the while" as she was being cross-examined because "the interest in the Negro

Question in the United States on the part of people in Denmark, Scandinavia and most European countries is amazing. Some of it is Communist inspired," said Barnett's correspondent: "the people in these countries believe that so long as America mistrusts its black population, it has little right to flaunt the virtues of democracy before others."[80] Stung to the quick, Sampson—an attorney and a friend of Eleanor Roosevelt[81]—assailed Worthy bitterly.[82] He had "definite leanings toward Soviet Russia," she charged. He was then a student in Denmark and she blamed him for the fact that whenever she lectured there, she was heckled.[83] Undaunted, Worthy lambasted Sampson, saying that "quite understandably [she] resented my informing colored Americans about the fairy tales of paradise in Mississippi that she had been spreading behind their backs in Europe." Even the ANP noted that "within highly intellectual Scandinavia, her speeches on the race question were as much an object of withering ridicule" as anything heard in Scandinavia of late.[84] The ANP could only conclude that "the interest in the Negro Question in the United States on the part of the people in Denmark, Scandinavia and most European countries is amazing."[85]

Yet Barnett well knew that the United States would have difficulty in prevailing in the Cold War as long as Jim Crow stained the nation's escutcheon. He also knew that this presented yet another profit opportunity for his bulging investment portfolio. The remedy for the problem? Make more propaganda films starring Barnett to help rebut stereotypes.[86]

The rebuked Sampson then turned her ire on Josephine Baker, terming the French resident's denunciation of Jim Crow hypocritical, since she supposedly was not as upset with French colonialism[87]—a point the chanteuse denied vehemently.[88] This occurred after both Baker and Richard Wright were the sources for an ANP story that deplored the bias in the United States and contrasted this policy with France's. Baker was angered because during a recent trip to the United States, a number of hotels refused her service, and Wright was cited for the proposition that "more wealthy Negroes" should follow his path and move to Paris.[89]

Baker, far from being intimidated, then journeyed to Buenos Aires, where she eulogized Eva Peron and, said the ANP, "won countrywide acclaim in Argentina for her lectures on racial discrimination in the United States."[90] For his part, composer Andy Razaf was impressed with Baker, devising a ditty that praised her fight "across the foam" and "your greatest one at home."[91] For her troubles, she faced the prospect of being barred from entering the United States.[92]

Now firmly on the offensive, Sampson rebuked the AMEZ Bishop W. J. Walls, also of Chicago, for allowing Robeson to appear on a program with her at their convention.[93] Sampson was battered nonetheless, this time by attorney Nelson Willis.[94] Sampson felt compromised, perhaps, because Robeson subsequently was to be found alongside DuBois, Charlotta Bass, and many others, according to the ANP (including a "LARGE number of Negroes," it was stressed), "among the hundreds of people who attended" the reception at the Soviet embassy in Washington marking the thirty-fifth anniversary of the Bolshevik Revolution.[95]

Bass had long since diverted from the path trod by Barnett. The same could be said for Thyra Edwards, with whom he collaborated profitably during the Spanish Civil War, but by 1953, she had become an exile in Italy, learned the language, and passed away.[96] Also passing into history was a kind of left-wing radicalism, with which Barnett and the ANP had once engaged fruitfully.

For although Frederick Patterson found Miles Horton of the Highlander Folk School in Tennessee to be "liberal or socialistic in his views," he deemed him to be acceptably and "strongly anticommunist";[97] this was important because the Highlander Folk School was to gain notoriety as a training ground for activists associated with Dr. Martin Luther King Jr. and Rosa Parks. Still, this was a bridge too far for Barnett, who confessed that he "shied away" from Highlander Folk School because of the allegation that they were not sufficiently anticommunist,[98] thereby cutting ANP off from a vital connection with the emerging new anti–Jim Crow movement.

*   *   *

In a way, the more pressure the United States faced abroad, the more opportunities flowed to Barnett. It was in June 1954 that he was invited to a luncheon at Blair House in Washington in honor of Azikiwe of Nigeria. Present, boasted Barnett, were "top people from State, Export-Import and British Embassy," all of which "shows they are regarding Africa more highly."[99] In November 1954 Barnett was to be found at the Hotel Tudor in Manhattan and, as he told Glucksman, there too were to be found the finance minister of the Gold Coast and Sylvanus Olympio of Togoland, who "used to be general manager for Lever Brothers in French Togoland."[100]

Yet even in his rubbing shoulders with visiting African dignitaries, it was evident that the United States had yet to escape Jim Crow. When His Imperial Majesty Haile Selassie of Ethiopia visited Chicago in 1954, his stay was "cut down to one day because the Drake Hotel where he is to stay," said Barnett ruefully, "was fearful of 'too much African society'" showing up. Besides, said Barnett, now firmly enmeshed in a broadening circle of African leaders, "I found it difficult to work up much interest in his Amharic Majesty if he looks down on his darker brothers,"[101] a reference to a longstanding rumor.

But again, this is just one side of a complicated coin. Barnett had access to these eminences and was willing to parlay this influence for the right price. Ruth Sloan, formerly of the State Department, was thinking along parallel lines. She was an ANP source to begin with.[102] But suddenly she left Foggy Bottom in order to form a business targeting Africa, in a manner that Barnett found complementary,[103] as the gold rush in an impending decolonized Africa sped up.

Barnett was doing sufficiently well that he could welcome Sloan into the market with little apprehension. Soon Barnett was able to report ecstatically to Glucksman that "few films have been worked harder than the Chesterfield films which the company sent to Haiti." The "estimate given to me," he confided, was that tens of thousands "had seen them."[104]

✳   ✳   ✳

Barnett's high-level contacts with Africa continued to pay dividends. He added to his growing collection of artifacts by obtaining a "spear from the Kikuyu" while commenting disappointingly that "prices in East Africa have advanced considerably." One reason was that one of his retail contacts "went out of business during the Mau Mau trouble."[105]

Barnett, whose spouse—after all—was a renowned performer, had long evinced a dedicated interest in the arts, and it was thought this too could pay off abroad.[106] When Edith Sampson was queried about an official U.S. sponsorship of a global touring company of *Porgy and Bess*, the so-called Negro folk opera, she expressed reservations and asked that Barnett be consulted.[107]

Barnett continued to pull strings to make sure that his spouse received performing opportunities, not just in Africa, but increasingly in Europe too.[108] Her ability to sing in six languages made his job easier.[109] Because of his spouse, Barnett continued to be a force in the performing arts: When the actor Minto Cato was accused of nebulous ties to the Communist Party, she beseeched Barnett to publicize her ardent denials.[110]

But productions on stage were not the medium to which Barnett turned increasing attention. For some time his ANP had not only serviced newspapers but radio too.[111] Chicago's Margaret Burroughs referred derisively to the "Iron Curtain" that "exists in radio and television as far as the Negro people are concerned. Our rich life and humor, warmth, humanity and fighting spirit is not considered a fit subject for depictions on the air." This was occurring, she said, during "a year in which we find the greatest resurgence of the Ku Klux Klan since the days following World War I."[112]

Barnett was an early adopter of television, which by 1953 he found to be "like a narcotic. You can't look at it and work too," and so he was dumbfounded about "how to keep the thing out of the newsroom."[113] By 1954 Etta Moten was "one of the woman's page editors," as Barnett proudly observed on an NBC show in Chicago, "Melody Magazine."[114]

This opened the door to further commercial opportunities, such as promoting those companies that advertised on Moten's show in the columns of the ANP.[115] Barnett apprised CBS Radio of its shortcomings[116] and sought to leverage this on behalf of President Tubman of Liberia, bolstering his ties and investments there.[117]

Barnett continued to maintain a fruitful network of sources and colleagues abroad, a group that had expanded as the manacles of Jim Crow weakened. This included Mary Mills in Beirut, an officer in the U.S. military, who kept him apprised of riots in Iran "preceding the return to office of Mr. Mossadeq, there were many killed"; the "new king in Egypt"—and more.[118] As was his wont, Barnett did not simply husband his contacts but encouraged Earl Dickerson to reach Mills when he passed through Lebanon. She "established a school for nursing in Liberia," he told his friend, and "is a good friend of mine."[119] "You must have your hands full with NATO," Barnett told the nation's premier Negro envoy, Clifton Wharton, then serving in Lisbon, after thanking him for his gracious hospitality in "your lovely home."[120]

It probably did not hurt when Barnett informed Dale Cox of International Harvester, an internationally minded corporation, that the senior Wharton was a close "friend of mine," having served as "United States Consul General at Marseilles, France" while reigning as "the dean of Negro career men in the State Department Consular Service."[121] As the walls of Jim Crow began to crack from the global pressure on the United States because of this malignancy, it became possible for Negro elites to ascend on the career ladder, and Barnett was able to take advantage.

Barnett continued to play a role in this process, seeking to desegregate the State Department, getting those placed in posts who could be friendly to his own interests. The problem was that there was waning interest in Africa among ANP affiliates, which ironically could curb his investment opportunities on the continent. This was occurring—with even more irony—as Africans themselves, as colonialism began to retreat, were more interested in reaching the African American audience. As Barnett clamored to have more Negroes appointed to posts like Lisbon and Zurich, African Americans were concerned that the sinecure that had been Liberia was slipping from their grasp. "Preserving that post for our group" was a must, he said. There was a "fear on the part of colored career employees that the State Department and the white business firms," meaning Firestone and Republic Steel, had a differing priority.[122]

Barnett was insufficiently alert to realize that his own approach was part of the problem. With his typical acuity, he asked the Belgian authorities whether they possessed "definite description of or statistics on the schools of Belgian Congo for natives? How high do they go?" And, yes, "are there any bars to American Negroes entering Belgian Congo?" But then he compromised his approach by asking, of course, where he could secure "carvings and curios" at a "stabilized price."[123] The latter inquiry opened the door to his being presented with an attractive offer that would deflect more important concerns. The latter inquiry also exposed what was lost when the Robeson-led Council on African Affairs was forced to retrench, because it was contrary to their code to engage in business dealings with their adversaries. Eventually, Baron Dhanis of the Belgian legation in the United States replied after a lengthy delay that "if there is social discrimination in the Belgian Congo it is applied in the same manner either to Europeans or Congolese"[124]—which seemed to be a deliberate insult to Barnett's intelligence.

As of 1953 the ANP maintained a correspondent in Pakistan and Barnett continued to insist that "our papers ought to be interested in the proposition that [Pakistanis] represent a large segment of darker peoples albeit not of Indian extraction." Now chastened with his up-and-down relationship with New Delhi, Barnett felt his affiliates "ought especially be interested in Pakistanians [*sic*] because they seem to identify with Negroes much more readily than East Indians."[125]

Barnett also continued to be deluged with proposals from prospective writers, one of which in 1952 foretold the growing popularity of nonviolent resistance to Jim Crow.[126] Even potential novelists[127] and crossword puzzle creators[128] pelted Barnett with proposals, not to mention potential reporters from the frozen tundra of Alaska.[129] Some of these proposals were intriguing, for example, one that promised a "series of articles concerning the white church in the South and its connections with the Ku Klux Klan," an illustration, it was said, of the "degeneration of the Church."[130]

The problem, as ever, was how to pursue the historic militancy that had driven the anti–Jim Crow movement historically without running afoul of those who suspected that such an approach was just a guise and ruse on behalf of a pro-Red movement. As the *New York Times* put it at the time, the "major factor in the battle against domestic and international Communism is the elimination of discrimination."[131] This admonition from the paper of record contributed to excessive skittishness not only about Communists but also about activities that had been associated with them, such as anti–Jim Crow protest.

The ANP's own reports provided cautionary messages, as in their coverage of the story of labor lawyer Ruth Weyand Perry, who lost her government job on charges of being a Communist—and, not tangentially, after she married a prominent NAACP attorney, Leslie Perry, who then lost his post too.[132] This purge also affected Negro colleges, denuding them of white faculty who were suspected of being Red.[133] Simultaneously, their faculties were buttressed by those fleeing revolution abroad, serving to augment conservatism in Dixie where most of these campuses were sited.[134]

The lengthy list of those purged included Lee Lorch, one of the few whites in Little Rock in 1957 who stood openly on the side of desegregation and then was forced to evacuate to Canada.[135] "Southern whites who want to be decent," he told Barnett, "are up against a lot of problems" and "unless those who are attacked as a result of decent behavior are supported it will scare many others from standing up." But standing up for Lorch would have meant taking a stand on behalf of a presumed Communist, which would have compromised Barnett's other interests.[136] Soon Lorch was in exile in Canada: "we had to migrate here to make a living," he told Barnett. "We like it here," an abrupt change from his stay in Dixie.[137]

Those like Barnett felt compelled to honor the emerging anticommunist consensus in return for concessions, but it seemed that certain elites seemed not to trust them sufficiently to justify collaboration. This was the import of what Horace Mann Bond told Barnett, after sending him remarks that he had recently delivered at Howard University. He was upset that a major initiative in African Studies was sited not at Howard or another school of its type but at Northwestern University, "a place . . . that excludes Negro women from its dormitories and by deed gift excludes Negroes" from other areas. The irate Bond was determined to "make the name of the university as odious as possible in the African circles I know of," thus complicating U.S. foreign policy. Bond thought—correctly—"I would not at all be surprised if Northwestern soon announces a change in its policy with reference to segregation."[138] Still, Barnett's Chicago friend, the scholar St. Clair Drake, while thanking the ANP for "those very welcome bundles of African and West Indian papers" often arriving in his mailbox, continued to be "very careful in selecting participants" in his African Studies program to "make sure that no one with 'subversive' affiliations is included."[139]

The mistrust by elites was reciprocated in that the ANP continued to portray the rest of the world as being more welcoming to U.S. Negroes than their homeland. Two European journalists traveling in the United States in late 1952 were depicted in the ANP as being shocked and appalled by Jim Crow.[140]

Yet an ANP correspondent in Paris was sufficiently aware to detect the fact that, although African Americans were favored there for being an "underdog," Africans from the colonies were treated altogether differently, not to mention the "intensity" of "hatred" for "Indo-Chinese."[141] (Of course, a different policy prevailed on U.S. military bases in France, where U.S. Negroes were disfavored and Africans were not.)[142]

Robert Browne, the Negro economist, who was born in Chicago in 1924 and served in the U.S. military during World War II, was recruited by Barnett as a kind of correspondent. He wanted to know "about the general racial attitude in Spain" and whether the regime there was "favorable to colored people."[143] Browne's work would undoubtedly produce articles that would allow Barnett to pressure Washington for more Negro diplomats, as opposed to a change in policy.

This dynamic of maltreatment of U.S. Negroes at home while being toasted abroad extended to the region the ANP routinely described as being "behind the Iron Curtain" and included its very own correspondent, Rudolph Dunbar. By 1951 he was to be found in Sarajevo, Yugoslavia, invited by the minister of culture to conduct an orchestra. It was "memorable," he jubilated, a "success beyond my dreams," because "each concert was sold out." He sought to present the work of William Grant Still, the noted U.S. Negro composer. In Belgrade he was embraced as "Commarade" and was not allowed to pay on public transit. "[O]n all my travels," he exclaimed, "I have never encountered such benevolence."[144]

The question hardly considered then was this: What would happen if Communist influence waned? Would the rationale for anti–Jim Crow concessions shrivel accordingly?

CHAPTER 9

Barnett Bestrides the Globe

Alice Dunnigan was displeased.

Global attention was turning to an epochal meeting of mostly Asian and African nations in Bandung, Indonesia, signaling a turning point in world history, but she was unable to go.

"You might imagine how I feel with Louis Lautier gloating about his trip and that of his wife and Ethel Payne" doing the same, a reference to two of her peers in the small circle of Negro journalists. She "heard that the State Department was picking up his tab," meaning Lautier's; she "also heard that Nelson Rockefeller was underwriting the trip" of other journalists.[1] All she knew for sure was that she was not going and that did not make her happy.

Bandung was not just a turning point for the world. It was also a turning point for Barnett, then well into his sixties, and his agency. Already there were signs that the ANP was reaching its expiration date, impelled—ironically—by the paradoxical strains introduced by the move toward "integration." Bandung also signaled the coming era of decolonization and, with Africa surging to independence, Africans could now open government-to-government relations with Washington and there was less of a perceived need for those like Barnett to act as intermediaries and lobbyists and, in any case, those like Barnett were coming to be seen not as honest brokers or disinterested politicos but just one more in a long line of entrepreneurs lusting after the vast resources of Africa and the Caribbean. Simultaneously, decolonization also meant that the newly liberated nations could exert pressure on Washington to erode the more egregious aspects of Jim Crow, which helped to foment "integration" that in turn served to erode the rationale for the ANP.

Ironically, Barnett was able to gain the most traction in dealing with Ghana's Kwame Nkrumah, who also happened to be the African leader closest to those who had been sidelined by the postwar ascendancy of anticommunism—W. E. B. DuBois and Shirley Graham DuBois in the first instance—which meant he had to incur the possibility of a domestic assault because of a perceived softness on the bedrock issue of anticommunism as he reached for global gain. "We went to practically every one of the events for Prime Minister Nkrumah in Washington," said Barnett with accuracy in 1958.[2] Consorting with the leading Ghanaian who happened to be close to U.S. radicals, however, involved a perilous tightrope walk.

A snapshot of Barnett's dilemma was exposed in early 1955 when he traveled to Haiti, a frequent haunt of his. There he bumped into Walter White, during the latter's 14th visit there. Then Barnett drove to another spot on the island and, "as we entered a beautiful sunny nook, who should be sitting there but [DuBois] and his wife, Shirley Graham," both of whom were ideological rivals of White and had been there for three weeks, one of the few places they could visit without a U.S. passport.[3] This chance encounter with DuBois and his spouse was not coincidental in that it came as the ANP began to provide the Father of Pan-Africanism with more respectful[4]—and lengthy—coverage.[5]

This embrace was also a reflection of the changing political climate indicated by Bandung and the movement toward decolonization. The political climate also influenced Barnett's reaction to hot-button Cold War issues. After encountering DuBois in Haiti, he heard that Alfred Stern and his spouse—as a press account put it—"disappeared behind the Iron Curtain," presumed to be fleeing "spies." He was married to a daughter of Julius Rosenwald, the tycoon with whom Barnett had been associated and participated in this rich man's "race ventures" as a member of the board of the National Urban League.[6] Barnett not only knew him, he also knew that "the Sterns were closely associated with some of our most prominent citizens" and "he was a most helpful person in racial matters. I served on a board with him."[7] Like many Euro Americans presumed to be pro-Soviet, the Sterns were also more likely to consort with African Americans. But such personal associations not only made it harder for him to join the journalist wolf-pack then tearing the couple to pieces, particularly as international tensions eased, it also raised searching questions about Barnett's own loyalty, questions that his ties over the years to Frank Marshall Davis had done little to dissipate.

Bandung also took place during the same year as the tragic murder of the black Chicago teenager Emmett Till in Mississippi, lynched for racist reasons in an episode that stirred African Americans and the world. The ANP commissioned Langston Hughes to write a special poem in commemoration[8] and castigated a Jackson, Mississippi, periodical after they charged that the youth's father was "hanged in Italy, July 2, 1945 as a result of a trial on February 17, 1945 . . . on charges of raping two Italian women and shooting to death a third man."[9]

The ANP also was keen to underscore the intersection between the Till case and analogous events globally. Referring to recent events in Taiwan, Gordon Hancock reported that "our great nation is learning, much to its chagrin, that acquitting a white man in the slaying of a Chinaman is not the same as acquitting a white man in the slaying of a defenseless Negro." The "riots in Taipei" involving "as many as 30,000 participants" in the wake of this tragedy, showed not only that failure to repress white supremacist attitudes at home could reverberate abroad but also that "the average white American carries with him to the uttermost parts of the earth his race prejudice and he has carried it to Formosa."[10]

The ANP diligently reported stories showing how Jim Crow backfired to Washington's detriment when it sought application of this pernicious practice against those who were not U.S. Negroes.[11] This was particularly so during the Little Rock desegregation crisis of 1957.[12] When Autherine Lucy was confronted with howling mobs in her attempt to desegregate the University of Alabama in 1956, the ANP quoted a respected Mexican journal that compared the response there to something from the times of Hitler, and then went on to warn that "if we don't stand up for her, this will hit us when we cross the border."[13]

Again, this incident was used to reprove Jim Crow, which was contrasted invidiously with the practice prevailing south of the border. "If while visiting this country," said the ANP correspondent in Mexico, "you should ever meet with discrimination notify the Mexican Tourist Bureau and they may close the establishment."[14] Thus, continued Earl Morris, "American Negroes living in foreign countries"—of which he was one—"are indeed proud of the fact that their women are playing an important role in developing better racial relations" and were "doing more than their share." Those battling Jim Crow gained sustenance from his observation that "the Colored Peoples of other nations, as well as the fair minded peoples of all nations are cheering the Negro in his fight."[15]

Moreover, the agency continued to broadcast news from Moscow—for example, the premier of a film "Slaves in America"—depicting the horrors of Jim Crow and slavery's aftermath.[16] ANP readers also learned that Negro visitors to Moscow were often greeted with more tact and friendliness than they would receive in certain precincts in Dixie.[17] ANP readers would not have been shocked to read, as they did, of Howard B. Spears Jr., a twenty-six-year-old U.S. military veteran who applied for Soviet citizenship because he was fed up with racism at home. "I want to be treated like a human being," said this man who professed that he was not a Communist.[18]

Perhaps rising to the competitive bait, the ANP's peers sought not only to cover the news but to make it. Bill Worthy, who had harassed Edith Sampson in Denmark, broke the journalistic blockade by traveling to Red China and then made news further when he reported that Washington had pressured his newspaper, the *Afro-American*, to compel him to return.[19]

Sufficiently stirred, even the NAACP's Roy Wilkins called for free elections in Mississippi—after the Magnolia State's Senator James Eastland called for free elections in Poland.[20]

The agency also paid obeisance to anticommunist trends. "A Communist Blueprint for the conquest of Africa has been revealed," reported the agency breathlessly in late 1955.[21] Thus, 1956 also marked the onset of the crisis in Hungary and the Soviet intervention, wherein the ANP quoted Congressman Charles Diggs of Detroit saluting Budapest in their struggle against what the portly legislator termed "monstrous infamy."[22]

Nevertheless, it was the ANP that contrasted the often harsh reception accorded Puerto Ricans—U.S. citizens—as they migrated to the mainland with the warmness accorded Hungarians migrating to the U.S.[23] And it was the ANP that played up the story involving a white student, Andre Toth, a refugee from Hungary who sparked a "bitter controversy" by enrolling at the historically black Allen University in South Carolina, causing both the governor to react badly and Negroes to seek admission to the theretofore lily-white University of South Carolina.[24]

Nor was it deemed to be overly provocative when Gordon Hancock told readers that the "attempt to overmatch Russia, as it were, with one hand and hold the Negroes down with the other" was unsustainable. What gave ground was the latter, which facilitated the former; "there are elements of the Old South," Hancock cautioned nonetheless, "who would rather see Russia in charge of the world than to see the Negro liberated." Retrospectively, those "elements" described by the moderate columnist did not prevail,[25] though Hancock would not have been surprised to hear that as he was taking pen to paper, a Negro minister in Lexington, Kentucky, "posed as Adolf Hitler" by mail as a financial ruse and collected a cool $15,000 from the deluded, some of whom thought they were backing a "new revolt" against Negro equality.[26]

Although Negro visitors were embraced "behind the Iron Curtain," in Baton Rouge, said the ANP, a "new secret society, the Southern Gentlemen," demanded that this city "be placed off limits to Negro troops during large scale war maneuvers," involving 140,000 soldiers, the "largest game exercise since World War II"—ironically designed to confront Moscow.[27]

The confluence of the rise of Asia and Africa in Bandung and the continued pressure from Moscow gave momentum to the anti–Jim Crow resurgence embodied in the fightback after the Till murder, in a way that close readers of the ANP dispatches could discern.

*　*　*

Thus, though Barnett recognized the importance of this Indonesian meeting, he was not eager to send his top correspondent there. He downplayed Africa's influence there, reducing its newsworthiness and speculated that "through the kindness of Mr. Nehru's people," ANP would "get reports directly from Bandung." Moreover, "we hope to get the American point of view or sidelights from the group of Americans in Bandung who are over there as a result of the Tuskegee program of cooperation with the Indonesian government." Anyway, it was questionable what value her reporting could provide to readers because "we have as a people not become sufficiently acquainted [with] the problems of our African relatives to truly understand them nor to get excited about them," a view that undercut years of Pan-African journalism. It was not evident that Dunnigan was qualified for such a weighty assignment because "the Asian and East Indian attitude is so far from that which we know and it is so certain to dominate the conference that only a person skilled in statecraft and international reporting could expect to distil the true flavor." Apologetically, he concluded, "I hope you won't be too depressed."[28]

Dunnigan may not have been depressed, but she was dissatisfied. She had begun working for the agency full time in 1947 and was still with them helping to provide copy to "around 85" papers.[29] "I have been writing for newspapers and magazines since I was 13 years old," she commented tartly, and "I am now nearly 50." Her mettle as a journalist was confirmed once more when "just a few days ago at the Liberian Embassy reception, Mrs. John Foster Dulles," spouse of the secretary of state, "came to me, shook my hand and said she had great respect for me." More than most she knew that "writing is a profession" and an "art." More than most, she also knew "the insults that a woman meets when rambling around that time of night alone,"[30] even when pursuing journalism, and yet when she simply sought to apply her skills to an earth shattering event in Indonesia, Barnett was bereft of assistance. Why should she continue to sacrifice?

If the agency would not send her to Indonesia, what about Ghana? "Why can't 112 newspapers pool about $10 each?" she asked, and send her. "I am the 'Dean of Negro Newspaper Women' around Washington" yet "never get the recognition I so rightfully deserve."[31] Where was the justice?

"I lost my husband," she groaned, because of her tireless labor for ANP, which detracted from home life. "He said that I gave my work more time than I have for my home and family." She was disconsolate. "I'm going to end up . . . in the insane asylum or the graveyard," not least because "I never participate in any social activities, unless it is something from which I can get a story. I never relax to look at a comedy or a drama on television." She was forlorn. "I work day and night" while "a clerk typist makes almost twice as much money as I, the big-shot professional newspaper reporter [am] making" in that "they have a starting salary of about $3500" annually. Thus, she said gloomily, "many times I don't have anything in the house to eat on weekends."[32]

The stout, light-skinned journalist whose hair was beginning to gray[33] was more than ready to depart the ranks of the ANP. She had started in high school as a reporter in Kentucky and then pursued her trade further at Kentucky State University,[34] garnering more experience—but her rapidly balding boss, Barnett, was unyielding in refusing adamantly to facilitate her journey to Bandung.

Dunnigan may have heard that the National Council of Negro Women was sponsoring a tea at the Indonesian Embassy, which was emblematic of this nation's attempt to forge ties with African Americans and was a harbinger of a future warm welcome in Bandung.[35] Dunnigan countered by managing to interview U Nu, the Burmese prime minister, a "member of the darker races," she said, invoking pre-1945 rhetoric, when he arrived in Washington.[36]

The clever Barnett was simultaneously negotiating with another journalist to cover the Bandung event. Marguerite Cartwright approached him with a "proposed trip around the world" and sought a letter of introduction from him for the Bandung leg of her journey. She described herself as a U.S. Negro journalist and was impressed that Azikiwe's name remained on ANP letterhead.[37]

Insulting to Dunnigan was that Barnett knew the importance of Bandung; he just did not think she was qualified to report on this profound gathering. Reached in Haiti, Barnett did not downplay the gathering in Indonesia but instead insisted that it "may well be the beginning of a shift in relationship between the colored peoples of the world and the white masters."[38] It may be important to note, as he later told Dunnigan, that Cartwright's "husband was paying her expenses. She is married to a distinguished chemist who is a Caucasian."[39]

Then the shrewd Barnett turned to the affluent San Francisco publisher Carlton Goodlett of that fogbound city's leading Negro journal, and decided to "appoint you as our representative" in Bandung; contrary to what he had told Dunnigan, he told Goodlett that Liberia was participating and, indeed, the "Liberian delegation will be headed by a friend of mine," to wit, Momulu Dukuly.[40]

Dunnigan attempted to get Jakarta to foot her bill but "was too late to get on the 'bandwagon.' I also had secret contact with the U.S. Information Agency but here again I was too late," she said dejectedly. Typically, she had expended "much money in cab fares, long distance telephone calls and telegrams" to reach her goal but now felt "rather let out and left out," especially since her peers were planning to attend. She was wallowing in moroseness and berating Barnett as a result of being both underpaid and underappreciated.[41]

To allay Dunnigan's souring temperament, Barnett moved from downplaying Bandung's significance to warning that attending might only enhance her threadbare Red credentials to her detriment. "Because of our great national fear of Communism," he warned, "and the bogey we have built up about it, it will be difficult to keep the conference from seeming to have a pink tinge." And unlike the halcyon days of the war now long gone, this would "interpose considerable difficulty on the part of those seeking to cover it for Negro newspapers."[42]

As Barnett was moving to prevent her firsthand ANP coverage of this epochal event, the mainstream *Los Angeles Daily Mirror* had moved oppositely and appointed a Negro, James Jones, to cover Bandung,[43] which was just one more reason why ambitious African-American reporters found it easier to shun Barnett's agency in favor of the mainstream as Jim Crow barriers began to erode.

Ultimately, an unnamed ANP correspondent was able to tell readers that Bandung meant that "colonialism and white supremacy are as out of style as a stagecoach. .... [M]ost of the delegates here seemed to be more worried about economic exploitation and Jim Crow than about Moscow's global designs,"[44] which was not the kind of message crafted to win friends and influence the elites with whom Barnett was now currying favor.

Washington was the "chief prop of white supremacy," according to the ANP's A. J. Siggins, but, he advised, this doctrine was "doomed." The United States was seeking to "weaken India and all Asian and African states which do not support white imperialism." Did not Kerala, an Indian state, now have a "Communist government"?[45] South Korean strongman Syngman Rhee, according to the ANP, provided indirect credence to Siggins's view when he decried the proliferating of "white-Indian" films from Hollywood because "the Communists make a big exploitation of such films to show that the U.S. is a colonial power 'enslaving the colored races.'" His point? "Stop making films showing American Indians being killed by white men."[46]

*   *   *

Dunnigan should have realized that Barnett may have been hoarding his—and ANP's—ducats because of the proliferating investment opportunities that were opening in the new era of the helter-skelter retreat of Jim Crow and colonialism, with the two processes linked. He had joined with his old friend, Lloyd Kerford of Kansas, who—said Barnett—"operates what I believe to be" the "largest individual business owned by Negroes in the United States." It involved a Liberian mining concession in the midst "of one of the foremost iron mining projects in the world," clearly "equal to the best Swedish iron" to be exploited by an unnamed Swiss concern and the Republic Steel Company of Cleveland. The product would be brought to Baltimore, then transshipped to Ohio.[47]

Barnett was also in touch with Edward Logelin of the U.S. Steel Corporation "about the possibilities in the Republic of Liberia. I pointed out that far more than most countries, the personal interest of someone well placed officially was more advantageous. The Vice President of the country, who is my friend, is due in New York," he confided, and "I would be glad to arrange a discussion."[48]

Haile Selassie, His Imperial Majesty, was from the other side of the continent, but while visiting Los Angeles he told the ANP that Ethiopia would welcome investment from U.S. Negroes too,[49] a point that Barnett would also be able to parlay.[50]

In eastern Africa, Barnett was already looking ahead to Kenyan independence when he circulated a letter from anticolonial leader Tom Mboya, seeking to raise funds from ANP papers for his defense.[51] The grateful Kenyan hastened to "welcome" U.S. Negroes to his homeland, reminding them, "we, of course, welcome you warmly because you are so close to our hearts."[52] In his African initiatives Barnett continued to try to benefit his alma mater, as when he sought bibles for Tuskegee in Kiswahili,[53] a language spoken widely in East Africa.

As usual, Barnett was quite busy in Haiti.[54] That Barnett had only recently been decorated with one of the republic's highest honors would doubtlessly be a key to open those doors.[55]

*   *   *

Dunnigan's mood may have been influenced negatively by working conditions beyond what was foisted upon her by Barnett. She was perpetually ignored at White House press conferences though she would bounce up and down for the duration of a thirty-minute session seeking to pose questions. Each time President Eisenhower would ignore her existence. "The ANP reporter," said the ANP, "is not the only Negro who has been bypassed at the President's conferences" but, befitting Dunnigan, she was probably the most persistent. But since there was only one other Negro reporter at these confabs, the title was not imposing. The president was only conforming to Washington tradition in that FBI director J. Edgar Hoover "wouldn't even talk to a Negro," said the ANP.[56]

"To think that I, the only newspaper representative for 17 million Americans," Dunnigan complained, "am completely ignored at all of the President's conferences. That he will look me squarely into my eye and recognize somebody far beyond me. . . . [I]t makes one's blood boil." It was then that a "reporter for the Chinese service insisted on having coffee with me after the conference to discuss the president's obvious refusal to recognize me. I am perfectly honest when I said I jumped up so many times that my knees became weak and my legs ached." Her reaction? "We must put on our boxing gloves and come out fighting."[57] That she did. Tellingly, the Chinese reporter seemed more concerned about her plight than her Euro American counterparts.

For in addition to battling the White House, she also was involved in ever sharper conflicts with Dixiecrats in Congress. She recounted to Barnett "one of the most vicious hearings I have ever witnessed" on Capitol Hill. It was "crowded with rebels—real crackers," and "the witnesses and the Southern Congressmen constantly referred to our race as 'niggers' until it made one's blood boil," an occupational hazard for her. She was forced to "grit [her] teeth, clench [her] fist and almost feel like [she] could toss an atomic bomb on the entire southland," particularly when the "audience applauded loudly every time some distasteful remark was made about the 'niggers.'" Equally troublesome was the extraordinary sight of "observers" who "constantly heckled the Negro reporters at the press table." Worse, she realized that "the white boys" were "not going to print the story as it actually was" and she had to hope that her version of events "will be picked up by some foreign papers" and, perhaps, used at the "Asia-Africa conference" at Bandung. As ever, the ANP had to hope that global journals would circulate reports about the Negro for it would take the U.S. mainstream a while longer to do so.

In this instance, however, the eventuality of an accurate report of this disturbing congressional hearing was squelched by none other than Barnett himself. "But lo! And behold! When my story came out, it didn't tell any of the details. It was watered down and whacked off to about two or three paragraphs."[58] By way of explanation, Barnett told her that "you wanted to describe in burning language" how these racists "used the word 'nigger' but no first class colored paper uses the word."[59] Of course, Barnett may have edited severely her inflammatory reporting so as not to embarrass Washington elites and preserve his ability to circulate in rarified circles.

As Dunnigan explained things, dealing with President Eisenhower was similarly worrisome. White House aide Max Rabb approached her at an embassy party brusquely. "Alice, you're always asking the boss questions on some subject with which he is not familiar. This is very embarrassing to him." Dunnigan did not buy this explanation that he should screen her inquiries beforehand. "I was enraged," she said, "because out of the five hundred or more reporters, I was the only [one], to my knowledge, who was asked to check her questions with the White House." Still, she went along, but when she provided her questions to Rabb, he determined that they were inappropriate. So Eisenhower continued the pattern. "He would recognize people all around me, in front of me, in back of me, on either side but he always left me standing like the invisible man." Dunnigan sought to avoid the obvious, that "this issue was based on either race or sex discrimination." Still, the story was publicized by journals that included the *New York Post*, the *Afro-American*, and even the Communist *Daily Worker*.

As Dunnigan recalled, Barnett was irked by this publicity, even "when the 112 ANP newspapers picked up the story," and "it became widespread around the nation." Eisenhower continued to ignore her, and when in 1961 the incoming President John F. Kennedy "at his first press conference" recognized her, it became a national event. It was shortly after finally asking a question to a president that Dunnigan left the ANP for greener pastures.[60] This too was an ironically paradoxical turning point: as this Negro journalist's status was upgraded, she then found it easier to depart the ANP.

Barnett should have seen this coming. Even before Dunnigan's hurried exit, Barnett was irked because "as soon as [we] train a man up, one of the big papers come[s] along and hires him at a price we cannot afford to meet."[61] Barnett should have been the first to recognize that the new era of "integration" was not all upside, namely, that as investment opportunities opened for him, job opportunities opened for his valued employees, thereby destabilizing his institution, the ANP. Such was the paradox of Jim Crow's retreat.

*   *   *

Barnett also had opened a new front in the ANP's global coverage by turning the agency's attention south of the border; often, where ANP correspondents dared to tread, Barnett's commercial interests were sure to follow. Their correspondent, Earl Morris, dismissed "rumors that Guatemala has a racial discrimination policy. That is not true, as we see it," because "there are many black Guatemalans" and "several (a few hundred, I was told) Negroes from the States who are working in that country."[62] The value of heading a news agency as a launching pad for investment was exhibited when Barnett heard directly from a well-placed Costa Rican who wanted to write for ANP and then briefed him on the progress made of late by those of African descent in his country, which could open the door to opportunities for African Americans like Barnett.[63]

In Mexico, where he was based, Morris reported on the popularity of Negro ballplayer Monte Irvin, "so popular here that people have asked me if he is a Mexican," which was part of the "Mexican attitude of trying to identify himself with the Negro," in contrast to "the lack of pride of some Negroes in [the] States in regard to their color and their hair."[64] Another Negro celebrity who spent considerable time in Mexico was Willard Motley. This "famous author," said Morris, "lives in Cuernavaca." His "latest books have all been translated into seven or more languages." Thus, said the ANP correspondent in words that mirrored Barnett's, "I should like to see more Negroes looking towards Latin America as a possible depository for investment money."[65]

This was an invitation for more U.S. Negroes to arrive, and another Morris report provided encouragement and investment advice—albeit sarcastically, perhaps ironically—to Barnett's long-time favorite: hair-straightening enterprises.[66]

Morris was peculiarly suited for his role. He claimed descent from those Africans who had merged with "Seminole Indian[s]" who had fought the United States to a standstill in the 1850s before being forced to move south of the border. He was a member of Mexico's journalists union. Part of his job seemed to be to encourage emigration; thus, he regaled readers with the story of Morris Williams, a Negro travel agent there who arranged tours for U.S. Negroes to Mexico and who exhorted, "I want to live the rest of my life in Mexico," to which Morris instantly—and artlessly—replied, "Yo también, estoy muy gusto" or "Me too, I am happy to say."[67]

Despite his roots in Mexico, Morris had resided in Chicago where he worked for Barnett's colleague, P. L. Prattis. Thus, he touted the accomplishments in Mexico of "the Jones Brothers . . . two former Chicagoans, Edward and George," who arrived in Mexico City "several years ago" but now controlled a "lucrative business," which was an advertising broadside for others to act similarly.[68] It was Edward Jones who informed him that "one of the richest men here in Mexico City is a Negro. He owns more taxicabs than anyone here." This man, Joseph Harris, a Jamaican, had an heir, his son, Oswald. The elder Harris was the "black Horatio Alger" in that he headed south "years ago as a poor man" but now also had "extensive lumber holdings."[69] Morris also touted James Keys, a "tall Negro" with "the manner of a prince, he was carrying a riding crop." He had been in Mexico for more than three decades and spoke several languages, including an indigenous language (besides Spanish). He was practicing podiatry in an unconventional way.[70]

Harold Streeter, yet another ex-Chicagoan residing in Mexico, who worked as an exporter, told Morris with emphasis that "Negroes in Latin American countries have integration. They have had FULL CITIZENSHIP," he exclaimed, "from the first day their country started."[71]

A popular radio commentator in Guadalajara was the U.S. Negro Nat Harris, who broadcast in Spanish and English on radio station XEHL.[72] It is not surprising that Morris found that an increasing number of U.S. Negro students were coming to Mexico to study, and his columns were a call for more to follow.[73] They were followed duly by a choir from Texas's historically black Wiley College who were "royally received" in Mexico, making for a "triumphant success" in Morris's words. The eagle-eyed in Washington may have noticed that the Hollywood screenwriter John Bright, who had escaped the Red Scare by emigrating to Mexico, aided their gaining publicity.[74]

His cheerleading for emigration notwithstanding, Morris did not stint in telling ANP readers that it was not atypical for a Negro to get a visa to Mexico for a "three day period" while a "Caucasian" routinely received a visa for a "15 day period."[75] But the major thrust of his proemigration reporting was his accentuation of the warm welcome U.S. Negroes would receive there from "Afro-Mexicans, Afro-Cubans, Panamanians, Puerto Ricans and other Latin Negroes" who "discuss everything from world sports to world [peace]." There were those "American Negroes" who were "surprised to learn that Negroes in other parts of the world are deeply interested in world affairs and they feel that American Negroes are their brothers" and "recognize that we all had African ancestors and that those ancestors as slaves had been scattered throughout the Western Hemisphere."[76] Morris did his best to wed African Americans to Mexico in his reporting, stressing, for example, the ties of the latter's leader, Benito Juarez, to U.S. Negroes.[77] In some ways, Morris was the archetypical ANP correspondent, as revealed when he wondered why Liberia did not have a legation in Mexico, especially since "two of the most popular nations represented in Mexico are Haiti and Ethiopia."[78]

Thus, a visiting Josephine Baker wowed Mexico City as she "could switch from Spanish to French to English and Italian with ease," as well as "speak the Spanish of the Cubans, Argentines and Mexicans."[79] Katherine Dunham was greeted with similar rhapsody, enjoying "great popularity" in that "each of her dance sequences has a particular pull to each Negroid group living in" Mexico City. Both Baker and Dunham, said Morris awkwardly, "are showing Negroes that they are blood brothers," while "making articulate the cry of freedom for Negroes everywhere."[80]

As a result, Morris was ecstatic when the "Second Pan American Games" took place in Mexico in 1955.[81] He was equally uplifted when Dr. Martin Luther King Jr. came to Mexico. Yes, he wrote, he was treated "like a king." He was feted and "held press conferences almost daily on the racial situation in the U.S.," providing "Alabama and the U.S. a black eye."[82]

Another so surnamed, Clennon King of Dixie, sought asylum in Mexico when he ran afoul of what was described as Mississippi's "anti-Negro policy."[83] The reverberations of Morris's journalism were suggested when a journal in Mexico City sponsored "the young Negro bullfighter [from New York], Don Christian as well as his appointment to the position of Bullfighting Editor of our literary magazine."[84]

On the other hand, when Allan Shivers, a prominent conservative Texas politician, was bruited for a high-level post in Mexico, Morris recalled that Barnett "sent this correspondent a memo and gave us carte blanche meaning that I was free to drop London Bridge or the Atomic Bomb" to block this maneuver, which he promptly did—successfully.[85]

Once more, it would be a mistake to view Morris's reporting as wholly representative of the agency's output or the region's embrace of African Americans. Hence, the archbishop of Panama weakly denied that that he denounced the rising "rock and roll dance craze" as "only indulged in by Negroes and Africans," this on the cusp of the arrival in town of the Harlem stars "Frankie Lymon and the Teenagers."[86] Yet because of Morris's aggressive reporting, which had regional implications, it became easier for Barnett to inquire subsequently about the "part which colored Americans are playing in the disturbances which are taking place in the Panamanian situation,"[87] a reference to an elongated series of protests about control of the Panama Canal.

*　*　*

The capstone of Barnett's integration into the highest levels of U.S. society arrived when he developed a relationship with Vice President Richard M. Nixon. In pursuing this tie, he rejected the advice of his fellow publisher Nathaniel Sweets of the *St. Louis American* after Nixon was elected; Sweets asserted that Nixon was a "pious demagogue" and "most dangerous to a democracy." Extraordinarily, continued Sweets, Nixon "seems the counterpart of the brash young cohorts that arose to power at Hitler's elbow."[88] When Nixon traveled to Caracas after he became friendly with Barnett, the ANP did not slack in reporting on the raucous reception accorded the vice president.[89]

But Barnett was not in accord with Sweets's astringent view—at least that was the way it seemed. Barnett, said his coworker Enoch Waters, "despised Richard Nixon," though this seemed to be hardly the case when he dropped by the White House. He sought photos of himself in the company of the vice president for display on his wall-of-fame in his office.[90]

But Barnett was not only a prominent entrepreneur but a shaper of the news and a friend of a rising class of African leaders, which could prove valuable to Nixon, just as shrouding his distaste for the vice president could be valuable to the ANP chief.[91] Barnett was a man to be courted in Washington and, thus, in 1957 Nixon's faithful secretary, Rose Mary Woods, conveyed the words of her boss that it was "sweet" of Barnett "to attend the luncheon" that was given in Washington "in honor of the Queen and Prince Philip" of London; "you were invited both as friends and as representatives of the Negro race,"[92] it was added meretriciously. A sign of changing times was the presence on the guest list during the royal couple's visit to Chicago not just of Barnett but of John H. Johnson and the affluent Dr. Theodore Lawless too.[93]

Earlier that year Barnett and Etta Moten had been part of the vice president's delegation that traveled to Accra to witness the historic moment when Ghana attained independence. Along for the ride was Congressman Diggs and, said Barnett, a "separate plane carrying 30 newspaper, radio and television people."[94] There Barnett and Nixon bonded: the ANP chief was pleased with the latter's "hand shakes" and his "ready smile"; "Mrs. Barnett is a sincere admirer of Mrs. Nixon,"[95] Barnett observed gratuitously.

Barnett's alleged "intimate" tie to Prime Minister Nkrumah also was conveyed by the publisher himself to Vice President Nixon. Nixon may have known that in 1956 Barnett congratulated his "dear friend" Kwame Nkrumah on his appearance on U.S. television. "[T]here was a tremendous audience," he said with enthusiasm, "perhaps 30 or 40 million." He delicately complimented him by telling him "you are far better looking than the shots revealed."[96]

He reminded the U.S. leader that at a Pan-African gathering in Accra that took place months after Ghana's independence, Premier Nikita Khrushchev in Moscow sent a "personal cable of three pages," and Chou en-Lai of China "had sent a two page wire," but "only the West was silent." Barnett also said, "I conferred with him two or three times," referring to the prime minister, and mentioned in passing that Etta Moten "had the opportunity of cultivating Mrs. Nkrumah."[97]

This was a gathering attended by Shirley Graham DuBois and others usually marginalized. Vice President Nixon gave thanks to "Dear Claude" for his apparent aid in influencing Nkrumah to do a "most statesmanlike job of preventing extremism from taking over" at this gathering. "It was a pleasure to have you say that my message was of some help in this respect," he said feelingly. "It was the efforts of such able 'ambassadors' as yourself and Mrs. Barnett who provided the really effective support to the task of proving that our policies in no way run counter to the legitimate aspirations of the peoples of Africa."[98]

His familiarity with Nixon may have compromised him with many Africans while an emerging cadre of black nationalists in Harlem were upset with Accra's alleged ties to Communists, which by implication ensnared Barnett in this uncomfortable company.[99]

Undeterred, Barnett sought to convert his ties to Accra into lucrative contracts for himself and his allies. His importance had zoomed in the region, not only because of his relationship with Nkrumah and his Liberian connections but, while calling himself familiarly "Claude," he told the prime minister that he "delivered your note to President Touré" in neighboring Guinea-Conakry.[100]

The rise of anticolonialism helped to pull Barnett to the left a bit or, perhaps, express his lack of appreciation for the colonial powers, whose economic interests he was now challenging. "France owns more of the African continent than any other foreign power," he declared accusingly, while hailing the "brilliant leadership of 36 year old Sekou Toure," whose sterling example illustrated that the "American Negro suddenly is compelled to realize that his fate and that of his 19,000,000 brothers in French West Africa are inevitably and inextricably bound."[101]

Barnett pointed Prime Minister Nkrumah to a "prominent firm of attorneys in Washington" who could represent Accra's interests for a handsome fee; this firm, he said, was "associated" with "our mutual friend, Dr. Horace Mann Bond." Barnett also thought he could assume the lucrative role of middleman in the pending construction of the Volta Dam, a major Ghanaian project.[102]

It was the starry-eyed Bond, dazed by the opportunities opening in independent Africa, who told Barnett that his proposed investments "ought to make someone a lot of money."[103] At this juncture Bond was "involved in the African American Corporation that with Swedish assistance has been exploring" Liberia along the eastern frontier with Guinea. This was of "great strategic and economic importance," he insisted. As if these African nations were still colonies, he "proposed [a] Ghana-Guinea federation," albeit "retained within the U.S. orbit" because "it would be a major defeat, perhaps fatal, if Guinea fell into Communist hands," a distinct possibility. It is revealing that Bond took the time to deny that he was a "complete crackpot" in asserting such claims. He went on to "guarantee the ready cooperation of the men who now dominate the African countries I have mentioned—Ghana, Guinea, Liberia, Nigeria" and threw in for sweeteners the ability to attract the dedicated attention of the "Southern delegation" in the U.S. Congress.[104]

Barnett was not persuaded by Bond's words, for he accused his friend of a "flight into the realm of fantasy," though he did note that the prospect of a cornucopia of riches opening in independent Africa was not deluding Bond alone. Also part of this budding group was W. Arthur Lewis of St. Lucia, soon to be knighted, who entertained Barnett's son-in-law with cocktails and whose hasty departure from Accra, due to what the ANP leader called "his disagreement with the administration in Ghana over the importance of Volta," was an early sign of frostier relations with the North Atlantic bloc.[105]

Bond also had joined with Barnett and others in what was called "the Ghanus Corporation." The "immediate problem," Barnett was told, was "to obtain from the Ghana government an arrangement, along the lines of an option, which we can use in contacting the aluminum interests."[106]

In short, Barnett was not providing disinterested advice to Accra, in the past pattern of the now defunct Council on African Affairs, but was enmeshed in what seemed to be a conflict of interest. What Barnett told the prime minister was the breezy "I have a good personal friend in a high place, who also has a friendly interest in Ghana" and "they feel the dam proposal to be too big for a young, small country."[107] Nkrumah in reply was blunt: "[T]here is no real alternative [to] the Volta River Project."[108] R. M. Akwei in Ghana's U.S. legation echoed Accra when he said with similar bluntness that his government was "not able to grant the option requested."[109]

Barnett did not relent, instructing the prime minister about his thirteen years in a "consultation capacity as special assistant to the U.S. Secretary of Agriculture. As such," he was in "close contact" with those in the corridors of power in Washington and knew better than most that Ghana should seek aid "not through a government agency"; the "best way"[110] was via private interests, where his own financial interests rested comfortably.

Cultivating the prime minister further, he shared his distaste for Robert Ruark, who wrote popular novels lauding colonialism in Kenya. "I have always despised his writing on Africa," Barnett said seethingly; he was "the darling of the White Settlers of Kenya." He solicited a condemnation of the novelist from Nkrumah before reconsidering as he wondered whether it was "within good taste for the head of a country to express his full opinion."[111]

Barnett's attempt at intimacy with the Ghanaian leader went a step too far when he began making inquiries about his new bride: "[F]olk want to know," said the ANP founder, "whether she is beautiful" and "how a man who is idolized by all the women in his nation dare go outside to claim a consort,"[112] a reference to her Egyptian origins. Nkrumah, Barnett was told chillily by the prime minister's spokesman, "regards his marriage as a very private affair."[113]

The erstwhile educator Horace Mann Bond was not as tentative about his views; he was "beginning to feel like a commuter to New York and [a] Habitué of Wall Street." It was not only the Ghana mission but "our Liberian iron ore project" too; as for the latter, he emphasized, it was *almost* in the bag and in a big way." Just as Barnett leveraged his role in the ANP for private gain in Africa, Bond confessed that he was doing the same in his capacity as "President of the American Society for African Culture."[114] Even so, Bond was "willing to yield" to Barnett half his prospective share of Ghana investments, since the publisher was on such "very intimate grounds with Nkrumah" and was better positioned to deliver results as a consequence.[115] The journalist Marguerite Cartwright echoed this view when she told Barnett directly that after speaking to the prime minister in Accra she found that he and "all of the Africans hold you in such high esteem."[116] Moreover, to Barnett's advantage, George Padmore, one of Nkrumah's closest advisers, found Etta Moten to be utterly charming.[117]

Barnett had other influential backers. The influential Washington lobbyist with whom the two Negroes were associated—Arthur Condon—warned the U.S. envoy in Accra that "the Soviets have been emphasizing their interest in producing and marketing aluminum" and simultaneously were "the gravest possible menace to the very existence of Cuba"; thus, he had little hesitation in pushing for the "Barnett-Bond group" to gain influence in Ghana.[118]

Former U.S. Senator James Duff also was part of the "Bond-Barnett group," and he told the prime minister directly that "active political support for the Volta River Project among Americans of African descent would have the political effect" desired and be a "persuasive factor in Washington political circles."[119]

Richard Jones, the U.S. ambassador in Liberia, told "Claude" about the "interesting discussion" he held with the prime minister "about you. . . . I told him you were the man," and thus Barnett had reason to believe that his mission would reach fruition.[120] He also found the time to acquaint Accra with "our son-in-law Alvis Lee Tinnin," who worked for "Olin Mathieson, the big chemical concern" involved in "bauxite production in Guinea." His daughter and son-in-law were more than willing to move to Africa in pursuit of these ventures, and he prayed that "adverse feeling" toward Washington would not "affect us."[121] Rarely neglecting the interests of his family, when he contacted Trevor Shaw in the Congo seeking information, Barnett did not hesitate to remind him that his son-in-law had "completed work for his doctorate in French at Yale" and would "be in Leopoldville . . . this summer" in search of opportunities.[122]

Thus, he continued to remain in touch with Nixon after he left office, even proffering political advice to this man he deemed to be a "dear friend."[123] "I keep faith with people like Etta and yourself," Nixon assured soothingly, "and with my own conscience."[124]

Despite the flap over the Volta River Project, African Americans invested profitably in Ghana.[125] And Barnett continued to be a facilitator of this process, one example being the reception he hosted that was attended by hundreds of the best and brightest in Chicago at the Hotel Sheraton in honor of Ghana's Chief Justice.[126] Later Barnett was the master of ceremonies at yet another bash for Nkrumah, who was visiting a plush Chicago hotel. Etta Moten sang and Mayor Richard Daley gave the dignitary a medallion of appreciation as the capacity audience applauded loudly. Nkrumah gave hope to African Americans when he proclaimed that Africans would not be "liberated [and] free . . . until self-respect and honor are accorded men of color everywhere."[127]

*   *   *

By 1957 Barnett was just back from North Africa, as well, and was enthused to learn that the "big oil companies are drilling in Libya" and in Sudan "they grow the long staple cotton," something he learned in conferring with "the Vice Minister of Foreign Affairs. . . . I was introduced to him at the entrance to the Prime Minister's reception in Khartoum." He wanted to link him with Sam Bledsoe, a public-relations consultant and Barnett crony and former lobbyist for the U.S.'s Cotton Council.[128]

While in Sudan he enjoyed a "delightful party in the gardens at Khartoum," featuring "perfect weather, the delightful dinner, the lovely surroundings before the palace."[129] And while in Libya he brought back an expensive tray for President

Eisenhower that he placed in his hands during a festive occasion,[130] an occasion that brought him to a site where he was becoming a fixture: the White House.[131] The craftsman Feuzi Ness was "one of the finest brass workers in the Middle East"; it was he, said Barnett, who made this artwork "so large and so delicate." Barnett, in limning that Ness's "admiration for President Eisenhower" was "tremendous," advised "proper exploitation of this gift throughout the Middle East and Africa, as well as South America and perhaps some of Europe."[132]

Barnett had been stunned when he visited his Tripoli shop and Ness "suddenly launched into a panegyric of praise of President Eisenhower."[133] Barnett continued the festival of love when he told the president's aide that "it was great being in the White House and chatting with the President." His up-close look convinced him "his photos do not do him justice."[134]

Barnett also was convinced that his photo opportunity with the president "impressed folk back" in Libya. "It is probably the first time," he said enthusiastically, "they ever saw a President of the United States shaking hands with one of his brown fellow citizens." He requested a photo "autographed by the President, for hanging on my wall,"[135] which doubtlessly would impress visitors, enhancing his social and political capital.

While in North Africa, Barnett spent time with the couple he referred to as "Dr. and Mrs. J. Max Bond." There Barnett found himself in a "hotbed of anti-French demonstrations, especially as I sat in a large Libyan poolroom and tavern with an Arab friend of mine, the craftsman who made the wonderful tray" that so delighted the president. But as Barnett and the Libyan craftsman "sat drinking tea with peanuts," a "tipsy Arab approached me" and "began a tirade against France, NATO and white people. As about 40 or 50 Arabs gathered around us he made the most vehement speech against white people I have ever heard in my life."[136]

Apparently he did not share with these Africans the exchange he had with Hassen J. Abraham, an Islamic leader from South Bend after the latter expressed distaste for unfairness to Moslems in Palestine, Algeria, and elsewhere. "The world wide tinge of unappreciation [*sic*] for people who are not what our Caucasian friends call 'white,'" seemed to be growing. Naturally, Barnett assured, "this organization has not been guilty."[137]

While in northern Africa, apparently he did not see Elsie Austin, billed by the ANP as "the first woman of color to graduate from the University of Cincinnati's College of Law" and besides, "charming . . . lovely . . . vivacious." She had traveled to Haifa and Kampala in her capacity as a member of the Baha'i faith,[138] a religion that originated in Persia in the mid-nineteenth century.[139] Their leadership had contacted Barnett about her while she was residing in Tangier and he was told do not "refer to her work or her present interests and not to her Baha'i interests" because of possible religious persecution.[140]

One did not have to be a cynic to think that when the ANP reported on the death sentence handed out to three members of the Baha'i faith,[141] it was possible that it could lead to a business opportunity in North Africa—perhaps a public-relations contract to improve their image?—especially when it was reported that in calling for a "spiritual conquest of the entire African continent by the Baha'is," a special role was carved out for the "American Negro Baha'i" designated to "carry [the] 'faith' to Brothers in Distant Africa."[142]

Ironically, as Barnett's investment opportunities were expanding, the prospects for the crown jewel of his kingdom—the ANP—were contracting.

CHAPTER 10

Pan-Africanism Is the News

By 1961 Alice Dunnigan received an offer to join the staff of Vice President Lyndon B. Johnson. "My salary for one day," she mused, "would equal that which ANP pays for one week." It was "quite tempting."[1] By the end of the year, she had departed the agency and was working for the newly installed President's Committee on Equal Employment Opportunity,[2] a body that concretized the assumed new consensus on racial equality, a consensus that happened to open a severe gash in the flesh of the ANP. Like a troubled couple on the verge of divorce, Dunnigan could not resist bringing up old slights as she exited. She wailed still about "not being able to attend the historic Bandung conference" and "being deprived" of joining Nixon on his Africa tour.[3]

This sad twist of events may not have been foreseeable at the highest levels of ANP because by early 1960 the agency announced an expansion, a news service "specially designed for African papers." Their dispatches, it was said immodestly but not inaccurately, were "used by practically all Negro publications" in the United States and "more than 300 newspapers and magazines on the African continent, several of them with circulations of 50,000 or more," and there was an urgent demand for ANP's reports in a decolonizing Africa. During his extensive travels in Africa, Barnett found "little intercommunication between African states and [noticed] that all are interested in news about the Negro in the United States," and the ANP was determined to solve this conundrum. Like its domestic counterpart, the dispatches of the African service were mimeographed and dispatched by air mail from Chicago weekly.[4]

It was not just Barnett who was trying to take advantage of decolonization. A competing Negro publisher, Louis E. Martin, traveled to Nigeria in 1960 during the year of independence on assignment on behalf of Premier Obafemi Awolowo of western Nigeria tasked to establish the first commercial and educational television network services—said the ANP—in Africa. In a direct challenge to its neighborhood competitor, Martin also hoped to expand the base of the foreign news service of the *Chicago Defender*.[5]

The ANP did not shrink from this competition. Barnett had higher goals in mind than just market share and profit-making (though the two were rarely distant from his calculations). The purpose was "establishing a bridgehead of understanding and cooperation between Africans and people of African descent in the United States." He and his spouse had just joined John H. Johnson to hold a lunch for Ghana's envoy, where he recollected that "when Etta and I went to Ghana, Nigeria and Tunisia" recently, "it was my 8th trip ever" to the continent; thus, said the collector, "our art items have grown," necessitating donation of "a collection to Tuskegee."[6]

Doing good and doing well went hand in hand for Barnett and Moten. "Our collection has grown in size and I think in quality," he said in 1963. His last addition was "one of the most beautifully carved tusks I have seen and we acquired two paintings, all in the Congo, which were excellent indeed."[7]

By 1963 the agency was said to serve "150 newspapers and publications in the West Indies and Africa in both English and French" with new natty offices at 918 F Street NW in Washington, D.C.[8] Actually, this number may be an underestimate because just as the agency often filched from Reuters, African periodicals did the same to the ANP.[9]

There was a real hunger for the uniqueness of ANP dispatches filed by a skilled crew of writers, including David Talbot in Addis Ababa. Born in British Guiana, he held degrees from New York University; he formerly edited the *Ethiopia Herald* and was known to be close to His Imperial Majesty Haile Selassie.[10] At the triumphal inaugural meeting of independent African nations in Addis Ababa in 1963, the ANP announced that William Payne also would be their correspondent there; he was one of a number of ANP reporters covering the sprawling continent.[11]

African Americans were standing in line, seeking an opportunity to work for the ANP in Africa. Akbar Muhammad, the son of Elijah Muhammad of the Chicago-based Nation of Islam, told Barnett from his residence in Cairo of his "readiness to be an ANP correspondent here."[12]

Barnett worked out an entente with Albert Bolela, director of information in what became the Democratic Republic of the Congo.[13] Then Barnett turned to that nation's neighbor across the Congo River, telling Sylvain Bemba of the Congo Information Agency in Brazzaville that the ANP was "interested" in having him serve the ANP. "We have been to Brazzaville," he said, "and had the privilege of interviewing President Fulbert Youlou."[14]

Due north in Mali, the authorities expressed interest in subscribing to ANP services.[15] Still, with all these attainments, a Togolese official remonstrated with Barnett because the latter's "World News Service" was lacking in the "quality of the French language" dispatches, seemingly "written by someone whose mother tongue is English or who, at all costs, thinks in English."[16]

Still, there was an appetite in Africa for what the agency offered. In 1962 the ANP circulated an article on boxer Joe Louis to almost two hundred papers on the continent. "They are avid on sports" said Barnett. With his usual network-ing skills, Barnett helped to spark an avid interest in Africa in sports that was to benefit U.S. campuses in coming decades.[17]

But it did not take long for the mainstream press to realize that the ANP was sitting on a journalistic goldmine with its direct pipeline to one of the biggest stories of the decade, if not the century: decolonization and how it intersected with the battle against Jim Crow. As early as 1959, one of the agency's chief clients, P. B. Young of the *Norfolk Journal & Guide,* chose to discontinue his subscription to the ANP and switched to United Press International. "There was a time," he explained to a disappointed Barnett, "when a wire service was of little use to a Negro newspaper. Today, however, they pick up everything and consider news concerning the activities of the Negro race a *must* apparently."[18]

Thus, Charlayne Hunter was filing stories for ANP in 1962[19]—but soon was writ-ing for the *New York Times* and the *New Yorker.* Such was the case for C. Gerald Fraser, who too wound up at the *Times* but began his career telling ANP readers about tragic events in Rwanda and Burundi, writing in 1964 that "almost unno-ticed are the bloody convulsions . . . where Africans are killing Africans by the thousands."[20]

Barnett was being squeezed from another angle too. He had developed a side-line in public relations, but that sphere was being invaded also. It was in 1959 that Barnett found out that a mainstream "public relations firm . . . evidently stumbled upon the fact that there is profit in the Negro field."[21] This was in the context of promotion of an early antiapartheid film, "Come Back Africa," which was to be shown at the United Nations with the assistance of the megastar Harry Belafonte, who too was seeking to "invade our field."[22]

Barnett was in an advance wave of African Americans descending upon Africa seeking to take advantage of the perceived gold rush delivered by decoloniza-tion. Barnett frankly told a fellow Chicago entrepreneur, a purveyor of hair-care products to Negroes, in a 1962 exchange about "considering invading Africa in a big way with your products" and would "be glad to talk" about opening doors.[23] For her part, Etta Moten was touting "Africa's 'Fashion for Freedom,'" pushing a trend that would sweep the United States in coming years. "Hand woven Kente" cloth met her glowing approval,[24] as she was in the vanguard of a fashion trend with political implications that assumed increasing significance in coming years.

It seemed like it was the best of times. "You should hurry with your memoirs," Barnett was told, because "publishers are reaching for anything they can get these days" in this unwinding era of "integration." "They'll buy anything grammatical these days. Horace Cayton has a publisher for his autobiography," said P. L. Prattis of a Chicago intellectual of much lesser rank than Barnett.[25]

But by 1964 Barnett was funereal. It "pains us," he told David Talbot, that he could no longer be paid. "We have had to suspend the World News Service," he announced to his Addis correspondent in March 1964.[26] "To admit that you worked yourself out of a job is not easy," he confessed, "even though that has been our goal from the start" (though rarely articulated). "The Negro newspaper has done a magnificent job for the Race," which was generally true. He said in brutal recognition of the magic of the marketplace, "only the superior organs can survive" and now "the best trained craftsmen are being absorbed by daily newspapers. The dailies," he said ruefully, "are using more and more news about Negroes, Africans and Negro causes" and, thus, the agency would cease operations by 15 July.[27]

There was a temporary burst of energy by the ANP, but by December 1964 Robeson—an avid consumer of their dispatches—was told that Barnett had abandoned ship and the ANP was "now headquartered in New York City under new management,"[28] which was a simple prelude to extinction. The agency had been purchased by a representative of Barnett's rival, Alfred Duckett, a columnist with the *Chicago Defender*, who also was closely associated with Nelson Rockefeller, giving false hope that the ANP would survive.[29]

                                    *   *   *

Even without the defection of his star staffer, Dunnigan, Barnett had reason to believe that by 1961 the end was nigh for his prized creation, the ANP. For it was during that year that the Ghana News Agency (GNA) was beginning to cut into what ANP thought would be its new bonanza on a newly independent continent. The GNA was—at least in a de facto sense—sworn to allegiance to Accra, just as Reuters and BBC were slanted toward London and Agence France Presse leaned toward Paris and Associated Press and United Press International reflected Washington; the ANP straddled a mushy middle in that it was comfortable with leaders in Accra and Conakry who increasingly were viewed in Washington as insufficiently anticommunist, while many on the continent felt the exact opposite.[30]

As for the latter, militant Africans would have been intrigued to read Barnett's 1962 message to Edward R. Murrow, then leading the United States Information Agency, viewed on the continent widely as Washington's official propaganda arm. "Please know," Barnett said, "that [the ANP] will be always at your service. It seems especially important that [we] maintain close relationship with USIA since . . . we also serve with news our overseas release to more than 100 African newspapers and leaders."[31]

Decolonization, a natural corollary of the emerging ideology of "integration," also ensured that ANP's expiration date would fast approach. P. L. Prattis dolefully admitted what was not precisely true: "neither of us could have foreseen," he said, that "something called integration was going to get the best of us."[32]

But, as often happens, his hindsight was misleading; the fact that integration could imperil certain Negro institutions was utterly foreseeable. Moreover, it was not as if all nonblack elites welcomed integration in a manner that would have been helpful to its black proponents. In what was to become an ongoing pattern, in 1964 the NAACP chose to picket the major newspaper in Cleveland after the group had been condemned in editorials for their views in favor of school desegregation and their critique of banking practices.[33] The ANP and its allies were in a vise: caught up in a historical trend toward integration they did not fully understand while battling those more powerful who resisted the trend. That the ANP had deserted Robeson and his allies in their time of need also left Barnett and his allies dangerously exposed when pressure against the latter was ratcheted up.

Another viselike pressure that the ANP found hard to resist was the other major force of that conflicted era: anticommunism. Barnett's friend and business partner, the attorney Earl Dickerson, was friendly to those of the left. Yet Governor Otto Kerner of Illinois blocked a government appointment for him, dropping the innuendo that he was tied to Communists because Dickerson had known Eslanda Robeson at the University of Illinois and befriended the Negro Communist leader Claude Lightfoot "when he was a young boy in the streets of Chicago."[34]

Unlike the past, the Negro press was now reluctant to hire talented writers with radical associations. "What do you know about Ishmael Flory?" asked Prattis. "I am tempted to have him do some articles for us. He writes well and is quite knowledgeable" and was "very smart" but, alas, had "many Communist associations" at a time when these "folk here are scared like hell of Commies."[35] A conservative leader in 1963 warned the ANP to steer clear of *Freedomways,* a journal that styled itself as striding in Robeson's large footsteps.[36]

Seemingly caught in a spider's web of anti–Jim Crow contradictions, ANP thrashed about with one columnist arguing frankly, "Why I like the ghetto." He offered a "frank defense of living in an all-Negro neighborhood as opposed to an integrated community," but this aspiration was not congruent with the negative connotation generally associated with "ghetto," suggestive of the theoretical and practical snares in which the agency found itself.[37]

As this high drama was unfolding, Barnett continued to live the good life in Chicago, making it difficult to grasp the far-reaching changes just over the horizon. "When you step into the living room of the Barnetts' residence," said an impressed observer, "you will find yourself standing on a luxurious rug from Morocco," while "near the chair on which you sit" rested "an elephant table from Ghana"; the "brass chandelier is from Tunis." Wherever one wandered— "bedroom, bathroom, kitchen and even in the corridors," there were artifacts from Africa, including a marvelous collection of "artistic carvings in ivory and wood, bronze, metal and leather work, woven cloths and rugs, even paintings."

Africa had been good to and for Barnett, even as his agency was going down the drain.[38]

*   *   *

Barnett and the ANP did bring added attention to independent Africa, which brought both into closer touch with a steady stream of African American migrants to the continent. A dentist couple from Virginia—Dr. Sarah Lee and Dr. Robert Lee—arrived in Ghana in 1956. "All during our college days," she said, "Dr. Lee and I were surrounded by native African students" and this led to their being "identified with African activists,"[39] an association they continued during their lengthy exile. Robert had attended school with Kwame Nkrumah in Pennsylvania.[40]

Why Africans and African Americans were becoming ever closer was suggested when Howard University's Mordecai Johnson was invited to a NATO congress and announced to rippling chuckles that he thought he was invited "because I am one of those under-developed peoples": "my father was a slave" and "my mother was born in slavery."[41] This was part of a heightened desegregation of the U.S. State Department, exemplified when this bureaucracy recruited O. Rudolph Aggrey of North Carolina, whose roots were in Ghana and who graduated from Hampton in 1946, an event extolled by the ANP.[42]

U.S. General Mark Clark, one of the nation's highest-ranking military men, was not shy in saying why he thought Africans should be cultivated. These nations were destined, along with Asia, to dominate the United States through the United Nations: "I foresee in the future a time when the balance of power [tilts] against the United States,"[43] he predicted soberly. Washington's concern about Africa's direction was ratified further when Barnett met with a top State Department official, Loy Henderson, about increasing Negro personnel—"particularly in Africa," in the ANP's words.[44] Influencing the selection of personnel as a substitute for influencing policy became the new mantra of the new era of integration. This material change had a class bias in that influencing the selection of personnel inexorably empowered a middle class while influencing policy tended to benefit the poor and working class of African descent.

The worry about Communist influence also caused Washington to open its doors wider to a flood of incoming students from Africa. At Fisk University, four African students and one from the Caribbean gave an international shading to the list of top-ranking students during the 1961–62 academic year.[45] At Tuskegee, which challenged Fisk in attracting foreign students, there were about fifty matriculating in 1961, including eight from Kenya.[46] White House aide Brooks Hays lauded Hampton Institute of Virginia for the role it played in preventing "Communists from getting a foothold in West Africa," referring specifically to their efforts in Sierra Leone, Nigeria, and Liberia—though not Ghana.[47] Hampton also brought African students, many of whom were putative or actual royalty, to their campus to be "educated," particularly in the pivotal year of 1963 when Kenya arrived at independence.[48]

"There are about 200 African students studying" in Chicago, said an ANP staffer. "They spend from two to six years here," said Enoch Waters in 1963. They depart with the "impression that Negroes are inhospitable, unconcerned and unfriendly." Thus, he asked, "will you accept an African student as a dinner guest? Will you entertain an African student for a weekend?" This query was made to Richard Durham of the journal of the then ascending Nation of Islam. Actually, despite this affiliation, Durham also was firmly in the grasp of the left, meaning that this invitation would not necessarily serve anticommunist purposes.[49] (Ironically, Durham's post illustrated why the Nation of Islam's periodical was soon to garner readers fleeing the mainstream Negro press, not least because *Muhammad Speaks* was more inclined to hire writers of the left, as they were being scorned by the mainstream.) A notable student courted by the ANP was Bonito Olympio, son of Togo's founder, who passed through Chicago in 1962; his brother Elipidio studied architecture at Princeton.[50]

Still, this overture to Durham was part of a burgeoning relationship between Africans and African Americans impelled by the kind of Pan-Africanism that the ANP had long advocated. The relationship was further solidified when the Algerian musician Khalil Nimini Ben Bezaleel performed in a benefit for the now-teetering *California Eagle*, which had long since passed from the control of the left-leaning Charlotta Bass. The concert, movingly titled "Songs of the Blacks," found Ben Bezaleel performing in English, Arabic, French, English, Swahili, and Spanish. The artist had a Sudanese mother and was honored for his distinguished service during the world war as a fighter for the Free French.[51]

Monrovia continued to be a regional headquarters of sorts for Barnett. By early 1960 it was reported that he was part of a huge delegation of African Americans dispatched to the inauguration of William Tubman as president of Liberia, accompanied by General Benjamin O. Davis, journalist Marguerite Cartwright, Republican Party official Val Washington, Congressman Charles Diggs, and scores more.[52]

It seemed that a turning point in the centuries-long journey of Africans and African Americans had zoomed to a new zenith when Barnett and other delegates jetted to Liberia on a chartered plane that included Lensdell K. Christie, president of the Liberia Mining Corporation.[53] This was the publisher's fifth trip to Africa in recent years but surely one of the most elaborate as four DC-7 jets landed in West Africa. Tubman symbolized this new relationship in that he was a descendant of the early settlers who had roots in Augusta, Georgia: his mother migrated to Liberia in 1872 and his spouse, the former Antoinette Padmore, carried a surname that bespoke a certain kind of Pan-African royalty.[54] Barnett's presence signaled that he had become a crucial intermediary between Washington and Africa. This position was solidified when the mayor of Dakar, Senegal, arrived in Chicago and it was Barnett who took him and his wife down to meet Mayor Richard Daley.[55]

Gordon Hancock of the ANP may not have had this eminent delegation in mind when he railed against the "Negro Emissary Movement," Washington's practice of tabbing Negroes to travel abroad and repair the nation's image battered by repetitive stories about Jim Crow. This was another turnabout from the time when Negroes begged to get visas and were greeted with stony silence from a State Department that turned a deaf ear to their urgent appeals. Hancock pooh-poohed the idea that these repairers would have any impact because the torrent of headlines from places like Little Rock spoke louder than the messages delivered by self-interested envoys. These headlines were "Negro Exhibit Number One," he argued, which inevitably made for ineffective emissaries. "To have the Negro abroad building up and the Negro-phobes at home tearing down, strikes me as getting nowhere," he scoffed.[56]

Continuing along the path trod by Hancock, the ANP reported that "Communism's evangelists are pouring accounts" of Jim Crow into the global mass media stream. The message? "Negroes are being treated worse than dogs."[57] The "airwaves of [the] world," said the ANP, were deluged with "propaganda about American Negroes" then provided chapter and verse from Moscow and elsewhere.[58] Hancock had the temerity to trump the card often played against Negro dissidents by asking grumpily, "did the Communists inspire the Nat Turner [slave] rebellion"? In fact, he said, "a long time before Lenin appeared on the scene in Russia the Negro was full of unrest."[59]

The ANP's thrust in Africa, alas, was colored inevitably by the interests of those who controlled the agency. Etta Moten was invited to Israel as a guest of the government at an International Seminar for Socialist Youth Leaders. (This group included, for example, German Social Democrats and French Socialists, though anticommunist critics in the United States might have thought otherwise.) An official told her that "African countries have a new upsurge of confidence in Israel," because this country, it was said, "is the 'only white country they feel they can really trust.'"[60] Moten was friendly with Golda Meir, the Milwaukeean who became Israel's prime minister. At one point in 1964 the two women were stopped, recalled Moten, at the Rhodesian border while traveling together. "She was the heroine of the occasion," said the performer. "When they ordered 'all blacks out of the bus,' she said, 'We all get out.'" Her affection for the Israeli leader was matched by her warmth toward Meir's compatriots in that there were "probably no audiences like the Israelis, except perhaps the Russians."[61]

This evaluation of Israel as a trustworthy "white" nation implicitly slapped Moten's homeland, a move made more pointedly by a man who was to be regarded as one of the leading African-American novelists, John A. Williams. In Barcelona Williams interviewed an African from a European colony for the ANP who found it ironic that the dictatorship in power in Madrid was more progressive toward blacks in Spain than the "democracy" of the United States was toward its darker citizens.[62]

* * *

In 1961 the ANP's Waters took a four-month tour of twenty-two African nations, part of a process wherein he had spent six of the fifteen months leading up to 1962 in Africa, for a grand total of twenty-eight countries visited as part of an ANP scouting mission.[63] By early 1964 he was enjoying a bon voyage, headed to Kampala "to serve as a technical advisor for a new African paper," said the invitation to his party.[64]

This tall, dark-skinned man with a receding hairline, a veteran of twenty-eight years in Chicago journalism[65] headed to Uganda, seeking to launch a new journal. "I have been inundated by young men wanting to be reporters," he informed Barnett, "some of whom can't speak English. There are no trained or experienced African journalists here,"[66] which created a Pan-African opportunity for the ANP.

Soon he was to be found in Addis Ababa, where he encountered another aspect of how and why the ANP changed. There he met with Homer Smith—otherwise known as Chatwood Hall—the agency's former correspondent in the Soviet Union, now serving as the editor of an English-Amharic magazine and residing comfortably with what Waters termed his "friendly Russian wife and two children."[67] The market for pro-Moscow dispatches for the ANP had dissipated while the market for reports from an emerging Africa was ascending. Smith and Waters were part of a regular trickle of African Americans to a newly independent Africa, exemplifying the Pan-Africanism that the ANP embodied just as it was entering desuetude.[68]

An emblem of this tendency arrived in 1963 when William Leo Hansberry was named dean and director of the institute bearing his name at a leading Nigerian university. One of his students at Howard University in Washington, D.C., in 1927 had been a tall, thin African youth named Nnamdi Azikiwe, who at this point was leading this most populous of African nations.[69] Further solidifying the Pan-African promise was the awarding of a gold medal and $10,000 to Professor Hansberry from the Ethiopian government.[70]

Hansberry, who had close ties to Chicago, may well have suspected that Barnett had a role in this honor because earlier the ANP chief had arranged a "luncheon for the Crown Prince of Ethiopia" hosted by Chicago's mayor. "I happened to be sitting with a group representing some of the larger industries," said Barnett, including U.S. Steel and International Harvester, who had an interest in cultivating ties with what may have been independent Africa's most important nation.[71] The deft Barnett knew that it was Ethiopia that was the "only African country to participate actively" in the war in Korea, having "furnished several contingents" and, thus, merited special attention.[72]

If Waters's experience was a guide, these migrants were greeted with open arms. For in Nairobi Waters spoke of how well he was being treated when it was found out that he was African American (the same held true in Mogadishu). The former Chicagoan was present at a rally of fifteen thousand in Kenya designed to raise funds for an airlift of African students; he said that white Americans and Europeans were treated differently because they assumed an air of superiority toward Africans.[73] Similarly, ANP readers were informed that "U.S. Negroes are the 'most preferred' foreigners in Africa,"[74] a vindication of ANP's Pan-Africanism even as the agency was passing into history.

This supposed favoritism toward African Americans did not extend to their nation of origin. Uganda's Milton Obote denounced the United States at the founding meeting of the Organization of African Unity, an event that unfolded as sickening scenes of assaults on protesting children in Alabama deluged the airwaves. He was appalled by the "Iron Curtain" in Birmingham and the horrific sight of "snarling dogs [set] upon our kith and kin." Africa's "freedom and independence would be a mere sham," he charged furiously, "if our black brethren elsewhere in Africa and the United States still remain in political, social and economic bondage." This was a blockbuster, said the ANP accurately, which reflected a wider sentiment in Addis Ababa that equated apartheid and Jim Crow. "You see," said African delegates to the U.S. visitors, "we have not forgotten you."[75] African leaders warned menacingly that U.S. bases in Africa—including those in strategically sited Libya—would be threatened unless this oppression ceased forthwith.[76] "World reaction," said the ANP properly, played a "big role in forcing [Washington] to move decisively on civil rights." Much of the "impetus has been provided by the reaction of the world outside the American borders," as in East Berlin, Paris, Vienna—and Addis.[77]

It was the ANP, virtually alone at this pivotal gathering in Ethiopia, who noticed the large number of U.S. Negroes who were present. There was Shirley Graham DuBois, who was part of the Ghanaian delegation, and William Alexander of New York, who filmed the gathering for the Ethiopian government and had been filming regularly for the Liberian authorities. There was Akbar Muhammad, a fluent speaker of Arabic, a skill that proved instrumental when this son of Chicago lobbied actively with delegates for a stronger resolution on Jim Crow. William Gardner Smith of Philadelphia was there too, though he was representing Agence France Presse of Paris, which termed itself the "world's largest news agency." Of course, he was fluent in French, which too was useful when lobbying delegates. Another U.S. Negro, Calvin Raullerson, who eventually was to serve the U.S. faithfully as an administrator with the Peace Corps, arrived with the Nigerian delegation, and Edward Welch jetted in from Kampala with the delegation of the International Confederation of Free Trade Unions. Charles Howard of the *Afro-American* was there, as was Sidney Williams of Chicago, an activist who had known Barnett for years.[78]

Even His Imperial Majesty of Ethiopia, sensitive to his relations with Washington, chose to provide an ANP correspondent with a rare and exclusive interview in which he echoed the inextricable linkage between colonialism and Jim Crow.[79]

The turnout was a vindication of Barnett's and the ANP's Pan-Africanism in that their presence guaranteed that the Organization of African Unity's anti–Jim Crow message would be both strengthened and transmitted widely, helping to ensure that this iniquitous system would soon erode decisively.

*   *   *

This contradictory pattern—punching Uncle Sam at times, then embracing the United States too—had characterized the ANP of late and was to do so until its final moment. When Soviet Premier Khrushchev was slated to visit the United States, the agency quoted a number of Negro war veterans who wanted the Communist leader to "talk to the Negroes" and ask how many were "registered voters" (a pitiful sum then because of state malfeasance) and how many high-level jobs they held too (also paltry). If he had visited Natchitoches, he should be sure to visit the city's entrance where stood a statue simultaneously lionizing and denigrating an ill-kempt African scratching his head with the inscription "to the Good Darky."[80] Let the Soviet leader visit Atlanta, commented Gordon Hancock with sarcasm, then "ask him what he thinks about segregation."[81]

Khrushchev hardly disappointed in castigating U.S. racism in words aimed at the African delegations at the United Nations.[82] He told the aghast diplomats that "they could not have gotten a New York hotel room without U.N. documents [and] could not be assured of getting service in restaurants," and asked pointedly, "is that not a disgrace for a civilized government."[83]

Moscow was blamed when pamphlets were circulated in Addis Ababa scorning the United States because of its maltreatment of African diplomats[84] and lynching of U.S. Negroes.[85] Of course, the devastatingly negative propaganda in Africa about the United States was not wholly a Moscow creation. What was the impact in Africa of violence targeting "Freedom Riders" or anti–Jim Crow riders on public transport, asked the ANP rhetorically? "NEGATIVE" was the loud message transmitted with emphasis from Lagos. "Americans are foolish to think," said a Nigerian organ, "that Africans appreciate being accorded any special privileges because they are not 'American Negroes.' . . . Africans resent this attitude on the part of U.S. whites."[86]

Senegalese visitors to Chicago, said the ANP, also resented special privileges accorded to them and denied to African Americans,[87] and Father Alexis Kagame of Ruanda-Burundi was among those who found Jim Crow in Boston distasteful.[88] Ambassador Angie Brooks of Liberia received no special privileges in Raleigh, North Carolina. To the contrary, she raised with the UN the issue of an eatery there that refused to serve her with her nephew, Joseph Outland, a student at Shaw University. This was in the midst of mass protests engineered by Shaw students.[89]

It is not surprising that more U.S. Negroes began to see a benefit in masquerading as Africans in order to escape the strictures of Jim Crow, giving a boost to Pan-Africanism and a growing identification with the continent. In what was becoming a now normative occurrence, John Norman Rhem, a twenty-six-year-old Negro from Philadelphia, began calling himself Sham Sud Deen and began to dress in lavish embroidered robes and turbans and traveled under the title of "Secretary General of Radio Free Africa" in Egypt. He charged up to $1000 for lectures to the unwitting.[90]

What needs to be considered more carefully is how Washington retreated from Jim Crow in order to placate visiting Africans, giving a boost to Pan-Africanism—and such masquerades.[91] By 1963 Washington was chagrined when Africans diplomats continued to endure difficulty in finding adequate housing and escaping bias generally, leading the State Department to back avidly an antidiscrimination housing law in the District of Columbia.[92]

Similarly, Barnett's ascending, now surpassing, rival, John H. Johnson of Chicago, visited Ivory Coast with Attorney General Robert F. Kennedy, where they found that Africans were "deeply concerned over the inhuman and intolerable conditions of the Negroes in the South."[93]

The ANP continually stressed overseas comments highly critical of U.S. racist praxis.[94] A Dutch journalist in Atlanta pleaded with the United States to change because, he cried, "the fate of Western Civilization depends upon the United States."[95] A Belgian tourist in Williamsburg, Virginia, found it "mystifying" when he was forced to relinquish his seat in the Negro section of a local bus. "We don't have that, even in the Congo," was his befuddled response.[96] A similar response came from a British student in Jackson, Mississippi, jailed after he sought to have a Negro accompany him to a concert performed there by the Royal Philharmonic Orchestra from London.[97]

In a copycat maneuver, Swedish soprano Birgit Nilsson refused to perform in Jackson because of Jim Crow arrangements. She was then emulated by baseball hero Stan Musial and the wildly popular television show *Bonanza*, which also refused to appear in this land of apartheid.[98] Nilsson may have heard that, just before her admirable act of disobedience, the black performer Sammy Davis Jr. was booed lustily at the Democratic National Convention in Los Angeles by Dixie delegates upset with his relationship with the Swedish actor May Britt; he collapsed in tears, said the ANP.[99]

Global pressure against the Magnolia State mounted when Dr. Ram Nachar Lolia of India, a leader of the Socialist Party and a parliamentarian, was turned away abruptly from a suburban Jackson restaurant, though he was wearing clothes that indicated his national origin. The State Department apologized, but the blow to the nation's Cold War prestige was harder to dismiss.[100]

An ANP reporter was present at the Soviet embassy when Premier Khrushchev met with William Clark, described as a Negro laborer from Newark, who "won national attention plus a Soviet scholarship for his 13 year old daughter" after writing Moscow about "discrimination in this country," including lynching, which he had "witnessed with his own eyes in Georgia, his native home." Also present was the U.S. Communist leader William Patterson.[101] Months later, John Benjamin Witt, a U.S. army deserter in Germany, fled to Czechoslovakia via Austria because of "racial prejudice," according to his spouse.[102] Gordon Hancock indirectly supported these exiles when, in the midst of the trial in Israel of Nazi war criminal Adolph Eichmann, he argued that "it could happen here,"[103] meaning the United States, meaning genocide against Negroes.

When the United Nations General Assembly passed a resolution in December 1960 on ending colonialism by a vote of 89–0 —with the United States abstaining—Dr. Zelma Watson George, a black woman, "created a sensation," said the ANP, when she "arose from her seat and applauded vigorously," an action interpreted widely as "indicating her disagreement" with Washington's vote.[104] Promptly, she was asked to resign from the U.S. delegation.[105]

Also suggesting that bringing more Negroes into the diplomatic corps might lead to an unanticipated problems was the decision by Edith Sampson to advocate admission of China into the United Nations, years before it became official policy.[106]

Mordecai Johnson, speaking at Howard University's 1960 graduation told the three thousand assembled that "not all Communists are white. . . . [T]here are about 650 million who are black and brown and yellow. . . . [Thus,] America has got to help the very people they despise, the black, the brown and the Chinese."[107] Chief Justice Earl Warren, said the ANP, found that the "first thing asked of him" during his trip to the Soviet Union concerned "the Negro Problem."[108] When W. E. B. DuBois spoke in Accra in 1960, receiving a standing ovation while proclaiming that socialism was the "panacea of the world's evils" and heaping praise on the Soviet Union and China, not only did the ANP report the event, but it was Barnett who reported it.[109]

As the ANP wound down, it was Barnett who often chose himself to do the reporting from and on Africa. In 1960 he wrote a lengthy three-part series on West Africa that included a one-hour interview with Modibo Keita, the founding father of independent Mali. A young Senegalese friend of the publisher married to an African American, Lovie Johnson of Chicago, served as interpreter. The African leader told him that this was the first opportunity to "express himself to the people of the United States" as he recollected that "at the beginning of the 19th century the American Negro was engaged in the fight for the liberation of the black man," including Malians, and thus it was "desirable" for "Africans and the Negroes from overseas [to] give each other a hand" in an expression of Pan-African solidarity.[110] It was Barnett who told cheering crowds in Nigeria that "full American citizenship" for African Americans would mean they would use their "growing political influence on behalf of the new emerging nations of Africa," validating Keita's viewpoint.[111]

It was Barnett who selected himself to confer with Colonel Joseph Mobutu, soon to be Congo's dictator for decades, who seized the opportunity to assail Communists vociferously. Mobutu granted Barnett and Moten a private interview.[112] Barnett then interviewed another opponent of Prime Minister Patrice Lumumba when he conferred with Joseph Kasavubu in Manhattan with his son-in-law, Alvis Tinnin, interpreting Kasavubu's French.[113]

Nevertheless, when Lumumba was murdered in early 1961, Barnett was among the first to raise his voice in stern protest.[114] He happened to be in town when Lumumba was detained. It was "not possible for us to see . . . Mr. Lumumba, whose house was surrounded by two different varieties of soldiers," who then murdered him.[115] It was through the ANP that U.S. readers discovered that the slain leader was expelled from a U.S. Methodist missionary school when he was twelve[116] and it was the ANP that provided maximum coverage to the raucous demonstrations in the United States of African students who blamed Washington for this assassination, just as they denied being "Communist inspired."[117]

The assassination of Lumumba should have been a sobering event for Barnett and his cohort, exposing the reality that the government they often served in Washington had interests inimical to those of a truly independent Africa. "I was aching to get to the Congo and to do some stories for you," said the Chicago academic St. Clair Drake to "Dear Claude." He cabled Ralph Bunche to that end, who directed him to the Congo Minister of External Affairs. Naïvely, Professor Drake "had thought that Ralph might have been able to cut the red tape, but I realized he was in a very difficult situation"[118]—but so were Drake and Barnett when it came to the Congo, though they did not seem to realize it at the time.

The growing disappointment with U.S. policy in Africa was unveiled when at the 4 July holiday celebration in the Congo, half the African Americans chose to boycott. This included UN officials, teachers, technicians, secretaries, and "housewives"; only ten from this group chose not to boycott. "Six or seven, however, were military men," said the ANP, "who indicated that they were not permitted to join a boycott"; naturally, "no Congolese were invited."[119]

It was Barnett who conferred with the putative leader of the pro-Lumumba bloc, Sékou Touré in Guinea-Conakry, who promptly sent via the ANP "brotherly greetings" to U.S. Negroes.[120] By early 1962, the peripatetic Barnett and Moten were back in West Africa, where she was designated as the godmother of Nkrumah's son.[121]

The Janus-faced Barnett, however, was also a transmission belt conveying intelligence to the White House about his visits with the Ghanaian leader. It was on White House stationery that a presidential aide wrote that he was "looking forward" to receiving a "blow-by-blow description of Prime Minister Nkrumah's visit" with Barnett.[122]

"We gave Nkrumah a wonderful parade down South Parkway to the City Hall," said the Chicago publisher, "with people out despite the rain and that night a dinner at the Sheraton Blackstone which I chaired." It was "50–50 racially," and the prime minister "enjoyed his stay in Chicago more than in any other city."[123] The bipartisan Barnett also was briefed by leading Democrat Senator Hubert H. Humphrey, who pledged to keep the agency chief "fully informed on my activities, especially as they relate to people of color"[124]—and, in return, implicitly expected reciprocity.

The agile Barnett had maintained ties to the left bound to incur the favor of the Ghanaian leader, informing him how he had commissioned "Mrs. Paul Robeson" to provide "excellent coverage" on matters close to Nkrumah's heart.[125] As she saw it, Barnett was "so impressed with the respect and affection of the Africans paid me" and "the way Nkrumah treated me," that he consented to allow her to write for ANP.[126] When British Commonwealth nations met in London in 1961, she was welcomed by officialdom, "perhaps more than any other reporter," she said. "I had direct personal access to the heads of delegations. Paul and I spent a marvelous hour with Nkrumah," which led to a "series of articles" she wrote for ANP.[127] But this magnanimity toward the Robesons could have been compromising for Barnett because at the same time she was making "regular broadcasts over Radio Afrika (Moscow)," which elicited a "marvelous reaction," she said, "from both Africa and Moscow."[128] Such ties meant that Barnett could not be wholly trusted by Washington.

"We have the highest regard for Mrs. Robeson," said Barnett; "when we were together in Africa," he continued, "she accepted an invitation to write and sent us a number of articles" and "we used every bit of her material." As for her spouse, the agile Barnett confided that "Paul's friendship I have cherished through the years."[129]

By 1961 Barnett had extended his remit to East Africa, reminding the founding father of the nation that was to become Tanzania that he was hopeful that "our overseas service reaches you." Julius Nyerere was informed further about "Mrs. Barnett, whom you will remember meeting in Nigeria and perhaps New York with me."[130] Barnett, who attended Kenyan independence ceremonies in 1963 as guest of the incoming government,[131] also admired Jomo Kenyatta, a "crag of a man" and his fellow leader, Mbiyu Koinange, characterized as "our good friend."[132]

"We still have many African visitors," Barnett boasted. "Within recent weeks we have had half a dozen from French African areas—a quartet from Kenya," the "Premier of Eastern Nigeria," and many more.[133] Earlier, the social secretary of the Kennedy White House, Letitia Baldridge, urged Barnett to attend a "stag luncheon at the White House" for the "Prime Minister of Nigeria."[134]

It was hard to say whether Barnett was closer to the Ghanaian or the Nigerian leaders. It was "at a reception in the home of the Chief Justice of Nigeria in Lagos," Barnett told Samuel Pierce, future cabinet member, when he met Governor Nelson Rockefeller of New York. "My wife and I were house guests of the Chief Justice and Lady Ameola, who were hosts," and completing the circle, was the governor, who was a patron of Tuskegee.[135]

In consorting with African leaders, Barnett and Moten were simply part of a larger trend. It was in October 1962 that Dr. King conferred in Manhattan with Algeria's Ben Bella. They discussed, said the ANP, the "effect of the U.S. race problem on the emerging African nations." According to an aide, the two leaders "talked mostly about the relations between the American racial problem and colonialism" with the U.S. leader accepting an invitation to travel to Algiers with his departure to be effected "as soon as possible."[136] Dr. King also joined Roy Wilkins and scores of other leaders at a meeting weeks later designed to shape U.S. policy toward Africa, a meeting that featured what was described as a "bitter attack" on apartheid.[137]

This pressure of the international community, which ANP played a preeminent role in generating, was an essential corrosive serving to ensure that Jim Crow would lapse into a death spiral from which it could not escape easily. At the

Barnett and his artistic spouse, Etta Moten, board a flight in New York, circa 1963–64. His varied connections also benefited his wife's career as an actor and singer. Courtesy of the Chicago History Museum.

time of the path-breaking March on Washington of 1963, hundreds picketed U.S. embassies in Europe, by far the largest turnout for which was in Paris, led by the black actor William Marshall.[138] The march dominated the news in Paris, said the ANP, and marches on U.S. legations also took place in Bonn and Munich. The youth wing of the socialist-oriented New Democrat Party led protests in Ottawa, and unions protested in China. In Cairo dozens attempted to deliver a protest to the U.S. Embassy, which was a reflection of a larger protest in Africa that was particularly conspicuous in settler regimes such as Kenya, the Rhodesias, and Southern Africa generally. Ben Bella in Algeria expressed solidarity too.[139]

These gusts of favorable winds from abroad not only served to erode Jim Crow at home. When George Weaver was designated by the International Labor Organization to assume a post fighting job bias internationally, the ANP could claim more than a small share of the credit.[140]

But, alas, just as it seemed that the ANP was reaching new heights of influence, buoyed by the decolonization of Africa, which it long had championed, the agency found itself on the brink of collapse.

CHAPTER 11

The Jim Crow Paradox

Not all was rosy in relations between Africans and African Americans, a trend exposed when Kwame Nkrumah's Ghana nationalized two insurance companies owned by U.S. Negroes Robert Freeman and Vertner Tandy.[1]

"American Negroes in Ghana disturbed by editorials attacking them as enemies of Africans"—and "treacherous" and "selfish" in the bargain—was a story well disseminated.[2] Indicative of a deepening rift that had asserted itself in Black America, Claude Barnett admitted that his agency had "held information" that indicated that W. E. B. DuBois, who resided in Ghana from 1961 until his death in August 1963, "was responsible for this continued series of attacks on American Negroes in the Ghana newspapers."[3] As time passed, Barnett turned on the elderly Pan-Africanist with a vengeance, which did not necessarily improve the agency's image in Accra and Conakry.[4]

Barnett complained directly to Nkrumah about these "slanderous attacks,"[5] but there was more at play than personal ties and charm could cure. Then the U.S. financial press chimed in denigrating Accra's "Monument to Folly," that is, that "the U.S. should not subsidize Ghana's Power Venture," referring to a dam project deemed essential to the nation's development.[6] St. Clair Drake, the black anthropologist from Chicago, was then in Accra, and he disclosed the bad news that the U.S. State Department thought that Nkrumah had toed the Soviet line on anticolonialism,[7] leaving the inference that Ghana could return to Washington's good graces only by backing colonialism.

By early 1964, a U.S. Negro, Adger Emerson Player, was deemed by the ANP to be "the American hero of the recent Ghana anti-American demonstration." He boldly engaged in a "flag-hoisting act," unfurling the stars and stripes. He was renounced as a traitor by the Ghana press, along with all U.S. Negro diplomatic personnel then labeled as "skunks and Judases." The ANP cited the local press for the proposition that "Black Americans work twice as hard as the whites in spreading vicious rumors and attempting to corrupt our youth with money, gifts, and false tales about the happy lot of black Americans." Player, on the other hand, received a personal commendation from the White House for his purported courage in foiling attempts to drag the U.S. flag through the dust.[8]

This was a structural problem: The decline of forces represented by Robeson meant that forces symbolized by Barnett, who were surely interested in Pan-Africanism but also were seeking profitable investments, meant they were conflicting with African leaders like Nkrumah who had a socialist orientation: this was bound to create waves. And it was bound to undermine ANP's role as an honest broker or even as a cynical promoter of Washington's policies, all of which was hastening the agency's demise.[9] Part of the paradox of Jim Crow was that as it eroded at a time when the Robesons were in retreat and the Nkrumahs of the world were ascending, conflict was bound to arise between Africans and African Americans, thus eroding too the global leverage that had been so instrumental in collapsing Jim Crow in the first place.

Soon ANP was reporting Accra's fervent denials to ANP that it had sent troops to Havana at a time of deteriorating relations with Washington for both developing nations.[10] The news worsened when Sylvanus Olympio, the premier leader in Ghana's neighbor Togo, was, according to ANP, "shot at the gate of the United States Embassy," and then after his tearful funeral his father died of an apparent heart attack.[11] The impactful message delivered to Accra was hard to ignore. Sooner still, U.S. Negroes in Ghana became disturbed by editorials attacking them as enemies of Africans and depicting them as devious, greedy, and as the enemy.[12] Even an exclusive interview that Nkrumah accorded to Barnett upon his arrival in Accra was insufficient to heal what was becoming an aching wound.[13]

U.S. relations with left-leaning African leaders were in freefall, and Sékou Touré in Conakry wrote a three-page letter to Barnett, detailing these difficulties, as if the Chicagoan had more influence at the State Department than he actually possessed.[14] "We are anxious to present Guinea in the most favorable light here," said the agency chief. [15]

Barnett replied, but healing the rifts was quickly becoming mission impossible. Continuing as both a shaper and reporter of news, the ANP dispatch on the "exchange of correspondence" between Chicago and Conakry included informed speculation about how and whether the Guineans influenced the sacking of John Morrow as U.S. ambassador there.[16] Morrow was African American and Barnett knew "his brother in the White House [staff] very well." This controversy was tied to "rumors for years," said Barnett, "that the white firms would prefer to have a white ambassador or that the State Department wanted to add that post to its list of career posts," eroding what was thought to be a U.S. Negro stranglehold on plum diplomatic posts in Africa.[17] A writer for the *Washington Post,* said Barnett, demanded that the State Department "should not send American Negroes to Africa," a reflection of this region's quick transition from colonial backwater to Cold War battlefield, thereby necessitating representation by those defined as white.[18]

The point was that eventually Barnett would not be wholly trusted by Washington nor by militant Africans—and for good reason. This too ensured the ANP's demise. West Africa was undergoing strain brought by the felt desire to elude the snares of neocolonialism or domination by the North Atlantic powers, a destiny that Moscow also opposed, which meant the introduction of Cold War tensions. But some pressures also were indigenous, a reality adduced when the Creole community of Sierra Leone, often descendants of those with roots in the United States, Britain, and the Caribbean and those rescued from slave ships, sought to secede, creating further regional ripples.[19] Yet when the agency received an official notice from the U.S. Postmaster General, instructing that it was holding "foreign mail addressed to you . . . which contains foreign political propaganda," it was apparent that the ANP was not seen as simon pure by Washington.[20] When the ANP office in Chicago was burglarized, with seven typewriters taken, leading to polygraph tests for employees, it would have been understandable if Barnett had suspected that—contrary to what he was told—the culprit had been a political foe.[21]

Though Barnett had questioned the circumstances of Lumumba's assassination publicly, he also sought assiduously to whip up "a rumor going about that one of the African nations has passed over to [the UN] a complete plan of the Russians to use the Congo as a steppingstone toward taking over all of Africa south of the Sahara," adding accurately that "this would make a real story." He also inquired "about the colored delegations" at the UN to "see what the people think about the treatment of the African students who are protesting the pressures and mishandling of the Soviet [Union], especially the three medical students who were in Moscow but raised their protest after they got into West Germany." Barnett said this report was "confidential," but when he signed off with instructions to provide greetings to "Presidents Nkrumah, Toure [and] Olympio, extend them my best wishes and tell them I am on my way to Nigeria,"[22] the possibility for a leak of unsupported "rumors" to these powerful men, not all of whom were anti-Soviet and would have reason to be suspicious of U.S. nationals who were anti-Soviet, was suddenly possible.

As so often happened, an ANP dispatch then reflected Barnett's thinking, for it was reported that "African students are being used as stooges for communism, posing a threat to free Africa." This was the accusation of "an African former student at Moscow State University," who complained—strangely—that "study of the Russian language was compulsory" at this Russian language school.[23] Barnett, who was a recipient of what amounted to intelligence reports,[24] was at times not sufficiently diplomatic to be discreet in private correspondence, which raised questions about his ability to be trusted wholly by either side of the Cold War divide.[25]

"How much more democratic are my people's newspapers than are the general newspapers of our country!"[26] This was Robeson's claim. Yet even the lessening of Red Scare tensions and the rise of an assertive anti–Jim Crow movement were not enough to push agencies like the ANP decisively toward those like Nkrumah—and Robeson himself, for that matter.

In the context of questioning Ghana, the ANP also invoked Cuba, an island that had a revolution in 1959 helping ultimately to bring Communists to power; this brought ructions to Washington, too. Initially, it seemed that the ANP was impressed that Fidel Castro's rebel army was "thoroughly integrated," a sentiment reinforced when Congressman Adam Clayton Powell endorsed their rebellion.[27]

Powell's endorsement notwithstanding, Barnett was ambivalent about the ouster of Fulgencio Batista in Havana; the dictator "had given us an interview in the past," said the ANP founder as he reprimanded Dunnigan for visiting Santo Domingo without talking to him—or "fail[ing] to say a word about Trujillo's dictatorship." He wondered what "Castro's ambassador thinks Castro's attitude toward colored people is? Photographs show that he had some before the executioner's squad."[28]

But then the perception arose that Moscow's influence had now penetrated deeply into the U.S. backyard, a notion that arose as early as 1960 when a leader in North Carolina, Robert F. Williams, was described by the ANP as a "Negro supporter of Fidel Castro."[29] Columnist Gordon Hancock, who had stood tall for the longest, finally collapsed into an ideological heap when he found it "distressing to see our great country stand by while Castro hands Cuba over to Khrushchev." The "confiscation of our properties in Cuba," he warned, "is but a prelude to the confiscation of our property in the United States."[30] When one considers the propertylessness of too many Negroes, it is evident that he was speaking only for a narrow sliver of individuals, reflective of the narrowing base of the ANP as "integration" enriched some while causing spokesmen like Hancock to hasten the agency's demise by speaking for an ever smaller constituency.

Nevertheless, when Williams turned up in Havana in 1962 addressing a large gathering as—in the ANP's words—"a representative of the oppressed peoples of the United States who are sick with the United States Government intervention in Cuba," the direst fears of Hancock and his like were glimpsed.[31] A few months later the Bay of Pigs invasion sought to topple the regime in Havana, which included Nestor Fitzgerald Williams, a twenty-one-year-old U.S. Negro "ransomed," said the ANP, "for Fidel Castro's rock bottom price of $25,000."[32] The presence of this young man in Cuba was suggestive of the difficulty that some were having in adjusting to a new reality offshore. The influx of fleeing Cubans was creating an "economic crisis for Negroes" in Miami; they were arriving at the rate of a thousand per week by early 1963, though the ANP was quick to observe that "very few Negro Cuban refugees are coming to Miami. And even if they came," it was said with bitter resignation, "they would be discriminated against also."[33] It was also the ANP that reported that Havana was playing "Robin Hood to Cuban Negroes"; in other words, the regime "took homes from white families and gave them to Negroes."[34] The profound implications of this story for the mainland, however, were not teased out.[35]

Instead, the ANP's correspondent in neighboring Jamaica joined the fray by smearing the island's left-wing leader, Richard Hart, who was accused of "swearing to spread Moscow's doctrine in independent Jamaica." He "slashes across the face of capitalism, coddles socialism and communism," it was said contemptuously. It was "certain that he will get Fidel Castro's guidance and British Guiana Cheddi Jagan's (his long time friend) advice and perhaps instruction from the Iron Curtain. Although Hart has yet to stir up big trouble in Jamaica, his ideas may very well be hatched into hatred among the Ras Tafarians," a new world religion influenced by Ethiopia.[36] Hart was pummeled repeatedly, with the ANP dismissively referring to Hart's recent book as failing to generate interest "save [from] some Ras Tafarians."[37]

This attack on the left was not accompanied by an embrace by the right. Clennon King was in flight from Dixie and sought asylum in Jamaica just after independence in 1962. He told Kingston about "the hell on earth" that had been "created for African-Americans," though commenting that "white Cubans are being accepted as refugees in Jamaica while black Americans are rejected." He wondered whether he was being viewed negatively because "the press and radio have mentioned my public appearance for UNIA [Marcus Garvey's organization] here." He had "fear that the great homeland of Garvey is in danger of exchanging the shackles of British imperialism for those of the USA." He urged Kingston to create an example by granting him asylum because "if African-Americans were allowed welcome and unrestricted refuge in nearby nations like Jamaica, the U.S. would lose, ¾ of its African population within 20 years."[38]

There was a spate of bad news for the agency that did not halt its slide toward oblivion. In Chicago, radio station WYNR was assailed by Congressman Roman Pucinski after it dropped foreign language programming in Polish by his mother in favor of Negro programming. Etta Moten, the station's community relations director, was accused of putting pressure on the station by bringing Congressman Adam Clayton Powell into the fray.[39]

It was not as if Africans were rallying en masse to the ANP as they were assaulted. Instead J. M. Oyangi in Nairobi issued a blistering philippic deriding the American Negro as a "danger to development of African culture. He is Victim Number One of the inferiority complex and the African must guard himself against this person who seeks to destroy nature by trying to change his or her appearance to look like a white man or woman," an apparent reference to straightening hair and lightening skin. U.S. Negroes, he said, "after they had been suppressed by the whites in America for decades had suffered a terrible nervous breakdown. . . . [T]hese poor fellows . . . are indeed misguided and should be put under the care of a psychiatrist, a psychologist or a philosopher." Sadly, "some of the few Negresses we have in Kenya have aggravated this situation. Their attitude of superiority towards the Africans, especially toward African women has caused an atmosphere of hatred towards all Negroes. These women have gone as far as encouraging our women to straighten their hair."[40] Oyangi's compatriot, Mohamed Koor, conceded that this coruscating writer "may be wrong" but "these are the current feelings out here."[41]

What was worse? Being denigrated by Africans or assailed by a powerful congressman? When NAACP attorney Thurgood Marshall was quoted in colonial Kenya to the effect that the Nation of Islam was the equivalent of apartheid, it did not necessarily aid the image of the U.S. Negro abroad.[42]

Due east in Pakistan, newspapers ran banner headlines when the athlete then known as Cassius Clay joined the Nation of Islam while Marshall's presumed opposite, Senator Richard Russell of Georgia, echoed the attorney when he vowed that the boxer "will pay for this," for he will suffer "harassment, humiliation and insults such as he has never experienced."[43]

To a degree, Senator Russell kept his word, but that did not bar the growth of various forms of Islam among African Americans. The ANP provided detailed scrutiny of the odyssey of Malcolm X, the defrocked Nation of Islam minister who by May 1964 had arrived in Chicago, just back from a lengthy journey abroad. He "didn't reflect a true separationist [sic] view," it was reported, but "an international outlook" in that he "kept calling for closer collaboration and identification between the American Negroes and their 'African brothers.'" He said that he intended to "file a protest in the United Nations through representatives of the African nations and called on Negroes to link and identify themselves with the other darker peoples of the world, who are now in the majority," a throwback to Bandung. He "plugged for Pan-Africanism," said the agency that pioneered this field. "He said he was given a royal reception in Saudi Arabia" and "in Accra" too, a turnabout from the assailing of U.S. Negroes there: contrastingly, Malcolm conferred amiably with Nkrumah.[44] Washington was displeased when Malcolm termed the newly formed Peace Corps as being little more than a "spy ring and missionaries of neo-colonialism."[45]

This relatively unbiased view of Malcolm was a turnabout from earlier ANP coverage of the Nation of Islam. The Nation of Islam's public relations consultant, Masco Young of Philadelphia, told Barnett in 1960 that "Elijah Muhammad's Muslims . . . have been literally butchered in the press."[46] Young's attempt to rectify the situation, for example, by publicizing the fact that Elijah Muhammad was "kissed by Egypt's Great Imam," would not necessarily win plaudits,[47] suggestive of the group's steep uphill climb. Even Barnett felt compelled to inform Young stiffly that "we would not be interested in any phase of the so-called 'Muslim' program."[48]

The ANP's Gordon Hancock captured a growing segment of Negro thinking when he opined that "in the last analysis Russia and the United States will somehow become allies on racial grounds rather than annihilate each other and leave

China [and]dark people to dominate the world of the future."[49] Unfortunately, this widespread view often led some Negroes to underestimate the raw rancor imbedded in the Washington–Moscow conflict, which—in turn—made it difficult to plot an effective global strategy.

As things turned out and not for the first time, the ANP provided a misleading prediction in that a few years later, President Nixon journeyed to China, leading to an anti-Soviet entente that was to transform the planet in relatively short order. The attacks on U.S. Jim Crow by African leaders doubtlessly helped African Americans, but it probably did not help Barnett with Washington for the superpower could wonder legitimately just whose side he was on.

∗   ∗   ∗

As ANP was going down the drain, so was Barnett. "My trip to Mayo's [hospital]," he announced in mid-1957, "was apparently quite useful. They gave me the works and ended by saying I was in good shape. When I returned from Africa there was a swelling in one ankle which my doctor could not fathom. Neither did Mayo's," though "they decided [the cause was] the long sitting on the plane in one position—I did very little moving—one jump being 14 hours with only a brief stop."[50]

By September 1961, after another spate of intense travel, Barnett responded that he was "doing no work but Etta is a wonderful nurse," after a "chunk was taken out of [his] elbow." Fortunately, "the office seems to run reasonably well without me."[51] "While the heat in Africa improved my arm and its attendant injuries," he said in 1962, "I came back to our unseasonably bitter cold," he said of Chicago, "and lost all its advantages."[52] By 1966 he was retired and, Moten lamented, unable to "walk or help himself in any way." "I have become an expert on bed baths"; as a result, her disabled spouse spent time reading and smoking "his big cigars."[53]

By 1967 he was dead, and perishing along with him was the eminence he had developed so assiduously as a leading press baron and Negro leader. The ephemeral nature of his celebrity was in part a function of the Jim Crow paradox that he symbolized. That is, Barnett—and he was hardly alone—did not seem to grasp the import of the historical forces unleashed when Jim Crow began to erode. He did not understand consistently that "integration" came with a price, not only in terms of the agency he founded—the ANP—but also in terms of the transient nature of his own reputation.

NOTES

Introduction

1. Claude Barnett to *Chicago Daily News*, 3 December 1958, Box 180, Folder 1, Claude A. Barnett/Associated Negro Press Papers, Chicago History Museum (hereafter cited as CAB-CHM), 1

2. Letter from Kwame Nkrumah, 3 September 1958, Reel 66, No. 144, Part I, Press Releases, Claude A. Barnett/Associated Negro Press Papers, North Carolina State University–Raleigh (hereafter cited as CAB).

3. Memorandum from Claude Barnett, 12 December 1960, Reel 1, No. 1170, Part III, Series K, CAB.

4. Adlai Stevenson to Claude Barnett, 10 February 1961, Reel 9, No. 360, Part III, Series I, Race Relations, CAB.

5. Claude Barnett to Adlai Stevenson, 26 January 1961, Reel 9, No. 366, Part III, Series I.

6. Press release, 17 July 1963, Box 212, Folder 1, CAB-CHM.

7. E. S. Gillespie, Vice President of Public Relations, Supreme Life Insurance Company, to Claude Barnett, 16 March 1961, Reel 6, No. 695, Part III, Subject Files on Black Americans, CAB.

8. Claude Barnett to Nnamdi Azikiwe, Governor General of Lagos, 30 March 1961, Reel 6, No. 710, Part III, Subject Files on Black Americans.

9. Claude Barnett to Luther Foster, 23 June 1954, Reel 2, No. 766, Part III, Series G, Philanthropic and Social Organizations, CAB.

10. Fact Sheet on Barnett, circa 1959, Box 109, Folder 1, CAB-CHM.

11. Claude Barnett to Chair of Wendell Phillips Dabney Testimonial Committee, 2 November 1949, Reel 21, No. 326, Part II, Organizational Files, CAB.

12. Claude Barnett to Alice Dunnigan, 9 April 1955, Reel 5, No. 1012, Part II, Organizational Files.

13. Claude Barnett to Lawrence Burr, 21 June 1946, Reel 5, No. 1103, Part III, Series G.

14. Dean Acheson to Claude Barnett, 25 March 1954, Box 208, Folder 2, CAB-CHM.

15. Memorandum from Claude Barnett, 19 March 1965, Box 168, Folder 8, CAB-CHM.

16. See, e.g., Gerald Horne, *Black and Red: W.E.B. Du Bois and the Afro-American Response to the Cold War, 1944–1963* (Albany: State University of New York Press, 1986); Gerald Horne, *Black Revolutionary: William Patterson and the Globalization of the African American Freedom Struggle* (Urbana: University of Illinois Press, 2013).

17. Note in Todd Vogel, ed., *The Black Press: New Literary and Historical Essays* (New Brunswick, NJ: Rutgers University Press, 2001), 59.

18. John H. Sengstacke to Etta Moten, 3 August 1967, Box 67, Robert S. Abbott Papers, Vivian Harsh Research Collection of Afro-American History and Literature, Carter G. Woodson Regional Library, Chicago Public Library.

19. Press release, 15 May 1957, Reel 62, No. 853, Part I, Press Releases, CAB.

20. P. B. Young to Claude Barnett, 10 November 1950, Box 142, Folder 4, CAB-CHM.

21. Claude Barnett to Alice Dunnigan, 21 April 1950, Box 208, Folder 1, CAB-CHM.

22. Lawrence D. Hogan, *A Black National News Service: The Associated Negro Press and Claude Barnett, 1919–1945* (Rutherford, NJ: Fairleigh Dickinson University Press, 1984), 25, 32.

23. A. S. Scott to Claude Barnett, 12 March 1934, Reel 14, No. 499, Part II, Organizational Files.

24. Westbrook Pegler column, 20 April 1946, Box 146, Folder 3, CAB-CHM.

25. Memorandum from Alice Dunnigan, 24 April 1957, Reel 62, No. 620, Part I, Press Releases, CAB.

26. Claude Barnett Speech to "Brothers in Alpha, our families and friends," no date, Reel 3, No. 251, Part III, Series K, CAB. See also Hogan, *Black National News Service*, 17: In 1890 a short-lived "Associated Correspondents of Race Newspapers" was organized.

27. Adam Green, *Selling the Race: Culture, Community, and Black Chicago, 1940–1955* (Chicago: University of Chicago Press, 2007), 94.

28. Claude Barnett to Thomas W. Young of the Guide Publishing Company, 13 February 1950, Box 142, Folder 2, CAB-CHM.

29. Truman K. Gibson, *Knocking Down Barriers: My Fight for Black America* (Evanston, IL: Northwestern University Press, 2005), 51, 59.

30. Claude Barnett to Harold Hochschild, 11 November 1964, Box 174, Folder 7.

31. Enoch P. Waters, *American Diary: A Personal History of the Black Press* (Chicago, IL: Path Press, 1987), 420.

32. On how this trend manifested in the field of education, see, e.g., Alison Stewart, *First Class: The Legacy of Dunbar, America's First Black Public High School* (Chicago: Lawrence Hill, 2013); David Cecelski, *Along Freedom Road: Hyde County, North Carolina, and the Fate of Black Schools in the South* (Chapel Hill: University of North Carolina Press, 1994).

33. Christopher B. Daly, *Covering America: A Narrative History of a Nation's Journalism* (Amherst: University of Massachusetts Press, 2012), 309. See also Juan Gonzales and Joseph Torres, *News for All the People: The Epic Story of Race and the American Media* (New York: Verso, 2011).

34. Quoted in Hayward Farrar, *The Baltimore Afro-American, 1892–1950* (Westport, CT: Greenwood, 1998), xi.

35. Gunnar Myrdal, *An American Dilemma: The Negro Problem and Modern Democracy,* vol. 2 (New York: Harper and Bros., 1944), 924.

36. Claude Barnett, "The Negro Press in the War Effort," no date, circa 1940s, Box 144, Folder 5, CAB-CHM.

37. Press release, March 1948, Reel 37, No. 343, Part I, Press Releases, CAB. Note: At times, the precise date of material—particularly press releases—from this vast collection were unclear, as in this case; hence, month and year are cited.

38. Dr. Martin Luther King Jr. to Claude Barnett, 24 January 1962, Reel 4, No. 177, Part III, Series J, Religion, CAB.

39. Claude Barnett to "Dear Martin Luther," King, 9 September 1963, Reel 4, No. 182, Part III, Series J.

40. David Talbot to Claude Barnett, 23 September 1963, Box 172, Folder 2, CAB-CHM.

41. Claude Barnett to Lee Lorch, 29 October 1957, Reel 3, No. 08, Part III, Series B, CAB.

42. Fact Sheet on Barnett, 20 October 1958, Box 109, Folder 1, CAB-CHM.

43. Irene Roland to Walter Scott, 6 September 1955, Box 142, Folder 5, CAB-CHM.

44. Finding Aid, no date, Etta Moten Papers, Vivian Harsh Research Collection of Afro-American History and Literature, Carter G. Woodson Regional Library, Chicago Public Library.

45. Items, circa 1964, Box 110, Folder 4, CAB-CHM.

46. Claude Barnett to George Davis of the Federal Theater of Chicago, 24 June 1936, Reel 10, No. 1027, Part III, Series C, Economic Conditions, Subject Files on Black Americans, CAB.

47. Richard Wright to Claude Barnett, 19 May 1948, Reel 2, No. 803, Part III, Series D, Entertainers, Artists and Authors, CAB.

48. Richard Wright to Claude Barnett, 28 December 1940, Reel 2, No. 796, Part III, Series D.

49. Henry Allen Moe, Guggenheim Foundation to Claude Barnett, 4 November 1948, and Barnett to Moe, circa 1948, Reel 5, No. 244–245, Part II, Organizational Files, CAB.

50. Greetings from Frank Marshall Davis, 16 December 1949, Reel 5, No. 264, Part II, Organizational Files.

51. Gerald Horne, *Fighting in Paradise: Labor Unions, Racism, and Communists in the Making of Modern Hawaii* (Honolulu: University of Hawaii Press, 2012).

52. Zora Neale Hurston to Claude Barnett, 25 February 1939, Reel 2, No. 744, Part III, Series D, CAB.

53. Zora Neale Hurston to Claude Barnett, 24 November 1942, Reel 2, No. 746, Part III, Series D.

54. Zora Neale Hurston to "Dear Claude," no date, Reel 2, No. 760, Part III, Series D.

55. Mary Church Terrell to P. L. Prattis, 24 March 1931, Reel 7, No. 248, Part II, Organizational Files, CAB.

56. Press release, April 1929, Reel 1, No. 509, Part I, Press Releases, CAB.

57. Ezekiel Mphahlele to Langston Hughes, 10 February 1955, and Langston Hughes to Claude Barnett, 1955, Box 175, Folder 3, CAB-CHM.

58. Press release, May 1936, Reel 12, No. 996, Part I, Series A, Press Releases, CAB.

59. Nathaniel Nakasa to Claude Barnett, 16 August 1960, Box 176, Folder 3, CAB-CHM.

60. Rudolph Dunbar to Claude Barnett, 26 July 1945, Box 200, Folder 2, CAB-CHM.

61. Albert Anderson of the ANP to Vernon Jordan, 23 October 1962, Box 130, Folder 4, CAB-CHM.

62. Roy Wilkins to "Dear Claude," 24 November 1930, Reel 18, No. 557, Part II, Organizational Files: "What has the ANP against the Jews? . . . several careless references," e.g., "bank failure" involved "dragging in the fact that the Flowers brothers are Jews. . . . from a business standpoint, it would be poor policy for Negro papers to emphasize the race [*sic*] of gougers, for a good part of their income is from Jewish advertisers."

63. Amy Ashwood Garvey to Claude Barnett, no date, circa 1935, Reel 4, No. 305, Part III, Series G, Philanthropic and Social Organizations.

64. Claude Barnett to Ivy Anderson, [also known as Ivie Anderson], 26 February 1935, Reel 6, No. 003, Part III, Series D.

65. Claude Barnett to Marian Anderson, 19 March 1934, Reel 5, Part III, Series D, CAB.

66. Merze Tate to Claude Barnett, 16 May 1945, Box 198, Folder 4, CAB-CHM. See also Merze Tate to Claude Barnett, 16 May 1945, Reel 1, No. 443, Part III, Series F, CAB: "I am toying with the idea of visiting friends and soldiers in England, France, Switzerland and possibly Germany. . . . I travelled in Western Europe and studied at Geneva in the summer

of 1931 and returned to Europe in 1932 where I remained for three years studying at Oxford, Paris, Geneva and Berlin."

67. Fay Jackson to Claude Barnett, 11 April 1937, Box 198, Folder 11, CAB-CHM.

68. Charles "Luckey" Roberts to "Dear Claude" Barnett, 29 October 1962, and attached profile, Reel 1, No. 394, Part III, Series D, CAB.

69. Rosemary Woods to Etta Moten, 11 November 1957, Box 208, Folder 1, CAB-CHM.

70. Claude Barnett to Majorie Joyner, United Beauty School Owners and Teachers Association, no date, Reel 2, No. 689, Part III, Series A, Subject Files on Black Americans, CAB.

71. B. T. Bradshaw, President-Treasurer of Virginia Mutual Benefit Life Insurance Company, 25 July 1950, Reel 4, No. 167, Part III, Series A, CAB.

72. Horne, *Black Revolutionary*, passim.

73. ANP to F. H. M. Murray, *Washington Tribune*, 19 February 1933, Box 147, Folder 9, CAB-CHM.

74. Claude Barnett to Rudolph Dunbar, 3 July 1944, Box 200, Folder 1, CAB-CHM.

75. ANP style sheet, no date, Box 109, Folder 5, CAB-CHM.

76. P. B. S. Young to ANP, 27 April 1936, Box 108, Folder 2, CAB-CHM. This veteran journalist objected to "us[ing] of the word 'spade' and the word 'Spook,'" both found in ANP releases. He also criticized the word "Duskyamerican": "there can be no justification for our use of such words as spade, spook, ofay, blackamoor, Dusk[y]american, sepia, cracker, or nigger. . . . we raise holy hell when such epithets are used by the opposite race with reference to us."

77. Claude Barnett to Ruth Sloan, USIS, 25 October 1951, Reel 3, No. 538, Part III, Series D, CAB.

78. "Final Treatment Outline," 15 August 1951, Reel 3, No. 490, Part III, Series D, CAB.

79. Claude Barnett to E. H. Ellis, 26 November 1951, Reel 3, No. 649, Part III, Series D, CAB.

80. Press release, 30 March 1953, Reel 3, No. 690, Part III, Series D, CAB.

81. Claude Barnett to E. M. Glucksman, 13 May 1959, Reel 4, No. 589, Part III, Series D, CAB.

82. Claude Barnett to E. H. Ellis, McCann-Erickson, 23 November 1956, Box 168, Folder 6, CAB-CHM.

83. Claude Barnett to Central Veneer Company, Indianapolis, 5 September 1950, Box 168, Folder 6.

84. Gabriel Dennis to Claude Barnett, 28 March 1938, Box 184, Folder 5, CAB-CHM.

85. Claude Barnett to "Dear Lester" Walton, 9 August 1941, Box 184, Folder 5, CAB-CHM.

86. Claude Barnett to Gabriel Dennis, 7 February 1950, Box 184, Folder 5, CAB-CHM.

87. Press release, June 1940, Reel 20, No. 1050, Part I, Press Releases, CAB.

88. Claude Barnett to Marian Anderson, 21 December 1935, Reel 5, No. 102, Part III, Series D, CAB.

89. Claude Barnett to Alfred Xuma, 18 December 1945, Box 168, Folder 9, CAB-CHM.

90. Hastings Banda, Prison-Gwelo, Southern Rhodesia, to Claude Barnett, 21 January 1960, Box 174, Folder 6, CAB-CHM: "Some of my former teachers at the University of Chicago are in correspondence with me."

91. Bill Mullen, "Claude A. Barnett (September 16, 1889–August 2, 1967)," in Steven C. Tracy, ed., *Writers of the Black Chicago Renaissance* (Urbana: University of Illinois Press, 2011), 54.

92. Adam Green, *Selling the Race: Culture, Community, and Black Chicago, 1940–1955* (Chicago: University of Chicago Press), 99. Press release, July 1957, Reel 63, No. 173, Part I, Press Releases, CAB.

93. ANP to F. H. M. Murray, 19 September 1933, Box 147, Folder 9, CAB-CHM.

94. Press release, April 1962, Reel 76, No. 620, Part I, Press Releases, CAB.

95. *Crain's Chicago Business*, 9 September 2014.

96. Bank statement, 29 June 1956, Box 124, Folder 2, CAB-CHM. Note: Barnett's tax returns in this collection are not available to researchers.

97. *Crain's Chicago Business*, 14 April 2015.

98. John Maxwell Hamilton, *Journalism's Roving Eye: A History of American Foreign Reporting* (Baton Rouge: Louisiana State University Press, 2009), 333. See also Hogan, *Black National News Service,* 32: A "multiple of four or five is a generally accepted figure used by students of the American press to determine the readership of a single copy of a black paper."

99. Armistead Scott Pride, "A Register and History of Negro Newspapers in the U.S." (PhD diss., Northwestern University, 1950), 143.

100. Mark Slagle, "Mightier than the Sword? The Black Press and the End of Racial Segregation in the U.S. Military, 1948–1954" (PhD diss., University of North Carolina–Chapel Hill, 2010), 29, 28, 69: "An Internal Revenue Service ruling on allowable advertising deductions on the wartime excess profits tax left companies with the choice of buying more advertisements or letting their surplus income be taxed by the federal government. As a result, many white owned businesses chose to advertise in black newspapers for the first time. . . . [F]lush with cash from these new advertisers, black publishers now had to worry about keeping them."

101. Farrar, *Baltimore Afro-American,* 8, 16–17.

102. Claude Barnett to Hon. and Mrs. T. Hoskkyns-Abrahall, 10 March 1948, Reel 1, No. 894, Part III, Series G, Philanthropic and Social Organizations, CAB.

103. Green, *Selling the Race,* 94.

104. Claude Barnett to Frederick D. Patterson, 14 October 1953, Reel 3, No. 18, Part III, Series G, CAB.

105. Claude Barnett to Thomas Dabney, 17 September 1960, Reel 5, No. 89, Part II, Organizational Files, CAB.

106. Press release, February 1944, Reel 27, No. 743, Part I, Press Releases, CAB.

107. William Rutherford to Claude Barnett, 12 October 1949, Box 198, Folder 6, CAB-CHM.

108. "Confidential" FBI Report, 9 May 1945, 100–17497, Claude Barnett FBI File, Gerald Horne Papers, Schomburg Center, New York Public Library.

109. Alice Allison, Dunnigan, *Alone Atop the Hill: The Autobiography of Alice Dunnigan, Pioneer of the National Black Press* (Athens: University of Georgia Press, 2015), 105.

110. Enoch P. Waters, *American Diary: A Personal History of the Black Press* (Chicago: Path Press, 1987), 154.

111. Press release, May 1961, Reel 73, No. 852, Part I, Press Releases, CAB.

112. W. E. B. DuBois to Claude Barnett, 27 February 1939, Reel 6, No. 68, Part III, Series I, CAB.

113. Claude Barnett to W. E. B. DuBois, 4 March 1939, Reel 6, No. 69, Part III, Series I, CAB.

114. Roy Wilkins to "Dear Claude," 28 July 1939, Reel 2, No. 930, Part III, Series H, CAB.

115. Alvin White, ANP Correspondent to Claude Barnett, 9 August 1941, Box 140, Folder 6: "Rayford Logan called today. . . . He too is hot with Walter [White, NAACP leader]. Says Walter had dinner at the White House one day before the president left. . . . [W]hen White comes to town, he slips in and out and stays at the Hay-Adam House, down near the White House, a very exclusive spot—favored by diplomats, presidential invitees."

116. Claude Barnett to William V. Lawson, Director of Public Relations, National Association of Manufacturers, 20 February 1942, Reel 1, No. 117, Part III, Series C, CAB. See also Dunnigan, *Alone atop the Hill*, 164.

117. C. C. Spaulding to Claude Barnett, 24 April 1940, Reel 5, No. 767, Part III, Series A, CAB.

118. Claude Barnett to Harvey Firestone, 17 January 1933, Box 181, Folder 3, CAB-CHM.

119. W. D. Hines, Firestone Tire and Rubber, to Claude Barnett, 20 June 1938, Box 190, Folder 1.

120. Claude Barnett to John Hamilton, 20 November 1937, Reel 2, No. 751, Part III, Series H, CAB.

121. Hogan, *Black National News Service*, 95.

122. "Grassroots Editor" Newsletter, January 1965, Box 109, Folder 5, CAB-CHM.

123. See Gerald Horne, *The Deepest South: The U.S., Brazil and the African Slave Trade* (New York: New York University Press, 2005); Gerald Horne, *Race to Revolution: The U.S. and Cuba during Slavery and Jim Crow* (New York: Monthly Review Press, 2014).

124. Amy Alexander, *Uncovering Race: A Black Journalist's Story of Reporting and Reinvention* (Boston: Beacon, 2011), 10, 50.

125. *Washington Examiner*, 27 July 2015. In 1965 the *Los Angeles Times* had no black reporters when Watts erupted in a transformative conflagration. A black messenger for the paper was recruited promptly as a journalist to report from the zone of conflict, which stretched far beyond Watts. Today African Americans "make up 3.4% of the staff across the newsroom, including designers, Web developers and a handful of reporters," which is a mite better that "most of the state's publications that reported data," which "had no African American reporters." See *Los Angeles Times*, 14 August 2015. See also Gerald Horne, *Fire This Time: The Watts Uprising and the 1960s* (New York: Da Capo, 1997).

Chapter 1. Beginnings

1. Barnett Memoir, "Fly Out of Darkness," no date, Reel 2, No. 390, Part III, Series K, Personal and Financial, Claude A. Barnett/Associated Negro Press Papers, North Carolina State University–Raleigh (hereafter cited as CAB).

2. Memorandum, 2 January 1920, Reel 1, No. 03, Part III, Series H, Politics and Law, CAB.

3. Memorandum, 24 February 1920, Reel 1, No. 19, Part III, Series H, CAB.

4. Betty Lou Kilbert Rathbun, "The Rise of the Modern American Negro Press, 1880–1914" (PhD diss., State University of New York–Buffalo, 1978), 104, 114–15, 225, 226, 240.

5. Ibid.; Lawrence D. Hogan, *A Black National News Service: The Associated Negro Press and Claude Barnett, 1919–1945* (Rutherford, NJ: Fairleigh Dickinson University Press, 1984), 57, 59.

6. ANP Annual Report, 1919–1920, Box 108, Folder 1, Claude A. Barnett/Associated Negro Press Papers, Chicago History Museum (hereafter cited as CAB-CHM).

7. ANP to Pullman Company, 17 March 1923, Reel 9, No. 02, Part III, Series A, CAB.

8. Memorandum, no date, Reel 9, No. 04, Part III, Series A, CAB. See also Memorandum, 30 July 1925, Reel 9, No. 15, Part III, Series C, CAB.

9. Memorandum, 26 January 1929, Box 108, Folder 2, CAB-CHM.

10. Memorandum, 18 September 1934, Reel 9, No. 182, Part III, Series A, CAB.

11. Report by William Pickens, 8 May 1926, Reel 3, No. 400, Part II, Organizational Files, CAB.

12. Claude Barnett to W. J. Cameron, Ford Motor Company, 14 July 1937, Reel 10, No. 612, Part III, Series A, CAB.

13. Claude Barnett to Alvin White, 17 September 1941, Box 140, Folder 6, CAB-CHM.

14. Claude Barnett to W. J. Cameron, 3 April 1935, Reel 1, No. 07, Part III, Series C, Economic Conditions, CAB. See also G. James Fleming, President's Committee on Fair Employment Practices, Detroit Field Office to Claude Barnett, 14 July 1943, Box 137, Folder 6, CAB. See also *California Eagle*, 18 April 1941.

15. Claude Barnett to R. H. Bowden, 4 November 1938, Reel 9, No. 212, Part III, Series A, CAB.

16. Claude Barnett to Randy Trice, 22 December 1938, Reel 9, No. 215, Part III, Series A, CAB.

17. Congressman Arthur Mitchell to C. L. Townes, circa 1938, Reel 9, No. 218, Part III, Series A, CAB.

18. Claude Barnett to Al Holsey, 4 March 1933, Reel 14, No. 189, Part III, Subject Files on Black Americans, CAB.

19. "The Light," 29 October 1927, Reel 3, No. 555, Part II, Organizational Files, CAB.

20. Claude Barnett to Edgar McDaniel of Poro College–St. Louis, 27 January 1931, Reel 3, No. 03, Part III, Series C, CAB.

21. Brochure on Poro College, 1922, Reel 3, No. 148, Part III, Series C, CAB.

22. Aide, Poro College, to Claude Barnett, 13 September 1924, Reel 2, No. 924, Part III, Series C, CAB.

23. R. Irving to Claude Barnett, 7 July 1928, Reel 7, No. 157, Part III, Series C, CAB.

24. Undated memorandum, circa 1920, Box 108, Folder 1, CAB-CHM.

25. ANP Stationery, 17 October 1922, Box 108, Folder 1, CAB-CHM.

26. Walter Cohen to Claude Barnett, 8 June 1928, Box 333, Folder 3, CAB-CHM.

27. Enoch P. Waters, *American Diary: A Personal History of the Black Press* (Chicago: Path Press, 1987), 420–21.

28. Herbert Hoover to Claude Barnett, 16 June 1928, Box 333, Folder 3, CAB-CHM.

29. R. H. Rutherford to Claude Barnett, 28 March 1928, Reel 1, No. 186, Part III, Series H, CAB.

30. Letter to A. H. Kirchhofer, Republican National Committee, 25 September 1958, Reel 1, No. 442, Part III, Series H, CAB.

31. Preston Lauterbach, *Beale Street Dynasty: Sex, Song and the Struggle for the Soul of Memphis* (New York: Norton, 2015), 267.

32. "Negro Newspapers: Their Political Affiliations and Attitudes . . . 1930–1932," Reel 1, No. 875, Part III, Series H, CAB.

33. Oscar Stauffer, Landon-for-President Committee to Claude Barnett, 13 June 1936, Reel 2, No. 693, Part III, Series I, CAB.

34. P. L. Prattis to Claude Barnett, 29 June 1938, Reel 7, No. 292, Part II, Organizational Files, CAB.

35. R. R. Reed to Alvin Holsey, Secretary of the Colored Republican Committee, 4 September 1928, Reel 1, No. 313, Part III, Series H, CAB.

36. Report by "Publicity Committee, Colored Voters Division," 1928 campaign, marked "confidential," Reel 1, No. 883, Part III, Series H, CAB.

37. Pamphlet by Ida B. Wells-Barnett, 20 September 1928, Reel 1, Part III, Series H, CAB.

38. Henry Lewis Suggs, "P. B. Young and the 'Norfolk Journal & Guide,' 1910–1964" (PhD diss., University of Virginia, 1976), 191.

39. Hilary Mac Austin, "The 'Defender' Brings You the World: The Grand European Tour of Patrick B. Prescott, Jr.," in Darlene Clark Hine and John McCluskey Jr., *The Black Chicago Renaissance* (Urbana: University of Illinois Press, 2012), 57–75, 58.

40. Press release, 18 September 1929, Reel 7, No. 548, Part III, Series I, Race Relations, CAB.

41. Press release, May 1930, Reel 2, No. 812, Part I, Press Releases, CAB.

42. Marian Anderson to Claude Barnett, 18 October 1930, Reel 5, No. 59, Part III, Series D, CAB.

43. Press release, January 1930, Reel 1, No. 372, Part I, Press Releases, CAB.

44. Press release, August 1932, Reel 6, No. 72, Part I, Press Releases, CAB.

45. Press release, March 1933, Reel 7, No. 101, Part I, Press Releases, CAB. See also press release, May 1933, Reel 7, No. 409, Part I, Press Releases, CAB: "Turks bar jazz band . . . as a result Jim Fikos and his five man orchestra are out of a job at the Pora Hotel." And so they move on to Iraq.

46. Press release, August 1935, Box 198, Folder 4, CAB-CHM.

47. Press release, 4 January 1938, Box 198, Folder 4, CAB-CHM.

48. Press release, February 1939, Reel 5, No. 880, Part III, Series J, CAB.

49. Horace Mann Bond to Claude Barnett, 21 February 1934, Reel 2, No. 466, Part III, Series I, CAB.

50. Press release, February 1934, Reel 8, No. 514, Part I, Press Releases, CAB.

51. Samuel Goldsmith, Emergency Committee for Palestine-Chicago to Claude Barnett, 1 November 1938, Reel 1, No. 127, Part III, Series K, CAB.

52. Claude Barnett to Lord Lothian, 5 December 1940, Reel 7, No. 97, Part III, Series I, CAB.

53. *Dynamite*, 27 August 1938, Reel 3, No. 340, Part III, Series K, CAB.

54. William Pickens to "Dear Claude," 29 July 1932, Reel 6, 616, Part III, Series I, CAB.

55. Press release, circa 1929, Reel 1, No. 202, Part I, Press Releases, CAB.

56. Press release, circa June 1929, Reel 1, No. 723, Part I, Press Releases, CAB.

57. Press release, May 1935, Reel 10, No. 745, Part I, Press Releases, CAB. See also press release, November 1938, Part I, Press Releases, CAB: A Negro in Louisiana speaks French fluently "and English with some difficulty." See also press release, August 1936, Reel 13, No. 826, Part I, Series A, CAB: Elderly Negro woman in eastern Maryland speaks "perfect French."

58. Jinx Coleman Broussard, *African American Foreign Correspondents: A History* (Baton Rouge: Louisiana State University Press, 2013), 66.

59. Press release, 17 March 1929, Reel 1, No. 281, Part I, Press Releases, CAB.

60. Ruediger Bilden to Claude Barnett, 19 May 1936, Reel 5, No. 720, Part III, Subject Files on Black Americans, CAB.

61. Press release, September 1930, Reel 3, No. 255, Part I, Press Releases, CAB. See also press release, October 1930, Reel 3, No. 324, Part I, Press Releases, and press release, January 1934, Reel 8, No. 392, Part I, Press Releases, both in CAB.

62. Suggs, "P. B. Young and the 'Norfolk Journal & Guide,'" 158.

63. Press release, May 1930, Reel 2, No. 799, Part I, Press Releases, CAB.

64. Joseph Harris to Claude Barnett, 7 September 1932, Reel 2, No. 110, Part III, Series I, CAB.

65. James R. Hooker, *Black Revolutionary: George Padmore's Path from Communism to Pan-Africanism* (New York: Praeger, 1967).

66. Press release, no date, circa 1932, Reel 6, No. 2, Part III, Series I, CAB.

67. Press release, November 1928, Reel 1, No. 143, Part I, Press Releases, CAB.

68. "Proceedings of the Twenty-Second Annual Meeting of the National Negro Business League," Atlanta, 17–19 August 1921, Reel 8, No. 660, Part III, Series C, CAB.

69. R. R. Moton to Thomas Jesse Jones of Phelps–Stokes Fund, 18 November 1925, Box 190, Folder 1, CAB-CHM.

70. Claude Barnett to Elder Dempster Steamship Company, 17 January 1931, Reel 3, No. 02, Part III, Series C, CAB.

71. Press release, December 1933, Reel 8, No. 231, Part I, Press Releases, CAB.

72. Press release, March 1929, Reel 1, No. 345, Part I, Press Releases, CAB. The ANP was not consistently favorable toward Garvey.

73. Press release, February 1934, Reel 8, No. 471, Part I, Press Releases, CAB.

74. Press release, August 1936, Reel 13, No. 508, Part I, Series A, CAB.

75. Press release, October 1931, Reel 4, No. 871, Part I, Press Releases, CAB.

Chapter 2. Haiti and the Bolshevik Revolution

1. Press release, August 1930, Reel 3, No. 115, Part I, Press Releases, CAB.

2. Press release, December 1929, Reel 2, No. 120, Part I, Press Releases, CAB.

3. Press release, December 1929, Reel 2, No. 182, Part I, Press Releases, CAB.

4. Press release, June 1931, Reel 4, No. 364, Part I, Press Releases, CAB.

5. Press release, September 1932, Reel 6, No. 329, Part I, Press Releases, CAB.

6. Press release, January 1929, Reel 1, No. 193, Part I, Press Releases, CAB.

7. Press release, December 1929, Reel 2, No. 120, Part I, Press Releases, CAB.

8. Press release, March 1930, Reel 2, No. 609, Part I, Press Releases, CAB.

9. Press release, June 1930, Reel 2, No. 1026, Part I, Press Releases, CAB.

10. Press release, June 1930, Reel 2, No. 1094, Part I, Press Releases, CAB.

11. Press release, April 1931, Reel 4, No. 72, Part I, Press Releases, CAB.

12. Press release, April 1931, Reel 4, No. 72, Part I, Press Releases, CAB.

13. Press release, February 1930, Reel 2, No. 532, Part I, Press Releases, CAB.

14. Press release, February 1930, Reel 2, No. 439, Part I, Press Releases, CAB.

15. Press release, February 1930, Reel 2, No. 476, Part I, Press Releases, CAB.

16. Press release, June 1931, Reel 4, No. 363, Part I, Press Releases, CAB.

17. Press release, June 1932, Reel 5, No. 881, Part I, Press Releases, CAB.

18. Press release, July 1937, Reel 15, No. 20, Part I, Press Releases, CAB.

19. Claude Barnett to Emmett Scott, 21 November 1933, Reel 4, No. 168, Part III, Series B, CAB.

20. Claude Barnett to Leston Huntley, circa 1934, Reel 3, No. 460, Part III, Series B, CAB.

21. Albon Holsey to Claude Barnett, 23 May 1934, Reel 14, No. 250, Part III, Series B, CAB.

22. Press release, April 1933, Reel 8, No. 907, Part I, Press Releases, CAB.

23. Claude Barnett to Albon Holsey, 29 May 1934, Reel 14, No. 252, Part III, Series B, CAB.

24. Press release drafted by Emmett Scott, 21 December 1939, Reel 5, No. 375, Part III, Series I, CAB.

25. Press release, May 1934, Reel 8, No. 1043, Part I, Press Releases, CAB.

26. Press release, July 1937, Reel 5, No. 87, Part III, Series C, CAB.

27. L. D. Reddick to Claude Barnett, 2 June 1941, Reel 4, No. 500, Part III, Series I, CAB.

28. Claude Barnett to Inez Smith, 5 October 1938, Box 203, Folder 5, CAB-CHM.

29. Press release, December 1933, Reel 8, No. 174, Part I, Press Releases, CAB.

30. Jose Garcia Ynerarity to Claude Barnett, 10 October 1930, Box 203, Folder 4, CAB-CHM.

31. Press release, Reel 3, No. 211, Part I, Press Releases, CAB.

32. Joaquin A. Bercerril to ANP, 12 May 1937, Box 203, Folder 1, CAB-CHM.

33. ANP to *The Black Man*, 18 July 1930, Box 206, Folder 7, CAB-CHM.

34. Victor H. Daniel to Claude Barnett, 13 April 1933, Box 207, Folder 2, CAB-CHM.

35. Press release, November 1931, Reel 3, No. 1120, Part I, Press Releases, CAB.

36. Press release, May 1935, Box 207, Folder 3, CAB-CHM.

37. "The Light," 26 February 1927, Reel 1, No. 401, No. 403, Part II, Organizational Files, CAB.

38. Press release, March 1930, Reel 2, No. 562, Part I, Press Releases, CAB.

39. Press release, September 1930, Reel 3, No. 231, Part I, Press Releases, CAB.

40. Memorandum, 20 July 1939, Box 108, Folder 3, CAB-CHM.

41. Claude Barnett to William Patterson, 15 June 1938, Reel 14, No. 834, Part II, Organizational Files, CAB.

42. Ibid. See also Mark Slagle, "Mightier than the Sword? The Black Press and the End of Racial Segregation in the U.S. Military, 1948–1954" (PhD diss., University of North Carolina–Chapel Hill, 2010), 69.

43. Press release, August 1932, Reel 6, No. 63, Part I, Press Releases, CAB.

44. Press release, November 1938, Reel 17, No. 1084, Part I, Press Releases, CAB.

45. Press release, September 1932, Reel 6, No. 276, Part I, Press Releases, CAB.

46. Press release, September 1932, Reel 6, No. 243, Part I, Press Releases, CAB.

47. Press release, August 1932, Reel 6, No. 68, Part I, Press Releases, CAB.

48. Press release, January 1931, Reel 3, No. 854, Part I, Press Releases, CAB.

49. Press release, February 1931, Reel 3, No. 995, Part I, Press Releases, CAB.

50. Claude Barnett to Paul Robeson, 19 July 1938, Reel 3, No. 30, Part III, Series J, CAB. See also ANP letter, 18 May 1936, Box 108, Folder 3, CAB-CHM. Listed on letterhead then were Frank Marshall Davis at headquarters in Chicago; Chatwood Hall in Moscow; Jameson G. Coka in Johannesburg; Reginald Pierrepointe in the "West Indies"; Adolph Gereau in the U.S. Virgin Islands; Ernest Jameson in "Christobal, Canal Zone"; Dunbar in London.

51. Press release, October 1932, Reel 6, No. 392, Part I, Press Releases, CAB.

52. Press release, Reel 6, No. 199, Part I, Press Releases, CAB.

53. Memorandum, 30 July 1939, Reel 1, No. 148, Part III, Series K, CAB.

54. Press release, March 1930, Reel 1, No. 601, Part I, Press Releases, CAB.

55. Press release, November 1932, Reel 6, No. 676, Part I, Press Releases, CAB.

56. Press release, June 1931, Reel 4, No. 357, Part I, Press Releases, CAB.

57. Press release, June 1931, Reel 4, No. 397, Part I, Press Releases, CAB.

58. Press release, May 1931, Reel 4, No. 342, Part I, Press Releases, CAB.

59. Press release, May 1931, Reel 4, No. 229, Part I, Press Releases, CAB.

60. Press release, February 1935, Reel 10, No. 139, Part I, Press Releases, CAB.

61. Press release, July 1931, Reel 4, No. 554, Part I, Press Releases, CAB.

62. Press release, December 1932, Reel 6, No. 747, Part I, Press Releases, CAB.

63. Press release, August 1932, Reel 6, No. 31, Part I, Press Releases, CAB.

64. Loren Miller to Claude Barnett, 31 March 1933, Box 146, Folder 5, CAB-CHM.

65. Clarence Scott to Claude Barnett, 27 March 1953, Reel 16, No. 53, Part II, Organizational Files, CAB.

66. Jasper T. Duncan to Claude Barnett, 27 November 1933, Reel 24, No. 480, Part II, Organizational Files, CAB.

67. Press release, April 1932, Reel 5, No. 714, Part I, Press Releases, CAB. See e.g. Susan Pennybacker, *From Scottsboro to Munich: Race and Political Culture in 1930s Britain*, Princeton: Princeton University Press, 2009.

68. Claude Barnett to John Spivak, 13 December 1933, Reel 4, No. 482, Part III, Series H, CAB.

69. Claude Barnett to Eugene Gordon, 20 January 1936, Box 201, Folder 4, CAB-CHM.

70. Claude Barnett to John Spivak, 24 October 1935, Reel 4, No. 505, Part III, Series H, CAB.

71. Claude Barnett to Florence Webster, 18 October 1936, Reel 13, No. 841, Part III, Series A, CAB.

72. Protest letter, September 1935, Reel 11, No. 360, Part I, Press Releases, CAB.

73. Claude Barnett to Nancy Cunard, 28 August 1935, Box 198, Folder 11, CAB-CHM.

74. Rudolph Dunbar to Claude Barnett, 7 March 1941, Box 200, Folder 1, CAB-CHM.

75. Press release, June 1933, Reel 7, No. 500, Part I, Press Releases, CAB.

76. Press release, January 1934, Reel 8, No. 324, Part I, Press Releases, CAB.

77. Press release, February 1935, Reel 10, No. 110, Part I, Press Releases, CAB.

78. Thyra Edwards to Claude Barnett, 25 August 1936, Box 137, Folder 4, CAB-CHM.

79. Press release, February 1937, Reel 14, No. 152, Part I, Press Releases, CAB.

80. Claude Barnett to Soviet Embassy, 17 June 1936, Reel 6, No. 131, Part II, Organizational Files, CAB.

81. Press release, February 1937, Reel 14, No. 212, Part I, Press Releases, CAB.

82. Press release, April 1937, Reel 14, No. 707, Part I, Press Releases, CAB.

83. Press release, June 1937, Reel 14, No. 1044, Part I, Press Releases, CAB.

84. Press release, June 1937, Reel 14, No. 1109, Part I, Press Releases, CAB.

85. Press release, July 1938, Reel 17, No. 285, Part I, Press Releases, CAB.

86. Press release, October 1937, Reel 11, No. 185, Part III, Series A, CAB.

87. Press release, July 1937, Reel 15, No. 80, Part I, Press Releases, CAB.

88. Press release, July 1937, Reel 15, No. 59, Part I, Press Releases, CAB.

89. Press release, July 1937, Reel 15, No. 159, Part I, Press Releases, CAB.

90. Press release, July 1937, Reel 15, No. 221, Part I, Press Releases, CAB. See also press release, April 1938, Reel 16, No. 1026, Part I, Press Releases, CAB.

91. Mordecai Johnson to Fred Moore of *New York Age*, 7 June 1933, Reel 6, No. 228, Part III, Series H, CAB.

92. Press release, June 1936, Reel 6, No. 193, Part III, Series H, CAB.

93. Press release, August 1936, Reel 11, No. 508, Part I, Press Releases, CAB.

94. Claude Barnett to Eugene Talmadge, 7 December 1935, Reel 2, No. 569, Part III, Series H, CAB.

95. Press release, September 1936, Reel 13, No. 697, Part III, Series H, CAB.

96. Thyra Edwards to Claude Barnett, 15 June 1937, Box 137, Folder 5, CAB-CHM. See also Gregg Edwards, *Thyra J. Edwards, Black Activist in the Global Freedom Struggle* (Columbia: University of Missouri Press, 2011).

97. Thyra Edwards to Claude Barnett, 15 October 1937, Box 137, Folder 5, CAB-CHM.

98. Press release, 20 November 1929, Reel 2, No. 64, Part I, Press Releases, CAB.

99. Press release, June 1929, Reel 1, No. 696, Part I, Press Releases, CAB.

100. Press release, September 196, Reel 13, No. 763, Part I, Press Releases, CAB.

101. Press release, October 1936, Reel 13, No. 894, Part I, Press Releases, CAB.

102. Claude Barnett to Frederick D. Patterson, 13 January 1941, Reel 7, No. 554, Part III, Press Releases, CAB.

103. Claude Barnett to Noel Sargent, National Association of Manufacturers, 23 August 1940, Reel 1, No. 60, Part III, Series C, CAB.

104. Press release, December 1937, Reel 16, No. 28, Part I, Press Releases, CAB.

105. Memorandum, 10 July 1939, Box 137, Folder 5, CAB-CHM. See also press release, January 1938, Reel 16, No. 150, Part I, Press Releases, CAB: Bethune, Randolph, Pickens, Tobias, et al., "plan conference to plead cause of Loyalist Spain."

106. John A. Williams to Claude Barnett, 13 January 1958, Box 198, Folder 4, CAB-CHM.

107. Press release, February 1937, Reel 14, No. 145, Part I, Press Releases, CAB.

108. Fay Jackson to "Dear Chief," 28 April 1937, Reel 1, No. 1072, Part III, Series D, CAB.

109. Press release, January 1938, Reel 16, No. 190, Part I, Press Releases, CAB. See also Press release, June 1938, Reel 17, No. 201, Part I, Press Releases, CAB: Black Communist, William Patterson, praises Kee.

110. Press release, May 1937, Reel 14, No. 992, Part I, Press Releases, CAB.

111. Press release, June 1938, Reel 17, No. 190, Part I, Press Releases, CAB.

112. Press release, September 1938, Reel 17, No. 852, Part I, Press Releases, CAB.

113. Press release, October 1937, Reel 15, No. 724, Part I, Press Releases, CAB.

114. Press release, October 1937, Reel 15, No. 734, Part I, Press Releases, CAB.

115. Brochure, no date, Box 132, Folder 7, CAB-CHM.

116. P. L. Prattis to Claude Barnett, 18 October 1935, Box 138, Folder 9, CAB-CHM.

117. Press release, January 1938, Box 142, Folder 6, CAB-CHM.

118. Clipping, 3 April 1938, Box 142, Folder 6, CAB-CHM.

119. ANP to Fay Jackson, 17 December 1933, Box 108, Folder 2, CAB-CHM.

120. ANP to P.B. Young, 2 October 1934, Box 108, Folder 3, CAB-CHM:

121. Vincent Fitzpatrick to Claude Barnett, 27 February 1937, Box 198, Folder 4, CAB-CHM.

122. *Oklahoma City Black Dispatch*, 20 March 1937, Box 198, Folder 4, CAB-CHM.

123. Loren Miller to Claude Barnett, 5 January 1928, Box 146, Folder 5, CAB-CHM.

124. J. D. Bass to "Dear Friend Claude," 28 December 1933, Box 146, Folder 5, CAB-CHM.

125. Claude Barnett to John Spivak, 24 October 1935, Reel 4, No. 505, Part III, Series H, CAB.

126. Claude Barnett to Everett Saunders, Republican National Committee—Chicago, 28 September 1932, Reel 2, No. 322, Part III, Series H, CAB.

127. Claude Barnett to "Dear Fay" Jackson, 1 February 1936, Reel 2, No. 584, Part III, Series H, CAB.

Chapter 3. World War Looms

1. Finding Aid, no date, Etta Moten Barnett Papers, Vivian Harsh Research Collections of Afro-American History and Literature, Carter G. Woodson Regional Library, Chicago Public Library.

2. Interview with Etta Moten, 25 September 1991, Box 11, Timuel Black Papers, Vivian Harsh Research Collections of Afro-American History and Literature, Carter G. Woodson Regional Library, Chicago Public Library [hereafter cited as Timuel Black papers].

3. Interview with Etta Moten, 11 November 1998, Box 11, Timuel Black Papers.

4. Enoch P. Waters, *American Diary: A Personal History of the Black Press* (Chicago: Path Press, 1987), 423.

5. Zora Neale Hurston to "Dear Claude," no date, Reel 2, No. 760, Part III, Series D, [hereafter cited as CAB].

6. Claude Barnett to President Roosevelt, 29 January 1934, Reel 2, No. 462, Part III, Series H, CAB.

7. Claude Barnett to Bert Ross, 5 August 1935, Box 199, Folder 2, Claude A. Barnett/ Associated Negro Press Papers, Chicago History Museum [hereafter cited as CAB-CHM].

8. Eslanda Robeson to Etta Moten, 3 March 1935, Box 199, Folder 2, CAB-CHM.

9. Karen Hudson, *Paul Williams, Architect: A Legacy of Style* (New York: Rizzoli, 1993).

10. Claude Barnett to Will Hays, 23 July 1935, Reel 3, No. 03, Part III, Series D, CAB.

11. Claude Barnett to Edwin Meyers, 18 May 1937, Reel 3, No. 16, Part III, Series D, CAB.

12. Edwin Meyers to Claude Barnett, 30 June 1937, Reel 3, No. 18, Part III, Series D, CAB.

13. Claude Barnett to Edwin Meyers, 6 July 1937, Reel 3, No. 19, Part III, Series D, CAB.

14. Claude Barnett to Etta Moten, 4 November 1937, Reel 3, No. 22, Part III, Series D, CAB.

15. Claude Barnett to Ed Sullivan, 10 August 1938, Reel 3, No. 34, Part III, Series D, CAB.

16. Claude Barnett to "Miss Thompson," 25 September 1935, Reel 3, No. 49, Series D, CAB.

17. Claude Barnett to S. M. Lazarus, 29 January 1943, Part III, Series D, CAB.

18. Claude Barnett to Ed Sullivan, 10 August 1938, Reel 3, No. 34, Series D, CAB.

19. Claude Barnett to William Pickens, 4 March 1936, Reel 6, No. 920, Part III, Series I, CAB.

20. Claude Barnett to Herbert Hoey, 29 April 1936, Reel 13, No. 837, Part III, Series A, CAB.

21. Letter to Claude Barnett, 16 September 1937, Reel 13, No. 867, Part III, Series C, CAB.

22. Fay Jackson to "Dear Chief," circa 1937, Reel 1, No. 1002, Part III, Series D, CAB.

23. Claude Barnett to William D. McAdams, 21 June 1941, Reel 6, No. 436, Part III, Series D, CAB.

24. A. A. Schomburg to Claude Barnett, 15 May 1936, Reel 4, No. 612, Part III, Series I, CAB.

25. Claude Barnett to Jesse Thomas, 28 March 1936, Reel 7, No. 858, Part III, Series E, CAB.

26. Claude Barnett to Harry Romm, 24 March 1937, Reel 13, No. 849, Part III, Series C, CAB.

27. Claude Barnett to Harry Romm, 6 May 1937, Reel 13, No. 851, Part III, Series C, CAB.

28. Press release, January 1938, Reel 16, No. 452, Part I, Press Releases, CAB.

29. Press release, October 1938, Reel 17, No. 970, Part I, Press Releases, CAB.

30. Claude Barnett to Hon. John Coffee, 10 November 1941, Reel 3, No. 172, Part III, Series H, CAB.

31. Press release, March 1939, Reel 18, No. 645, Part I, Press Releases, CAB.

32. Letter from Brazilian embassy, 6 March 1939, Box 207, Folder 4, CAB-CHM.

33. Press release, March 1940, Reel 20, No. 565, Part I, Press Releases, CAB.

34. Press release, March 1945, Reel 30, No. 604, Part I, Press Releases, CAB.

35. Claude Barnett to Alvin White, 24 October 1941, Box 140, Folder 6, CAB-CHM.

36. Memorandum by Alvin White on interview at Brazilian embassy, 29 October 1941, Box 140, Folder 6, CAB-CHM.

37. Claude Barnett to "Dear Katherine Dunham," 18 November 1941, Reel 2, No. 803, Part III, Series D, CAB.

38. Claude Barnett to Bill Grady, 18 November 1941, Reel 3, No. 282, Part III, Series D, CAB.

39. Press release, December 1928, Reel 1, No. 54, Part I, Press Releases, CAB (emphasis is in the original).

40. Press release, December 1928, Reel 1, No. 54, Part I, Press Releases, CAB.

41. Press release, January 1931, Reel 3, No. 765, Part I, Press Releases, CAB.

42. Press release, November 1938, Reel 18, No. 21, Part I, Press Releases, CAB. See also José Ángel Ceniceros, Departamento de Asuntos Comerciales y de Protección, Secretario de Relaciones Exteriores to ANP, 18 February 1935, Box 207, Folder 4, CAB-CHM.

43. Claude Barnett to William Taylor, Howard Law School, 25 March 1935, Reel 3, No. 362, Part III, Series B, CAB. See also Claude Barnett to William Taylor, 25 March 1935, Box 207, Folder 4, CAB-CHM.

44. Press release, September 1939, Reel 18, No. 566, Part I, Press Releases, CAB.

45. Press release, October 1940, Reel 21, No. 644, Part I, Press Releases, CAB.

46. Press release, July 1936, Reel 13, No. 329, Part I, Press Releases, CAB.

47. Press release, July 1936, Box 207, Folder 5, CAB-CHM.

48. Edwin Embree to William Pickens, 5 March 1941, Reel 3, No. 981, Part III, Series G, CAB.

49. Clipping, no date, Reel 1, No. 619, Part III, Series D, CAB.

50. Press release, January 1930, Reel 2, No. 379, Part I, Press Releases, CAB.

51. Press release, November 1943, Reel 27, No. 67, Part I, Press Releases, CAB.

52. Press release, April 1941, Reel 21, No. 387, Part I, Press Releases, CAB.

53. Press release, April 1937, Reel 14, No. 620, Part I, Press Releases, CAB.

54. Press release, August 1939, Reel 19, No. 423, Part I, Press Releases, CAB.

55. Claude Barnett to Alvin White, 10 July 1939, Box 140, Folder 4, CAB-CHM.

56. Press release, October 1939, Reel 19, No. 798, Part I, Press Releases, CAB.

57. Caterina Jarboro to Claude Barnett, 19 January 1936, Reel 5, No. 371, Part III, Series D, CAB.

58. Marian Anderson to Claude Barnett, 18 January 1934, Reel 5, No. 69, Part III, Series D, CAB.

59. *Moscow Daily News*, 17 June 1935, Reel 5, No. 201, Part III, Series D, CAB.

60. Press release, March 1937, Reel 5, No. 394, Part III, Series D, CAB.

61. Marian Anderson to Claude Barnett, 23 October 1935, Reel 5, No. 87, Part III, Series D, CAB.

62. Press release, February 1935, Reel 10, No. 247, Part I, Press Releases, CAB.

63. ANP to Fay Jackson, 3 November 1936, Reel 1, No. 956, Part III, Series D, CAB.

64. Fay Jackson to "Dear Chief," circa 1937, Reel 1, No. 1002, Part III, Series D, CAB. She found men in London generally to be "inhuman towards women. I think," she stressed, "it is because ALL ENGLISHMEN ARE SISSIES, essentially if not actually. I mean, London is the motherland of Pansy men. . . . they hold hands. They gossip. . . . they HATE women and enjoy only in the company of each other."

65. Fay Jackson to "Dear Chief," 28 April 1937, Reel 1, No. 1072, Part III, Series D, CAB. "Black men. It is a mania with these English women," referring to Nancy Cunard. "I call the

African boys over here and in Paris—and she's had most of them—Nancy's Empire." What needs to be scrutinized is the extent to which the global reach of these black evangelists may have served to erode Jim Crow. See Clipping, 10 May 1964, Reel 1, No. 1008, Part III, Series J, CAB. Father Divine had followers in Australia and Switzerland; his spouse was Euro Canadian (Clipping, 8 March 1960, Reel 1, No. 959, Part III, Series J, CAB). "More than 5000 Swiss citizens regard" Father Divine as "God." See also Clipping, 12 February 1960, Reel 1, No. 876, Part III, Series J, CAB. Another popular Negro evangelist, Charles M. "Sweet Daddy" Grace, born in Cape Verde, died a millionaire (*Washington Post*, 7 March 1960). Grace was "perhaps the travelingest [*sic*] and richest preacher in history. . . . born Marcelino Manoel da Grace on January 25, 1881."

66. Press release, July 1940, Reel 21, No. 107, Part I, Press Releases, CAB.

67. Press release, February 1937, Reel 14, No. 152, Part I, Press Releases, CAB.

68. Press release, no date, Reel 1, No. 923, Part III, Series D, CAB.

69. W. E. B. DuBois remarks at "New School Negro in American Life Series," no date, Reel 6, No. 208, Part III, Series I, CAB.

70. Noah Williams to "Mrs. Jessee," 21 January 1935, Reel 7, No. 801, Part III, Series J, CAB.

71. Press release, July 1937, Reel 15, No. 41, Part I, Press Releases, CAB. (Here can be found an early ANP dispatch by the novelist.)

72. Richard Wright to Claude Barnett, 5 February 1941, Reel 2, No. 646, Part III, Series D, CAB (emphasis is in the original).

73. Claude Barnett to Richard Wright, 8 February 1941, Reel 2, No. 797, Part III, Series D, CAB.

74. Claude Barnett to Alvin White, 5 March 1941, Box 140, Folder 6, CAB-CHM.

75. Claude Barnett to Cordell Hull, 10 April 1941, Reel 2, No. 802, Part III, Series D, CAB.

76. Zora Neale Hurston to Claude Barnett, 25 February 1939, Reel 2, No. 744, Part III, Series D, CAB.

77. Press release, July 1938, Reel 17, No. 423, Part I, Press Releases, CAB.

78. Claude Barnett to Zora Neale Hurston, 11 March 1939, Reel 2, No. 746, Part III, Series D, CAB.

79. Press release, December 1938, Reel 18, No. 87, Part I, Press Releases, CAB. The ANP also found that the former French colony that was Quebec had "less" racism "on the surface" than the United States. There, black people "have no political" nor "economic power." Almost all Quebec's blacks resided in Montreal: See press release, September 1941, Reel 23, No. 04, Part I, Press Releases, CAB.

80. Press release, February 1937, Reel 14, Part I, Press Releases, CAB.

81. Press release, July 1937, Reel 15, No. 37, Part I, Press Releases, CAB.

82. Press release, September 1938, Reel 17, No. 869, Part I, Press Releases, CAB.

83. Press release, February 1939, Reel 18, No. 285, Part I, Press Releases, CAB.

84. Press release, June 1939, Reel 18, No. 1198, Part I, Press Releases, CAB.

85. Press release, September 1939, Reel 19, No. 531, Part I, Press Releases, CAB.

86. Rudolph Dunbar, 7 March 1941, Box 200, Folder 1, CAB-CHM.

87. Press release, September 1939, Reel 19, No. 532, Part I, Press Releases, CAB.

88. Press release, June 1930, Reel 2, No. 917, Part I, Press Releases, CAB.

89. Press release, July 1938, Reel 17, No. 371, Part I, Press Releases, CAB.

90. Press release, December 1937, Reel 16, No. 96, Part I, Press Releases, CAB.

91. Dr. Charles Drew to Claude Barnett, 29 September 1941, Reel 5, No. 583, Part III, Series E, CAB.

92. Claude Barnett to Alvin White, 19 September 1941, Box 140, Folder 6, CAB-CHM.
93. Press release, October 1938, Reel 17, No. 970, Part I, Press Releases, CAB.
94. Rudolph Dunbar to Claude Barnett, 20 June 1941, Box 200, Folder 1, CAB-CHM.
95. Claude Barnett to Morris Fishbein, 4 June 1938, Reel 1, No. 121, Part III, Series E, CAB. See also Dean of Howard Medical School to Anthony Thompson, 13 October 1936, Reel 3, No. 154, Part III, Series E, CAB: "14 Negroes have published some 75 scientific articles in the various branches of medicine in 30 different scientific journals in the United States, England, Germany, France and Puerto Rico."
96. Remarks by Dean H. M. Smith of the Chicago Baptist Institute, January 1938, Reel 16, No. 142, Part I, Press Releases, CAB: "The most effective protest that the United States can make to the brutal race prejudice of modern Germany is to see that lynching, Jim Crow practices and nationwide economic discrimination against Negroes is stamped out of American life."
97. Press release, July 1938, Reel 17, No. 220, Part I, Press Releases, CAB.
98. Press release, July 1938, Reel 17, No. 245, Part I, Press Releases, CAB.
99. Press release, June 1938, Reel 17, No. 27, Part I, Press Releases, CAB.
100. Press release, November 1938, Reel 18, No. 41, Part I, Press Releases, CAB.
101. Press release, March 1939, Reel 18, No. 430, Part I, Press Releases, CAB.
102. Press release, June 1938, Reel 18, No. 06, Part I, Press Releases, CAB.
103. Press release, May 1939, Reel 18, No. 950, Part I, Press Releases, CAB.
104. Press release, November 1941, Reel 3, No. 169, Part III, Series F, CAB. Lee's remarks were "a bit off the groove," it was said, in that he declared that "stopping Hitler was important but there were other things even more so to him as a 'New Negro' and that he had rather fight Gov. Talmadge [Georgia] or Sen. Bilbo [Mississippi]" and "as a New Negro he disbelieved either in Booker T. Washington or Abraham Lincoln."
105. Press release, February 1941, Reel 22, No. 24, Part I, Press Releases, CAB.
106. Press release, June 1941, Reel 22, No. 772, Part I, Press Releases, CAB.
107. Press release, July 1941, Reel 22, No. 834, Part I, Press Releases, CAB.
108. Press release, July 1941, Reel 22, No. 919, Part I, Press Releases, CAB.
109. Press release, October 1941, Reel 23, No. 246, Part I, Press Releases, CAB.
110. Press release, March 1941, Reel 22, No. 136, Part I, Press Releases, CAB.

Chapter 4. War Changes

1. *Atlanta Daily World,* no date, circa World War II, Box 111, Folder 1, Claude A. Barnett/Associated Negro Press Papers, Chicago History Museum [hereafter cited as CAB-CHM].
2. Claude Barnett to Ernest Johnson, 1 March 1944, Box 138, Folder 2, CAB-CHM.
3. Gerald Horne, *Race War! White Supremacy and the Japanese Attack on the British Empire* (New York: New York University Press, 2003).
4. Patrick Washburn, *A Question of Sedition: The Federal Government's Investigation of the Black Press during World War II* (New York: Oxford University Press, 1986), 63; Lee Finkle, *Forum for Protest: The Black Press during World War II* (Rutherford, NJ: Fairleigh Dickinson University Press, 1975). See also Paul Alkebulan, *The African American Press in World War II: Toward Victory at Home and Abroad* (Lanham, MD: Lexington, 2014).
5. Claude Barnett to Presley Winfield, 26 February 1942, Box 127, Folder 2, CAB-CHM.
6. Report on America First Committee, no date, Reel 3, No. 644, Part III, Series F, Claude A. Barnett/Associated Negro Press Papers, North Carolina State University–Raleigh [hereafter cited as CAB].

7. Claude Barnett to Jackson Davis, 3 February 1942, Part III, Series G, CAB.

8. Quoted in Lawrence D. Hogan, *A Black National News Service: The Associated Negro Press and Claude Barnett, 1919–1945* (Rutherford, NJ: Fairleigh Dickinson University Press, 1984), 163.

9. A. T. Spaulding to P. L. Prattis, 2 March 1942, Box 144, Folder 2, CAB-CHM.

10. Lester Granger to Sylvan Gotshal, President of United Jewish Appeal, 8 September 1943, Reel 1, No. 942, Part III, Series I, CAB: "Daily we read with growing horror of the ruthless savagery unleashed against helpless Jews in Nazi-occupied Europe. We who have known deprivation and suffering in our native land, America, stand against the maniacal fury and bestial atrocities practiced against the Jewish people by Hitler and his foul associates."

11. Press release, July 1939, Reel 19, No. 251, Part I, Press Releases, CAB. Pickens complimented Martha Gruening, who "financed out of her own personal pocket the presentations of the great Pageant of Ethiopia" and who "made the first thorough investigation of lynching" in 1919. Jewish Americans, he said, have done "much more than their numerical proportion" in fighting Jim Crow.

12. William Pickens to Lord Lothian, 5 December 1940, Box 173, Folder 8, CAB-CHM.

13. William Grant Still to Claude Barnett, 17 February 1943, Reel 5, No. 09, Part III, Series D, CAB.

14. Press release, May 1943, Reel 25, No. 901, Part I, Press Releases, CAB.

15. Press release, February 1943, Reel 25, No. 464, Part I, Press Releases, CAB.

16. Claude Barnett to C. A. Scott, et al., 7 April 1942, Reel 1, No. 415, Part III, Series F, CAB.

17. Claude Barnett to P. B. Young, 2 April 1942, Reel 1, No. 375, Part II, Organizational Files, CAB.

18. Thyra Edwards to Claude Barnett, 18 May 1944, Reel 6, No. 175, Part II, Organizational Files, CAB.

19. Claude Barnett to Truman Gibson, 21 May 1941, Reel 1, No. 483, Part III, Series F, CAB.

20. Claude Barnett to P. L. Prattis, 7 April 1942, Box 139, Folder 1, CAB-CHM.

21. Press release, August 1942, Reel 24, No. 653, Part I, Press Releases, CAB. See also press release, Reel 25, No. 181, Part I, Press Releases, CAB. William Pickens scribbled on this page, "I hear Negroes saying that the colored citizens of the United States should emulate the people of India" in their civil disobedience during the war: he disagreed.

22. Claude Barnett to Alvin White, 10 June 1942, Box 141, Folder 1, CAB-CHM.

23. Ernest Johnson to Claude Barnett, 20 June 1944, Box 138, Folder 3, CAB-CHM.

24. Ira Lewis to "Dear Claude," 9 June 1942, Reel 22, No. 859, Part II, Organizational Files, CAB.

25. Claude Barnett to Ira Lewis, 9 June 1942, Reel 22, No. 861, Part II, Organizational Files, CAB.

26. Ernest Johnson to Claude Barnett, 4 June 1943, Box 138, Folder 2, CAB-CHM.

27. Ernest Johnson to William Hassett, 30 June 1943, Box 138, Folder 2, CAB-CHM.

28. Ernest Johnson to Claude Barnett, 21 September 1943, Box 138, Folder 2, CAB-CHM.

29. Press release, March 1942, Reel 23, No. 1025, Part I, Press Releases, CAB. See also press release, June 1943, Reel 25, No. 1098, Part I, Press Releases, CAB

30. Ernest Johnson to Claude Barnett, 18 July 1943, Box 138, Folder 2, CAB-CHM.

31. Ernest Johnson to Claude Barnett, 14 October 1954, Reel 6, No. 890, Part II, Organizational Files, CAB.

32. Press release, June 1942, Reel 24, No. 371, Part I, Press Releases, CAB. Savannah Crowder of Winston-Salem announced the engagement of her niece, Virginia Lee Sim-

mons, to Prince Akiki K. Nyabongo of Uganda of the "Kingdom of Toro." See also press release, July 1942, Reel 24, No. 511, Part I, Press Releases, CAB. I. T. A. Wallace-Johnson of Sierra Leone married Edith Henrietta Downes, born in the United States and raised in Jamaica.

33. Press release, November 1945, Reel 3, No. 832, Part III, Series J, Press Releases, CAB.

34. Press release, March 1945, Reel 30, No. 695, Part I, Press Releases, CAB.

35. Press release, August 1943, Reel 26, No. 607, Part I, Press Releases, CAB.

36. Claude Barnett to Ernest Johnson, 14 October 1943, Box 138, Folder 2, CAB-CHM.

37. Claude Barnett to Ernest Johnson, 15 August 1944, Box 138, Folder 3, CAB-CHM.

38. Ernest Johnson to Claude Barnett, 25 March 1944, Box 138, Folder 3, CAB-CHM.

39. Claude Barnett to Carl Murphy, 20 October 1943, Reel 3, No. 155, Part III, Series F, CAB.

40. Ernest Johnson to Claude Barnett, 14 June 1945, Box 138, Folder 3, CAB-CHM.

41. Turner Catledge to "Dear Claude," 18 November 1945, Box 142, Folder 4, CAB-CHM.

42. Claude Barnett to Turner Catledge, 22 May 1945, Box 142, Folder 2, CAB-CHM.

43. Claude Barnett to "Mr. Catledge," 23 May 1945, Box 142, Folder 2, CAB-CHM.

44. James Wesley Johnson, "The Associated Negro Press" (PhD diss., University of Missouri, 1976), 105.

45. Press release, April 1945, Reel 30, No. 926, Part I, Press Releases, CAB.

46. Claude Barnett to "Gentlemen," "Office of Facts and Figures," 15 January 1942, Reel 5, No. 235, Part II, Organizational Files, CAB.

47. Claude Barnett to "Mr. Turner," 20 November 1945, Box 142, Folder 4, CAB-CHM.

48. Postcard from Jeanne Pelletier to CBS, 7 March 1942, Box 145, Folder 1, CAB-CHM.

49. Memorandum from Claude Barnett, 1942, Box 108, Folder 3, CAB-CHM.

50. Claude Barnett to W. Colston Leigh, 14 September 1945, Box 200, Folder 1, CAB-CHM. See also press release, July 1947, Reel 35, No. 76, Part I, Press Releases, CAB: Dunbar, "internationally famous symphonic conductor . . . to conduct symphonic group" in Paris.

51. "Statement and Recommendations of Roscoe Dunjee to the Steering Committee of the National Negro Business League," 17 November 1944, Reel 8, No. 248, Part III, Series A, CAB.

52. Claude Barnett to N. W. Hopkins, 25 March 1944, Reel 6, No. 465, Part III, Series D, CAB.

53. Claude Barnett, "The Role of the Press, Radio and Motion Picture and Negro Morale," *Journal of Negro Education,* Summer 1943, Reel 2, No. 357, Part III, Series K, CAB.

54. Memorandum from Albert G. Barnett, circa 1942, Box 108, Folder 4, CAB-CHM. See also press release, December 1940, Reel 21, No. 989, Part I, Press Releases, CAB. Pickens over the years gave more than 10,000 speeches "to many millions."

55. Press release, January 1945, Box 108, Folder 4, CAB-CHM.

56. Clipping, 20 February 1943, Reel 11, No. 898, Part III, Series C, CAB.

57. Claude Barnett to Commander Armstrong, Great Lakes Training Station, 21 January 1944, Reel 1, No. 45, Part III, Series F, CAB. [Armstrong first name not available.]

58. Jesse Thomas to Claude Barnett, 19 October 1945, Reel 7, No. 1095, Part III, Series E, CAB.

59. Rudolph Dunbar to Claude Barnett, 20 November 1944, Box 200, Folder 2, CAB-CHM.

60. Audley Connor Jr. to "Dear Sir," 21 June 1945, Reel 6, No. 06, Part III, Series E, CAB.

61. Ernestine Ruiz to Claude Barnett, Reel 2, No. 504, Part III, Series F, CAB.

62. Jesse Thomas to Claude Barnett, 20 November 1945, Reel 7, No. 1102, Part III, Series E, CAB.

63. Brochure by LCP, 1945, Box 199, Folder 2, CAB-CHM.

64. Speech by Claude Barnett, 6 June 1942, Box 143, Folder 6, CAB-CHM.

65. Claude Barnett to Carl Murphy, 20 October 1943, Reel 3, No. 155, Part III, Series F, CAB.

66. List of Foreign Correspondents, 1943, Reel 1, No. 1037, Part III, Series F, CAB. The list included Rudolph Dunbar and Nancy Cunard in London, James Randall in Great Britain, Ben Azikiwe in Lagos, C. G. Whittingham in the Panama Canal Zone, J. M. "Scoop" Jones in the Southwest Pacific, Jameson Coka in Johannesburg, M. G. F. Hoffman in Honolulu, Chatwood Hall in Moscow, and Everett Moore in Iran.

67. Claude Barnett to Florence Murray, Editor–"Negro Handbook," 1 February 1944, Reel 2, No. 58, Part III, Series F, CAB. "We now have additional correspondents," including Sergeant Evelio Grillo, "somewhere in India"; Will V. Neely, "somewhere in South Pacific"; Conrad Clark, "somewhere in South Pacific"; Frank Godden, "Somewhere in Africa"; and Henri O'Bryant Jr., "United States Navy."

68. Press release, April 1945, Reel 30, No. 861, Part I, Press Releases, CAB.

69. Enoch P. Waters, *American Diary: A Personal History of the Black Press* (Chicago: Path Press, 1987), 372.

70. Jack Lockhart, Office of Censorship, to Claude Barnett, 8 January 1944, Reel 2, No. 13, Part III, Series F, CAB.

71. Claude Barnett to Jack Lockhart, 19 January 1944, Reel 2, No. 38, Part III, Series F, CAB: "The enclosed story is scheduled for release Friday from our office in Chicago. We mention the fact that there are 28,000 soldiers in Italy, but do not designate the place, which is Naples. If for any reason anything in this story needs changing, will you please notify us in Chicago?"

72. Rudolph Dunbar to Claude Barnett, 14 April 1944, Box 200, Folder 1, CAB-CHM.

73. Claude Barnett to Attorney General Francis Biddle, 16 June 1943, Reel 1, No. 414, Part II, Organizational Files, CAB.

74. Press release, 19 April 1943, Box 108, Folder 4, CAB-CHM.

75. J. Edgar Hoover to Charles A. Barnett, 22 May 1943, Box 108, Folder 4, CAB-CHM. This letter left open the possibility that letters to the ANP from locations other than the U.S. South were being tampered with.

76. J. Edgar Hoover to Claude Barnett, 22 May 1943, Reel 11, No. 165, Part III, Series C, CAB.

77. Armistead Scott Pride, "A Register and History of New Newspapers in the U.S." (PhD diss., Northwestern University, 1950), 42, 44.

78. Press release, June 1943, Reel 25, No. 1124, Part I, Press Releases, CAB.

79. Walter White to "Dear Claude," 16 June 1943, Box 143, Folder 6, CAB-CHM.

80. ANP Memorandum, 19 April 1943, Box 108, Folder 4, CAB-CHM.

81. Thurman Arnold to ANP, 2 March 1943, Box 143, Folder 6, CAB-CHM.

82. DuBois column in the *Chicago Defender*, 1943, Box 144, Folder 4, CAB-CHM. The date of the column is unclear in this source.

83. Picture and inscription, circa 1943, Reel 3, No. 1043, Part III, Series F, CAB.

84. Press release, December 1944, Reel 3, No. 461, Part III, Series F, CAB.

85. Press release, January 1943, Reel 25, No. 249, Part I, Press Releases, CAB.

86. Press release, May 1944, Reel 28, No. 259, Part I, Press Releases, CAB.

87. Press release, July 1944, Reel 28, No. 1028, Part I, Press Releases, CAB. Reporting from Vilna [Vilnius], Lithuania, Hall wrote that it was "precisely" here that "young black Abram Hannibal, fresh from his native Abyssinia, was christened in [the] Orthodox Church in 1707 with Peter the Great and the Queen of Poland standing as his godparents."

88. Press release, February 1944, Reel 27, No. 734, Part I, Press Releases, CAB.

89. Press release, January 1945, Reel 30, No. 241, Part I, Press Releases, CAB.

90. Press release, July 1942, Reel 24, No. 549, Part I, Press Releases, CAB.

91. Press release, October 1944, Reel 29, No. 714, Part III, Press Releases, CAB.

92. Press release, November 1944, Reel 29, No. 969, Part I, Press Releases, CAB.

93. Press release, April 1945, Reel 30, No. 851, Part I, Press Releases, CAB. For more on Patterson, see also an article from Federated Press, no date, Reel 1, No. 655, Part III, Series D, CAB.

94. Press release, June 1943, Reel 26, No. 33, Part I, Press Releases, CAB.

95. Press release, December 1943, Reel 26, No. 369, Part I, Press Releases, CAB.

96. Press release, November 1943, Reel 26, No. 162, Part I, Press Releases, CAB. Hall added, "all the Jews had been murdered. . . . [T]ens of thousands of Jews lived here before the Hitler hordes."

97. Press release, September 1943, Reel 26, No. 731, Part I, Press Releases, CAB.

98. Press release, September 1943, Reel 26, No. 929, Part I, Press Releases, CAB.

99. Press release, February 1944, Reel 27, No. 933, Part I, Press Releases, CAB: "Negro guerrillas fought fiercely in ravine and forest" to help preserve Soviet power there.

100. Press release, January 1944, Reel 27, No. 628, Part I, Press Releases, CAB.

101. Press release, August 1944, Reel 29, No. 145, Part I, Press Releases, CAB.

102. Press release, November 1944, Reel 29, No. 790, Part I, Press Releases, CAB. Hall wrote, "Key Nazis eye refuge in Africa," particularly in Portuguese colonies, but "the natives will boil and eat them."

103. Press release, August 1944, Reel 29, No. 99, Part I, Press Releases, CAB.

104. Press release, August 1944, Reel 29, No. 212, Part I, Press Releases, CAB.

105. Press release, September 1944, Reel 29, No. 344, Part I, Press Releases, CAB.

106. Press release, November 1944, Reel 29, No. 820, Part I, Press Releases, CAB. Press release, February 1945, Reel 30, No. 455, Part I, Press Releases, CAB. German soldiers put on "black face" to infiltrate U.S. Negro forces in Italy but few are fooled and they were "cut down" by the latter.

107. Press release, September 1943, Reel 26, No. 853, Part I, Press Releases, CAB. Still, Berlin contradicted itself by arguing that Negro folkways had become those of the United States, rendering the U.S. itself illegitimate.

108. Press release, August 1945, Reel 31, No. 610, Part I, Press Releases, CAB.

109. Press release, January 1945, Reel 30, No. 241, Part I, Press Releases, CAB.

110. Claude Barnett to Major Roscoe Giles, Fort Huachuca, Arizona, 11 July 1944, Reel 2, No. 224, Part III, Series F, CAB: "got a cable from Rudolph Dunbar today." See also press release, August 1944, Reel 29, No. 230, Part I, Press Releases, CAB: "New York Negro of Netherlands extraction fighting" in Normandy. Joseph Richardson of Staten Island was with Dutch forces. See also press release, March 1944, Reel 27, No. 1050, Part I, Press Releases, CAB. Trezvant Anderson of ANP met a Dutch soldier in Britain, Alvin Patrick, born in St. Eustasius in the Caribbean, who migrated to the United States in 1928 and resided in the Bronx. He volunteered for the Dutch army in 1943 while in Canada.

111. Claude Barnett to Ernest Johnson, 30 March 1943, Box 138, Folder 2, CAB-CHM.

112. Ernest Johnson to Claude Barnett, 10 May 1943, Box 138, Folder 2, CAB-CHM.

113. Letter to Alvin White, 18 March 1942, Box 141, Folder 1, CAB-CHM.

114. Ernest Johnson to Claude Barnett, 3 June 1943, Reel 6, No. 565, Part II, Organizational Files, CAB.

115. A. O. Akiremi to ANP, 18 September 1933, Box 176, Folder 6, CAB-CHM.

116. Claude Barnett to Félix Éboué, 29 March 1933, Box 176, Folder 6, CAB-CHM.

117. Félix Éboué to Claude Barnett, 11 May 1933, Box 176, Folder 6, CAB-CHM.

118. Claude Barnett to Félix Éboué, 13 February 1941, Box 176, Folder 6, CAB-CHM.

119. Elizabeth Scruggs to Claude Barnett, 17 June 1945, Reel 2, No. 467, Part III, Series F, CAB. She was writing on behalf of Fred Cousins "now being held in confinement as the result of an incident in India" with minimal due process. He had been subject to court-martial in what was seen as a frame-up. Cousins asked her to contact Barnett and other "influential friends of mine." See also Elizabeth Scruggs to Claude Barnett, circa June 1945, Reel 2, No. 483, Part III, Series F, CAB. Cousins had been tried in Calcutta and was confined in Turlock, California, at this time.

120. Claude Barnett to Truman K. Gibson, 16 October 1943, Reel 7, No. 467, Part III, Series A, CAB.

121. Dorothy Porter to "Dear Claude," 27 October 1943, Reel 1, No. 312, Part III, Series K, CAB.

122. Frank Marshall Davis to Truman K. Gibson, 4 April 1942, Reel 9, No. 240, Part III, Series A, CAB. There was a similar concern about German seamen. See clipping, no date, Reel 10, No. 104, Part III, Series A, CAB: "Race seamen rescue stranded Americans . . . close on the heels of press reports that pro-German sympathy of many seamen on American liners [was] making it difficult for the Government to bring stranded Americans back from Europe."

123. Press release, October 1940, Reel 21, No. 667, Part I, Press Releases, CAB.

124. Press release, June 1943, Reel 26, No. 01, Part I, Press Releases, CAB.

Chapter 5. Red Scare Rising

1. Charles Johnson to Claude Barnett, 15 January 1937, Reel 1, No. 111, Part III, Series A, Claude A. Barnett/Associated Negro Press Papers, North Carolina State University–Raleigh [hereafter cited as CAB].

2. Claude Barnett to Benjamin Hubert, President–Georgia State College, 28 April 1941, Reel 2, No. 27, Part III, Series A, CAB.

3. Claude Barnett to Sherman Briscoe, 3 July 1941, Reel 2, No. 87, Part III, Series A, CAB.

4. Sherman Briscoe to Claude Barnett, 29 September 1941, Reel 2, No. 133, Part III, Series A, CAB.

5. Julius Pettigrew to President Roosevelt, 17 October 1941, Reel 2, No. 156, Part III, Series A, CAB.

6. Claude Wickard to Claude Barnett, 25 February 1942, Reel 2, No. 257, Part III, Series A, CAB.

7. Claude Barnett to Attorney Robert Cobb, Jefferson City, Missouri, 15 February 1942, Reel 2, No. 252, Part III, Series A, CAB.

8. Claude Barnett to Assemblyman Gus Hawkins, 18 May 1942, Reel 2, No. 369, Part III, Series A, CAB.

9. E. B. Evans, Negro Extension Work—Prairie View A&M University to Claude Barnett, Reel 3, No. 579, Part III, Series A, CAB.

10. James P. Davis to Claude Barnett, 30 December 1947, Reel 7, No. 806, Part III, Series A, CAB.

11. Horace Mann Bond to Claude Barnett, 1 December 1943, Box 127, Folder 3, Claude A. Barnett/Associated Negro Press Papers, Chicago History Museum [hereafter cited as CAB-CHM].

12. Sherman Briscoe to Claude Barnett, 23 August 1943, Reel 3, No. 57, Part III, Series A, CAB.

13. Frank Pinder to Claude Barnett, 12 January 1944, Reel 3, No. 290, Part III, Series A, CAB.

14. Press release from the U.S. Department of Agriculture, 21 February 1944, Reel 2, No. 345, Part III, Series A, CAB.

15. Press release, February 1944, Reel 2, No. 367, Part III, Series A, CAB.

16. Press release, November 1943, Reel 27, No. 09, Part I, Press Releases, CAB.

17. M. L. Wilson to Claude Barnett, 27 February 1946, Reel 4, No. 383, Part III, Series A, CAB.

18. Press release, May 1944, Reel 28, No. 442, Part I, Press Releases, CAB.

19. Press release, August 1943, Reel 26, No. 538, Part I, Press Releases, CAB.

20. Press release, October 1941, Reel 23, No. 83, Part I, Press Releases, CAB.

21. Press release, September 1944, Reel 29, No. 479, Part I, Press Releases, CAB.

22. Claude Barnett to Sergeant David D. Kravitz, 11 August 1945, Reel 6, No. 321, Part III, Series A, CAB.

23. See letters, October 1941, Box 203, Folder 1, CAB-CHM.

24. Claude Barnett to Etienne Du Puch, Nassau, Bahamas, 15 March 1944, Box 203, Folder 1, CAB-CHM: "this is the second or third story which we have sent you on imported laborers from the Caribbean."

25. Claude Barnett to Vicente Machado Valle, 27 October 1943, Box 206, Folder 6, CAB-CHM (emphasis in the original). The same letter with the same date also was sent to Napoleon Viera-Altamirana, Director of the *Diario de Hoy*, San Salvador, El Salvador; Ramon Blanco of *El Imparcial* in Guatemala City, Guatemala; Jorge Hipolito Escobar of *El Tiempo* in Asunción, Paraguay; Renato Silva of Chile; Antonio Ribera of *El Liberal* in Bogotá, Colombia; and Ebel Romeo Castillo of *El Telegrafo* of Guayaquil, Ecuador. A week later the same letter was sent to Gonzalo Baez Camargo of *Excelsior* of Mexico City; Xavier Sanchez Cavito of *El Nacional* of Mexico City; Abelardo Bonilla of *Diario de Costa Rica*; Ricardo Vernazza of *El Tiempo* of Montevideo, Uruguay; Elias Antonio Pacheco Chavez Nieto of *A Noite* of São Paulo, Brazil; Dr. Andrew Goncalve Carrazoni of *A Noite* of Rio de Janeiro, Brazil; Jose Aguati of *Noticias Graficas* of Buenos Aires, Argentina; Jorge Maclean Estanos of "President's Press Bureau" of Lima, Peru; Nelson Garcia Serrano of *La Razen* of Montevideo, Uruguay; Lis De Zavala of *La Razon* of La Paz, Bolivia; Pedro Joaquin Chamorro of *La Prensa* of Managua, Nicaragua; Enrique Ruiz Vernacci of *Panama-America*; and others.

26. Claude Barnett to Luis Esteban Rey, Caracas, 5 October 1943, Box 207, Folder 9, CAB-CHM.

27. Luis Esteban Rey to Claude Barnett, 25 November 1943, Box 207, Folder 9, CAB-CHM.

28. See article by Wright, press release, July 1937, Reel 15, No. 41, Part I, Press Releases, CAB.

29. Press release, August 1937, Reel 15, No. 337, Part I, Press Releases, CAB.

30. Press release, April 1939, Reel 18, No. 822, Part I, Press Releases, CAB.

31. Press release, April 1943, Reel 25, No. 836, Part I, Press Releases, CAB.

32. Press release, July 1939, Reel 19, No. 157, Part I, Press Releases, CAB.

33. Alvin White to Claude Barnett, circa 1939, Box 140, Folder 4, CAB-CHM.

34. Alvin White to Claude Barnett, no date, circa 1939, Box 141, Folder 1, CAB-CHM.

35. Alvin White to Claude Barnett, 1940, Box 140, Folder 4, CAB-CHM.

36. Claude Barnett to Alvin White, 24 April 1939, Reel 6, No. 389, Part III, Series H, CAB.

37. Claude Barnett to Alvin White, 24 April 1939, Box 140, Folder 3, CAB-CHM.

38. Press release, July 1940, Reel 21, No. 190, Part I, Press Releases, CAB. See also Claude Barnett to Alvin White, 2 December 1939, Box 140, Folder 1, CAB-CHM.

39. Press release, July 1944, Reel 28, No. 1059, Part I, Press Releases, CAB.

40. Press release, August 1944, Reel 29, No. 155, Part I, Press Releases, CAB.

41. Press release, March 1945, Reel 30, No. 683, Part I, Press Releases, CAB.

42. Press release, January 1945, Reel 30, No. 75, Part I, Press Releases, CAB.

43. Gerald Horne, *Black Liberation/Red Scare: Ben Davis and the Communist Party* (Newark, NJ: University of Delaware Press, 1994).

44. Claude Barnett to Luther Peck, 7 May 1943, Reel 8, No. 276, Part I, Press Releases, CAB.

45. Press release, September 1943, Reel 26, No. 849, Part I, Press Releases, CAB.

46. Press release, August 1942, Reel 24, No. 689, Part I, Press Releases, CAB.

47. Press release, October 1946, Reel 33, No. 1074, Part I, Press Releases, CAB.

48. Press release, May 1947, Reel 34, No. 978, Part I, Press Releases, CAB.

49. Claude Barnett to Jackson Davis, 19 October 1946, Reel 1, No. 535, Part III, Series G, CAB:

50. Ernest Johnson to A. Philip Randolph, Box 138, Folder 2, CAB-CHM: "You are undoubtedly the biggest man I have ever met and had occasion to interview as a reporter. Why you're so big, they tell me you've got three secretaries to run interference for you— besides a buzzer on the front door."

51. P. L. Prattis to Virginius Dabney, Editor, *Richmond Times-Dispatch,* 7 July 1943, Box 139, Folder 1, CAB-CHM: "The *Courier* has consistently OPPOSED the March ever since agitation for it began in 1941" (emphasis in the original).

52. Press release, September 1946, Reel 33, No. 993, Part I, Press Releases, CAB.

53. Press release, March 1948, Reel 37, No. 212, Part I, Press Releases, CAB.

54. Press release, April 1949, Reel 40, No. 385, Part I, Press Releases, CAB.

55. Claude Barnett to E. C. Goode, 8 March 1943, Reel 5, No. 457, Part III, Series D, CAB.

56. FBI Report, 24 January 1947, 100–335141–18, Gerald Horne Papers, Schomburg Center, New York Public Library [hereafter, Gerald Horne papers].

57. Press release, March 1948, Reel 37, No. 130, Part I, Press Releases, CAB.

58. Press release, May 1946, Reel 32, No. 1214, Part I, Press Releases, CAB.

59. "Manuscript of a Washington Newsletter," 3 September 1945, Box 143, Folder 7, CAB-CHM.

60. Claude Barnett to George Padmore, 26 July 1947, Box 199, Folder 2, CAB-CHM.

61. George Padmore to Claude Barnett, 18 August 1948, Box 199, Folder 2, CAB-CHM.

62. Frank Marshall Davis to Malcolm Smith, 28 May 1947, Reel 5, No. 241, Part II, Organizational Files, CAB.

63. Claude Barnett to Frank Marshall Davis, 20 February 1949, Reel 5, No. 264, Part II, Organizational Files, CAB.

64. P. L. Prattis to Coriene Robinson Morrow, 2 April 1954, Reel 7, No. 405, Part II, Organizational Files, CAB.

65. Coriene Robinson Morrow to P. L. Prattis, 17 March 1954, Reel 7, No. 398, Part II, Organizational Files, CAB.

66. James Nicholson, Executive Vice President, American National Red Cross to Claude Barnett, 28 January 1952, Reel 15, No. 617, Part II, Organizational Files, CAB.

67. Press release, April 1950, Reel 42, No. 1237, Part I, Press Releases, CAB.

68. Claude Barnett to U.S. Department of Agriculture, 16 February 1949, Reel 5, No. 267, Part III, Series A, CAB.

69. Frank Marshall Davis to Claude Barnett, 2 March 1949, Box 136, Folder 3, CAB-CHM.

70. Sam Bledsoe to Claude Barnett, 13 April 1948, Box 132, Folder 5, CAB-CHM.

71. Sam Bledsoe to Claude Barnett, 13 April 1948, Reel 4, No. 292, Part II, Organizational Files, CAB.

72. Claude Barnett to Alice Dunnigan, 30 August 1947, Box 136, Folder 5, CAB-CHM.

73. Sam Bledsoe to Claude Barnett, 7 April 1948, Box 132, Folder 5, CAB-CHM.

74. FBI Report, 16 April 1945, 100–6146, Gerald Horne Papers.

75. FBI Report, 16 May 1950, 100–335141, Gerald Horne Papers.

76. FBI Report, 8 January 1946, 100–335141–17, Gerald Horne Papers.

77. FBI Report, 25 October 1945, 100–335141–16, Gerald Horne Papers.

78. Press release, April 1946, Reel 32, No. 993, Part I, Press Releases, CAB. See also Roi Ottley, *No Green Pastures* (New York: Scribner's, 1951). This occasional writer for the ANP in his tour of postwar Europe was impressed with France, less so with Italy and Britain, and enthusiastically impressed with Moscow's approach to the Negro.

79. Press release, March 1946, Reel 32, No. 905, Part I, Press Releases, CAB.

80. Press release, March 1946, Reel 32, No. 913, Part I, Press Releases, CAB.

81. Press release, March 1946, Reel 32, No. 806, Part I, Press Releases, CAB. .

82. Press release, September 1944, Reel 29, No. 299, Part I, Press Releases, CAB.

83. Press release, March 1945, Reel 30, No. 521, Part I, Press Releases, CAB.

84. Press release, September 1944, Reel 29, No. 484, Part I, Press Releases, CAB.

85. Claude Barnett to E. Washington Rhodes, *Philadelphia Tribune*, 21 September 1950, Reel 22, No. 310, Part II, Organizational Files, CAB.

86. Harry Levette to Claude Barnett, 26 February 1949, Reel 2, No. 035, Part III, Series D, CAB.

87. Frank Godden to Claude Barnett, 25 October 1947, Box 108, Folder 5, CAB-CHM: "The restrictions here in California against non-whites don't seem to have a chance to survive. . . . I don't believe that one will [find] any city in the country where the Negroes have been able to penetrate themselves in 'exclusive districts' as they have here in Los Angeles."

88. Frank Marshall Davis to Alvin White, 11 June 1947, Box 342, Folder 3, CAB-CHM.

89. Frank Marshall Davis to Claude Barnett, 4 January 1949, Box 136, Folder 3, CAB-CHM. See also Davis to Barnett, 11 January 1949, Box 136, Folder 3, CAB-CHM.

90. Alvin White to Claude Barnett, 1947, Box 342, Folder 3, CAB-CHM.

91. Press release, June 1948, Reel 37, No. 1124, Part I, Press Releases, CAB.

92. Alvin White to Claude Barnett, July 1949, Box 342, Folder 3, CAB-CHM.

93. Press release, April 1949, Reel 4, No. 554, Part III, Series G, CAB.

94. W. M. Black, *Los Angeles Herald Examiner,* to Claude Barnett, 23 May 1950, Box 128, Folder 1, CAB-CHM.

95. Sam Bledsoe to F. D. Patterson, 7 April 1948, Box 132, Folder 5, CAB-CHM.

96. Channing Tobias to Claude Barnett, 5 November 1948, Reel 3, No. 396, Part III, Series G, CAB.

97. Press release, November 1946, Reel 34, No. 45, Part I, Press Releases, CAB.

98. Press release, November 1946, Reel 34, No. 92, Part I, Press Releases, CAB.

99. Press release, August 1947, Reel 35, No. 671, Part I, Press Releases, CAB.

100. Press release, Reel 35, No. 1108, Part I, Press Releases, CAB.

101. Press release, August 1947, Reel 35, No. 747, Part I, Press Releases, CAB.

102. Press release, August 1947, Reel 35, No. 744, Part I, Press Releases, CAB.

103. Press release, December 1946, Reel 34, No. 405, Part I, Press Releases, CAB.

104. Press release, December 1947, Reel 36, No. 381, Part I, Press Releases, CAB.

105. Press release, January 1946, Reel 32, No. 420, Part I, Press Releases, CAB.

106. See, e.g., Gerald Horne, *Fire This Time: The Watts Uprising and the 1960s* (Charlottesville: University of Virginia Press, 1995).

107. William Hawkins to F. D. Patterson, 2 September 1948, Reel 6, No. 417, Part III, Series H, CAB.

108. F. D. Patterson to Claude Barnett, 2 September 1948, Reel 6, No. 418, Part III, Series H, CAB.

109. Claude Barnett to C. C. Spaulding, 28 July 1948, Reel 5, No. 914, Part III, Series C, CAB.

110. Press release, January 1948, Reel 36, No. 664, Part I, Press Releases, CAB.

111. Press release, October 1948, Reel 39, No. 20, Part I, Press Releases, CAB.

112. Alvin White to Claude Barnett, 8 June 1948, Box 141, Folder 3, CAB-CHM: White "is the cock of the walk—but he is going to get a rude awakening. . . . [H]e is a Truman man not so pure and far from simple—dating way back to the days of the Truman committee when he" was accused of "blocking a certain thing in the Truman committee."

Chapter 6. Back to Africa

1. Betty Lou Kilbert Rathbun, "The Rise of the Modern American Negro Press, 1880–1914" (PhD diss., State University of New York–Buffalo, 1978), 247, 272, 275.

2. Lawrence D. Hogan, *A Black National News Service: The Associated Negro Press and Claude Barnett, 1919–1945* (Rutherford, NJ: Fairleigh Dickinson University Press, 1984), 196–97.

3. Alice Dunnigan to Claude Barnett, 13 December 1949, Box 136, Folder 5, Claude A. Barnett/Associated Negro Press Papers, Chicago History Museum (hereafter cited as CAB-CHM).

4. *St. Louis Post-Dispatch*, 2 September 1948, Reel 20, No. 351, Part II, Organizational Files, CAB.

5. James Wesley Johnson, "The Associated Negro Press," Phd diss., University of Missouri–Columbia, 1976, 23.

6. Faye Marley to Claude Barnett, 16 July 1947, Reel 6, No. 88, Part III, Series E, Claude A. Barnett/Associated Negro Press Papers, North Carolina State University–Raleigh (hereafter cited as CAB).

7. Stetson Kennedy to Claude Barnett, 26 June 1948, Box 108, Folder 5, CAB-CHM: "Do you think it would be possible for ANP to pay me an honorarium of even $10 weekly for

a story every week? Klan busting, etc. is not the most profitable of enterprises and even that would help keep the pot boiling."

8. Press release, June 1946, Reel 33, No. 217, Part I, Press Releases, CAB: Negro medics raise $1000 in Harlem for Yugoslav Red Cross; press release, July 1946, Reel 33, No. 453, Part I, Press Releases, CAB: "Influx of Ethiopians to Harlem recently"; press release, November 1945, Reel 31, No. 1152, CAB: "Harlem canteen houses Indonesian seamen."

9. Press release, July 1947, Reel 35, No. 88, Part I, Press Releases, CAB.

10. Press release, August 1946, Reel 33, No. 662, Part I, Press Releases, CAB: "Indian newspapers and leaders score lynching of Negroes in Georgia."

11. Albon Holsey to Claude Barnett, 27 December 1946, Reel 15, No. 103, Part III, Series B, CAB.

12. Claude Barnett to Albon Holsey, 3 January 1947 Reel 15, "110, Part III, Series B., CAB

13. Claude Barnett to Judge J. H. Coussey, 8 December 1949, Box 178, Folder 2, CAB-CHM.

14. Press release, April 1947, Reel 34, No. 664, Part I, Press Releases, CAB.

15. Cedric Dover to Claude Barnett, circa 1947, Box 1, Cedric Dover Papers, Emory University–Atlanta.

16. Claude Barnett to Hoskyns-Abrahall, 8 December 1949, Box 178, Folder 2, CAB-CHM.

17. Press release, August 1946, Reel 33, No. 675, Part I, Press Releases, CAB: "Sweden condemns America's injustice to Negroes." See also press release, March 1946, Reel 32, No. 771, Part I, Press Releases, CAB: "the position of the Negro in America is attracting attention in the Paris press." Cf. Claude Barnett to Robert M. Williams, Stockholm, 10 August 1946, Reel 6, No. 192, Part III, Series J, CAB.

18. Press release, August 1947, Reel 1, No. 546, Part III, Series D, CAB.

19. Press release, April 1948, Reel 37, No. 681, Part I, Press Releases, CAB.

20. Press release, November 1946, Reel 34, No. 149, Part I, Press Releases, CAB: "Two American Negro workers at present working in Russia, including Robert Robinson at the country's biggest ball-bearing works in Moscow" and Richard Williams in Ukraine's aluminum works. Added waspishly, was that in contrast to the United States, "There are hundreds of Red Caps [porters] at Russia's railway station[s] but not one can be found who has studied medicine, law or dentistry." See also Press release, October 1946, Reel 34, No. 04, Part I, Press Releases, CAB: "Vivian Mason of Norfolk, a U.S. Negro woman, arrives in the Soviet Union for a meeting of the International Federation of Democratic Women."

21. Press release, July 1947, Reel 35, No. 222, Part I, Press Releases, CAB:

22. Press release, November 1947, Reel 36, No. 284, Part I, Press Releases, CAB: Johnson "in Vienna" was "the guest of Emperor Franz Josef," and "King Edward of England was critical of Tommy Burns's dodging of Johnson and told the big fella with the golden smile as much. . . . King Alfonso of Spain, a dyed-in-the-wool boxing fan, once questioned Johnson for hours on the subject of glove technique."

23. Press release, July 1947, Reel 35, No. 148, Part I, Press Releases, CAB.

24. Press release, July 1947, Reel 35, No. 245, Part I, Press Releases, CAB.

25. Press release, May 1948, Reel 37, No. 791, Part I, Press Releases, CAB.

26. Press release, September 1947, Reel 35, No. 837, Part I, Press Releases, CAB: Two Egyptians, "Achmed Kotb and Mostafa Momen" arrive at the United Nations, New York to "ask aid of U.S. Negroes in fight for 'unity' of [the] Nile."

27. Gerald Horne, "The Haitian Revolution and the Central Question of African-American History," *Journal of African-American History* 100, no. 1 (Winter 2015): 26–58.

28. Press release, April 1947, Reel 33, No. 717, Part I, Press Releases, CAB.

29. Claude Barnett to Henri Bonnet, French ambassador to the U.S., 8 January 1949, Box 173, Folder 4, CAB-CHM.

30. Press release, May 1947, Reel 34, No. 843, Part I, Press Releases, CAB.

31. Press release, October 1947, Reel 36, No. 01, Part I, Press Releases, CAB.

32. Lt. Col. Marcus Ray to Claude Barnett, 20 September 1949, Reel 2, No. 731, Part III, Series F, CAB. See also press release, August 1948, Reel 38, Part I, Press Releases, CAB: Sixteen "more Jamaicans arrived" in Liberia "to take up permanent residence," including "the dry-cleaner here" who was "doing a profitable business," along with nurses, a plumber, steno-typist, and teachers. Press release, October 1948, Reel 39, No. 34, Part I, Press Releases, CAB: "60,000 Jamaicans petition for return to Africa . . . despite a gloomy picture of Liberia" provided by recent migrants there.

33. Press release, November 1947, Reel 36, No. 227, Part I, Press Releases, CAB. Cf. press release, August 1948, Reel 38, No. 955, Part I, Press Releases, CAB. Press release, September 1948, Reel 38, No. 968, Part I, Press Releases, CAB.

34. Press release, November 1947, Reel 36, No. 369, Part I, Press Releases, CAB.

35. W. E. B. DuBois, "Race Relations in the United States, 1917–1947," Reel 6, No. 104, Part III, Series I, CAB.

36. Charles Johnson to Claude Barnett, 17 October 1946, Reel 2, No. 760, Part III, Series B, CAB. Johnson also was designated by Washington to aid in remaking the "education and cultural systems" of occupied Japan: Clipping, April 1946, Reel 2, No. 859, Part III, Series B, CAB.

37. Press release, August 1949, Reel 2, No. 62, Part III, Series J, CAB.

38. Claude Barnett to Charles Ross, 17 January 1948, Reel 3, No. 345, Part III, Series H, CAB.

39. Report, 18 August 1947, Reel 8, No. 400, Part III, Series C, CAB.

40. Press release, July 1949, Reel 4, No. 959, Part III, Series G, CAB.

41. J. Max Bond to Claude Barnett, 19 November 1948, Reel 8, No. 450, Part III, Series H, CAB.

42. Claude Barnett to J. Max Bond, 25 November 1948, Reel 8, No. 451, Part III, Series H, CAB. See Claude Barnett to Alice Dunnigan, 22 February 1950, Box 136, Folder 5, CAB-CHM.

43. Managing Director of the *Gleaner* of Jamaica to Claude Barnett, 9 January 1947, Reel 6, No. 334, Part III, Series C, CAB.

44. Jocelyn Francis to Claude Barnett, 15 January 1947, Reel 6, No. 337, Part III, Series C, CAB. See also Claude to Ellis and Earl, 25 January 1947, Reel 6, No. 343, Part III, Series C, CAB.

45. Earl Dickerson and W. Ellis Stewart to Claude Barnett, 3 February 1947, Reel 6, No. 347, Part III, Series C, CAB.

46. Gerald Horne, *Mau Mau in Harlem? The U.S. and the Liberation of Kenya* (New York: Palgrave, 2009); Gerald Horne, *From the Barrel of a Gun: The U.S. and the War against Zimbabwe* (Chapel Hill: University of North Carolina Press, 2001).

47. Claude Barnett to W. E. F. War, Colonial Office–London, 6 September 1947, Reel 2, No. 543, Part III, Series G, CAB.

48. Claude Barnett to Thomas C. Wasson, 15 July 1946, Reel 7, No. 679, Part III, Series C, CAB.

49. Claude Barnett to Kenneth Meeker, Chief Liberia Division, State Department, Box 190, Folder 3, CAB-CHM.

50. Claude Barnett to Albon Holsey, Haytian Afro-American Chamber of Commerce, 26 July 1946, Reel 15, No. 40, Part III, Series B, CAB. See also *Kansas City Call*, 15 December 1950: "Sen. Elmer Thomas asked Congress to appropriate money to buy the Kerford caves in Atchison, Kansas"; and *Wall Street Journal*, 22 December 1960: "More firms use old mines for storage, production, farming. . . . Pentagon has bomb shelter for tools."

51. Claude Barnett to Albon Holsey, 28 July 1946, Box 190, Folder 1, CAB-CHM.

52. C. B. Powell, *New York Amsterdam News,* to Claude Barnett, 23 July 1946, Box 168, Folder 5, CAB-CHM. In the same file see also Manuel Garlikov, *Daily Bulletin* of Dayton, to Claude Barnett, 20 July 1946: Both express an inability to fund coverage in Africa. Also in the same file, see Ulysses Boykin, *Detroit Tribune,* to Claude Barnett, 5 July 1946: "I made a survey" and readers want more material on South Africa "because Detroit's AME Bishop George W. Baber has been assigned there and colorful Ethiopia because of its tie in Soviet interest"—funding, however, was left to the ANP.

53. E. Martin Lancaster to Claude Barnett, 12 August 1946, Reel 12, No. 223, Part III, Series C, CAB.

54. Alonzo H. Phillips to Claude Barnett, 31 October 1945, Box 191, Folder 6, CAB-CHM.

55. Claude Barnett to Basil O'Connor, 18 March 1947, Reel 1, No. 503, Part III, Series K, CAB.

56. Peggy Peterson to "Dear Claude," 23 November 1947, Reel 1, No. 526, Part III, Series K, CAB: "My great uncle General T. Morris Chester was Superintendent of Schools in Liberia in the 18 fifties [*sic*]; he married and stayed there a few years; he was a friend of Alex. Dumas and Ira Aldridge and was wined and dined by Emperor Alexander of Russia. . . . [M]y uncle was Minister to San Domingo and Haiti, perhaps I also have cousins there."

57. Enoch P. Waters, *American Diary: A Personal History of the Black Press* (Chicago: Path Press, 1987)*,* 418.

58. Jacob Reddix to Claude Barnett, 19 April 1946, Box 190, Folder 3, CAB-CHM.

59. Sidney Williams to Claude Barnett, 26 March 1947, Reel 8, No. 998, Part III, Series I, CAB.

60. Press release, February 1956, Reel 59, No. 286, Part I, Press Releases, CAB.

61. George Burchum to Claude Barnett, 26 September 1947, Box 190, Folder 3, CAB-CHM.

62. Claude Barnett to Eli Oberstein, 4 March 1947, Reel 6, No. 573, Part III, Series D, CAB.

63. Lester Walton to Claude Barnett, 26 November 1935, Box 188, Folder 1, CAB-CHM.

64. Clipping, 4 October 1940, Box 188, Folder 2, CAB-CHM,

65. *Weekly Mirror* [Monrovia], 17 August 1945; *Chicago Defender*, 26 June 1945.

66. Lester Walton to Claude Barnett, 29 January 1946, Box 188, Folder 2, CAB-CHM.

67. Lester Walton to Claude Barnett, 8 February 1947, Box 188, Folder 2, CAB-CHM.

68. Press release, December 1945, Reel 32, No. 207, Part I, Press Releases, CAB.

69. Press release, December 1945, Reel 32, No. 83, Part I, Press Releases, CAB; press release, January 1946, Reel 32, No. 361, Part I, Press Releases, CAB.

70. Claude Barnett to E. K. Featherstone, 6 October 1947, Box 192, Folder 5, CAB-CHM.

71. Claude Barnett to Nnamdi Azikiwe, 11 March 1947, Box 192, Folder 5, CAB-CHM.

72. Claude Barnett to E. K. Featherstone, 23 September 1947, Box 192, Folder 5, CAB-CHM.

73. Claude Barnett and Etta Moten, "A West African Journey," 1 September 1947, Reel 2, No. 323, Part III, Series K, CAB.

74. Claude Barnett to Channing Tobias, 21 May 1947, Reel 3, No. 285, Part III, Series G, CAB.

75. Claude Barnett to Channing Tobias, 9 June 1947, Reel 3, No. 287, Part III, Series G, CAB.

76. Claude Barnett to Dale Cox, 24 February 1948, Reel 4, No. 271, Part III, Series I, CAB.

77. Claude Barnett to Georges Apedo-Amah, 24 February 1948, Box 177, Folder 9, CAB-CHM.

78. Dale Cox to Claude Barnett, 12 April 1948, Reel 4, No. 285, Part III, Series I, CAB.

79. V. P. Bourne-Vanneck to Claude Barnett, 5 October 1947, Reel 20, No. 271, Part II, Organizational Files, CAB.

80. Claude Barnett to Helen Gambrill, 17 November 1947, Reel 7, No. 172, Part III, Series E, CAB.

81. Christopher W. M. Cox to Colonial Office, 10 December 1948, Box 199, Folder 2, CAB-CHM.

82. Press release, April 1947, Reel 34, No. 550, Part I, Press Releases, CAB.

83. Barnett apparently was embraced by London. See Charles Hall, Elks–Washington, D.C., to Claude Barnett, 4 December 1946, Reel 1, No. 48, Part III, Series G, CAB: "Received a letter from an English blonde in which she mentioned having met you at a cocktail party in London. Fine going for a man from Matoon [*sic;* Illinois]—or is it Macomb?"

84. Claude Barnett to Mary Brady, Harmon Foundation, 18 March 1947, Reel 1, No. 742, Part III, Series G, CAB.

85. Claude Barnett to BOAC, 10 July 1948, Reel 3, No. 458, Part III, Series D, CAB. Barnett shot twelve hundred feet of motion pictures in Africa, including three hundred at the Booker T. Washington Institute in Liberia: Claude Barnett to Hon. and Mrs. T. Hoskyns-Abrahall, Ibadan, Reel 1, No. 894, Part III, Series G, CAB.

86. Claude Barnett to Mr. L. W. Harrison, 20 March 1948, Reel 5, No. 716, Part III, Series G, CAB.

87. Claude Barnett to Hon. and Mrs. T. Hoskyns-Abrahall, 10 March 1948, Box 178, Folder 1, CAB-CHM.

88. Correspondence between Claude Barnett and E. E. Sabban-Clare, Colonial Attaché, 30 March 1948, Box 178, Folder 1, CAB-CHM.

89. Jackson Davis to Claude Barnett, 3 August 1945, Reel 1, No. 497, Part III, Series G, CAB.

90. Claude Barnett to W. E. F. Ward, 6 September 1947, Reel 2, No. 543, Part III, Series D, CAB.

91. L. A. Roy, Phelps-Stokes Fund, to Claude Barnett, 29 September 1947, Reel 2, No. 552, Part III, Series G, CAB.

92. Claude Barnett to Channing Tobias, 18 October 1947, Reel 3, No. 317, Part III, Series G, CAB.

93. Rudolph Dunbar to Claude Dunbar, September 1948, Box 200, Folder 2, CAB-CHM.

94. Richard Wright to Claude Barnett, 19 May 1948, Reel 2, No. 803, Part III, Series D, CAB.

95. Memorandum from Claude Barnett, 1 June 1948, Reel 2, No. 806, Part III, Series D, CAB.

96. Claude Barnett to District Magistrate, 8 November 1947, Box 179, Folder 7, CAB-CHM.

97. See thick sheaf of clippings on the Barnett-Moten art collection, Box 168, Folder 10, CAB-CHM, and the numerous receipts for art purchases in Box 169, Folder 1, CAB-CHM.

98. See thick sheaf of clippings on the 1947 tour, Box 170, Folder 3, CAB-CHM.

99. Claude Barnett and Etta Moten, "A West African Journey," 1 September 1947, Reel 2, No. 497, Part III, Series G, CAB.

100. Minutes of Board of Liberia Company, 1 December 1947, Box 190, Folder 3, CAB-CHM.

101. Remarks by Claude Barnett, 2 January 1948, Box 190, Folder 3, CAB-CHM.

102. Claude Barnett to Channing Tobias, 30 July 1948, Reel 3, No. 371, Part III, Series G, CAB.

103. Channing Tobias to Claude Barnett, 16 September 1948, Reel 3, No. 391, Part III, Series G, CAB.

104. Brochure on Department of Commerce conference, 1–3 April 1948, Reel 12, No. 318, Part III, Series C, CAB.

105. Claude Barnett to Robert Resor, 14 May 1948, Box 190, Folder 5, CAB-CHM.

106. Robert Resor to Claude Barnett, 17 August 1948, Box 190, Folder 5, CAB-CHM.

107. Claude Barnett to Channing Tobias, 9 November 1948, Reel 3, No. 397, Part III, Series G, CAB.

108. Claude Barnett to F. D. Patterson, 23 December 1947, Reel 8, No. 470, Part III, Series B, CAB.

109. Jacob Dosoo Amenyah to "Sir," 19 May 1947, Box 178, Folder 1, CAB-CHM.

110. Frederick Douglass Patterson to Claude Barnett, 5 March 1948, Reel 8, No. 486, Part III, Series B, CAB.

111. Claude Barnett to Harold Cooper, 13 January 1948, Reel 1, No. 836, Part III, Series G, CAB.

112. Dorothy Porter to Claude Barnett, 25 February 1949, Reel 1, No. 624, Part III, Series K, CAB.

113. Claude Barnett to Hoskyns-Abrahall, 8 December 1949, Box 178, Folder 2, CAB-CHM.

114. Nnamdi Azikiwe, Zik's Press Ltd.–Lagos to Claude Barnett, 7 June 1948, Box 194, Folder 1, CAB-CHM: "I need badly news and photo-blocks or mates of (1) Negro athletes, boxers and tennis stars (but none of football, baseball and basketball); (2) Negro actresses, actors and musicians."

115. Telegram from J. E. Appiah, WASU, 13 January 1947, Reel 1, No. 585, Part III, Series G, CAB.

116. Claude Barnett to Oscar Chapman, 29 October 1949, Reel 11, No. 248, Part III, Series C, CAB.

117. Oscar Chapman to Claude Barnett, 2 November 1949, Reel 11, No. 249, Part III, Series C, CAB.

118. Donald Chisholm, Nigerian Printing and Publishers, *Daily Times*–Lagos to Claude Barnett, 4 April 1949, Reel 1, No. 578, Part II, Organizational Files, CAB.

119. Claude Barnett to Hon. and Mrs. T. Hoskyns-Abrahall, 10 March 1948, Box 178, Folder 1, CAB-CHM.

120. Claude Barnett to Blackwell Smith, President of Liberian Company, 9 March 1948, Box 190, Folder 3, CAB-CHM.

121. Claude Barnett to Stanley Adams, Assistant to President and General Manager, Liberia Company, 23 April 1948, Box 190, Folder 4, CAB-CHM.

122. Claude Barnett to T. Hoskyns-Abrahall, 4 December 1948, Reel 1, No. 937, Part III, Series G, CAB. This letter also can be found at Reel 3, No. 425, Part III, Series H, CAB.

123. Johnson, "Associated Negro Press," 148.

124. M. A. McCall, U.S. Department of Agriculture, to Claude Barnett, 4 November 1949, Reel 4, No. 616, Part III, Series A, CAB.

125. Claude Barnett to Dr. M. V. Lambert, Dean of Nebraska Experimental Station, 6 September 1949, Reel 5, No. 427, Part III, Series A, CAB: "What was your general impression of the possibilities before the Africans in Kenya and the adjacent areas where you visited them [?]. Africans claim that they are not being afforded adequate means of schooling and that a program of exploitation exists . . . in Uganda especially the newspapers and planters are opposed to permitting natives to go out of the country for schooling, even to England and India. . . . [There was a] tendency in Kenya and Northern Rhodesia to encourage European farmers to settle who promptly expropriate the land and become a landed gentry riding along on the native's back."

126. Ibid.; Barnett to Hoskyns-Abrahall, 4 December 1948.

127. Press release, September 1949, Reel 38, No. 967, Part I, Press Releases, CAB, in which John Sengstacke, Louis Martin, and a bevy of other Negro press leaders praise Truman.

Chapter 7. Cold War Coming

1. Press release, October 1949, Reel 41, No. 940, Part I, Press Releases, Claude A. Barnett/Associated Negro Press Papers, North Carolina State University–Raleigh (hereafter cited as CAB).

2. Press release, March 1949, Reel 40, No. 287, Part I, Press Releases, CAB.

3. Press release, June 1949, Reel 40, No. 991, Part I, Press Releases, CAB.

4. Press release, September 1949, Reel 41, No. 628, Part I, Press Releases, CAB.

5. Press release, July 1949, Reel 41, No. 138, Part I, Press Releases, CAB.

6. Press release, November 1950, Reel 5, No. 579, Part III, Series D, CAB: James T. (Popeye) Bellafont, twenty-nine, of Columbia, South Carolina, and leader of the Mutual Association of Colored People, has launched an anti-Robeson campaign: "I like to dress the best I can. That's another reason I want to see Robeson [shut up]. I run into so many people who think just because I'm dressed up I'm connected with Robeson or the Communists."

7. Alice Dunnigan to Claude Barnett, 30 January 1948, Box 136, Folder 5, Claude A. Barnett/Associated Negro Press Papers, Chicago History Museum (hereafter cited as CAB-CHM).

8. Alice Dunnigan to Claude Barnett, 21 June 1948, Box 136, Folder 5, CAB-CHM: "The courtesy which was extended to me by the leading white newspaper men in this country who were aboard the President's train," somehow "did not come from the Negro reporters aboard." Further, both sides' "story" they reported came from an "exclusive from me," she said. Then there were Barnett's "rewrites" of her prose, which amounted to "misinterpretations of my stories." "Somehow," she continued "the Negro press will not publish the facts exactly like the white press publishes the things which they send in—I wonder why."

9. Alice Dunnigan to Claude Barnett, 25 June 1948, Box 136, Folder 5, CAB-CHM.

10. Alice Dunnigan to Claude Barnett, no date, Box 136, Folder 5, CAB-CHM.

11. Press release, November 1951, Reel 47, No. 417, Part I, Press Releases, CAB. Alice Dunnigan to Claude Barnett, no date, Box 136, Folder 5, CAB-CHM. Dunnigan was

one of the most articulate opponents of sexism during this often-conformist era: A fall festival she attended was a "swell affair, cabaret style" but then there was a "fashion show, a leg contest. . . . [I]magine my surprise when I was called up to the front to be one of the judges of the leg contest. Sure this is irregular for a woman to judge another woman's legs. Frankly I have never taken a second look at another woman's legs unless they were very unusual."

12. Press release, January 1951, Reel 1, No. 651, Part III, Series E, CAB.

13. Claude Barnett to Lucille Chambers Norman, 13 June 1953, Reel 2, No. 595, Part III, Series E, CAB.

14. Claude Barnett to "Dear Pat and Catherine," 21 December 1950, Reel 1, No. 738, Part III, Series K, CAB.

15. Alice Dunnigan to Claude Barnett, no date, Box 136, Folder 5, CAB-CHM: "Here is the thing, which has hurt me to the quick—when I recently found out you were adding to this current, undercover dirt, by taking sides with my known enemies by also belittling me and telling Mrs. [Mary McLeod] Bethune and perhaps others that I was no good, and that I was [not] worthy [of] my hire. . . . [Y]ou told her that I was not worth any more money and that you retained me because you could get the work done cheap. Mrs. Bethune has told everyone who came in contact with her and I have been a laughingstock for those enemies who [are] in the same stall with the First Lady of the Negro Race."

16. Alice Dunnigan to Claude Barnett, 12 July 1948, Box 136, Folder 5, CAB-CHM.

17. Claude Barnett to Alice Dunnigan, 27 May 1950, Box 136, Folder 5, CAB-CHM.

18. Alice Dunnigan to Claude Barnett, 1951[?], Box 137, Folder 1, CAB-CHM.

19. W. C. Hueston to Claude Barnett, 24 February 1948, Reel 1, No. 167, Part III, Series G, CAB.

20. Clipping, 1949[?], Box 136, Folder 5, CAB-CHM.

21. Gerald Horne, *Black and Red: W.E.B. Du Bois and the Afro-American Response to the Cold War, 1944–1963* (Albany: State University of New York Press, 1986).

22. Press release, June 1948, Reel 38, No. 446, Part I, Press Releases, CAB.

23. Press release, August 1948, Reel 38, No. 480, Part I, Press Releases, CAB.

24. Press release, June 1948, Reel 37, No. 1006, Part I, Press Releases, CAB.

25. Press release, June 1948, Reel 38, No. 99, Part I, Press Releases, CAB.

26. Press release, September 1949, Reel 41, No. 647, Part I, Press Releases, CAB.

27. Press release, May 1948, Reel 37, No. 860, Part I, Press Releases, CAB. Compare press release, October 1948, Reel 39, No. 83, Part I, Press Releases, CAB: "On the Palestine Question, Mr. [Walter] White was not for a separate state and said that he looked upon Palestine only as a temporary refuge for all," including "Jews, Arabs." Compare also the words of ANP columnist A. J. Siggins: "Israel was a mistake from the Jewish angle as well as from the U.S.A., British and French angle. . . . [T]he Jews have been a martyred race for many centuries. They have now made martyrs and that will prove to be worse than a crime—[it is] a blunder" (press release, May 1957, Reel 62, No. 865, Part I, Press Releases, CAB). See also press release, April 1958, Reel 64, No. 1077, Part I, Press Releases, CAB: "The people of Israel are loud in their expressions of gratitude to Negro Americans who have contributed so generously to the nation," e.g., Dr. Theodore Lawless, a Chicago physician; musician Lionel Hampton; et al. Dr. Lawless donated $400,000 for the dermatology wing of a hospital that bears his name. William Booker of the historically black Virginia State University, who was a supply sergeant during World War II, worked for the UN beginning in 1946 and by 1948 was in Palestine. By 1958 he was in Lebanon and by 1960 in Kano,

Nigeria (press release, November 1960, Reel 72, No. 124, Part I, Press Releases, CAB). See also press release, December 1962, Reel 5, No. 879, Part III, Series J, CAB: Joan West, 18, from St. Albans, Queens, New York is "fluent in Hebrew" and "first Negro to enroll at Hebrew University," where she also studies French and Arabic. It would be worthwhile to have a comprehensive study of relations between U.S. Negroes and Israel.

28. Press release, June 1948, Reel 37, No. 1128, Part I, Press Releases, CAB. Claude Barnett to R. K. Gardner, 3 November 1948, Box 173, Folder 8, CAB-CHM: "When the Palestine matter was up at Lake Success, can you tell me what position Liberian, Haitian and Ethiopian delegations took?" See also Hassen Abraham, South Bend, Indiana Federation of Islamic Associations to Claude Barnett, 5 July 1957, Box 173, Folder 1, CAB-CHM: "Many news agencies are inclined to use the words 'Islam' and 'Muslim' to infer fanaticism and mysticism. . . . [N]o support in the American press for the rights of Palestinian refugees."

29. Claude Barnett to W. V. S. Tubman, 17 January 1951, Box 185, Folder 2, CAB-CHM.

30. Press release, September 1951, Reel 3, No. 504, Part III, Series G, CAB.

31. Patsy Graves to Claude Barnett, 20 July 1951, Reel 6, Part III, Series A, CAB: Mary McLeod Bethune criticized by mainstream on anticommunist grounds.

32. Clipping, 23 October 1951, Reel 3, No. 613, Part III, Series G, CAB.

33. Press release, June 1954, Reel 54, No. 858, Part I, Press Releases, CAB.

34. Claude Barnett to Channing Tobias, 29 September 1951, Reel 3, No. 544, Part III, Series G, CAB.

35. Claude Barnett to Channing Tobias, 31 October 1951, Reel 3, No. 547, Part III, Series G, CAB. See also Leopold Senghor to Claude Barnett, 12 August 1954, Box 198, Folder 9, CAB-CHM.

36. Press release, April 1950, Reel 2, No. 257, Part III, Series C, CAB: Rose Morgan of New York and Chicago, president of Rosa-Meta sweeps into Paris; her "famed beauty and cosmetic combination" envisioned an "empire of beauty salons and salons serving 80 million Africans." See also press release, April 1950, Reel 2, No. 257, Part III, Series C, CAB.

37. B. T. Bradshaw to Claude Barnett, 25 July 1950, Reel 4, No. 167, Part III, Series C, CAB.

38. Gerald Horne, *Black Revolutionary: William Patterson and the Globalization of the African American Freedom Struggle* (Urbana: University of Illinois Press, 2013).

39. Channing Tobias to Claude Barnett, 17 November 1951, Reel 3, No. 551, Part III, Series G, CAB.

40. Claude Barnett to Negro Press, 13 November 1954, Box 194, Folder 9, CAB-CHM.

41. Claude Barnett to Ruth Sloan, State Department, 5 March 1951, Box 209, Folder 1, CAB-CHM.

42. Claude Barnett to Horace Mann Bond, 10 December 1949, Reel 1, No. 670, Part III, Series K, CAB. Claude Barnett to Emmanuel Racine, 7 June 1952, Box 205, Folder 4, CAB-CHM. See also press release, April 1950, Reel 3, No. 825, Part III, Series J, CAB.

43. Claude Barnett to Channing Tobias, 23 November 1951, Reel 3, No. 552, Part III, Series G, CAB.

44. Claude Barnett to George McCray, 1 May 1950, Box 168, Folder 5, CAB-CHM.

45. Press release, April 1950, Reel 10, No. 218, Part III, Series C, CAB.

46. Press release, June 1951, Reel 13, No. 364, Part III, Series C, CAB.

47. A. J. Siggins to Claude Barnett, 28 April 1951, Box 200, Folder 4, CAB-CHM.

48. Claude Barnett to Gabriel Dennis, 30 June 1951, Box 185, Folder 5, CAB-CHM.

49. Claude Barnett to William V. S. Tubman, 26 March 1951, Box 185, Folder 2, CAB-CHM.

50. Claude Barnett to Nnamdi Azikiwe, 13 November 1951, Box 193, Folder 1, CAB-CHM.

51. Press release, July 1951, Reel 6, No. 35, Part III, Series H, CAB.

52. Press release, April 1951, Reel 6, No. 298, Part III, Series H, CAB.

53. Claude Barnett to Kelsey Pharr, 15 November 1952, Reel 3, No. 331, Part III, Series C, CAB. Barnett went further to press a fellow Negro mogul to endorse Dickerson: Claude Barnett to Norman Houston, president of the Golden State Insurance Company in Los Angeles, 15 November 1952, Reel 4, No. 191, Part III, Series C, CAB.

54. Claude Barnett to Gabriel Dennis, 17 September 1952, Box 185, Folder 1, CAB-CHM.

55. Claude Barnett to Gabriel Dennis, 16 December 1952, Box 185, Folder 1, CAB-CHM.

56. Claude Barnett to Channing Tobias, 12 January 1952, Reel 3, No. 572, Part III, Series G, CAB.

57. Claude Barnett to President Truman, 4 August 1951, Reel 3, No. 551, Part III, Series H, CAB.

58. Claude Barnett to Dean Acheson, 4 August 1951, Box 208, Folder 1, CAB-CHM.

59. Claude Barnett to Ruth Sloan, 7 April 1949, Box 208, Folder 6, CAB-CHM.

60. Claude Barnett to Dean Acheson, 16 March 1954, Reel 3, No. 762, Part III, Series H, CAB.

61. Press release, April 1949, Reel 40, No. 423, Part I, Press Releases, CAB: Invitees included Jeanette Welch Brown of the National Council of Negro Women and William H. Jernagin of the Federal Council of Churches.

62. Press release, August 1951, Reel 46, No. 519, Part I, Press Releases, CAB.

63. Press release, February 1951, Reel 3, No. 291, Part III, Series C, CAB.

64. Press release, January 1952, Reel 3, No. 254, Part III, Series C, CAB.

65. Press release, September 1950, Reel 9, No. 513, Part III, Series C, CAB.

66. Alex Poinsett, Johnson Publishing Company, to Claude Barnett, 23 June 1953, Reel 4, No. 549, Part III, Series E, CAB. The Red Cross replied with an ambiguous denial: Ramone Eaton, Red Cross to Alex Poinsett, 2 July 1953, Reel 6, No. 550, Part III, Series E, CAB.

67. Claude Barnett to James T. Nicholson, 15 February 1952, Reel 5, No. 437, Part III, Series C, CAB.

68. James T. Nicholson, Executive Vice-President of American Red Cross, 28 January 1952, Reel 5, No. 583, Part III, Series E, CAB.

69. Charlotte Hawkins Brown to Claude Barnett, 13 April 1951, Reel 5, No. 733, Part III, Series B, CAB.

70. See also Claude Barnett to Robert Lucas, 27 September 1950, Reel 1, No. 227, Part III, Series D, CAB.

71. Robert Lucas to Claude Barnett, 22 December 1950, Reel 1, No. 225, Part III, Series D, CAB.

72. Claude Barnett to Sidney Jones, 11 February 1950, Reel 8, No. 556, Part III, Series H, CAB.

73. J. F. Adams to Claude Barnett, 10 September 1953, Box 200, Folder 4, CAB-CHM.

74. Robert Butts to Claude Barnett, 20 October 1951, Box 201, Folder 1, CAB-CHM: "I might add to the Malaya caption that the British have been leading the war against the Communist bandits for over three years. . . . [T]hey also destroy plants, cut rubber trees and disrail [sic] trains." See also Claude Barnett to British Information Service, 11 March

1953, Box 202, Folder 2, CAB-CHM: Barnett's query: how many African troops were then fighting for London in Malaya?

75. Memorandum from Stafford E. D. Barff, 26 May 1961, Box 201, Folder 3, CAB-CHM.

76. Claude Barnett to Luc Grimard, 11 April 1950, Box 203, Folder 6, CAB-CHM.

77. Dean Acheson to Claude Barnett, 22 August 1951, Box 208, Folder 1, CAB-CHM.

78. Claude Barnett to Congressman Dawson, 29 November 1950, Reel 8, No. 592, Part III, Series H, CAB.

79. J. Max Bond to Claude Barnett, 30 July 1954, Box 205, Folder 1, CAB-CHM.

80. "Doc" Young to Claude Barnett, 22 April 1950, Feel 15, No. 370, Part II, Organizational Files, CAB.

81. Claude Barnett to "Doc" Young, 1 May 1950, Reel 15, No. 371, Part II, Organizational Files, CAB.

82. Claude Barnett to M. V. Holmes, 28 July 1953, Box 128, Folder 5, CAB-CHM: "We have a correspondent in Haiti. His name is Emmanuel Racine."

83. Claude Barnett to H. L. Collins, Commonwealth News Agency–London, 10 May 1950, Box 199, Folder 5, CAB-CHM: "Oddly enough our papers have less interest in East Africa. There is fairly good concern about West Africa."

84. Ernest Jamieson to Claude Barnett, 15 April 1950, Box 206, Folder 6, CAB-CHM. The ANP's uniqueness and a surfeit of writers enhanced the agency's bargaining power—at least for a while. See H. Stephen Currie to Claude Barnett, 7 May 1954, Box 109, Folder 1, CAB-CHM: "I am a native of Nairobi Kenya Colony" and a "graduate of American schools." His query: Would ANP "accept some articles from me. . . . [M]y name before being adopted by the late Bishop George E. Curry was Ahmed Mohammed Ali, Vth. I would prefer working under my original name."

85. Claude Barnett to Joseph Gathings, 16 June 1951, Reel 2, No. 38, Part III, Series E, CAB.

86. Claude Barnett to Jean F. Brierre, 17 February 1951, Box 205, Folder 7, CAB-CHM.

87. Claude Barnett to "Dear Bill," 1 June 1950, Reel 8, No. 573, Part III, Series H, CAB.

88. Claude Barnett to "Dear Pat and Catherine," 21 December 1950, Reel 1, No. 738, Part III, Series K, CAB.

89. Roberta McGuire to Claude Barnett, 21 April 1950, Reel 5, No. 284, Part III, Series G, CAB.

90. Claude Barnett to Kelsey Pharr, no date, Reel 3, No. 339, Part III, Series C, CAB.

91. Claude Barnett to Harold Sims, African Desk–State Department, 11 April 1950, Box 208, Folder 6, CAB-CHM.

92. Claude Barnett to Dear "Pat and Catherine," 8 January 1951, Reel 1, No. 749, Part III, Series K, CAB.

93. Claude Barnett to Edward Dodd, 30 June 1953, Reel 16, No. 136, Part III, Series B, CAB.

94. Press release, July 1949, Reel 41, No. 138, Part I, Press Releases, CAB.

95. Arturo H. Le Conte to Claude Barnett, 14 July 1949, Box 207, Folder 4, CAB-CHM.

96. Press release, October 1947, Box 207, Folder 4, CAB-CHM.

97. "Pamphlet Tells How Negroes Fought Communism in Canal Zone," 10 September 1952, Box 207, Folder 5, CAB-CHM.

98. Claude Barnett to Hon. Señor de Gonzales-Arevalo, Foreign Minister, 28 September 1949, Box 207, Folder 4, CAB-CHM.

99. "Alice" to Claude Barnett, no date, circa 1949, Box 207, Folder 4, CAB-CHM: She was told that Guatemala "has had a law for the past 30 years which prohibited the entrance

of Negroes into that country" but "since the revolution in 1944 the repeal of that law has been under consideration" and "a repeal is expected."

100. Press release, September 1949, Reel 41, No. 736, Part I, Press Releases, CAB.

101. Claude Barnett to Paul Fernandez, Minister of Foreign Affairs–Brazil, 19 April 1950, Box 207, Folder 4, CAB-CHM. See also Barnett to "Conselho Nacional de Migracão e Colinacão," Rio de Janeiro, 1 May 1950, Box 207, Folder 4, CAB-CHM.

102. Press release, August 1950, Reel 43, No. 921, Part I, Press Releases, CAB.

103. Luis Barreiros, São Paulo to ANP, 1 April 1955, Box 207, Folder 6, CAB-CHM: "As [a] Brazilian journalist permanently writing for pro-Negro journalistic campaigns" now wants to write for the ANP.

104. Bishop R. R. Wright Jr., St. Peter's AME, Georgetown, to Claude Barnett, 5 February 1952, Box 207, Folder 4, CAB-CHM.

105. Remarks of Cheddi Jagan, no date, Box 207, Folder 4, CAB-CHM.

106. Fenner Brockway to Claude Barnett, 19 October 1953, Box 199, Folder 6, CAB-CHM.

107. Claude Barnett to Alice Dunnigan, 21 April 1950, Reel 5, No. 630, Part II, Organizational Files, CAB.

108. Claude Barnett to Lucille Chambers Norman, 13 June 1953, Reel 1, No. 595, Part III, Series E, CAB.

109. Press release, June 1949, Reel 40, No. 935, Part I, Press Releases, CAB: In Bolivia there is "growing distrust and dislike of American whites" and "an undertone beneath the tin strike violence which flared out here last week. When the tin miners deserted the mines they attacked and maltreated the white American engineers employed there. Two of the Americans were killed. . . . '[Y]ou dirty Gringoes,' the Bolivians shouted. . . . [B]oth white men and women were maltreated by the infuriated natives."

110. Press release, July 1954, Box 207, Folder 4, CAB-CHM. See also press release, August 1953, Reel 52, No. 829, Part I, Press Releases, CAB: "Panama lifts race barriers on visitors."

111. Claude Barnett to Major Lawton Collins, U.S. Army, 31 January 1950, Reel 2, No. 788, Part III, Series F, CAB.

112. Major General Edward Witsell to Claude Barnett, no date, Reel 2, No. 791, Part III, Series F, CAB.

113. Claude Barnett to General Thomas Handy, 2 February 1952, Reel 2, No. 863, Part III, Series F, CAB.

114. Claude Barnett to Dwight D. Eisenhower, 6 February 1952, Reel 2, No. 865, Part III, Series F, CAB.

115. Brief in Case of Lieutenant Leon Gilbert, circa 1951, Reel 2, No. 1184, Part III, Series F, CAB.

116. Press release, February 1951, Reel 45, No. 306, Part I, Press Releases, CAB.

117. Press release, April 1951, Reel 45, No. 757, Part I, Press Releases, CAB.

118. Press release, February 1951, Reel 45, No. 698, Part I, Press Releases, CAB.

119. Claude Barnett to P. B. Young, 28 August 1951, Reel 24, No. 1098, Part II, Organizational Files, CAB.

120. Claude Barnett to President W. V. S. Tubman, Liberia, 17 January 1951, Box 185, Folder 2, CAB-CHM.

121. Claude Barnett to Truman Gibson, 16 January 1952, Reel 6, No. 709, Part III, Series C, CAB.

122. *New York Times*, 1 November 1949.

123. Virginia Stettinius to Claude Barnett, 18 November 1949, Box 191, Folder 4, CAB-CHM.

124. Claude Barnett to Roderick Harris, 7 August 1950, Box 191, Folder 4, CAB-CHM.

125. A. G. Gaston to Claude Barnett, 20 November 1953, Reel 4, No. 204, Part III, Series C, CAB.

126. A. G. Gaston to Claude Barnett, 20 November 1953, Reel 4, No. 203, Part III, Series C, CAB.

127. Claude Barnett to Lloyd Kerford, 29 March 1949, Reel 6, No. 731, Part III, Series C, CAB.

128. Claude Barnett to "Miss Brady," 10 January 1951, Reel 2, No. 08, Part III, Series G, CAB.

129. Letter from Foreign Mission Board of National Baptist Convention, to Claude Barnett, 4 March 1950, Reel 3, No. 344, Part III, Series J, CAB.

130. Reverend J. S. Brookens, AME Church–Mobile to President Truman, 27 June 1949, Reel 8, No. 800, Part III, Series J, CAB.

131. Press release, March 1951, Reel 9, No. 203, Part III, Series J, CAB.

132. A. G. Gaston to Claude Barnett, 11 January 1954, Reel 4, No. 205, Part III, Series C, CAB.

133. Claude Barnett to A. G. Gaston, 16 January 1954, Reel 4, No. 207, Part III, Series C, CAB.

134. Earl Dickerson to Supreme Liberty Life, 9 November 1953, Reel 6, No. 433, Part III, Series C, CAB.

135. C. C. Spaulding to Claude Barnett, 25 August 1950, Reel 5, No. 947, Part III, Series C, CAB.

136. C. C. Spaulding to John H. Johnson, 17 March 1949, Reel 5, No. 924, Part III, Series C, CAB.

137. Claude Barnett to Gabriel Dennis, 15 May 1951, Box 185, Folder 1, CAB-CHM.

138. Frank Pinder, Monrovia, to Claude Barnett, 16 May 1950, Box 186, Folder 1, CAB-CHM.

139. Claude Barnett to Gabriel Dennis, 7 October 1952, Box 185, Folder 1, CAB-CHM.

140. William Rutherford to Claude Barnett, 9 September 1950, Box 212, Folder 1, CAB-CHM.

Chapter 8. Negroes as Anticommunist Propagandists?

1. Press release, January 1953, Reel 10, No. 852, Part III, Series A, Claude A. Barnett/Associated Negro Press Papers, North Carolina State University–Raleigh (hereafter cited as CAB). See also *Newsweek*, 19 April 1954: 200 Negro newspapers exist in the United States with a total circulation of 2 million. All but one are weeklies, semiweeklies, or biweeklies. The *Pittsburgh Courier* is the largest with a circulation of 186,646, and in second place is the *Afro-American*.

2. *Arkansas Gazette*, 4 October 1956: "Negro radio station KOKY will go on the air Monday. . . . Arkansas' first station to feature all Negro personalities and programs."

3. George Murphy to Claude Barnett, 11 March 1955, Box 137, Folder 2, Claude A. Barnett/Associated Negro Press Papers, Chicago History Museum (hereafter cited as CAB-CHM).

4. Press release, August 1955, Reel 57, No. 845, Part I, Press Releases, CAB.

5. P. L. Prattis to Claude Barnett, 30 April 1956, Reel 7, No. 411, Part II, Organizational Files, CAB.

6. Claude Barnett to Alvin White, 1 May 1954, Reel 9, No. 780, Part II, Organizational Files, CAB.

7. Alvin White to Claude Barnett, 20 July 1956, Box 141, Folder 5, CAB-CHM: "George Levitan, the Jew who owns *Sepia* down there in Fort Worth has Ben Burns," a former Johnson employee and "Levitan has dough—lots of it . . . and with Burns burning to even up the score with Johnson—look out. . . . [T]he Johnson empire is in for a real battle."

8. Robert Peterson, *Only the Ball Was White: A History of Legendary Black Players and All-Black Professional Teams* (New York: Oxford University Press, 1992).

9. Press release, September 1949, Reel 41, No. 641, Part I, Press Releases, CAB.

10. Press release, January 1951, Reel 45, No. 51, Part I, Press Releases, CAB.

11. Press release, February 1951, Reel 45, No. 116, Part I, Press Releases, CAB.

12. Claude Barnett to Thomas W. Young, President, The Guide Publishing Company of Norfolk, 13 February 1950, Box 142, Folder 4, CAB-CHM.

13. Claude Barnett to S. Edward Gilbert, 24 August 1955, Reel 1, No. 585, Part III, Series E, CAB.

14. Press release, July 1953, Reel 52, No. 285, Part I, Press Releases, CAB.

15. Press release, July 1950, Reel 43, No. 862, Part I, Press Releases, CAB.

16. Claude Barnett to Irene Diggs, 24 November 1953, Box 168, Folder 3, CAB-CHM.

17. Claude Barnett to Irene Diggs, 7 December 1955, Box 168, Folder 3, CAB-CHM.

18. Press release, December 1949, Reel 42, No. 284, Part III, Press Releases, CAB.

19. Press release, May 1950, Reel 43, No. 477, Part I, Press Releases, CAB.

20. Charlotta Bass to Claude Barnett, 11 November 1950, Box 146, Folder 5, CAB-CHM.

21. Claude Barnett to Charlotta Bass, 18 November 1950, Box 146, Folder 5, CAB-CHM.

22. Press release, May 1951, Reel 45, No. 997, Part I, Press Releases, CAB.

23. *California Eagle*, 3 May 1951.

24. Ruth Washington to Claude Barnett, 18 November 1950, Box 146, Folder 5, CAB-CHM.

25. Richard Craddick, Public Information Officer, USS Saratoga to Claude Barnett, 15 September 1956, Reel 2, No. 1000, Part III, Series F, CAB: He is unable to act as ANP correspondent. He is "aboard this floating city" and it may violate regulations to do so. "The other and confidential reason . . . is that we have been anchored at the foot of GTMO Bay, Cuba, for the past three weeks" and "the only reason we would continue to Haiti after we get repaired is because of political reasons. That's the straight scoop."

26. Claude Barnett to Eugene Gordon, 24 January 1953, Box 142, Folder 2, CAB-CHM.

27. Alastair Revie, Scotsman Features Ltd., to Claude Barnett, 21 April 1954, Box 142, Folder 2, CAB-CHM: "Might you be interested in letting us handle on a percentage basis some of your material in the 43 countries of Europe and the British Empire."

28. Claude Barnett to Mark Etheridge, 2 September 1955, Box 142, Folder 4, CAB-CHM.

29. Mike Land to Claude Barnett, 16 July 1956, Reel 6, No. 688, Part III, Series E, CAB.

30. Ellsworth Bunker to Claude Barnett, 20 November 1956, Reel 6, No. 700, Part III, Series E, CAB.

31. Claude Barnett to Harold Hochschild, 29 August 1956, Box 174, Folder 7, CAB-CHM.

32. Harold Hochschild to "Dear Claude," 20 April 1961, Box 174, Folder 7, CAB-CHM.

33. Claude Barnett to Harold Brayman, Director of Public Relations–Du Pont, 16 October 1953, Box 141, Folder 5, CAB-CHM.

34. Gerald Horne, *Paul Robeson: The Artist as Revolutionary* (London: Pluto, 2016).

35. Press release, August 1956, Reel 3, No. 479, Part III, Series J, CAB.

36. Claude Barnett to Frederick Patterson, 4 February 1954, Reel 3, No. 33, Part III, Series G, CAB.

37. Press release, May 1949, Reel 40, No. 832, Part I, Press Releases, CAB.

38. Claude Barnett to Corienne Morrow, 29 March 1954, Reel 5, No. 244, Part III, Series H, CAB.

39. Press release, December 1948, Reel 39, No. 584, Part I, Press Releases, CAB. See also press release, January 1949, Reel 39, No. 985, Part I, Press Releases, CAB; and press release, January 1949, Reel 39, No. 985, Part I, Press Releases, CAB.

40. Press release, September 1949, Reel 41, No. 775, Part I, Press Releases, CAB.

41. Press release, September 1949, Reel 41, No. 798, Part I, Press Releases, CAB.

42. Press release, April 1949, Reel 40, No. 585, Part I, Press Releases, CAB.

43. Alvin White to Claude Barnett, circa 1952, Box 141, Folder 4, CAB-CHM.

44. Press release, October 1949, Reel 41, No. 940, Part I, Press Releases, CAB.

45. Press release, October 1950, Reel 44, No. 385, Part I, Press Releases, CAB

46. Press release, January 1950, Reel 42, No. 624, Part I, Press Releases, CAB.

47. Press release, April 1950, Reel 43, No. 101, Part I, Press Releases, CAB.

48. Press release, November 1949, Reel 41, No. 1093, Part I, Press Releases, CAB.

49. Press release, August 1951, Reel 45, No. 574, Part I, Press Releases, CAB.

50. Claude Barnett to Alice Dunnigan, 24 November 1954, Box 146, Folder 5, CAB-CHM.

51. Claude Barnett to E. M. Glucksman, 13 November 1954, Reel 4, No. 383. Part III, Series D, CAB.

52. Claude Barnett to E. M. Glucksman, 9 November 1954, Reel 4, No. 383, Part III, Series D, CAB.

53. Victor Roudin to Claude Barnett, 7 January 1952, Reel 3, No. 699, Part III, Series D, CAB.

54. E. M. Glucksman to Claude Barnett, 5 November 1951, Reel 3, No. 566, Part III, Series D, CAB.

55. Press release, December 1952, Reel 3, No. 688, Part III, Series D, CAB.

56. "Final Treatment Outline," 15 August 1951, Reel 3, No. 490, Part III, Series D, CAB.

57. Claude Barnett to E. M. Glucksman, 25 April 1952, Reel 4, No. 788, Part III, Series D, CAB.

58. Claude Barnett to E. M. Glucksman, 30 April 1952, Reel 4, No. 802, Part III, Series D, CAB.

59. Claude Barnett to E. M. Glucksman, 25 April 1952, Reel 4, No. 788, Part III, Series D, CAB.

60. Claude Barnett to B. F. Pew, L&M, 18 February 1956, Reel 2, No. 09, Part II, Organizational Files, CAB.

61. Claude Barnett to E. M. Glucksman, 29 July 1952, Reel 3, No. 849, Part III, Series D, CAB.

62. Text of ad, no date, Reel 2, No. 41, Part II, Organizational Files, CAB.

63. Claude Barnett to President David Jones, 18 November 1952, Reel 3, No. 954, Part III, Series D, CAB.

64. Claude Barnett to Joe Oliver, 10 January 1953, Reel 4, No. 95, Part III, Series D, CAB.

65. Claude Barnett to Robert N. Gilham, 6 June 1953, Reel 4, No. 98, Part III, Series D, CAB.

66. Claude Barnett to E. M. Glucksman, 27 October 1953, Reel 4, No. 226, Part III, Series D, CAB.

67. "Public Relations"—Lagos to Claude Barnett, 1 October 1953, Reel 4, No. 211, Part III, Series D, CAB.

68. Claude Barnett to Ethiopia's UN delegation, 11 November 1953, Reel 4, No. 238, Part III, Series D, CAB.

69. Claude Barnett to E. M. Glucksman, 9 November 1954, Reel 4, No. 381, Part III, Series D, CAB.

70. Victor Roudin to Claude Barnett, 29 April 1950, Reel 4, No. 800, Part III, Series D, CAB.

71. Proposal, no date, circa 1950s, Reel 11, No. 180, Part III, Series B, CAB.

72. Claude Barnett to Mary Beattie Brady, 15 November 1952, Reel 1, No. 848, Part III, Series B, CAB.

73. Marketing report, no date, Reel 4, No. 526, Part III, Series D, CAB.

74. Claude Barnett to R. M. Stephenson, 14 December 1953, Box 201, Folder 3, CAB-CHM.

75. Claude Barnett to William Rutherford, 16 September 1954, Box 212, Folder 1, CAB-CHM.

76. Press release, March 1952, Reel 48, No. 125, Part I, Press Releases, CAB.

77. Speech of Adam Clayton Powell, circa 1955, Reel 20, No. 414, Part II, Organizational Files, CAB. See, e.g., press release, April 1958, Reel 65, No. 240, Part I, Press Releases, CAB: Black Philadelphia attorney Raymond Pace Alexander to speak on Radio Free Europe "to the captive peoples." He "studied in Germany as a young man and speaks German, French and Italian."

78. Frank Stanley, *Louisville Defender*, to Claude Barnett, 20 July 1954, Reel 16, No. 400, Part II, Organizational Files, CAB.

79. Press release, September 1951, Reel 46, No. 964, Part I, Press Releases, CAB.

80. Letter to Claude Barnett (correspondent unclear), 3 February 1952, Box 214, Folder 1, CAB-CHM. See also press release, February 1952, Reel 47, No. 1106, Part I, Press Releases, CAB.

81. *Christian Advocate*, 24 April 1952, Box 214, Folder 1, CAB-CHM.

82. Press release, January 1955, Box 214, Folder 1, CAB-CHM.

83. Press release, January 1955, Reel 56, No. 196, Part I, Press Releases, CAB.

84. Press release, January 1955, Reel 56, No. 364, Part I, Press Releases, CAB.

85. Press release, February 1952, Reel 47, No. 1106, Part I, Press Releases, CAB.

86. Claude Barnett to E. M. Glucksman and Victor Roudin, 9 February 1952, Reel 3, No. 705, Part III, Series D, CAB.

87. Press release, January 1952, Reel 47, No. 675, Part I, Press Releases, CAB.

88. Press release, January 1952, Reel 47, No. 732, Part I, Press Releases, CAB. Cf. press release, May 1960, Reel 70, No. 368, Part I, Press Releases, CAB: At a reception honoring French President Charles de Gaulle at their embassy in Washington, de Gaulle told Baker, who was in attendance, "I am deeply indebted and grateful to you for being a faithful and sincere De Gaullist." Yet the ANP reported subsequently that "most blacks in the French Assembly support Leftist . . . most of the black members"—about 26—"sit with and support the strong Communist Party. . . . [N]ot a single black or brown face is to be seen in the rightist or De Gaulle bloc." See press release, June 1958, Reel 65, No. 500, Part I, Press Releases, CAB. Also see press release, February 1962, Reel 78, No. 382, Part I, Press Releases, CAB: De Gaulle seeks to crush "Number Two man in the French government, Gaston Monnerville, a black man from Guyana, who is president of the French Senate" and a leader of the Socialist Party.

89. Press release, July 1949, Reel 40, No. 1190, Part I, Press Releases, CAB.

90. Press release, June 1953, Reel 50, No. 744, Part I, Press Releases, CAB.

91. Press release, July 1951, Reel 46, No. 196, Part I, Press Releases, CAB.

92. Press release, April 1954, Reel 54, No. 314, Part I, Press Releases, CAB.

93. Press release, June 1952, Reel 48, No. 866, Part I, Press Releases, CAB.

94. Press release, December 1951, Reel 45, No. 13, Part I, Press Releases, CAB.

95. Press release, November 1952, Reel 50, No. 157, Part I, Press Releases, CAB. See also press release, November 1950, Reel 44, No. 653, Part I, Press Releases, CAB.

96. Eulogy for Thyra Edwards by Bernard Ades, 12 July 1953, Reel 6, No. 181, Part II, Organizational Files, CAB.

97. Frederick Patterson to Claude Barnett, 2 August 1955, Reel 3, No. 75, Part III, Series G, CAB.

98. Claude Barnett to Frederick Patterson, 6 August 1955, Reel 3, No. 79, Part III, Series G, CAB.

99. Claude Barnett to James Davis, 23 June 1954, Reel 8, No. 138, Part III, Series A, CAB. See also Luther Foster to Claude Barnett, 17 March 1955, Reel 9, No. 441, Part III, Series B, CAB.

100. Claude Barnett to E. M. Glucksman, 23 November 1954, Reel 4, No. 433, Part III, Series D, CAB.

101. Claude Barnett to Alvin White, 1 May 1954, Reel 9, No. 780, Part II, Organizational Files, CAB.

102. Ruth Sloan to Claude Barnett, 26 February 1952, Box 209, Folder 1, CAB-CHM.

103. Ruth Sloan to Claude Barnett, 15 December 1953, Box 209, Folder 1, CAB-CHM.

104. Claude Barnett to E. M. Glucksman, 21 March 1955, Reel 4, No. 433, Part III, Series D, CAB.

105. Claude Barnett to Mary Beattie Brady, 20 June 1950, Reel 2, No. 306, Part III, Series G, CAB.

106. Press release, August 1950, Reel 43, No. 1105, Part I, Press Releases, CAB.

107. Edith Sampson to Howland Sargent, Assistant Secretary of State, "Personal and Confidential," 24 July 1952, Reel 1, No. 234, Part III, Series D, CAB: Boxing champion Sugar Ray Robinson came to Paris and presented a copy of Harriet Beecher Stowe's novel to the wife of the French president: press release, July 1952, Reel 49, No. 228, Part I, Press Releases, CAB. See also press release, February 1951, Reel 45, No. 287, Part I, Press Releases, CAB: Robinson was reputed to be "very popular in Italy especially after his recent trip to Europe. His anticommunist statements endeared him to many freedom-loving Italians," according to the VOA.

108. Etta Moten to Nora Holt, 31 January 1952, Reel 2, No. 620, Part III, Series D, CAB.

109. Press release, February 1949, Reel 39, No. 1193, Part I, Press Releases, CAB. Her languages included "German, French, Italian, Spanish, [an] African dialect, and English. . . . [W]hile singing the African numbers she accompanied herself with a 'squeegee' drum, a gift from a Nigerian."

110. Minto Cato to Claude Barnett, 2 November 1953, Reel 1, No. 254, Part III, Series D, CAB.

111. Claude Barnett to John Henkes Jr., 2 January 1947, Reel 6, No. 572, Part III, Series D, CAB.

112. Press release, July 1950, Reel 43, No. 740, Part I, Press Releases, CAB.

113. Claude Barnett to Martin Sheridan, 28 February 1953, Box 111, Folder 4, CAB-CHM.

114. Claude Barnett to Pete Fischer, CBS Radio, 30 August 1954, Reel 6, No. 753, Part III, Series D, CAB.

115. Claude Barnett to Gordon Buck, Foote, Cane and Bolding (a Chicago advertising firm), no date, Box 129, Folder 2, CAB-CHM:.

116. Joseph V. Baker to Claude Barnett, 21 May 1952, Reel 6, No. 692, Part III, Series D, CAB.

117. Claude Barnett to Pete Fischer, 10 July 1954, Reel 6, No. 748, Part III, Series D, CAB.

118. Mary Mills to Claude Barnett and Etta Moten, 28 July 1952, Box 209, Folder 4, CAB-CHM.

119. Claude Barnett to Earl Dickerson, 26 April 1957, Reel 6, No. 972, Part III, Series C, CAB.

120. Claude Barnett to Clifford [*sic*] Wharton, 27 February 1952, Box 209, Folder 5, CAB-CHM.

121. Claude Barnett to Dale Cox, 17 April 1954, Reel 4, No. 286, Part III, Series I, CAB.

122. Claude Barnett to attorney Clayborne George, Cleveland, 19 April 1955, Reel 3, No. 793, Part III, Series H, CAB.

123. Claude Barnett to A. Freudman, 28 September 1950, Box 176, Folder 9, CAB-CHM.

124. Baron Dhanis, Attaché for Belgian Congo Affairs, Washington, D.C., to Claude Barnett, 13 May 1954, Box 176, Folder 9, CAB-CHM. See also Dr. Jan-Albert Goris of Information Center of Belgium and Belgian Congo, 3 October 1950, Box 176, Folder 9, CAB-CHM: "There are no bars to American Negroes going to the Congo. There have been several well-known American Negroes there in recent years. . . . [A]s far as we know there are none there at present."

125. Claude Barnett to Preston Valien, 24 March 1953, Reel 2, No. 472, Part III, Series B, CAB (the date was unclear and may have been 1963).

126. Juanita Nelson to Claude Barnett, 24 January 1952, Box 128, Folder 3, CAB-CHM: "I have been considering the idea of a column on non-violence which would discuss the use of this method in fighting racism as well as opposing other ills. Do you feel that newspapers which subscribe to your service would be interested in such a column?"

127. John Favicchio to Claude Barnett, 11 August 1953, Box 128, Folder 4, CAB-CHM: "Would you be interested in a 13,000 word novelette about an American Negro outfit stationed in England during World War II? It is primarily a love story between an American-Negro GI and an English lassie." It included the requisite "fights, knifings and killings."

128. Cecil Bennett to ANP, 19 May 1955, Box 128, Folder 4, CAB-CHM: "I have been creating crossword puzzles featuring the names of noted Negroes which I would like to have you consider for possible use in your syndicate."

129. William J. Burton to Claude Barnett, 19 May 1955, Box 128, Folder 4, CAB-CHM: "The Negro situation in Alaska is unique. In some respects it's far more advanced as compared with other stateside areas and yet in other ways it's far behind."

130. Charles R. Oaks to Claude Barnett, 6 December 1956, Box 129, Folder 2, CAB-CHM.

131. Clipping, *New York Times*, March 1953, Reel 13, No. 408, Part III, Series C, CAB.

132. Press release, December 1955, Reel 11, No. 733, Part III, Series C, CAB.

133. Press release, June 1949, Reel 2, No. 535, Part III, Series B, CAB: "Atomic scientist Rossi Lomannitz, 28, has left his job" at Fisk University because he was accused of being a Red.

134. Press release, August 1950, Reel 3, No. 171, Part III, Series B, CAB: Ya Lun Chou, a former Chinese official in the deposed anticommunist regime became head of the Division of Business at Hampton Institute. See Claude Barnett to Edwinna Harleston Whitlock, 25 February 1952, Box 142, Folder 4, CAB-CHM: "The *Charleston News and Courier* is the

most bitter paper in the United States against Negro rights and opportunities. It is worse than any paper in Mississippi." See also press release, October 1948, Reel 38, No. 1108, Part I, Press Releases, CAB: "Negro pastor to teach in China. . . . Rev. Darius L. Swann . . . to the foreign languages department of the University of Nanking. . . . born in Amelia, Virginia 24 years ago" and a graduate of Johnson C. Smith University in 1945.

135. Lee Lorch to Claude Barnett, 17 March 1957, Reel 3, No. 03, Part III, Series B, CAB.

136. Lee Lorch to Claude Barnett, 29 October 1957, Reel 3, No. 07, Part III, Series B, CAB.

137. Lee Lorch to Claude Barnett, 2 January 1960, Reel 3, No. 22, Part III, Series B, CAB.

138. Horace Mann Bond to Claude Barnett, 4 April 1951, Reel 3, No. 524, Part III, Series B, CAB.

139. St. Clair Drake to Claude Barnett, 2 November 1952, Reel 5, No. 792, Part III, Series B, CAB.

140. Press release, November 1952, Reel 49, No. 218, Part I, Press Releases, CAB.

141. Press release, December 1952, Reel 50, No. 420, Part I, Press Releases, CAB.

142. Press release, August 1954, Reel 55, No. 253, Part I, Press Releases, CAB: At this base, the policy was "not anti-colored but anti-Negro," for North Africans were welcomed. German bases were adjudged to have a more enlightened policy generally.

143. Claude Barnett to Robert Browne, 10 January 1953, Box 168, Folder 1, CAB-CHM.

144. Press release, February 1951, Reel 45, No. 146, Part I, Press Releases, CAB.

Chapter 9. Barnett Bestrides the Globe

1. Alice Dunnigan to Claude Barnett, 8 April 1955, Box 137, Folder 2, Claude A. Barnett/Associated Negro Press Papers, Chicago History Museum (hereafter cited as CAB-CHM).

2. Claude Barnett to E. F. Morrow, 12 August 1958, Reel 3, No. 907, Part III, Series H, Claude A. Barnett/Associated Negro Press Papers, North Carolina State University–Raleigh (hereafter cited as CAB).

3. Press release, March 1955, Reel 56, No. 954, Part I, Press Releases, CAB.

4. Claude Barnett to W. E. B. Du Bois, 23 July 1957, Reel 6, No. 131, Part III, Series I, CAB.

5. Press release, August 1957, Reel 63, No. 597, Part I, Press Releases, CAB.

6. Clipping, 24 March 1957, Reel 21, No. 326, Part II, Organizational Files, CAB.

7. Claude Barnett to M. A. Bernard, 23 August 1957, Reel 21, No. 960, Part II, Organizational Files, CAB.

8. Press release, September 1955, Reel 58, No. 214, Part I, Press Releases, CAB.

9. Press release, October 1955, Reel 58, No. 395, Part I, Press Releases, CAB.

10. Press release, June 1957, Reel 62, No. 1054, Part I, Press Releases, CAB. See also Stephen G. Craft, *American Justice in Taiwan: The 1957 Riots and Cold War Foreign Policy* (Lexington: University Press of Kentucky, 2015).

11. Press release, September 1957, Reel 63, No. 685, Part I, Press Releases, CAB; Press release, March 1954, Reel 54, No. 16, Part I, Press Releases, CAB.

12. Press release, October 1957, Reel 63, No. 1006, Part I, Press Releases, CAB: Little Rock is a world issue though global "white supremacy" is even more important. "Bandung is far more important than a thousand Little Rocks," particularly for the fate of U.S. Negroes. (Press release, October 1957, Reel 63, No. 1001, Part I, Press Releases, CAB: "U.S. racial problem gets airing" at UN).

13. Press release, February 1956, Reel 59, No. 519, Part I, Press Releases, CAB.

14. Press release, October 1956, Reel 60, No. 332, Part I, Press Releases, CAB.

15. Press release, January 1957, Reel 60, No. 920, Part I, Press Releases, CAB.

16. Press release, May 1955, Reel 57, No. 116, Part I, Press Releases, CAB.

17. Press release, September 1955, Reel 58, No. 22, Part I, Press Releases, CAB: Dr. William Reed of North Carolina A&T University returns from the U.S.S.R. after visiting with farmers. "My name was in the press quite a bit," he said, pointing out that Bill Worthy, who had savaged Barnett's ally in Copenhagen, "traveled with me." Unlike Dixie, "I saw no signs of racial discrimination," which "is non-existent in Russia."

18. Press release, January 1956, Reel 59, No. 17, Part I, Press Releases, CAB.

19. Press release, April 1957, Reel 62, No. 564, Part I, Press Releases, CAB.

20. Press release, October 1956, Reel 60, No. 299, Part I, Press Releases, CAB.

21. Press release, December 1955, Reel 6, No. 27, Part III, Series H, CAB.

22. Press release, March 1957, Reel 62, No. 345, Part I, Press Releases, CAB.

23. Press release, May 1957, Reel 62, No. 865, Part I, Press Releases, CAB.

24. Press release, September 1957, Reel 63, No. 895, Part I, Press Releases, CAB.

25. Press release, March 1956, Reel 59, No. 570, Part I, Press Releases, CAB.

26. Press release, May 1956, Reel 60, No. 805, Part I, Press Releases, CAB. Hancock also advised Moscow that "if Russia will just sit tight and play her game with her accustomed shrewdness, the Old South with its Negro-phobia will deliver our nation to her on a platter" (Press release, June 1959, Reel 67, No. 1105, Part I, Press Releases, CAB).

27. Press release, November 1955, Reel 58, No. 554, Part I, Press Releases, CAB.

28. Claude Barnett to Alice Dunnigan, 9 April 1955, Box 137, Folder 2, CAB-CHM:

29. Alice Dunnigan to Claude Barnett, no date, Box 137, Folder 2, CAB-CHM.

30. Alice Dunnigan to Claude Barnett, 8 August 1955, Box 137, Folder 3, CAB-CHM.

31. Alice Dunnigan to Claude Barnett, no date, Box 137, Folder 3, CAB-CHM.

32. Alice Dunnigan to Claude Barnett, 31 December 1956, Box 137, Folder 1, CAB-CHM.

33. *Oklahoma City Black Dispatch*, 17 July 1954.

34. Press release, March 1955, Reel 56, No. 886, Part I, Press Releases, CAB.

35. Press release, October 1954, Reel 55, No. 810, Part I, Press Releases, CAB.

36. Press release, July 1955, Reel 5, No. 1028, Part II, Organizational Files, CAB.

37. Marguerite Cartwright to Claude Barnett, 7 March 1955, Reel 4, No. 920, Part II, Organizational Files, CAB.

38. Claude Barnett to Marguerite Cartwright, 22 May 1955, Reel 4, No. 925, Part II, Organizational Files, CAB.

39. Claude Barnett to Alice Dunnigan, 26 March 1955, Reel 5, No. 1007, Part II, Organizational Files, CAB.

40. Claude Barnett to Carlton Goodlett, 7 March 1955, Reel 13, No. 352, Part II, Organizational Files, CAB.

41. Alice Dunnigan to Claude Barnett, 8 April 1955, Reel 5, No. 1010, Part II, Organizational Files, CAB.

42. Claude Barnett to Alice Dunnigan, 9 April 1955, Reel 5, No. 1012, Part II, Organizational Files, CAB.

43. Press release, March 1955, Reel 56, No. 854, Part I, Press Releases, CAB. See also James L. Horace, President of Baptist General State Convention of Illinois to Claude Barnett, 3 June 1955, Reel 2, No. 450, Part III, Series J, CAB.

44. Press release, April 1955, Reel 56, No. 1088, Part I, Press Releases, CAB.

45. Press release, April 1957, Reel 62, No. 678, Part I, Press Releases, CAB. See also Alice

Dunnigan to Claude Barnett, 12 March 1959, Reel 6, No. 07, Part II, Organizational Files, CAB.

46. Press release, May 1957, Reel 62, No. 980, Part I, Press Releases, CAB. More attention should be paid to how global pressure influenced Hollywood's racial depictions. See also press release, August 1957, Reel 63, No. 488, Part I, Press Releases, CAB: "Jamaica leaders threaten ban on U.S. films casting Negroes in 'subservient and degenerate roles.'" The television show "Amos 'n' Andy," featuring an all-Negro cast, is protested when it is broadcast in Britain because of stereotypical portrayals. See press release, May 1954, Reel 54, No. 480, Part I, Press Releases, CAB; and press release, April 1954, Reel 54, No. 256, Part I, Press Releases, CAB.

47. Claude Barnett to Basil O'Connor, 10 April 1956, Reel 12, No. 481, Part III, Series B, CAB.

48. Claude Barnett to Edward Logelin, 18 June 1957, Reel 10, No. 06, Part III, Series C, CAB.

49. Press release, June 1954, Reel 54, No. 858, Part I, Press Releases, CAB.

50. Claude Barnett to Makonnen Work Aguegnehu, Press and Information Office of Ethiopia, 8 April 1957, Reel 5, No. 636, Part III, Series H, CAB.

51. Jacqueline Kienzle, Amalgamated Clothing Workers–Chicago to Claude Barnett, 6 May 1958, Reel 10, No. 122, Part III, Series C, CAB.

52. Press release, June 1959, Reel 67, No. 996, Part I, Press Releases, CAB.

53. Claude Barnett to Ed Grief, 31 July 1956, Reel 4, No. 249, Part II, Organizational Files, CAB: Please send "three copies of the Union Swahili New Testament (Agano Jipya) and Psalms (Zaburi). . . . I want one for an African literature corner my wife has established at Tuskegee."

54. Claude Barnett to "Kelsey," 25 November 1956, Reel 3, No. 338, Part III, Series C, CAB.

55. Frederick Patterson to Claude Barnett, 2 August 1955, Reel 3, No. 75, Part III, Series G, CAB.

56. Press release, April 1957, Reel 62, No. 620, Part I, Press Releases, CAB.

57. Press release, circa 1957, Reel 5, No. 1207, Part II, Organizational Files, CAB.

58. Alice Dunnigan to Claude Barnett, no date, circa 1955, Box 137, Folder 1, CAB-CHM.

59. Claude Barnett to Alice Dunnigan, 24 February 1955, Box 137, Folder 1, CAB-CHM.

60. Alice Allison Dunnigan, *Alone Atop the Hill: The Autobiography of Alice Dunnigan, Pioneer of the National Black Press* (Athens: University of Georgia Press, 2015), 196–99.

61. Claude Barnett to Frederick Patterson, 19 February 1957, Reel 3, No. 124, Part III, Series G, CAB.

62. Press release, May 1954, Reel 54, No. 476, Part I, Press Releases, CAB.

63. Edwin R. Morris to Claude Barnett, 26 September 1954, Box 207, Folder 9, CAB-CHM. See also press release, February 1957, Reel 62, No. 278, Part I, Press Releases, CAB: Congressman Thomas Ludlow of Toledo says El Salvador bars visas to the Reverend Oscar Phillipps of Medford, Massachusetts, and his spouse "solely because they are Negroes." The State Department was accused of acquiescing to this.

64. Press release, September 1954, Reel 55, No. 549, Part I, Press Releases, CAB.

65. Press release, April 1955, Reel 56, No. 1181, Part I, Press Releases, CAB.

66. Press release, July 1954, Reel 54, No. 1061, Part I, Press Releases, CAB: "If the Negroes who live in Vera Cruz, Chiapas, Tabasco, Michoacan, and Puebla [Mexico] had the same ideas about hair as we do in the United States, this would be a fertile field to spread

hair straightening propaganda and many of these black Mexican men would 'conk' their hair." See also press release, October 1954, Reel 55, No. 758, Part I, Press Releases, CAB. In another discourse on "bad" hair, Morris interviews "Dr. Clarence Cecil Rhodes, formerly of Oakland" and "now living in Guadalajara." See also press release, November 1955, Reel 58, No. 867, Part I, Press Releases, CAB: "Mexico is a land where women want kinky hair. Sun tanned United States women want straight hair. Mexican women spend millions of pesos each year to kink their hair."

67. Press release, November 1954, Reel 55, No. 1004, Part I, Press Releases, CAB.

68. Press release, November 1954, Reel 55, No. 1078, Part I, Press Releases, CAB.

69. Press release, December 1954, Reel 55, No. 1137, Part I, Press Releases, CAB.

70. Press release, November 1955, Reel 58, No. 732, Part I, Press Releases, CAB.

71. Press release, February 1956, Reel 59, No. 386, Part I, Press Releases, CAB.

72. Press release, January 1957, Reel 60, No. 791, Part I, Press Releases, CAB.

73. Press release, January 1955, Reel 56, No. 331, Part I, Press Releases, CAB.

74. Press release, May 1957, Reel 62, No. 826, Part I, Press Releases, CAB.

75. Press release, January 1955, Reel 56, No. 368, Part I, Press Releases, CAB.

76. Press release, February 1955, Reel 56, No. 450, Part I, Press Releases, CAB.

77. Press release, June 1956, Reel 60, No. 272, Part I, Press Releases, CAB: Juarez a "full blooded Indian . . . became a lowly banana peddler in the streets of New Orleans. It was during this time that he worked on the New Orleans docks that he became closely associated with Negroes."

78. Press release, October 1956, Reel 61, No. 116, Part I, Press Releases, CAB. He added, "As you probably know, American Negroes are automatically citizens of Liberia."

79. Press release, March 1955, Reel 56, No. 769, Part I, Press Releases, CAB.

80. Press release, July 1955, Reel 57, No. 658, Part I, Press Releases, CAB.

81. Press release, March 1955, Reel 56, No. 862, Part I, Press Releases, CAB: "Negro athletes from North, Central and South America attended." This was "the first time . . . different national representatives, male and female, of the descendants of Africa had ever been assembled in the same city, anywhere in the Western Hemisphere."

82. Press release, October 1958, Reel 65, No. 348, Part I, Press Releases, CAB.

83. Press release, January 1960, Reel 69, No. 310, Part I, Press Releases, CAB. Initially he chose to "request political asylum in Jamaica" and had been in touch with Amy Jacques Garvey as a consequence. From Albany, Georgia, he was fired from a historically black college in Mississippi in 1957. "I stand with the USA Muslims for a separate African-American nation" was his coda: See Rev. Clennon King to Director, Office of Immigration, Jamaica, 20 September 1962, Reel 6, No. 825, Part III, Series J, CAB.

84. Frank B. Rosebery to Claude Barnett, 13 February 1961, Box 207, Folder 6, CAB-CHM.

85. Press release, January 1958, Reel 64, No. 484, Part I, Press Releases, CAB.

86. Press release, 1 April 1957, Reel 62, No. 411, Part I, Press Releases, CAB. See also press release, March 1954, Reel 54, No. 16, Part I, Press Releases, CAB.

87. Claude Barnett to Miss Ambrozine E. Villiers, 10 November 1959, Box 207, Folder 6, CAB-CHM.

88. N. A. Sweets to Claude Barnett, 7 October 1952, Reel 3, No. 625, Part III, Series H, CAB.

89. Press release, May 1958, Reel 65, No. 483, Part I, Press Releases, CAB.

90. Claude Barnett to Mammu Tadese, 15 April 1957, Reel 5, No. 637, Part III, Series H, CAB.

91. Enoch P. Waters, *American Diary: A Personal History of the Black Press* (Chicago, IL: Path Press, 1987), 423.

92. Rose Mary Woods for Richard M. Nixon to Claude Barnett, 11 November 1957, Reel 5, No. 579, Part III, Series H, CAB.

93. Press release, November 1959, Reel 67, No. 1178, Part I, Press Releases, CAB.

94. Transcript, April 1957, Box 168, Folder 7, CAB-CHM.

95. Claude Barnett to Richard M. Nixon, 1 April 1957, Box 168, Folder 7, CAB-CHM.

96. Claude Barnett to Kwame Nkrumah, 1 May 1956, Box 172, Folder 2, CAB-CHM. This awkward phrasing was surprising but not unusual for Barnett, otherwise a consummate diplomat. That same year he provided condescending compliments to Prince Faisal al Saud of Saudi Arabia, praising his "perfect" English while commenting indelicately, "I have really wanted to talk with your black bodyguard," that is, "what his status is" and as well the "treatment" of "your Nubian associates."

97. Claude Barnett to Vice President Nixon, 29 December 1958, Box 169, Folder 6, CAB-CHM.

98. Richard M. Nixon to "Dear Claude," 15 January 1959, Box 342, Folder 6, CAB-CHM.

99. Report on All African Peoples Conference in Ghana, 5–13 December 1958, by James Lawson of United African Nationalist Movement–Harlem, Reel 4, No. 974, Part II, Organizational Files, CAB: Nkrumah's key adviser, Padmore, was termed a "chief Communist apologist" while Marguerite Cartwright, who had worked for the ANP, was called a "close friend of Israel's Foreign Minister, Golda Meir" and "also active espousing the Russian viewpoint," not intended as complimentary. "The Padmore—Cartwright Axis almost seized control of the Conference and it was not until I pointed out that the No. 1 anti-Communist Marcus Garvey was the real Patron Saint (not W.E.B. Du Bois)," that this orientation shifted. At that point "Marxism was routed." He concluded by saying, "the U.S. must teach Capitalism to Africans as opposed to Communism." This ideological tendency among certain Black Nationalists has generally been ignored by scholars.

100. "Claude" to Prime Minister Nkrumah, 15 November 1958, Box 178, Folder 4, CAB-CHM.

101. Press release, October 1958, Reel 66, No. 803, Part I, Press Releases, CAB.

102. Claude Barnett to Prime Minister Nkrumah, 12 April 1958, Box 178, Folder 4, CAB-CHM.

103. Horace Mann Bond to Claude Barnett, 31 March 1958, Box 181, Folder 2, CAB-CHM.

104. Horace Mann Bond to Arthur Condon, 6 January 1959, Box 181, Folder 2, CAB-CHM.

105. Claude Barnett to Arthur Condon, 22 January 1959, Box 181, Folder 2, CAB-CHM.

106. Arthur Condon to Claude Barnett, 23 May 1958, Box 181, Folder 2, CAB-CHM.

107. Claude Barnett to Prime Minister Nkrumah, 20 March 1958, Box 181, Folder 2, CAB-CHM.

108. Prime Minister Nkrumah to Claude Barnett, 9 April 1958, Box 181, Folder 2, CAB-CHM.

109. Letter from R. M. Akwei, 5 November 1958, Box 181, Folder 2, CAB-CHM.

110. Claude Barnett to Kwame Nkrumah, 29 May 1958, Box 181, Folder 2, CAB-CHM.

111. Claude Barnett to Kwame Nkrumah, 7 March 1959, Box 172, Folder 3, CAB-CHM.

112. Claude Barnett to R. O. Mensah, Press Attaché, Ghana Embassy–U.S., 9 January 1958, Box 178, Folder 4, CAB-CHM.

113. R. J. Moxon, Ghana Information Services to Claude Barnett, 23 January 1958, Box 178, Folder 4, CAB-CHM.

114. Horace Mann Bond to Claude Barnett, 10 May 1958, Box 181, Folder 2, CAB-CHM.

115. Horace Mann Bond to Arthur Davies, 10 May 1958, Box 181, Folder 2, CAB-CHM.

116. Marguerite Cartwright to Claude Barnett, no date, circa 1957, Reel 4, No. 950, Part II, Organizational Files, CAB.

117. George Padmore, Office of the Advisor to the Prime Minister, to Claude Barnett, 21 March 1958, Box 178, Folder 2, CAB-CHM.

118. Arthur Condon to Daniel Chapman, 22 July 1958, Box 181, Folder 2, CAB-CHM.

119. James Duff to Kwame Nkrumah, 5 September 1958, Box 181, Folder 2, CAB-CHM.

120. Richard Jones to "Claude," 25 June 1958, Box 178, Folder 2, CAB-CHM.

121. Claude Barnett to R. J. Moxon, Ghana Information Service, 14 March 1961, Box 178, Folder 5, CAB-CHM.

122. Claude Barnett to Trevor Shaw, 27 February 1961, Box 177, Folder 2, CAB-CHM.

123. Claude Barnett to Richard M. Nixon, 4 October 1962, Reel 5, No. 617, Part III, Series H, CAB.

124. Richard M. Nixon to Claude Barnett, 20 October 1962, Reel 5, No. 611, Part III, Series H, CAB.

125. Press release, March 1959, Box 180, Folder 1, CAB-CHM: Tom A. Brown, U.S. Negro with roots in New York City and West Virginia, also was president of Caramafra Ghana Limited, which formed a million-dollar business in Accra involving refrigerator manufacturing. See also press release, July 1962, Box 180, Folder 1, CAB-CHM: Bill Mann, Negro engineer supervised building in rural Ghana. He was from New Bern, North Carolina, and attended Drexel University and the University of New Mexico.

126. Press release, January 1958, Reel 64, No. 408, Part I, Press Releases, CAB.

127. Press release, August 1958, Reel 65, No. 1008, Part I, Press Releases, CAB.

128. Claude Barnett to Sam Bledsoe, 1 April 1957, Reel 4, No. 385, Part II, Organizational Files, CAB.

129. Claude Barnett to Vice Minister for Foreign Affairs, Mirghani Hamza, 1 April 1957, Box 174, Folder 2, CAB-CHM.

130. Picture of Barnett and Eisenhower, 1 April 1958, Box 173, Folder 10, CAB-CHM.

131. Press release, April 1958, Reel 64, No. 1094, Part I, Press Releases, CAB.

132. Claude Barnett to E. F. Morrow, 13 January 1957, Reel 3, No. 869, Part III, Series H, CAB.

133. Claude Barnett to E. Frederick Morrow, 18 January 1958, Reel 3, No. 888, Part III, Series H, CAB. .

134. Claude Barnett to E. F. Morrow, 5 April 1958, Reel 3, No. 900, Part III, Series H, CAB.

135. Claude Barnett to E. F. Morrow, 21 April 1958, Reel 3, No. 904, Part III, Series H, CAB.

136. Claude Barnett to "Dr. and Mrs. J. Max Bond," 26 February 1960, Box 174, Folder 3, CAB-CHM.

137. Claude Barnett to Hassen J. Abraham, President of Federation of Islamic Association, 19 July 1957, Box 173, Folder 8, CAB-CHM.

138. Press release, no date, Reel 2, No. 86, Part III, Series I, CAB.

139. Article, 25 April 1963, Reel 2, No. 92, Part III, Series I, CAB.

140. Secretary of National Spiritual Assembly of the Baha'is to Claude Barnett, 11 March 1954, Reel 2, No. 75, Part III, Series I, CAB.

141. Baha'i Press Release, no date, Reel 2, No. 80, Part III, Series I, CAB.

142. Clipping, 2 May 1963, Reel 2, No. 93, Part III, Series I, CAB.

Chapter 10. Pan-Africanism Is the News

1. Memorandum from Alice Dunnigan, 1 May 1961, Box 137, Folder 4, Claude A. Barnett/ Associated Negro Press Papers, Chicago History Museum (hereafter cited as CAB-CHM).

2. Report, 14 November 1961, Box 137, Folder 4, CAB-CHM.

3. Alice Dunnigan to Claude Barnett, 1 May 1961, Reel 6, No. 84, Part II, Organizational Files, Claude A. Barnett/Associated Negro Press Papers, North Carolina State University–Raleigh (hereafter cited as CAB).

4. Press release, January 1960, Reel 69, No. 259, Part I, Press Releases, CAB.

5. Press release, April 1960, Reel 70, No. 260, Part I, Press Releases, CAB.

6. Claude Barnett to Mary Beattie Brady, 28 February 1963, Reel 2, No. 365, Part III, Series G, CAB.

7. Claude Barnett to Mary Beattie Brady, 11 March 1963, Reel 2, No. 369, Part III, Series G, CAB.

8. Press release, 1963?, Box 139, Folder 3, CAB-CHM.

9. Enoch Waters to E. W. Crampton, Uganda Argus–Kampala, 27 July 1962, Box 139, Folder 7, CAB-CHM.

10. Press release, August 1962, Reel 77, No. 173, Part I, Press Releases, CAB.

11. Press release, May 1963, Reel 79, No. 544, Part I, Press Releases, CAB. Among correspondents in Africa were James Clinton in Nigeria, Adolphus Patterson in Ghana, Mohammed Ahmed Koor in Kenya, Nicholas Mbicholo in Malawi, Michael Fernandez in Tanganyika, Polonius Paxton in South Africa, and Gabriel Makoso and M. R. Gripekoven in Congo–Leopoldville. Then there was Abraham Jacob in India, Wilbert Hemming in Jamaica, and Rudolph Dunbar—still—in London. In the United States there was A. J. Slaughter in Washington, Calla Scrivener in Los Angeles, and in Chicago there were Eddie Madison Jr., Henry Randall, and C. J. Livingston.

12. Akbar Muhammad to Claude Barnett, 4 March 1964, Box 173, Folder 5, CAB-CHM.

13. Claude Barnett to Albert Bolela, no date, Box 177, Folder 1, CAB-CHM.

14. Claude Barnett to Sylvain Bemba, 29 November 1962, Box 177, Folder 1, CAB-CHM.

15. Commission of Information, Government of Sudanese Republic and Federation of Mali to ANP, 5 April 1960, Box 173, Folder 1, CAB-CHM (in French, translation by author).

16. Russell Howe, Advisor–Minister of Information, Togo, to Claude Barnett, 14 July 1960, Box 177, Folder 9, CAB-CHM.

17. Claude Barnett to Dr. W. Montague Cobb, 24 May 1962, Reel 2, No. 154, Part III, Series E, CAB.

18. P. B. Young to Claude Barnett, 22 July 1959, Reel 4, No. 38, Part III, Series J, CAB (emphasis is in the original).

19. Press release, November 1962, Reel 77, No. 923, Part I, Press Releases, CAB. See also Charlayne Hunter-Gault, *In My Place* (New York: Farrar, Straus, Giroux, 1992).

20. Press release, February 1964, Box 172, Folder 9, CAB-CHM.

21. Claude Barnett to Richard Jackson, 24 November 1959, Reel 3, No. 448, Part III, Series J, CAB.

22. Richard Jackson to Claude Barnett, 23 October 1959, Reel 3, No. 447, Part III, Series J, CAB.

23. Press release, September 1962, Reel 1, No. 895, Part III, Series C, CAB.

24. Press release, April 1960, Reel 70, No. 159, Part I, Press Releases, CAB.

25. P. L. Prattis to Claude Barnett, 27 July 1964, Box 139, Folder 2, CAB-CHM.

26. Claude Barnett to David Talbot, 25 March 1964, Box 172, Folder 2, CAB-CHM.

27. Claude Barnett to Charles Livingston, 3 June 1964, Reel 2, No. 301, Part II, Organizational Files, CAB.

28. Lindsay Patterson to Paul Robeson, 1 December 1964, Box H-KA, Paul Robeson Papers, Howard University–Washington, D.C.; Frederick Patterson to Claude Barnett, 27 July 1964, Reel 2, No. 922, Part III, Series G, CAB: ANP "terminated on July 19."

29. *Chicago Defender*, 9 December 1964.

30. James Wesley Johnson, "The Associated Negro Press: A Medium of International News and Information, 1919–1967" (PhD diss., University of Missouri–Columbia, 1976), 248.

31. Claude Barnett to Edward R. Murrow, 3 October 1962, Box 139, Folder 3, CAB-CHM.

32. P. L. Prattis column, 1 August 1964, Box 139, Folder 2, CAB-CHM. Prattis also blamed ANP affiliates in that "in the original contracts drawn up, the member papers of the [ANP] were supposed to have made their hometown news available to ANP so that such news might be shared with other member papers. This part of the contract was never observed."

33. Clipping, 19 March 1964, Box 142, Folder 5, CAB-CHM.

34. Clipping, 19 October 1961, Reel 6, No. 978, Part III, Series C, CAB.

35. P. L. Prattis to Claude Barnett, 6 December 1959, Box 139, Folder 2, CAB-CHM.

36. Bruce Childreth to "Dear Sirs," 1963, Reel 7, No. 915, Part III, Series C, CAB.

37. Press release, June 1960, Reel 70, No. 830, Part I, Press Releases, CAB.

38. Press release, September 1960, Reel 70, No. 711, Part I, Press Releases, CAB.

39. Clipping, 25 March 1959, Reel 4, No. 834, Part III, Series B, CAB.

40. Clipping, 11 March 1959, Reel 4, No. 837, Part III, Series B, CAB.

41. Speech by Mordecai Johnson, 6 June 1959, Reel 3, No. 650, Part III, Series B, CAB.

42. Press release, April 1959, Reel 67, No. 694, Part I, Press Releases, CAB:

43. Press release, April 1960, Reel 70, No. 175, Part I, Press Releases, CAB.

44. Press release, December 1960, Reel 72, No. 408, Part I, Press Releases, CAB.

45. Fisk press release, no date, Reel 2, No. 515, Part III, Series B, CAB.

46. Press release, July 1961, Reel 74, No. 492, Part I, Press Releases, CAB.

47. Press release, May 1963, Reel 3, No. 189, Part III, Series B, CAB.

48. Press release, December 1963, Reel 3, No. 219, Part III, Series B, CAB.

49. Enoch Waters to Richard Durham, 19 April 1963, Reel 7, No. 967, Part II, Organizational Files, CAB.

50. Press release, November 1962, Reel 78, No. 69, Part I, Press Releases, CAB.

51. Press release, February 1963, Reel 13, No. 108, Part II, Organizational Files, CAB.

52. Press release, January 1960, Reel 69, No. 259, Part I, Press Releases, CAB.

53. Press release, January 1960, Reel 69, No. 259, Part I, Press Releases, CAB.

54. Press release, January 1960, Reel 69, No. 346, Part I, Press Releases, CAB. See press release, January 1960, Reel 69, No. 478, Part I, Press Releases, CAB; and press release, June 1960, Reel 70, No. 909, Part I, Press Releases, CAB.

55. Claude Barnett to Enoch Waters, 13 October 1965, Reel 7, No. 1011, Part II, Organizational Files, CAB.

56. Press release, January 1960, Reel 69, No. 402, Part I, Press Releases, CAB.

57. Press release, March 1960, Reel 69, No. 1054, Part I, Press Releases, CAB.

58. Press release, March 1960, Reel 69, No. 1114, Part I, Press Releases, CAB.

59. Press release, March 1960, Reel 69, No. 1154, Part I, Press Releases, CAB.

60. Press release, March 1959, Reel 67, No. 376, Part I, Press Releases, CAB.

61. Etta Moten to Eva Jessaye, 3 August 1966, Box 173, Folder 1, CAB-CHM.

62. Press release, January 1959, Reel 68, No. 968, Part I, Press Releases, CAB.

63. Press release, December 1961, Reel 75, No. 764, Part I, Press Releases, CAB.

64. Invitation, 12 February 1964, Box 142, Folder 5, CAB-CHM.

65. *Editor and Publisher,* 12 May 1962, Box 140, Folder 1, CAB-CHM.

66. Enoch Waters to Claude Barnett, 13 March 1964, Box 139, Folder 7, CAB-CHM.

67. Press release, September 1961, Reel 74, No. 900, Part I, Press Releases, CAB.

68. Press release, September 1961, Reel 74, No. 944, Part I, Press Releases, CAB: Mal Whitfield, champion U.S. sprinter—and African American—now heading the Physical Education Department at the University of Nigeria.

69. Press release, October 1963, Reel 80, No. 846, Part I, Press Releases, CAB.

70. Press release, July 1964, Reel 82, No. 1173, Part I, Press Releases, CAB.

71. Claude Barnett to Mayor Richard J. Daley, 27 October 1959, Reel 9, No. 280, Part III, Series H, CAB.

72. Claude Barnett to Gladys Graham, 23 June 1960, Reel 6, No. 477, Part II, Organizational Files, CAB.

73. Press release, September 1961, Reel 74, No. 1038, Part I, Press Releases, CAB. Apparently this charge did not include the cousin of Mississippi's segregationist governor, Ross Barnett, who served as a missionary in Africa and accused her kin of hampering her work (press release, November 1962, Reel 78, No. 122, Part I, Press Releases, CAB).

74. Press release, July 1961, Reel 74, No. 492, Part I, Press Releases, CAB.

75. Press release, May 1963, Reel 79, No. 722, Part I, Press Releases, CAB.

76. Press release, May 1963, Reel 79, No. 793, Part I, Press Releases, CAB.

77. Press release, June 1963, Reel 79, No. 860, Part I, Press Releases, CAB.

78. Press release, June 1963, Reel 79, No. 991, Part I, Press Releases, CAB. Williams was described as a dynamo. He "broadcast several times for a Negro radio station in Chicago" and was "selling Kente cloth ties" too. "He stole the show at the reception given by the Emperor" when he persuaded His Imperial Majesty "to pose for pictures with Miriam Makeba," the antiapartheid chanteuse, and himself.

79. Press release, August 1963, Reel 80, No. 275, Part I, Press Releases, CAB.

80. Press release, August 1959, Reel 68, No. 269, Part I, Press Releases, CAB.

81. Press release, September 1959, Reel 68, No. 648, Part I, Press Releases, CAB.

82. Press release, October 1960, Reel 71, No. 1005, Part I, Press Releases, CAB.

83. Press release, October 1960, Reel 71, No. 1042, Part I, Press Releases, CAB. According to the ANP, UN Secretary General Dag Hammarskjöld, soon to perish in a plane crash, was a student of U.S. Negro culture, particularly spirituals. He accompanied his deputy Ralph Bunche to performances of plays by the premier playwright Lorraine Hansberry and campaigned against housing bias in New York City in order to open opportunities for UN staff (press release, October 1961, Reel 74, No. 1173, Part I, Press Releases, CAB).

84. Press release, April 1961, Reel 73, No. 483, Part I, Press Releases, CAB.

85. Press release, March 1961, Reel 73, No. 231, Part I, Press Releases, CAB.

86. Press release, May 1961, Reel 73, No. 931, Part I, Press Releases, CAB.

87. Press release, July 1961, Reel 74, No. 381, Part I, Press Releases, CAB.

88. Press release, November 1961, Reel 75, No. 266, Part I, Press Releases, CAB.

89. Press release, May 1963, Reel 79, No. 506, Part I, Press Releases, CAB.

90. Press release, March 1962, Reel 76, No. 409, Part I, Press Releases, CAB. See also press release, November 1937, Reel 1, No. 830, Part III, Series J, CAB: "'Dr.' J. H. Oden who describes himself as an 'American Ethiopian Prince' and claims descent from King Solomon as well as being a cousin to Haile Selassie meets with the mayor of Cincinnati." (Actually, he was from Paducah, Kentucky.) "Resplendent in a golden turban and a purple gold-fringed robe over a brown business suit," he "plans to chase Father Divine out of business."

91. See, e.g., Gerald Horne, *Mau Mau in Harlem? The U.S. and the Liberation of Kenya* (New York: Palgrave, 2009).

92. Press release, February 1963, Reel 78, No. 1003, Part I, Press Releases, CAB.

93. Press release, August 1961, Reel 74, No. 617, Part I, Press Releases, CAB.

94. Press release, June 1961, Reel 73, No. 1007, Part I, Press Releases, CAB.

95. Press release, July 1961, Reel 74, No. 430, Part I, Press Releases, CAB.

96. Press release, August 1962, Reel 77, No. 165, Part I, Press Releases, CAB.

97. Press release, December 1963, Reel 81, No. 222, Part I, Press Releases, CAB.

98. Press release, April 1964, Reel 82, No. 295, Part I, Press Releases, CAB.

99. Press release, July 1960, Reel 71, No. 56, Part I, Press Releases, CAB.

100. Press release, June 1964, Reel 82, No. 730, Part I, Press Releases, CAB.

101. Press release, November 1960, Reel 72, No. 202, Part I, Press Releases, CAB. See also press release, January 1962, Reel 75, No. 814, Part I, Press Releases, CAB. Clark is listed here as "Vice Chairman of the Committee for Promotion of Education of Negroes in Russia."

102. Press release, March 1961, Reel 72, No. 91, Part I, Press Releases, CAB.

103. Press release, May 1961, Reel 73, No. 689, Part I, Press Releases, CAB.

104. Press release, December 1960, Reel 72, No. 594, Part I, Press Releases, CAB.

105. Press release, January 1961, Reel 72, No. 919, Part I, Press Releases, CAB.

106. Press release, November 1961, Reel 75, No. 452, Part I, Press Releases, CAB. With prescience she opined that in the immediate future China would be more of a threat to the Soviet Union than to the United States. She upheld the anti-Moscow line, however, by charging that the war in Korea was "necessary to save us from World War III," in that it was "the first step in the Russian plan to 'liberate' Southeast Asia," something she knew because the Soviet delegation at the UN sought to "convert her to Communism."

107. Press release, June 1960, Reel 70, No. 830, Part I, Press Releases, CAB.

108. Press release, August 1959, Reel 68, No. 336, Part I, Press Releases, CAB.

109. Press release, July 1960, Reel 71, No. 05, Part I, Press Releases, CAB.

110. Press release, September 1960, Reel 71, No. 581, Part I, Press Releases, CAB. See also interview with Modibo Keita, no date, Box 177, Folder 6, CAB-CHM.

111. Press release, November 1960, Reel 71, No. 147, Part I, Press Releases, CAB.

112. Press release, October 1960, Reel 71, No. 1115, Part I, Press Releases, CAB.

113. Press release, November 1960, Reel 72, No. 340, Part I, Press Releases, CAB.

114. Press release, February 1961, Reel 72, No. 1090, Part I, Press Releases, CAB.

115. Claude Barnett to Trevor Shaw, 27 February 1961, Box 177, Folder 2, CAB-CHM.

116. Press release, March 1961, Reel 73, No. 16, Part I, Press Releases, CAB.

117. Press release, March 1961, Reel 73, No. 31, Part I, Press Releases, CAB.

118. St. Clair Drake to "Dear Claude," 14 September 1960, Box 176, Folder 9, CAB-CHM.

119. Press release, July 1963, Reel 79, No. 1164, Part I, Press Releases, CAB.

120. Press release, November 1960, Reel 72, No. 276, Part I, Press Releases, CAB.

121. Press release, January 1962, Reel 75, No. 1033, Part I, Press Releases, CAB.

122. E. F. Morrow to Claude Barnett, 22 September 1958, Reel 3, No. 909, Part III, Series H, CAB.

123. Claude Barnett to E. M. Glucksman, 30 August 1958, Reel 9, No. 212, Part III, Series H, CAB.

124. Senator Hubert H. Humphrey to Claude Barnett, 28 December 1959, Reel 3, No. 927, Part III, Series H, CAB.

125. Claude Barnett to Prime Minister Nkrumah, 16 December 1958, Box 169, Folder 6, CAB-CHM.

126. Eslanda Robeson to "Fredie Dear," 8 February 1959, Box 3, Eslanda Robeson Papers, Howard University (hereafter cited as Eslanda Robeson Papers).

127. Eslanda Robeson to "Fredie Dear," 25 March 1961, Box 3, Eslanda Robeson Papers.

128. Eslanda Robeson to Freda Diamond, 14 May 1961, Box 3, Eslanda Robeson Papers.

129. Claude Barnett to Carleton Goodlett, 27 August 1959, Box 146, Folder 13, CAB-CHM.

130. Claude Barnett to Prime Minister Nyerere, 30 October 1961, Box 173, Folder 1, CAB-CHM.

131. Press release, December 1963, Reel 81, No. 261, Part I, Press Releases, CAB.

132. Claude Barnett to Mohamed Koor, 16 January 1964, Box 172, Folder 6, CAB-CHM.

133. Claude Barnett to Frederick Patterson, 23 October 1962, Box 186, Folder 3, CAB-CHM.

134. Letitia Baldridge to Claude Barnett, 18 July 1961, Reel 3, No. 951, Part III, Series H, CAB.

135. Claude Barnett to Samuel Pierce, 14 April 1964, Reel 3, No. 978, Part III, Series H, CAB.

136. Press release, October 1962, Reel 77, No. 775, Part I, Press Releases, CAB.

137. Press release, February 1962, Reel 78, No. 382, Part I, Press Releases, CAB.

138. Clipping, 22 August 1961, Reel 9, No. 642, Part III, Series C, CAB.

139. Press release, September 1963, Reel 80, No. 434, Part I, Press Releases, CAB.

140. Press release, March 1963, Reel 12, No. 893, Part III, Series C, CAB.

Chapter 11. *The Jim Crow Paradox*

1. Press release, October 1962, Reel 77, No. 923, Part I, Press Releases, Claude A. Barnett/ Associated Negro Press Papers, North Carolina State University–Raleigh (hereafter cited as CAB).

2. Press release, April 1963, Box 178, Folder 6, Claude A. Barnett/Associated Negro Press Papers, Chicago History Museum (hereafter cited as CAB-CHM).

3. Claude Barnett to Carleton Goodlett, 4 September 1963, Box 146, Folder 13, CAB-CHM.

4. Claude Barnett to Horace Mann Bond, 18 August 1960, Reel 9, No. 338, Part III, Series H, CAB: "Mrs. Du Bois and several Chicago women under the leadership of Christine Johnson and three labor women from Chicago tried to steer considerable leftish angles but the American women as a whole planned for a sane approach and won hands down. Nkrumah said that Dr. Du Bois was old and senile but he had invited him for sentimental reasons although he really claimed far more than he was entitled to on Pan-Africanism. He said Pan-Africanism was born at the All African Conference in Accra rather than Manchester—an interesting opinion. . . . Lumumba was in Washington as we returned from New York to Washington."

5. Claude Barnett to Kwame Nkrumah, 26 April 1963, Box 178, Folder 6, CAB-CHM.

6. *Barron's*, 8 May 1961, Box 181, Folder 2, CAB-CHM.

7. Press release, October 1960, Reel 71, No. 1062, Part I, Press Releases, CAB.

8. Press release, February 1964, Reel 81, No. 867, Part I, Press Releases, CAB.

9. Press release, October 1962, Reel 77, No. 923, Part I, Press Releases, CAB.

10. Press release, November 1962, Reel 78, No. 141, Part I, Press Releases, CAB.

11. Press release, January 1963, Reel 78, No. 693, Part I, Press Releases, CAB.

12. Press release, April 1963, Reel 79, No. 401, Part I, Press Releases, CAB.

13. Press release, January 1964, Reel 81, No. 424. Part I, Press Releases, CAB.

14. Sékou Touré to Claude Barnett, circa March 1961, Box 177, Folder 4, CAB-CHM.

15. Claude Barnett to Sékou Touré, 28 March 1961, Box 177, Folder 4, CAB-CHM.

16. Press release, March 1961, Box 177, Folder 4, CAB-CHM.

17. Claude Barnett to Bishop Bravid M. Harris, 20 June 1959, Box 183, Folder 1, CAB-CHM.

18. Claude Barnett to Frederick Patterson, 16 June 1961, Box 186, Folder 3, CAB-CHM.

19. Press release, May 1964, Reel 82, No. 606, Part I, Press Releases, CAB.

20. Notice, 16 March 1959, Reel 6, No. 251, Part III, Series H, CAB.

21. John E. Reid to Claude Barnett, 20 October 1959, Reel 9, No. 275, Part III, Series H, CAB.

22. Claude Barnett o Howard Jackson, 21 September 1960, Reel 3, No. 542, Part III, Series J, CAB.

23. Press release, circa 1960, Reel 5, No. 809, Part III, Series H, CAB.

24. Pastor, AME Church–Monrovia, to "Dear Claude," 10 December 1963, Reel 3, No. 967, Part III, Series H, CAB.

25. Claude Barnett to Horace Mann Bond, 18 August 1960, Reel 9, No. 338, Part III, Series H, CAB: "Stopped in Freetown where I had not been since 1947. . . . Ghana and Monrovia have outstripped her. . . . The Governor had me in for cocktails. . . . Sierra Leone is definitely pro-British."

26. Paul Robeson, *Here I Stand* (Boston: Beacon, 1988), 44.

27. Press release, January 1959, Reel 66, No. 354, Part I, Press Releases, CAB.

28. Claude Barnett to Alice Dunnigan, 24 February 1959, Reel 6, No. 04, Part II, Organizational Files, CAB.

29. Press release, August 1960, Reel 71, No. 329, Part I, Press Releases, CAB.

30. Press release, August 1960, Reel 71, No. 339, Part I, Press Releases, CAB.

31. Press release, January 1962, Reel 75, No. 1023, Part I, Press Releases, CAB.

32. Press release, August 1962, Reel 77, No. 74, Part I, Press Releases, CAB.

33. Press release, March 1963, Reel 79, No. 1, Part I, Press Releases, CAB.

34. Press release, May 1963, Reel 79, No. 525, Part I, Press Releases, CAB.

35. Claude Barnett to John Davis, 6 February 1963, Box 147, Folder 14, CAB-CHM: "A number of people have asked us about the influx of Cuban exiles and their effect upon the Negro residents, employment, etc. How many of the newcomers are of definite Negro descent? . . . [W]hat attitudes are apparent on the part of Cubans toward their Negro brothers from Cuba and those who are American?"

36. Article by Wilbert Hemming, 14 May 1963, Box 207, Folder 1, CAB-CHM.

37. Article by Wilbert Hemming, 21 January 1964, Box 207, Folder 1, CAB-CHM.

38. Clennon King to "Mr. Chang," Deputy Minister of Home Affairs, 25 September 1962, Reel 6, No. 828, Part III, Series J, CAB.

39. Press release, May 1963, Reel 79, No. 456, Part I, Press Releases, CAB.

40. Mohamed Koor to Claude Barnett, 24 August 1961, Box 172, Folder 6, CAB-CHM (article by Oyangi attached).

41. Mohamed Koor to Claude Barnett, 24 August 1961, Box 172, Folder 6, CAB-CHM.

42. Press release, July 1963, Reel 80, No. 32, Part I, Series C, CAB.

43. Press release, March 1964, Reel 81, No. 977, Part I, Press Releases, CAB.

44. Press release, May 1964, Reel 82, No. 647, Part I, Press Releases, CAB.

45. Clipping, 9 May 1964, Reel 2, No. 212, Part III, Series J, CAB.

46. Masco Young to Claude Barnett, 6 January 1960, Reel 2, No. 107, Part III, Series J, CAB.

47. Release by Masco Young, 11 January 1960, Reel 2, No. 108, Part III, Series J, CAB.

48. Claude Barnett to Masco Young, 13 February 1960, Reel 2, No. 109, Part III, Series J, CAB.

49. Press release, July 1964, Reel 82, No. 1195, Part I, Press Releases, CAB.

50. Claude Barnett to Mary Beattie Brady, 12 June 1957, Reel 2, No. 317, Part III, Series G, CAB.

51. Claude Barnett to Lloyd Kerford, 2 September 1961, Reel 7, No. 884, Part III, Series C, CAB.

52. Claude Barnett to Lucien Green, 10 April 1962, Reel 13, No. 575, Part III, Series B, CAB.

53. Etta Moten to Eva Jessaye, 3 August 1966, Box 173, Folder 8, CAB-CHM.

INDEX

Page references in *italics* refer to illustrations.

Abbott, Robert, 24, 30, 31; ANP and, 48; in Brazil, 33
Abkhazia, 41; Chatwood Hall in, 46
Abraham, Hassen J., 161, 221n28
Acheson, Dean, 119; on racial discrimination, 3
Addis Ababa: African nations conference (1963), 164; anti-American pamphlets in, 173
Africa: African American migration to, 171–72; African Americans' interest in, 102, 118, 165, 182; ANP coverage of, 33–34, 67, 107, 109, 122, 130, 163–66, 216n52; anticolonialism in, 137; cigarette sales in, 135; commercial importance of, 68, 102–3, 104, 105, 108, 139, 158; Communist influence in, 168, 183; decolonization of, 145, 179; French colonial, 116–17, 158; Nazis in, 76, 208n102; Negro troops in, 66; Soviet influence in, 183; U.S. bases in, 172; U.S. investments in, 105, 106; U.S. relations with, 175–76, 178; white ambassadors to, 182
African Americans: Africans and, 68, 105–9, 165, 168, 172, 181–82, 185–86, 205n32; anti-bigotry strategy, 100; as anti-Jim Crow emissaries, 170; Cuban refugees and, 184, 243n35; "Double V" campaign of, 65; European interest in, 138; Haitian interests of, 122; Indian interest in, 98, 127; insurance discrimination against, 126; Islam among, 186; kinship with Brazilians, 54; in Liberia, 141, 216n56, 234n78; medical care for, 61–62; migration to Africa, 171–72; in Paris press, 214n17; posing as Africans, 174, 240n90; and postwar anticommunism, 115–16; postwar opportunities for, 115; during postwar period, 115–16, 118–19; pro-Israel stance among, 115, 220n27; purchasing power of, 71; radicalism among, 34, 48;

relationship with Liberians, 104; Russian attitude toward, 49; solidarity among, 7; in Soviet Union, 41–42, 45–46; in Spanish Civil War, 47; view of Communism, 41–44, 86; and wartime Japan, 65; wartime Soviet alliances of, 74–75; World War II service, 66, 67, 72, 76. *See also* expatriates, black; soldiers, African American
African Methodist Episcopal Church, 126
African press: Barnett's aid to, 109; coverage of U.S., 109, 217n83
Africans: African Americans and, 68, 105–9, 168, 172, 181–82, 185–86, 205n32; Nazi massacre of, 76; at U.S. universities, 168–69; view of Jim Crow, 173
Afro-American (newspaper): circulation of, 17, 97; political pressure on, 147
Aiken, W. H., 130
Akwei, R. M., 159
Aldridge, Ira, 74–75; Russian tour of, 63
Alexander, Raymond Pace, 228n77
Alexis, Stephen, 33
All African Peoples Conference (Ghana, 1958), 235n99, 242n4
Amenyah, Jacob Dosoo, 108
America First Committee, black support for, 65
American Colonization Society, 35
American Metals Climax (firm), 131–32
American Red Cross: Barnett's service with, 131; segregated blood policy, 61, 120, 131, 222n66
Amos 'n' Andy (television show), 233n46
Anderson, Ivy, 12
Anderson, Marian, 12; European accompanist of, 15; European career of, 31, 57
Anderson, Trezzvant, 208n110; ANP contributions, 16
anticolonialism: in Africa, 137; Barnett's, 17, 34, 40–41, 112, 113, 118, 120, 132, 134, 136, 158, 219n125; U.N. resolution on, 175. *See also* decolonization

Rosenwald, Julius, 23, 146; grant to ANP, 19
Rowland, Irene, 29
Ruark, Robert: Kenyan novels of, 159
Russia: African Americans in, 41–42; attitude toward Negroes, 49; black publications in, 42
Rutherford, William, 127; ANP contributions, 18
Rwanda, genocide in, 165

saboteurs, German, 77–78
Sampson, Edith: on China, 175, 240n106; confrontation with Worthy, 137–38; Copenhagen visit of, 136; on *Porgy and Bess*, 140
Sandfords, Laddie, 12
Schmeling, Max, 62
Schomburg, Arthur, 33, 54
Schuyler, George, 44
Scott, A. S., 5
Scott, Clarence, 44
Scott, Cornelius A., 66
Scott, Emmett, 39
Scottsboro Nine, 59; ANP coverage of, 44; global aspects of, 44; support for, 42, 43
Scruggs, Elizabeth, 209n119
seamen, pro-German, 209n119
Sears (firm): Negro patronage of, 23
segregation: ANP on, 167; Wallace's opposition to, 95. *See also* Jim Crow
Selassie, Haile, 8, 139, 151, 164
Senghor, Leopold, 116
Sengstacke, John H., 3
Shaw, Trevor, 160
Shaw University, student protests at, 173
Shivers, Allan, 156
Sierra Leone: pro-British sentiment in, 242n25; secession effort of, 183
Siggins, A. J., 220n27; on white supremacy, 151
Sikeston (Missouri), racial unrest in, 80, 81
Sims, Harold, 123
singers, black: European careers of, 56–57
Slagle, Mark, 193n100
"Slaves in America" (film), 147
Sloan, Ruth: African business of, 139–40
Smith, Ada "Bricktop," 24
Smith, Ferdinand, 71
Smith, H. M., 55
Smith, Homer. *See* Hall, John Chatwood
Smith, William Gardner, 172
Smith, W. J., 47
Socialist Party, "News Service for Negro Papers," 43
soldiers, African American, 148; absence from Caribbean, 124–25; access to graves of, 33;

court-martialing of, 77, 209n119; in India, 68; in Korean War, 119–20, 130; miscegenation involving, 13; in Normandy invasion, 76, 208n110; in World War II, 72, 76, 207n71. *See also* armed forces, U.S.
South Africa: ANP correspondents in, 10; role in Namibia, 118
South America: ANP coverage of, 54; black racism in, 55–56; opportunity for blacks in, 33; racism in, 124
Southern Nigerian Defender, 17, 109
Soviet Union: African students in, 183; alliance with India, 127; ANP coverage of, 41, 42–43, 45–46, 75, 84; black residents of, 45–46, 99, 214n20; black visitors to, 147; exploitation of Jim Crow, 133, 173; human rights violations in, 114; influence in Africa, 183; influence in Middle East, 133; Jim Crow and, 74, 86; racial attitudes in, 89–90, 92–93, 212n78, 232n17; wartime black alliances of, 74–75
Spain, racial attitudes in, 143, 171
Spanish Civil War: ANP coverage of, 46–47; U.S. Negroes in, 47
Spaulding, A. T., 66
Spaulding, C. C., 126–27; on ANP cooperation, 19
Spears, Howard B., Jr., 147
State Department, U.S.: desegregation of, 141, 168; sponsorship of Barnett, 104, 107
Stern, Alfred, 146
Stettinius, Edward, 108; death of, 125; in Liberia Company, 107
Stevenson, Adlai: Barnett's cooperation with, 1, 2, 13, 14
Stewart, Ollie, 71
Still, William Grant, 66
Stoddard, Lothrop, 61
Stowe, Harriet Beecher, 229n107
Streator, George, 70
Streeter, Harold, 155
Streicher, Julius, 32
Strong, Edward, 47, 84
Sudan, Barnett's visit to, 160
Suez crisis, African Americans on, 132
Sullivan, Ed, 53
Sundaram, Lanka, 98
Sunday, Billy, 25
Supreme Liberty Life Insurance Company, 115; African contacts of, 2; Barnett's investment in, 126
Swann, Darius L., 231n134
Sweden, racial attitudes in, 115
Sweets, Nathaniel, 156

Williams, Richard, 214n20
Williams, Robert, 17, 45
Williams, Robert F., 184
Williams, Sidney, 103, 172, 239n78
Willis, Nelson, 138
Windsor, Duke of, 12, 13
Witt, John Benjamin, 175
Wiwanuka, Joseph, 133
women, black: exclusion from Northwestern, 143; workers, 113–14
Wood, Leonard, 25
Woods, Rose Mary, 13, 156–57
World Federation of Trade Unions (WFTU), 86
World War I, black soldiers' graves, 33
World War II: African American servicemen in, 72, 76, 207n71; ANP coverage of, 5, 58, 71–73; Barnett during, 79–82; black attitudes toward, 65; Jim Crow during, 74; Negro press coverage of, 71; Pan-Africanism during, 68; racial unrest during, 80–81; U.S. entry into, 65

Worthy, William, 232n17; confrontation with Sampson, 137–38; travel to China, 147
Wright, Ada, 44
Wright, Richard: ANP contributions, 8, 18, 58, 90, 107, 138; and Barnett, 8–9; Far Eastern proposal of, 58–59; in France, 59
Wright, R. R., Bishop, 124
WYNR (Chicago), Negro programming on, 185

X, Malcolm: ANP coverage of, 186

Ya Lun Chou, 230n134
Ynerarty, José García, 41
Yonan, Isaac, 34
Yorty, Sam, 131
Youlou, Fulbert, 1, 164
Young, A. S. "Doc," 122
Young, Masco, 186
Young, P. B., 48, 66, 165

GERALD HORNE is the John J. and Rebecca Moores Professor of History and African American Studies at the University of Houston. His many books include *Black Revolutionary: William Patterson and the Globalization of the African American Freedom Struggle*. He is a recipient of the Ida B. Wells and Cheikh Anta Diop Award for Outstanding Scholarship and Leadership in Africana Studies.

The University of Illinois Press
is a founding member of the
Association of American University Presses.

_____

University of Illinois Press
1325 South Oak Street
Champaign, IL 61820-6903
www.press.uillinois.edu